MW00534211

The Rape of Eve

The Transformation of Roman Ideology in Three Early Christian
Retellings of Genesis

Celene Lillie

Fortress Press
Minneapolis

THE RAPE OF EVE
The Transformation of Roman Ideology in Three Early Christian Retellings of
Genesis

Cover design: Rob Dewey

Hardcover ISBN: 978-1-5064-2336-4
Paperback ISBN: 978-1-5064-1436-2
eBook ISBN: 978-1-5064-1437-9

The paper used in this publication meets the minimum requirements of American
National Standard for Information Sciences — Permanence of Paper for Printed
Library Materials, ANSI Z329.48-1984.

Manufactured in the U.S.A.

This book was produced using Pressbooks.com, and PDF rendering was done by
PrinceXML.

Contents

Acknowledgments

This book is based on my doctoral dissertation, and as is always the case with such endeavors, there are more people to thank than pages in this work. I am filled with gratitude to everyone who has played a role in shaping me and bringing me to these thoughts and this work. All that is good here is shaped by their influence, and all the flaws are clearly mine.

First, I want to thank the staff at Union Theological Seminary, who always had moments for hellos, conversations, and words of encouragement in this long, arduous, and exciting process. I cannot imagine having completed this work without the people who kept me—and everything else—upright during my time at Union. The remarkable students at Union with whom and from whom I have learned also course through the pages of this work. Their brilliance has constantly inspired me and given me hope in those going out to do work in the world. If I started naming each one I would get myself into trouble, so if you are reading this, know I am taking about *you*! I hope I have believed in you all as much as you have believed in me.

This process would have been vastly different without the incredible doctoral colleagues I had the honor of working with over the years. I am particularly grateful for Davina Lopez's generosity as she mentored me after she had her PhD in hand. Gratitude is also extended to Liz Theoharris, Kirk Lyons, Derrick McQueen, Angela Parker, and Crystal Hall, with whom I have taught and collaborated and from whom I have learned much. A special note of thanks goes to conversation partners

Karri Whipple, my fellow traveler in all things ancient, particularly in the area of sexual violence and trauma, and Amy Meverden, my language colleague extraordinaire with whom everything from biblical literature to balancing life is on the table—you both are not only amazing colleagues but incredible friends. Finally, this process would not have been the same without Maia Kotrosits, my partner in early Christian crime, who has been there from the first day of New Testament 101. Not only this entire exploration but the entire doctoral process is infused with her presence—we have been through it all together, and I cannot wait to see what happens next.

Many thanks as well go to former students turned friends Lisa Holzberg, Renee Monrose, Lisa Bridge, and Toni Reynolds. Each one of you has played an ongoing and crucial role over the course of the last many years—from working on projects together to late-night conversations. You all have been more than incredible during the intense process of pulling this work from my body through both the dissertation and book phases. Special thanks go to Lisa Holzberg and Renee Monrose for being constant companions in my darkest times and constantly reminding me of the bigness of the world.

Next I need to thank Marlene Smith and John Shorb, constant and steadfast friends throughout the last many years, for sticking it out with me as I consistently fell off the map—to Marlene for always reminding me of the magic that exists along with the mayhem, and to John for being an ever-grounded and supportive presence in the midst of it all. Many thanks also to Elsa Peters, who not only has been the best editing buddy ever—and whose astute mark is on many of these pages—but is also great on a cross-country trip!

To my dear friends who have been there for so much of this life's journey: Jennie Finn, Shannon Small, Penelope Morrison, Kathie Gregory, and Kate Daily. I have been friends with each of these women for many, many moons—through all the growing up and figuring things out—I am so very, very blessed to have them in my life, no matter where and how far away we are. Amelia Martin and I found ourselves in New York City at the same moment, and I cannot imagine this process without her companionship, support, and willingness to let me use Eve in her wedding ceremony! Lauren Cioe, my soul sister, always finds time in the midst of the busyness to have the most important conversations, and is always, always there; Robyn Stout Sheridan always seems to be on a parallel journey no matter how long it has been since we last spoke; and Joshua Klein, one of my oldest and dearest friends, manages to show up when I seem to need him most—whether today or twenty years ago—and I could not be more grateful. Jane Prater played an utterly crucial role as my high school English teacher and has remained a friend and inspiration to this day—and true to her nature she keeps reading my writing. And Hope Swann was a mentor when I desperately needed one, and is the amazing woman who first introduced these texts many years before I could even have imagined studying for my life.

Thanks go to Virginia Burrus, who read my first paper on this topic during my doctoral course work and whose suggestions were crucial in pursuing this topic. Karen King's work provided many of the foundation stones upon which this work rests, and I have been privileged to count her as a mentor throughout my program. Many thanks to her for ongoing wisdom and also for insights at crucial moments of this process.

Working with Fortress Press has been a dream. Thanks to Maurya Hogan for her truly remarkable copyediting skills and to Alicia Ehlers for all of her help with production. Particular thanks to Neil Elliott, editor extraordinaire, who has been a delight to work with and has made this work better at every turn!

The utmost gratitude goes to my three dissertation committee members Michael Williams, Brigitte Kahl, and Hal Taussig, who believed in and encouraged this project. Michael Williams's engagement with, enthusiasm for, and constructive critique of this work was a huge act of generosity—his model of mentorship and collegiality has become something to strive for in my life. Brigitte Kahl has companioned me through the last eight years, and her influence has left its mark throughout this work—she has held my hand through everything from the writing of papers to the heights of the Galerius Rotunda, and for these things and many other I am truly grateful.

I took a class with Hal Taussig the second semester of my master's program and have been working with him ever since. My life was forever changed when I approached him and asked if he had ever thought about taking a student to study Nag Hammadi and other materials—and he took me in. I cannot imagine a more generous and gracious advisor—one who has counseled me, encouraged me, argued with me over the most important things, and given me the most amazing opportunities. And he has done these things not only for me but for countless other students, helping us all to flourish in conjunction with our greatest strengths and gifts and challenging us all the while. I would not be here doing what I am if it were not for Hal Taussig, and I am so grateful for his continual leaps of faith and his encouragement of so many to do the same.

Equally important throughout this journey has been my amazingly supportive family. My mother's extended family has often provided a respite in the midst of this process, and I want to give a special thanks to both my grandfather, Eugene Teusink, who passed away at the beginning of this process, and my uncle, Larry Teusink—both always asked amazing questions and engaged in meaningful conversation no matter how different what I do was from where they are. Additional thanks go to my aunt and uncle, Marilyn and Rick Duistermars—they have supported me and traveled with me in more ways than they probably could have ever imagined, and I am so blessed to have them in my life. To my parents, Ted and Carol Lillie, and my sister, Katie Lillie, to say that I could not have done this without them is an understatement, and words really cannot express my gratitude for their support. In addition, my mom read every word of this work and my sister kept the roof over my head so I could write it—I love you immensely.

Finally, I want to thank all of you who shared your stories with me as I wrote about Eve's—it has been an unfathomable honor to sit with you in pain and laughter, tears and healing. In the midst of finishing this manuscript my goddaughter Isla Hawk Eaton was born. It is my hope that she will grow up in a world where these stories of violence are a relic of the past. This book is dedicated to all those who are doing the work to make this world possible and to all those who find in Eve's story their own.

Abbreviations

Aen.	Vergil, *Aeneid*
AJA	*American Journal of Archeology*
ANNT	Hal Taussig, ed., A New New Testament: A Bible for the Twenty-first Century, Combining Traditional and Newly Discovered Texts (Boston: Houghton Mifflin Harcourt, 2013).
Ars	Ovid, *The Art of Love*
BHS	Biblia Hebraica Suttgartensia (Stuttgart: Württembergische Bibelanstalt, 1937).
CJ	*Classical Journal*
ClAnt	*Classical Antiquity*
ClQ	*Classical Quarterly*
CP	*Classical Philology*
Crum	W. E. Crum, A Coptic Dictionary (Oxford: Clarendon, 1939).
CW	*Classical World*
DH	Dionysius of Halicarnassus, *Roman Antiquities*
F.	*Fasti*
HSCP	*Harvard Studies in Classical Philology*
HTR	*Harvard Theological Review*
JECS	*Journal of Early Christian Studies*
JWSTP	Michael E. Stone, ed., Jewish Writings of the Second Temple Period: Apocrypha, Pseudepigrapha, Qumran Sectarian Writings, Philo, Josephus (Assen: Van Gorcum, 1984).
LCL	Loeb Classical Library

Lewis & Short	A Latin Dictionary: Founded on Andrews' Edition of Freund's Dictionary, revised and enlarged by Charlton T. Lewis and Charles Short, reprint of the 1879 ed. (Oxford: Clarendon, 1966).
Livy	Livy, *Ab Urbe Condita*
LSJ	Henry George Liddell and Robert Scott, A Greek English Lexicon, revised and augmented by Henry Stuart Jones (Oxford: Clarendon, 1940).
LXX	Septuagint
MD	*Materiali e discussioni per l'analisi dei testi classici*
Met.	Ovid, *Metamorphoses*
MT	Masoretic Text
Nat. Hist.	Pliny, *Natural History*
RoR	Reality of the Rulers
NHC	*Nag Hammadi Codices* (Leiden: Brill)
NHMS	Nag Hammadi and Manichaean Studies
NHS	Nag Hammadi Studies
NHSI	Marvin Meyer, ed., The Nag Hammadi Scriptures, International ed. (New York: HarperOne, 2008).
Od.	Horace, *Odes*
OnOrig	On the Origin of the World
Rep.	Cicero, *De republica*
Rom.	Plutarch, *Romulus*
Septuaginta	A. Rahlfs & R. Hanhart, Septuaginta, revised ed., (Stuttgart: Deutsche Bibelgesellschaft, 2006).
SHR	Studies in the History of Religions
Smith	Richard H. Smith, A Concise Coptic-English Lexicon, 2nd ed., Resources for Biblical Study 35 (Atlanta: Society of Biblical Literature, 1999).
SRJ	Secret Revelation of John
T&R	Plutarch, *Comparison of Theseus and Romulus*
TAPA	*Transactions of the American Philological Association*
Vulg.	Vulgate
ZPE	*Zeitschrift für Papyrologie und Epigraphik*

Introduction

I can still remember re-reading On the Origin of the World (Orig. World) (NHC XIII 2)[1] during the second year of my doctoral program. Although I had read it many times before, there was something different that occurred with this reading. This time the story felt startling and new, horrific and hopeful—as if I were somehow seeing the text for the first time. What particularly captured my attention was an episode that both haunted and mesmerized me: the story of the rulers' rape of Eve.[2] It was not only the violence of this episode that caught me but what happened to Eve and what happened between Adam and Eve in its wake.

The story in On the Origin of the World goes something like this: Wisdom sees Adam, created by the partially divine, partially material rulers of the world, abandoned by them and lying on the ground. He is

---

1. Just as the titles of the books of the Hebrew Bible and Christian Testament are neither italicized nor placed in quotation marks, I have opted to format other early Christian literature in this vein in the same manner. On the Origin of the World, one of the three texts from the Nag Hammadi Library central to this study, is among the codices buried sometime in the late fourth century and rediscovered in 1945. It is variously identified by its title On the Origin of the World or Treatise without Title, or by its place in the Library: XIII 2 indicates that it is the second text in the thirteenth codex. In this work, On the Origin of the World will be referred to by either its title or by the abbreviation OnOrig, and will include the page and line numbers of the codex, as is the standard practice.

2. Here I am specifically speaking about my reading of On the Origin of the World. It is important to note that in the larger dissertation my engagement is extended to the Secret Revelation of John and the Reality of the Rulers as well. While, in many ways, I see these as three distinct and separate stories of the rape of Eve with particular investments reflecting the texts in which the story is embedded, my analysis of the three texts has yielded many cohesive thematics that are shared by all three. Because of these shared points of contact, I find that I can refer to the rape of Eve as one story and three distinct stories. See chapter 3 below for a full analysis.

unable to stand because he lacks a soul, so Wisdom sends her daughter, Eve, as an instructor to help him arise. Eve goes to him and tells him to stand, and her word becomes manifest, and Adam rises. The rulers of the world see that Adam is alive and that Eve is the one who has given him life. Then, jealous of her power, the rulers decide to rape her. They do this not only to try to defile her but so that she will bear their children, who will become their subjects. The rulers also put a sleep on Adam, deceiving him and telling him that Eve came from his rib, attempting thus to make her subject to him and him lord over her.

But Eve, knowing their plan beforehand, laughs at them, blinding them and leaving her body with Adam while she herself enters and becomes the tree of knowledge. When the rulers recover, they see Eve's shadow and mistake it for her true self. The rulers then rape her body in all manner of ways, along with "defiling" her voice, which spoke the truth and made words manifest. As a result of the rulers' rape, Eve bears their children—children who are subject to the rulers because they are children of ignorance.

Despite the "success" of the rulers' plan, they are still fearful of Eve and Adam and worry that Adam and Eve will conquer them. So again the rulers plot, telling Adam and Eve that they may eat from any tree in the garden except the tree of knowledge—the tree where the true Eve is, the tree Eve has become. And, if they dare to eat from the tree, they will die. When Adam and Eve are once again alone in the garden, the serpent comes to them, but here the serpent is good, the instructor, the wisest of all creatures. The serpent tells Eve and Adam that the rulers' words are lies, that the fruit will open their minds, and that the rulers jealously want to keep them from this knowledge.

Eve believes the words of the serpent, goes to the beautiful tree, and loves it. Eve takes the fruit from the tree and eats it. She then gives fruit to Adam, and he eats as well. They eat of Eve's own tree, the tree that the spiritual Eve has entered and become. And with these acts of eating, they integrate what was lost through violence enacted by the rulers and become enlightened. In their enlightenment, they know that, indeed, it was the rulers who were evil. And they also see each other and love each other.[3]

There were so many things that struck me in this rereading of the text: the violence of the rulers' gang rape of Eve and the way in which it was predicated on a desire for subjection; the way in which, like so many survivors of violence, Eve dissociates in an attempt to save a piece of herself in the midst of this horrendous act; the rulers' act of raping "the seal of her voice" so that she cannot speak the truth. Also striking was the way On the Origin of the World played with and elaborated the well-known plot from Genesis: the serpent is good, leading Adam and Eve to knowledge; Eve's actions are not evil or defiant but an act of trust that leads her to become an actor in her own process of healing; and it is healing, rather than disobedience, that she extends to Adam when she offers him the fruit. This act of healing allows both Eve and Adam to see clearly that the rulers' actions have nothing to do with them—it is the rulers who are evil. And with this recognition, Adam and Eve can love each other, not according to the power dynamics that the rulers attempt to establish but as equal partners.

I also found the story psychologically savvy—not only did it seem to reproduce, though in a very compacted form, the psychological contours of individual experiences of rape and violent assault, but, because of its mythological form, it pointed to the larger experiences of peoples subjected to imperial and state violence. Here was a different type of narrative, an ancient narrative from the burgeoning Jesus/Christ communities that addressed the power dynamics of sexual and imperial violence head-on and offered a perspective that was not addressed in the contemporary world until Susan Brownmiller's landmark Against Our Will was published in 1975.[4] On the Origin of the World spoke directly and boldly about the experience of sexual violence as no other Christian text I had ever encountered. Not only that, but the text stated that woman's subordination to man is only a

---

3. OnOrig 115.35–119.19.
4. Susan Brownmiller, *Against Our Will: Men, Women, and Rape* (New York: Random House, 1975).

story, and that this type of violence is not the way things ought to be. This was an epiphany to me, and I felt that the text had many aspects that needed further engagement and exploration.

In 2008, I placed On the Origin of the World in dialogue with Karen King's groundbreaking analysis of the rulers as analogs to the Roman imperial powers in the Secret Revelation of John[5] and Davina Lopez's incisive inquiry into the relationship between the Roman imperial imagery of conquest and Pauline materials through what she terms "gender-critical" reimagination.[6] Using additional hermeneutical resources from feminist, postcolonial, and empire-critical perspectives, I wrote my first paper on this subject, entitled "On the Origins of the World: Rome and the Writing without Title," for a course taught by Virginia Burrus.[7] With this paper as a starting point, I expanded my initial research to include both the Secret Revelation of John (SRJ) and the Reality of the Rulers (RoR)[8] and presented a paper entitled "The Rape of Eve: Exploring the Social-Historical Context of the 'Gnostic' Myth" at the Society of Biblical Literature Annual Meeting in 2009.[9] Since these initial forays, I have not been able to let go of the stories of the rape of Eve—or perhaps they have not let go of me. These explorations planted the seeds for the years of research that have followed. This book explores several veins of this ongoing research.

It is my contention that the telling of the story of Eve's rape in the Secret Revelation of John, Nature of the Rulers, and On the Origin of the World occupies a unique place within the corpus of both biblical

5. Karen L. King, *The Secret Revelation of John* (Cambridge: Harvard University Press, 2006), particularly chapter 5, "Utopian Desire, Social Critique, and Resistance," 157–73.
6. Davina C. Lopez, *Apostle to the Conquered: Reimagining Paul's Mission* (Minneapolis: Fortress Press, 2008), see 6-17 on her "gender-critical" method; chapter 2, "The Fate of the Nations in Roman Imperial Representation," 26-55; and chapter 3, "The Fate of the Nations and the Naturalization of Conquest," 56–118.
7. Unpublished paper.
8. The rape of Eve is found in SRJ BG 61.7–63.12//III 30.22–32.6//II 23.35–24.34//IV 37.4–38.24, and RoR II 89.17-31, which is also found among the Nag Hammadi Codices. I will not italicize references to these texts and will refer to them either using their full title (Secret Revelation of John and Reality of the Rulers, respectively) or the abbreviations above, which reflecting this title (SRJ and RoR). As with On the Origin of the World, page and line numbers of the codex will be included in quotations. See also n. 1 above.
9. Celene Lillie, "The Rape of Eve: Exploring the Social-Historical Context of the 'Gnostic' Myth," paper presented at the Annual Meeting of the Society of Biblical Literature, New Orleans, Louisiana, 2009.

and extrabiblical texts, addressing sexual violence in a way not found in other ancient literatures. While acts of sexual violence occur in the Hebrew Bible,[10] much of the Christian Testament and other early church writings are concerned with issues of sexual morality, chastity, and purity.[11] The three stories of the rulers' rape of Eve not only give a description of sexual violence but also articulate a condemnation of this sexual violence, moving the locus of defilement from the victim to the perpetrator. This strategy on the part of these texts occasions for me a particular set of questions: What type of meaning are these texts trying to make through the rape of Eve narratives? What circumstances, texts, and ideologies might they be speaking with and to? What type of meaning do the rape of Eve narratives make within the texts in which they are embedded? I begin to explore these question in the study that follows.

My thesis is that one of the major discourses these stories are speaking with and to is Roman imperial discourses of rape. The founding narratives and myths of Rome inscribe and naturalize rape through the articulations of their beginnings—a discourse that forms a part of Rome's justification for the hierarchical and gendered dynamics on which society is predicated. These Roman narratives not only address the relational hierarchy between individual men and women and the ways in which Roman society is predicated on these relationships (i.e., primarily marriage) but extend to address the broader context of how Rome relates to its colonies.[12] The three stories of the rape of Eve, through both similar and unique strategies, perform interventions into this ideology of sexual hierarchy and violence,

10. For example, Amnon's rape of Tamar in 2 Samuel 13 or the gang rape of the unnamed women in Judges 19. See, e.g., Phyllis Trible, *Texts of Terror: Literary-Feminist Readings of Biblical Narratives* (Philadephia: Fortress Press, 1984); Susanne Scholz, *Sacred Witness: Rape in the Hebrew Bible* (Minneapolis: Fortress Press, 2007).

11. See, e.g., Peter Brown, *The Body and Society: Men, Women, and Sexual Renunciation in Early Christianity* (New York: Columbia University Press, 1988; 20th anniversary ed., 2008); Elaine Pagels, *Adam, Eve, and the Serpent* (New York: Random House, 1988); Kyle Harper, *From Shame to Sin: The Christian Transformation of Sexual Morality in Late Antiquity* (Cambridge: Harvard University Press, 2013). For a discussion of sexuality in the Jewish tradition, see Daniel Boyarin, *Carnal Israel: Reading Sex in Talmudic Culture*, New Historicism 25 (Berkeley: University of California Press, 1993).

12. For a particularly salient discussion of this, see David J. Mattingly, "Power, Sex, and Empire," in his *Imperialism, Power, and Identity: Experiencing the Roman Empire*, Miriam S. Balmuth Lectures in Ancient History and Archaeology (Princeton, NJ: Princeton University Press, 2011).

particularly through their characterizations of Eve and her relationship to the violent masculinity exhibited in the ruling powers.

In the following chapters, I name and summarize the interventions the three rape of Eve stories make into this ideology of sexual hierarchy and violence; summarize the similarities and unique strategies of the three rape of Eve stories; and name and summarize the three stories' characterizations of Eve and her relationship to the violent masculinity exhibited in the ruling powers. These goals are accomplished by means of three strategies. The first is to establish intertextual relationships between several Roman narratives and myths that contain rape as a major plot feature and the rape of Eve stories. The Roman narratives and myths include Mars's rape of Rhea Silvia, which produces the founders of Rome, Romulus and Remus; the Romans' seizure and forced marriage of the Sabine women as well as the ensuing conquest of their homelands; Sextus Tarquinius's rape of Lucretia, which provokes her suicide and presages the founding of the Roman Republic; the near-rape and killing of Verginia, which ended the Decemvirate and restored the consulship; and Apollo's pursuit of Daphne in book 1 of Ovid's *Metamorphoses*.

The second strategy is to engage in a close synoptic reading of the three rape of Eve narratives in order to investigate both similar and disjunctive investments of the three stories as found in the Secret Revelation of John, the Nature of the Rulers, and On the Origin of the World. The third strategy is to build on the intertextual and synoptic readings of the rape of Eve in order to use it as a focal point for thinking intratextually about the three texts in which it is embedded, that is, to think about the relationship between each individual telling of the rape of Eve and how it relates to the Secret Revelation of John, the Nature of the Rulers, and On the Origin of the World, respectively. It is important to note that, in reading this set of texts together, I am not attempting to establish dependence of the rape of Eve story on the Roman narratives, nor am I seeking an Ur-story or source-critical analysis in terms of the synoptic reading of the three rape of Eve texts. My goal in this study is to explore the intertextual relationships between the thematics of the texts in play, engaging particularly in the ways in which rape functions in these texts, how rape is portrayed, and the characterizations of the various actors within the texts.

Though theories of intertextuality that have emerged over the course of the last fifty years have been both wide reaching and varied,[13] I am particularly compelled by Daniel Boyarin's elucidation of intertextuality, in which he identifies three aspects of these varied deployments that are particularly helpful:

> The first is that the text is always made up of a mosaic of conscious and unconscious citation of earlier discourse. The second is that texts may be dialogical in nature—contesting their own assertions as an essential part of the structure of their discourse. . . . The third is that there are cultural codes, again either conscious or unconscious, which both constrain and allow the production (not creation) of new texts within the culture; these codes may be identified with the ideology of the culture, which is made up of the assumptions that people in the culture automatically make about what may or may not be true and possible, about what is natural in nature and in history.[14]

Using Boyarin's definition as a starting point, I set these texts side by side in an effort to explore some of the wider matrices that have helped shape the texts under consideration, particularly those matrices that constellate around rape. While the Roman narratives have often been treated through the optic of rape and its larger presence in Roman ideology,[15] there has been little sustained treatment of rape in terms of the Secret Revelation of John, the Nature of the Rulers, and On the Origin of the World, and what meaning-making purpose its presence may hold for these texts.[16] Through reading these texts together, I

---

13. For a thorough introduction to the history of intertextuality, including its theoretical beginnings in the works of Mikhail Bakhtin, Julia Kristeva (who coined the term), and Roland Barthes through its deployment in feminist, postcolonial, and postmodern theories, see Graham Allen, *Intertextuality*, New Critical Idiom (New York: Routledge, 2000).

14. Daniel Boyarin, *Intertextuality and the Reading of Midrash*, Indiana Studies in Biblical Literature (Bloomington: Indiana University Press, 1990), 12. Here Boyarin is raising specific ideas of intertextuality pertinent for theorizing midrash. While I am not arguing that SRJ, RoR, and OnOrig are formally midrash, it seems to me that in their deployment of text, countertext(s), and elaboration they exhibit many of the strategies found in midrash (see Boyarin, 15–19; see also Birger Pearson, "Gnostic Interpretation of the Old Testament in the *Testimony of Truth* (NHC IX,3)," HTR 73 (1980): 311–19, where he refers to portions of the Testimony of Truth as "gnostic midrash."

15. See the secondary sources in chapters 2 and 3 of this study.

16. To my knowledge, there are no full-scale treatments that focus exclusively on the rape of

attempt to explore new layers of meaning in the three renderings of
the story of the rape of Eve.

My strategy for this is to engage in close literary and philological
readings of each of the texts, weaving together intratextual,
intertextual, and synoptic readings. Intratextual readings of the texts
are twofold: to look at the overall thematics, structure, and
characterizations within each text[17] and to explore, as noted in Boyarin
above, the dialogical nature of the individual texts and the cohesion
and disjunctions within them individually.[18] This process is engaged
together with intertextual readings that, in terms of the Roman
narratives, seek to place them in their cultural and ideological milieus,
and, in terms of the rape of Eve texts, to read them particularly in
terms of the situated Roman materials.[19] In this vein, I have limited

Eve—particularly not in terms of comparative analysis with Roman sources. The closest book-
length treatment is Gedaliahu A. G. Stroumsa, *Another Seed: Studies in Gnostic Mythology*, NHS
24 (Leiden: Brill, 1984), who devotes an impressive chapter to the subject ("Chapter Two: The
Archons as Seducers," 35–70). While I disagree with many, though by no means all, of Stroumsa's
conclusions, his comparative work particularly with Enochic and rabbinic materials is invaluable.
Though I will not be addressing much of the comparative work he treats here, his intertextual
connections have clearly influenced this work. Additional work (for shorter treatments of the
rape of Eve in the course of longer treatments of SRJ, RoR, and OnOrig, see chapter 3 of this
study) on these issues includes the following: Pheme Perkins, "Sophia as Goddess in Nag Hammadi
Codices," in *Images of the Feminine in Gnosticism*, ed. Karen L. King (Philadelphia: Fortress Press,
1988), 96–112, who addresses the rape of Eve in a substantial portion of her essay; Karen L. King
("Ridicule and Rape, Rule and Rebellion," in *Gnosticism and the Early Christian World: In Honor of
James M. Robinson*, ed. James E. Goehring, Charles W. Hedrick, and Jack T. Sanders [Sonoma, CA:
Polebridge, 1990], 3–24) engages in a sustained reading of the rape of Eve along with Leo Curran's
work on rape in Ovid's *Metamorphoses* (see his "Rape and Rape Victims in the *Metamorphoses*,"
in *Women in the Ancient World: The Arethusa Papers*, ed. John Peradotto and J. P. Sullivan [Albany:
State University of New York Press, 1984], 263–86); Lillie, "Rape of Eve"; Nicola Denzey Lewis
(*Introduction to "Gnosticism": Ancient Voices, Christian Worlds* [New York: Oxford University Press,
2013]) has very recently engaged in some comparative work between the Sabine women, imperial
power, and the rape of Eve (see 142–45), though the analysis of this comparison is more suggestive
and not sustained.

17. Vernon Robbins's notion of "inner texture," which "concerns features like the repetition of
particular words, the creation of beginnings and endings, alternation of speech and storytelling,
particular ways in which the words present arguments, and the particular "feel" or aesthetic
of the text" has many parallels to my own strategies for reading texts intratextually. See his
Exploring the Texture of Texts: A Guide to Socio-Rhetorical Interpretation (Valley Forge, PA: Trinity Press
International, 1996), 3; see also 3–39 and his *Tapestry of Early Christian Discourse: Rhetoric, Society and
Ideology* (New York: Routledge, 1996), 27–30, 44–95.

18. See Alison R. Sharrock's introduction, "Intratextuality: Texts, Parts, and (W)holes in Theory," in
Intratextuality: Greek and Roman Textual Relations, ed. Alison Sharrock and Helen Morales (New York:
Oxford University Press, 2000), 1–42, for a discussion of intratextuality. As Sharrock notes, "a
text's meaning grows not only out of the readings of its parts and wholes, but also out of the
relationships between the parts, and the reading of these parts as parts" (6–7).

19. Throughout this study I will generally use terms such as *allusion* or *echo* to posit intertextual
relationships between texts. Robbins (*Exploring the Texture of Texts*, 40–68) distinguishes four

myself to using texts that could be described as myths or origin narratives that contain rape as a central feature. As has been well theorized, myths and origin narratives do not so much reflect a remote past as provide maps and ideals for the present and future.[20] This understanding of myth undergirds the objective of the intertextual investigation engaged in this study. Finally, reading these stories synoptically, that is, reading together several different versions of the same story,[21] helps to highlight both overlapping investments between texts and the unique assumptions and strategies that different tellings of the same narrative hold. These three reading strategies—intratextual, intertextual, and synoptic—are engaged with a conscious impulse toward gender-critical, empire-critical, postcolonial, feminist, and trauma studies, all of which both undergird and inform my readings of the texts.[22]

distinct facets of intertextuality, which he refers to as "intertexture" (oral-scribal, cultural, social, historical). In Robbins's schema (58–60), the terms *allusion* and *echo* apply specifically to the work of "cultural intertexture," *allusion* referencing a "statement that presupposes a tradition that exists in textual form" (58) and an *echo* referencing "a word or phrase that evokes or potentially evokes, a concept from cultural tradition" (60). Because his four categories of intertexture overlap, inform, and implicate one another in ways that are difficult to disentangle, and, in relation to this, the terms *allusion* and *echo* seem difficult to confine simply to the "cultural" milieu, I have opted not to use these distinctions in my own work. In addition, it seems impossible on many levels to obtain enough criteria to argue for distinctions between "allusion" and "echo," therefore I will use these interchangeably to posit intertextual relationships between texts.

20. See, e.g., Jonathan Z. Smith, *Map Is Not Territory: Studies in the History of Religions,* Studies in Judaism in Late Antiquity 23 (Leiden: Brill, 1978); and Smith, *Relating Religion: Essays in the Study of Religion* (Chicago: University of Chicago Press, 2004); Bruce Lincoln, *Discourse and the Construction of Society: Comparative Studies of Myth, Ritual, and Classification* (New York: Oxford University Press, 1989); Jan Assmann, *Cultural Memory and Early Civilization: Writing, Remembrance, and Political Imagination* (New York: Cambridge University Press, 2011).

21. See, the almost primal examples in Rudolf Bultmann, *The History of the Synoptic Tradition,* trans. John Marsh (Oxford: Blackwell, 1963).

22. Most influential on my thinking have been classics in the area of postcolonial studies such as Homi K. Bhabha's *The Location of Culture* (New York: Routledge, 1994), and Frantz Fanon's *Black Skin, White Masks,* trans. Richard Philcox (1967; repr., New York: Grove Press, 2008) and Fanon, *Wretched of the Earth,* trans. Richard Philcox (1963; repr., New York: Grove Press, 2004), along with two volumes in the area of postcolonial biblical studies edited by R. S. Sugirtharajah (*The Postcolonial Biblical Reader* [Malden, MA: Blackwell, 2006] and *Voices from the Margin: Interpreting the Bible in the Third World,* 3rd rev. ed. [Maryknoll, NY: Orbis Books, 2006]), and more recent works addressing settler colonialism such as Glen Sean Coulthard's *Red Skin, White Masks: Rejecting the Colonial Politics of Recognition* (Minneapolis: University of Minnesota Press, 2014), and Andrea Smith's *Conquest: Sexual Violence and Genocide* (Brooklyn: South End, 2005), which engages intersections between sexual violence and settler colonialism, have been extremely influential in shaping my own ongoing questions on the relationship between Roman conquest and sexual violence that lay at the heart of the rape of Eve. Veena Das's *Life and Words: Violence and the Descent into the Ordinary* (Berkeley: University of California Press, 2007), which takes up questions of gender and state-sponsored and rumor-driven violence in India, and Wendy S. Hesford's *Spectacular Rhetorics: Human Rights Visions, Recognitions,*

Because of the importance of establishing relationships within the three Genesis elaborations as well as between them and the Roman texts, this study primarily follows an inductive approach to its larger task. That is, the entire monograph must establish the synoptic, intertextual, and intratextual relationships as a part of its work, since little previous scholarship has been done on either the textual relationships between the Secret Revelation of John, the Nature of the Rulers, and On the Origin of the World or between these three texts and Roman texts. Therefore, a central task of this study itself is to establish relationships between these texts. Again, I do not seek to propose or establish source-critical relationships among the Genesis elaborations and the Roman texts, nor between the three Genesis elaborations themselves. Nor am I proposing that these texts (in any combination) are necessarily conscious of one another, though they certainly may be. Rather, my goals in terms of intertextuality, intratextuality, and synopticism are less specific but very important. The relationships I propose in this study are brought into sharpest relief through an inductive study of both the Roman texts and Genesis elaborations. That is, I have chosen very intentionally to use the larger family of studies of textual relationships characterized by the multiple levels and optics perhaps best described variously by Bultmann, Bakhtin, Kristeva, Barthes, and Robbins.[23] I believe that using this range of scholarship is the most responsible way of thinking about textual relationships rather than committing to one theoretical perspective and is the best way to approach and connect the texts on a variety of levels while avoiding the perils of adhering to one optic. This has meant that the inductive process of examining all the texts (particularly in chapters 1–3)—that is, through step-by-step description and analysis—is the only way to lay the foundation for

and Feminisms, Next Wave: New Directions in Women's Studies (Durham, NC: Duke University Press, 2011) have been theoretical conversation partners through my writing, both taking up issues at the intersections of violence, gender, and trauma. Along these lines Judith Butler's Precarious Life: The Powers of Mourning and Violence (New York: Verso, 2004) and Talal Asad's On Suicide Bombing, Wellek Library Lectures (New York: Columbia University Press, 2007) were early influences at the inception of this project.

23. Again, see Allen, Intertextuality.

subsequent scholarship of these various documents while attending to the complex similarities and distinctiveness of the texts.

Additionally, since the theorization of intertextuality is extremely important to note, as Boyarin emphasizes, "all interpretation and historiography is *representation* of the past by the present; that is, there is no such thing as value-free, true and objective rendering of documents. They are always filtered through the cultural, socio-ideological matrix of their readers."[24] To put it another way, the reader/interpreter is always a part of the intertextual matrix. For me, in terms of this project, this comes from my own commitments to speaking about and ending sexual violence. Whether through more personal experiences or the headlines making front-page news—from Steubenville to Isla Vista, assault in the military to the Violence Against Women Act; from domestic violence, rape, and assault in football culture to violence perpetrated by police forces; from the kidnappings of Boko Haram to the war rape in the Congo; to the reports of rape and sexual assault by U.S. military contractors in Colombia and the theology of rape of ISIS[25]—sexual violence has pulsed through my own life and the life of the writing of this work.

In terms of the ancient world and contemporary interpretations of it, there has been much controversy with regard to both translation and meaning of ancient texts and terminology and contemporary meanings of rape. Following Zola Marie Packman, I will call any act of sex by force rape. That is, any act of sex without consent will be considered rape.[26] As Roman law clearly shows, rape was a known concept in the ancient world; what was at issue was who was "rapable" and by whom.[27] For the purposes of this study, "rape" will not be

24. Boyarin, *Intertextuality*, 12.
25. This list could be expanded exponentially and reflects only a bare minimum of incidents and issues of sexual and gendered violence.
26. Zola Marie Packman, "Call It Rape: A Motif in Roman Comedy and Its Suppression in English-Speaking Publications," *Helios* 20.1 (1993): 42–55.
27. Suzanne Dixon, *Reading Roman Women* (London: Bristol Classical Press, 2001), 49–51; Jonathan Walters, "Invading the Roman Body: Manliness and Impenetrability in Roman Thought," in *Roman Sexualities*, ed. Judith P. Hallett and Marilyn B. Skinner (Princeton, NJ: Princeton University Press, 1997), 29–43; Susan Treggiari, *Roman Marriage: Iusti Coniuges from the Time of Cicero to the Time of Ulpian* (Oxford: Clarendon, 1991), 265, 278–79, 310.

considered something that can be perpetrated only against free women and girls, men and boys, but something that can be inflicted on all human beings, though the primary focus in the texts under consideration is the rape of women by men. Because of this, there is no reason to avoid the word *rape*—and every reason not to. Given my commitments on these fronts, I want to note my own clarity of the problematics involved in the passive phrasing "the rape of Eve"—as if there is no actor in the rape, as if it is only about Eve.[28] This is one of the many ways conventional language regarding rape fails to hold perpetrators accountable, and it is something I regret reproducing in my own phrasing of Eve's story. My difficulty has been in finding another succinct phrase to signify the story, given the different rapist(s) who act in the three accounts of Eve's rape.

Furthermore, in addressing the topic of rape, many scholars and commentators correctly emphasize the voyeuristic and titillating nature of engaging sexual violence even, and particularly, on the scholarly level.[29] These concerns are real, but to use these concerns as a way to evade and avoid the reality of sexual violence (much in the same way English translations of the Greek, Latin, Coptic, and Hebrew texts have done) is another way of perpetuating the structures and systems that promote, reward, and tolerate sexual violence.[30] I hope I have done both these concerns and demands justice in what follows.

Finally, in conceptualizing this project as a whole, several additional influences must be acknowledged. The first is Vincent Wimbush's *African Americans and the Bible* project.[31] His introductory essay to the volume, "Reading Darkness, Reading Scriptures,"[32] prompted me to ask a set of questions regarding the relationship between canonical and

---

28. See Curran "Rape and Rape Victims."
29. See Laura E. Tanner, *Intimate Violence: Reading Rape and Torture in Twentieth-Century Fiction* (Bloomington: Indiana University Press, 1994), esp. 1–16; cf. Susan Sontag, *Regarding the Pain of Others* (New York: Picador, 2003).
30. For a good discussion on the complexities of this from multiple perspectives, see Arthur Kleinman, Veena Das, and Margaret Lock, eds., *Social Suffering* (Berkeley: University of California Press, 1997).
31. Vincent L. Wimbush, ed., *African Americans and the Bible: Sacred Texts and Social Textures* (New York: Continuum, 2000).
32. Vincent L. Wimbush, "Introduction: Reading Darkness, Reading Scriptures," ibid., 1–43.

extracanonical christian[33] texts that had never occurred to me before. What if biblical interpreters put the canon down for a while and looked at extracanonical texts? What if interpreters tried to ask questions (inter- and intratextually) without recourse to canonical comparison? What might be learned about these other texts? What insights and new questions, in turn, might then be asked of the biblical canon? It was these questions that led me initially to focus on the three extracanonical retellings of Genesis containing the rape of Eve narratives.

The second influence is derives from the works of both Michael Williams[34] and Karen King[35] on the deconstruction of the category *gnosticism*. Williams's and King's work has thoughtfully and carefully detailed the texts in the wake of the Nag Hammadi discovery (or rediscovery) and has also traced the ideological investments historically used in both interpreting and classifying these texts. Their scholarship in particular has opened new spaces for a range of interpretational possibilities and connections that would have been difficult to contemplate before their insights. Indeed, their work planted the seeds for the connections made within this study.

Chapter Overview

In the following pages I explore the story/stories of the rulers' rape of Eve. The rape of Eve occurs in three different yet interrelated texts: the Secret Revelation of John, the Nature of the Rulers, and On the Origin of the World (also called the Treatise without Title). All three contain cosmogonies based on elaborations of the Genesis creation narrative;[36] all three follow a similar, but hardly identical, narrative arc

---

33. I employ the term *christian* with a lowercase *c* to denote the period of history when some notion of "christianity" existed, but in many diverse and divergent forms, as opposed to the distinct religion of Christianity that existed in a more consolidated form, particularly after Constantine made it the state religion. It should go without saying that Christianity, whether of the ancient world or contemporary times, was and is a diverse phenomenon.

34. Michael A. Williams, *Rethinking "Gnosticism": An Argument for Dismantling a Dubious Category* (Princeton, NJ: Princeton University Press, 1996).

35. Karen L. King, *What Is Gnosticism?* (Cambridge: Harvard University Press, 2003).

36. The Secret Revelation of John, the Reality of the Rulers, and On the Origin of the World contain a plethora of intertextual sites that heavily influence their elaborations of the Genesis narrative,

(generally based on the narrative flow of Genesis); and all three contain a story of the rape of Eve. This study focuses particularly on the varying accounts of Eve's rape by the rulers, using these accounts as a way to understand and explore the three texts of which the story is a part. In each of the three texts, the story of the rape of Eve is told a little differently—sometimes emphasizing similar themes in different ways and at other times focusing on aspects distinct to the particular text. In all three, the rape provides a pivotal moment in the text; in all three the story is marked by violence, domination, and power. My primary questions are the following: What is the purpose of the rape of Eve in these texts? What kinds of practices is it in conversation with? What type of meaning is the story trying to make?

My argument is that the story of the rape of Eve is a comment

---

including, but hardly limited to, wisdom literature (e.g., George W. MacRae, "Jewish Background of the Gnostic Sophia Myth," *Novum Testamentum* 12.2 (1970): 86–101), Johannine literature (e.g., King, *Secret Revelation of John*, 235–43, Enochic literature (e.g., Stroumsa), Pauline literature (e.g., Elaine Pagels, *The Gnostic Paul: Gnostic Exegesis of the Pauline Letters* [New York: Continuum, 1992]), and other biblical prophetic traditions (e.g., Nils A. Dahl, "The Arrogant Archon and the Lewd Sophia" in *The Rediscovery of Gnosticism: Proceedings of the International Conference on Gnosticism at Yale New Haven, Connecticut, March 28–31, 1978*, vol. 2, *Sethian Gnosticism*, ed. Bentley Layton, SHR 41 [Leiden: Brill, 1981], 689–712). As with New Testament literature, SRJ, RoR, and OnOrig also have intertextual relationships with myths and philosophies from their Greco-Roman milieu, such as traditional Greek mythology, stoic and Epicurean philosophy, Roman novels, and the like. In regard to SRJ, RoR, and OnOrig, particular scholarly attention has been paid to their intertextual relationship with Plato's *Timaeus*, and later Platonic and Neoplatonic philosophies. While I in no way dismiss the influence of Platonism and Neoplatonic philosophies on these texts, I find that they are generally overemphasized in an effort to bifurcate these formulations from a yet-to-be-established Christian orthodoxy. While highly elaborative, these texts are much more highly influenced by the Genesis narrative, which forms their narrative contours, as well as by other texts that clearly fall under the purview of Israel, spiritual Israel, and the emergent Jesus/Christ movements, than by a work such as the *Timaeus*. In fact, one of the most interesting intertextual aspects between works such as the *Timaeus* and SRJ, RoR, and OnOrig is the fact that the *Timaeus's* story of creation is born out of a discussion of the orderly (i.e., hierarchically arranged) state and war (17a–26e)—something, to my knowledge, not addressed in the comparative literature between these texts. As the connections between the ordered state and the ordered cosmos go hand in hand in the *Timaeus*, these connections also seem to be addressed in the three Genesis elaborations as they develop the relations between the divine and material realms, exploiting both the continuities and disjunctures between them, though the secondary literature focuses on the cosmological level. In addition, intertextualities between book 1 of Ovid's *Metamorphoses* and the three Genesis elaborations are much stronger on both a narrative and a thematic level (as I will argue in this study), than in the Timaeus (though, as noted in the previous sentence, there is more work to be explored here as well)—the connections between the narrative and thematics of Genesis and the *Metamorphoses* attested to by concurrent readings of the two from Lactantius in the fourth century CE to Milton's *Paradise Lost* in the seventeenth century. For these reasons, I have elected to limit myself to addressing the relationship of these three Genesis elaborations with Genesis itself, as well as with the other Roman narratives that constitute chapters 1 and 2 of this study, rather than looking at the *Timaeus*.

on Roman imperial rhetoric that connects gendered violence with territorial conquest. While this initial hypothesis has held true, subsequent research has complicated this picture. In the following pages I will argue that the rape of Eve is not only a story of and comment on imperial violence but, in its various iterations, comments on a long history of the connection between marriage and conquest, family and empire, force and fear of penetrability, and the legacy of sexual shame. These tellings of Eve's rape reuse many of the same models and virtues of the very structures they oppose but envision and frame them in different manners. While the acts they present are horrific, these narratives of the rape of Eve offer visions of a different world, a world based on partnerships between the divine and human realms as well as partnerships between human beings in the material world. What I mean by this is that the divine regularly intervenes and responds to humanity in the face of violence of the rulers and authorities, thus providing a paradigm and model for humans to interact with one another, particularly illustrated by the loving partnership shared by Adam and Eve. Throughout this study, I build a case, chapter by chapter, for the complex connections and critiques that the rape of Eve and the three texts in which it is embedded make against what they see as the violent gendered rhetoric of the empire.

In chapter 1, "'The king gave the sign to assault their spoils . . .': The Mytho-logic of Rape, Marriage, and Conquest," I engage close readings of three of the major founding myths of Rome as told by Dionysius of Halicarnassus, Plutarch, Livy, and Ovid, noting pertinent themes centered on the constellation of rape, marriage, and conquest. Dionysius of Halicarnassus, Livy, and Ovid all wrote during the reign of Augustus from 31 BCE to 14 CE, with Plutarch writing around the end of the first century CE. All three of the founding narratives selected have rape as one of their defining features. The first is Mars's rape of the vestal Rhea Silvia. This divine rape produces offspring who will become the founders of Rome, Romulus and Remus. The second story is the Romans' rape of the Sabine women, who are abducted in an act of deceit by the Romans in order to procure wives and offspring. Not only is it a story where rape is central, but it provides aetiologies of both marriage and conquest, connecting social values and relationships between men and women with the relationship of Rome to its territories. In addition, the rape of the Sabine women, particularly in Livy's version, provides a paradigm for the Roman ideal of *concordia*—a Roman value undergirding marriage, Roman society, and Rome's relationship with its territories. The third story is that of Sextus Tarquinius's rape of Lucretia, which ends the monarchy and ushers in the founding of the Roman Republic. Through her act of suicide, Lucretia becomes an *exemplum* of modesty, honor, and the ideal Roman wife. Finally, I look at the attempted rape and killing of Verginia, whose story brings about the end of the Decemvirate and restores the consulship.

Through both consideration of the individual texts and synoptic readings of them, I endeavor to show the concurrent and unique investments of the individual renderings. I pay attention also to intratextual dynamics in an effort to show the ways in which the Livy, Dionysius of Halicarnassus, and Plutarch narratives contain an ambivalence and discomfort with the rape and violence central to these stories as well as the ways in which Ovid exploits these ambivalences and discomforts to produce different types of meanings with his tellings. This chapter also engages in intertextualities with the broader Augustan milieu, briefly looking to both monumentalization of the founding myths and other material depictions that express some of the ideologies found within them. These explorations of the themes of rape, marriage, and conquest and the corresponding values predicated on them provide the basis for the intertextual scope of the following chapters.

Chapter 2, "'One loves, the other flees . . .': Daphne, Apollo, and Ovid's *Metamorphoses*," moves from founding myths to *fabulae* by continuing to explore the theme of rape in Ovid's *Metamorphoses*, book 1. The focal point of this chapter is the story of Apollo and Daphne, which has been proposed both in previous scholarship and in this study as a literary intertext of the rape of Eve narrative, particularly in regard to Nature of the Rulers,[37] although to my knowledge this connection has not previously been framed in the larger context of Ovid's book 1, particularly in regard to Augustan themes. In this chapter, I explore the myth of Apollo and Daphne within that larger intratextual context, comprising the creation of the world and the flood, which precedes the story of Apollo and Daphne and two rape narratives—that of Io by Jupiter and Syrinx by Pan—that follow it. This chapter, again, pivots on a close analysis of the narrative and pays particular attention to the violence of the divine realm, the three instances of sexual violence in book 1, and the complex Augustan themes infused throughout the work. Here I begin to make links with the founding Roman myths discussed in chapter 1 and highlight aspects of the texts introduced in both chapters 1 and 2, such as the characterizations of the gods and their imperial associations, which connect to the rape of Eve stories and the narratives in which they are embedded.

In chapter 3, "'And they lusted after her . . .': The Rape of Eve and the Violation of the Rulers," I turn to the texts that lie at the center of this study. This chapter has three major objectives. The first is to engage in a close reading and analysis of the rape of Eve story as found in the Secret Revelation of John, the Nature of the Rulers, and On the Origin of the World in an effort to identify the contours of the story as well as the thematics in each. The second is a synoptic reading of the three rape of Eve stories, drawing out connections and disjunctures among the three versions of the texts in order to begin to locate their particular investments and perspectives. While all three versions of the rape of Eve narratives have similar contours and address some common themes, they are by no means identical, and I do not treat them as such. In addition, I do not address issues of textual dependence or hypothesize an Ur-story that lies behind the three. Here the goal is to locate particular strategic moves in each of the three narratives in order to show both overlapping and unique themes in the three Genesis elaborations and to use these to look for intertextual

---

37. See Birger Pearson, "She Became a Tree: A Note to CG II, 4:89, 25–26," *HTR* 69.3–4 (1976): 413–15; and King, "Rape and Ridicule."

connections with the Roman narratives. Finally, this chapter explores the rape of Eve texts in conjunction with the Roman founding narratives discussed in chapter 1 and with book 1 of Ovid's *Metamorphoses*, discussed in chapter 2. Particular attention is paid to the ways in which rape, marriage, and conquest function in relation to the rape of Eve texts and to the ways in which the characterization of Eve provides an intertextual counterpoint to the women found in the Roman narratives discussed.[38]

Chapter 4, "'And so they convicted themselves . . .': The Rulers and Resistance" highlights several other significant intertextualities in an effort to complexify and reinforce the readings in the first three chapters. First, this chapter attends to the intertextual structuring of three elaborations of Genesis with Genesis itself, looking specifically at the relationship between the Genesis narrative and the framing of the rulers. Second, I turn to a comparative reading of the rulers and gods found in the Roman narratives addressed in chapters 1 and 2 with that of the rulers in the three Genesis elaborations. Third, I address recent comparisons, particularly in regard to the Secret Revelation of John, of the paterfamilias and the divine household as explicated in the three Genesis elaborations. Here I explore notions of the paterfamilias and the imperial family with the texts addressed in this study. Finally, this chapter uses these analyses to explore the rape of Eve stories in relation to this broader imperial framing and to address the interventions these stories make into imperial paradigms of gender and violence.

Chapter 5, "'But she could not be grasped . . .': Thinking through the Rape of Eve," returns specifically to the rape of Eve stories, analyzing them in conjunction with the previous four chapters. This chapter

---

38. As will be discussed further in chapter 3, I generally take the rape of Eve to be three separate stories, though each contains five features that are roughly similar: first, Eve is some kind of amalgam of the divine and material realms, connecting the two; second, Eve is raped by (a) ruling being(s) of the material world (though the actor(s) differ in the three texts); third, some type of splitting of the spiritual and psychical Eve happens before her rape (though this does not happen in all four SRJ manuscripts); fourth, Eve and Adam are granted knowledge after the rape that allows them to know and recognize each other; fifth, through Eve's lineage, savior figures are born. When the story is referred to simply as "the rape of Eve," it is in relation to these contours and does not extend beyond this.

takes another look at the places where the three rape of Eve narratives converge and diverge, framing these within the larger discussions of the Roman narratives. Of particular importance are ways in which the rape of Eve narratives reframe and resist the dynamics of rape that take shape within the Roman narratives, but also the ways in which they reproduce these dynamics as they take on these texts, displaying their own ambivalences in relation to the complex dynamics of rape, gender, sexuality, and subjugation.

In conclusion, I use as a starting point the character of Norea, the daughter of Eve in the Nature of the Rulers,[39] as a way to explore some of the broader theological investments of the texts and situate the rape of Eve narrative in terms of these. Looking at a broader range of secondary texts within the literature of spiritual Israel and the emerging Jesus/Christ movements, I attempt to situate the striking portraits of Eve and Norea in terms of sexuality and the figure of savior. In addition, I anticipate some possibilities for subsequent scholarship on the basis of the textual inquiries presented in this study.

This project follows one particular through-line of both the Roman imperial materials and the three cosmogonies: that of the connection between sexual violence, conquest, and the types of power it enacts. The texts engaged in each part of this study are filled with rich complexities, and this study presents only some of the possible connections between them. My hope is that this project provides a foundation and opens up spaces for further work on the stunning character of Eve as she is found in these texts.

---

39. See also chapter 3 on Norea.

1

_____

"The king gave the sign to assault their spoils . . ."

The Mytho-logic of Rape, Marriage, and Conquest

In many ways Rome's history—at least its mythic history—could be called a history of rape.[1] While this might seem both hyperbolic and

1. It is important to note at the outset that scholars often disagree as to how these rapes are presented. For example, can the rape of Ilia/Rhea Silvia actually be called a rape? See Mary R. Lefkowitz, *Women in Greek Myth*, 2nd ed. (Baltimore: Johns Hopkins University Press, 2007), 54-69, who describes liaisons between male gods and unwed, human women in bucolic locales as honorable both due to the offspring of these liaisons and because the gods are "making their approaches welcome" (59) and "pleasant to mortals" (54). She notes that these liaisons should not be called rape either "by ancient Greek standards as well as by ours" (54). If this assessment of the language is true (and I would argue it is not), maybe a better contemporary term would be "coerced consent." Is Ovid presenting his rapes in a sympathetic manner to expose sexual violence or just reinforcing an ingrained practice that sexual violence is acceptable and part and parcel of society? See, e.g., Amy Richlin, "Reading Ovid's Rapes," in *Pornography and Presentation in Greece and Rome*, ed. Amy Richlin (New York: Oxford University Press, 1992), 158-79; Molly Myerowitz, *Ovid's Games of Love* (Detroit: Wayne State University Press, 1985); Leslie Cahoon, "The Bed as Battlefield: Erotic Conquest and Military Metaphor in Ovid's *Amores*," TAPA 118 (1988): 293-307; Julie Hemker, "Rape and the Founding of Rome," *Helios* 12.1 (1985): 41-47; Sharon L. James, "Teaching Rape in Roman Love Elegy, Part II," in *A Companion to Roman Love Elegy*, ed. Barbara K. Gold (West Sussex, UK: Blackwell, 2012), 549-57, esp. 554.) While Mary-Kay Gamel is speaking of Roman elegy in particular, I think her statement applies well to the task at hand: "The variety of feminist readings . . . reflects the richness and ambiguity of these poems, and suggests that definitive conclusions on the questions are unlikely" ("Performing Sex, Gender and Power in Roman Elegy," in Gold, *Companion to Roman Love Elegy*, 339). These types of ambiguities make these narratives and stories particularly susceptible for reuse and reappropriation, but they

overly simplistic, the founding myths of Rome are punctuated at
pivotal moments by acts of sexual violence. This chapter traces the
contours of Rome's founding through these pivotal rape narratives and
explores the ongoing ways in which they both shape and are shaped
by a rhetoric of rape, looking at the function of sexual violence within
retellings of Rome's beginnings and then connecting these to broader
issues of the Roman imperial ideology of sexual violence and conquest.[2]

nonetheless should be read as rape narratives. As Genevieve Lively states, "However stylized,
sanitized, or normalized ancient literary representation of rape and sexual violence might seem,
I should not underestimate their power to cause new pain" ("Teaching Rape in Roman Elegy, Part
I," in Gold, *Companion to Roman Love Elegy*, 542–48, here 543). While she is speaking particularly
of the contemporary world, it is not difficult to imagine that those impacted by the realities of
violence in the ancient world would feel the same.

2. This chapter is heavily influenced by the exegetical work of Brigitte Kahl in her *Galatians Re-
Imagined: Reading with the Eyes of the Vanquished* (Minneapolis: Fortress Press, 2010) and Davina
Lopez's *Apostle to the Conquered* (whose extensive work on the Roman imperial ideology of gender
and conquest in particular has influenced this chapter as a whole) and their use of imperial
ideology to critically reimagine biblical texts from the vantage point of the vanquished and
oppressed. Both Kahl and Lopez draw on the work of Louis Althusser in their ideological analyses
of Paul. As Lopez notes, "Ideology, according to Louis Althusser's well-known formulation, is
'the imaginary relationship of individuals to their real conditions of existence.' For Althusser,
imaginary does not necessarily mean pretend. The *imaginary* designates what is created out of
the presentation of knowledge as inevitable and universal. It is a relentless display of reality
as unmediated and neutral and renders such reality invisible to criticism" (Lopez, *Apostle to the
Conquered*, 17–18, citing Louis Althusser, *Lenin and Philosophy and Other Essays*, trans. Ben Brewster
[New York: Monthly Review Press, 1971], 52; see also Kahl, *Galatians Re-Imagined*, 28, 116, 328n94).
In addition, Kahl links ideology with images saying, "The *eidos* (shape, form) of the images
is the visualization of ideology (not accidentally, both terms are semantically related to the
Greek verb *idein*, 'to see')" (28, 311n57). Lopez also notes the importance of images for ideology
stating, "While images are reflective of ideology, they also construct it and participate in its
dissemination" (19). In these ways, ideologies constructed by written texts cannot be separated
from their visual, material counterparts.

John Alexander Lobur (*Consensus, Concordia and the Formation of Roman Imperial Ideology*, Studies
in Classics [New York: Routledge, 2008]) draws particularly on the work of Clifford Geertz to define
ideology, which is also a helpful addition to the work of Lopez and Kahl. Lobur notes that Geertz
saw ideologies "'as systems of interacting symbols, as patterns of interacting meanings.' Ideology
uses symbols to construct models—'extrinsic sources of information in terms of which human
life can be patterned—extrapersonal mechanisms for the perception, understanding, judgment
and manipulation of the world.' (Clifford Geertz, "Ideology as a Cultural System, in D. E. Apter,
ed., *Ideology and Discontent* [New York: The Free Press, 1964], 56, 62.) According to Geertz, it is in
times of great crisis and turmoil that ideology plays its most crucial role, providing ever more
explicit answers 'in situations where the particular kind of information they contain is lacking,
where institutionalized guides for behavior, thought, or feeling are weak or absent.' The chaos of
the late Roman republic then, with its dysfunctional system, provided a perfect seedbed for the
development of ideology" (Geertz, 63) (Lobur, 2).

These entry points into ideology serve to highlight both its naturalizing and universalizing
capacities and its consolidating functions. These functions, as noted by Lobur, were important
tools for Augustus, as can be seen from the majority of sources used in this chapter, for the
consolidation and refounding of Rome in the wake of the civil wars and Actium. As David Quint
notes, "The advantage of ideology . . . is its capacity to simplify, to make hard and fast distinctions
and draw up sides" (*Epic and Empire: Politics and Generic Form from Virgil to Milton* [Princeton, NJ:

I begin with four moments in Rome's history that are critical to its establishment: the rape of Ilia/Rhea Silvia by Mars, through which the founders of Rome, Romulus and Remus, are born; the ravaging of the Sabine women by the Romans, through which the Roman men secure wives and the Romans conquer neighboring territory; the rape of Lucretia by Sextus Tarquinius, which brings an end to the monarchy; and the story of Verginia, which ends the Decemvirate and restores the consulship. The sources used for these narratives are primarily from the Augustan era, though Plutarch, writing at the end of the last decade of the first century CE or the beginning of the second, is used as well, showing the ongoing importance of these narratives and motifs during the Principate.

In conclusion, the chapter turns to another set of imperial texts, both visual and written, including the Basilica Aemelia, Augustus's Portico of the Nations, Hadrian's temple, the Sebasteion at Aphrodisias, and Calgacus's speech to the Britons, then looks at these in relation to the Vestals, the virgins who both literally and figuratively symbolize Rome's integrity. These examples are used to illustrate the intersections between rape, marriage, and conquest, showing the ways in which Roman integrity and conquest are mapped onto the bodies of women through the consistent "logic" between the mythic foundations of Rome and its later visual program of Roman imperial geography.[3]

Princeton University Press, 1993], 23) a point reflected in the ideological through-line presented in the sources throughout this chapter.

Also crucial to this study, and closely related to Rome's ideological program, is the important scholarship on the mapping of male masculinity as both being impenetrable and penetrating. See, e.g., Judith P. Hallett and Marilyn B. Skinner, eds., *Roman Sexualities* (Princeton, NJ: Princeton University Press, 1997), particularly Jonathan Walters's essay, "Invading the Roman Body: Manliness and Impenetrability in Roman Thought," 29–43; and Marilyn B. Skinner, *Sexuality in Greek and Roman Culture*, Ancient Cultures (Malden, MA: Blackwell, 2005).

3. As noted in the introduction, myth and origin narratives do not so much reflect a remote past as provide maps and ideals for the present and future; see J. Z. Smith, *Map Is Not Territory*; J. Z. Smith, *Relating Religion*; Lincoln, *Discourse and the Construction of Society*; and Assmann, *Cultural Memory and Early Civilization*.

Rape Stories and the Founding of Rome

Mars's Rape of Rhea Silvia

The two most thorough accounts of the mother of Romulus and Remus,[4] founders of Rome, are found in the accounts of Livy and Dionysius of Halicarnassus, both dating to around the time of Augustus.[5] According to Livy,

> [Proca] begat Numitor and Amulius; to Numitor, the elder, he bequeathed the ancient realm of the Silvian family. Yet violence [*vis*] proved more powerful than a father's wishes or respect for seniority. Amulius drove out his brother and ruled in his stead. Adding crime to crime [*addit sceleri scelus*], he killed [*interemit*] Numitor's male offspring; and Rhea Silvia, his brother's daughter, he appointed a Vestal under the pretense of honoring her, and by consigning her to perpetual virginity, deprived her of the hope of children. But the Fates were resolved, as I suppose, upon the founding of this great City, and the beginning of the mightiest of empires, next after that of the gods. The Vestal was violently pressed [*vi compressa*], and having given birth to twin sons, named Mars as the father of her doubtful offspring, whether actually so believing, or because it seemed less wrong if a god were the author of her fault. But neither gods nor men protected the mother herself or her children from the king's cruelty [*crudelitate*]; the priestess he ordered to be manacled and cast into prison, the children to be committed to the river. (Livy 1.3.10–1.4.4; Foster, LCL, with some alterations)

And Dionysius of Halicarnassus,

> When Amulius succeeded to the kingdom of the Albans, after forcibly excluding his elder brother Numitor from the dignity that was his by inheritance, he not only showed great contempt for justice [ὑπεροψίαν τῶν δικαίων] in everything else that he did, but he finally plotted [ἐπεβούλευσε] to deprive Numitor's family of offspring, both from fear [φόβῳ] of suffering punishment for his usurpation and also because of his desire never to be deposed of the sovereignty [τῆς ἀρχῆς]. Having long resolved

---

4. I use Rhea Silvia/Ilia interchangeably throughout. The appellation Ilia is used specifically to connect her with her Trojan roots.
5. Other accounts are found in Plutarch's *Romulus* 3 and Dio Cassius, *Frag.* 3.2, and contain fewer narrative details. The story is also found in Ovid and will be addressed in the next section. For a complete history of the Rhea Silvia narrative, see Fred C. Albertson, *Mars and Rhea Silvia in Roman Art* (Brussels: Latomus, 2012), 17–49. See also Catherine Connors, "Ennius, Ovid and Representations of Ilia," MD 32 (1994): 99–112; and Lopez, *Apostle to the Conquered*, 60–63.

upon this course, he first observed the place where Aegestus, Numitor's son, who was just coming to manhood, hunted, and having laid an ambush [προλοχίσας] in the most hidden part of it, he caused him to be slain [ἀποκτείνει] when he had come out to hunt; and after the deed was committed he contrived [παρεσκεύασε] to have it reported that the youth had been killed by robbers. Nevertheless, the rumor thus concocted could not prevail over the truth [τῆς . . . ἀληθίας] which he was trying to keep concealed, but many, though it was unsafe to do so, ventured to tell what had been done. Numitor was aware of the crime, but his judgment being superior to his grief, he affected ignorance, resolving to defer his resentment to a less dangerous time. And Amulius, supposing that the truth about the youth had been kept secret, set a second plan on foot, as follows: he appointed Numitor's daughter, Ilia,—or, as some state, Rhea, surnamed Silvia,—who was then ripe [ἀκμῇ] for marriage, to be a priestess of Vesta, lest, if she first entered a husband's house, she might bring forth avengers for her family. . . . Amulius was carrying out his plan under specious pretenses, as if he were conferring honor and dignity on his brother's family. . . [for] it was both customary and honorable among the Albans for maidens [κόρας] of the highest birth to be appointed to the service of Vesta. . . .

The fourth year after this, Ilia, upon going to a grove consecrated to Mars[6] to fetch pure water for use in the sacrifices, was violated [βιάζεταί] by somebody or other in the sacred precinct. Some say that the author of the deed was one of the maiden's suitors, carried away by his love [ἐρῶντα] for the slave girl [τῆς παιδίσκης]; others say that it was Amulius himself, and that, since his purpose was to destroy her quite as much as to satisfy his desire, he had arrayed himself in such armor as would render him most terrible to behold and that he also kept his features disguised as effectively as possible. But most writers relate a fabulous story to the effect that it was an image of the divinity [τοῦ δαίμονος εἴδωλον] to whom the place was consecrated; and they add that the misfortune [τῷ πάθει] was attended by many divine works [δαιμόνια ἔργα], including a sudden disappearance of the sun and a darkness that spread over the sky, and that the appearance of the image [τὸ εἴδωλον] was far more marvelous than that of a man both in stature and in beauty. And they say that the violator [τὸν βιασάμενον], to comfort the maiden (by which it became clear that he was a god), commanded her not to grieve [τῷ πάθει] what had happened, since she had been united in marriage to the divinity of the place and as a result of her rape [τοῦ βιασμοῦ] should bear two sons who would far excel all men in valor [ἀρετήν] and warlike [τὰ πολέμια] achievements. And having said this he was wrapped in a cloud and, being lifted from the earth, was borne upwards through the air. . . . [T]he maid, after her rape

---

6. See Lopez, *Apostle to the Conquered*, 62, for the significance of the rape occurring in the precinct of Mars.

[τὸν βιασμόν] feigned illness (for this her mother advised out of regard both for her own safety and for the sacred services of the gods) and no longer attended the sacrifices, but her duties were performed by the other virgins [παρθένων] who were joined with her in the same service to the state [λειτουργεῖν]. (DH 1.76–77; Cary, LCL, with some alterations)

Both of these accounts of the birth of Rome's founders are marked by violence, deception, and malice. The tales begin with the usurpation of Numitor's throne by his younger brother, Amulius.[7] Amulius takes Numitor's lawful place as the successor to the kingdom and, according to Livy, violently drives his brother out and claims his place as king. Livy describes Amulius's actions as "adding crime to crime" (*addit sceleri scelus*) as Amulius "kills" (*interemit*)[8] Numitor's sons and makes Rhea Silvia a Vestal (one of the six virgin keepers of Rome's hearth-fire[9]) under the guise of honoring her, though in reality it is an act meant to keep her a virgin and prevent her from having children. Amulius's actions against his brother and niece betray both his violence and his duplicity.

In Dionysius of Halicarnassus's longer version, emphasis is placed on Amulius's "contempt for justice" (ὑπεροψίαν τῶν δικαίων) and his plotting (ἐπεβούλευσε) against his brother as a result of his fear of punishment as well as his desire for power. In this account, Amulius stalks the hunting grounds of Aegestus, Numitor's son, and kills him, concocting a story that he was murdered by robbers. Though this lie could not "prevail over the truth [τῆς . . . ἀληθίας]," Numitor felt it was too dangerous to confront him. In the meantime, as in Livy's story, Amulius falsely honors Ilia/Rhea Silvia by making her a Vestal both to retain power for himself and his line and to avoid retribution.

Next, both authors relate the story of Ilia/Rhea Silvia's rape. Livy renders this with the compound *vi compressa*, depicting the vigor,

---

7. According to Plutarch's account, Amulius divided their inheritance into their dynastic rule and the booty brought from Troy. Numitor chose the kingdom, leaving Amulius the treasure. With his newfound wealth, he was quickly able to overpower Numitor and take the kingdom as well (*Rom.* 3.2). Dio states that an oracle had foretold Amulius's death at the hand of Numitor's children, prompting his actions against his brother and children.

8. Lewis & Short, s.v. *interimo*, "take out of the midst, to take away, do away with, abolish; to destroy, slay, kill."

9. See both this chapter and chapter 2 for further information on the Vestals.

strength, potency, and violence of the rapist's pressing/oppression.[10] *Vis* is a word often associated with military force, particularly apropos given the association of Ilia/Rhea Silvia's rape with Mars, the god of war.[11] Dionysius uses βιάζεται in the Greek, signaling the same "force or violence"[12] indicated by Livy in Mars's act. Both accounts hedge as to whether Mars was actually the perpetrator of this violence against Ilia/Rhea Silvia. Livy casts doubt on Rhea Silvia's words, saying he is unsure whether she actually believed that Mars was the perpetrator or if she claimed this "because it seemed less wrong if a god were the author of her fault [*auctor culpae*]" (Livy 1.4.2). Of note here is that Livy disbelieves what is framed as Rhea Silvia's account and places the blame for the violence perpetrated against her upon her, rather than her rapist.

Dionysius has other theories regarding her rape. His first proposal is that a suitor was "carried away by his love [ἐρῶντα]," or maybe better translated "lust," "for the slave girl [τῆς κόρης . . . τῆς παιδίσκης]" (DH 1.77.1), though the context raises the question of exactly what type of love this could have been. This is especially notable given the use of τῆς παιδίσκης ("slave") here, when, throughout the rest of the text, Ilia/Rhea Silvia is referred to as κόρη ("girl" or "maiden").[13] This is significant, as Ilia, the daughter of the king, is reframed as a slave, thus exposing both the power differential between her and the men in this narrative and her total vulnerability to this type of violence.[14] Dionysius also raises the possibility that it was Amulius himself who raped her, once again displaying his penchant for deception and violence. Disguising himself in armor to "render him[self] most terrible to behold," he raped her in order to "destroy her quite as much as satisfy his desire" (DH 1.77.1).

Despite their equivocation on just who has raped Ilia/Rhea Silvia, both Livy and Dionysius stress the "divine" nature of the rape,

---

10. See Lewis & Short,s.v. vis and *compresso*.
11. Ibid., s.v. *vis*.
12. See LSJ, s.v. βιάζω.
13. She is referred to simply as κόρη in 1.77.2, 4 and six times in 1.78.
14. On the sexual availability and vulnerability of slaves, see, e.g., Jennifer A. Glancy, *Slavery in Early Christianity* (New York: Oxford University Press, 2002), 50–53.

pregnancy, and birth of her twin sons. Livy notes, "the Fates were resolved . . . upon the founding of this great City, and the beginning of the mightiest of empires, next after that of the gods" (Livy 1.4.1). Dionysius's version moves beyond fate and is even more explicit regarding the divine nature of the incident. In his version, as Rhea Silvia goes to the grove of Mars to fetch water for sacrifices, the "image of the divinity [τοῦ δαίμονος εἴδωλον] to whom the place was consecrated" appeared, and this "image [τὸ εἴδωλον] was far more marvelous than that of a man both in stature and in beauty" (DH 1.77.2). And it was this divinity, Mars, who was the perpetrator of her "misfortune" [τῷ πάθει]; a "misfortune" attended to "by many divine works [δαιμόνια ἔργα] including a sudden disappearance of the sun and a darkness that spread over the sky" (DH 1.77.2). Rhea Silvia was "commanded" by Mars, her "violator" [τὸν βιασάμενον], "not to grieve [τῷ πάθει] what had happened, since she had been united in marriage to the divinity of the place and as a result of her rape [τοῦ βιασμοῦ] should bear two sons who would far excel all men in valor [ἀρετήν] and warlike [τὰ πολέμια] achievements" (DH 1.77.2)—just like their father, the god of war. Despite the fact that Ilia is told not to grieve, Dionysius's text makes her violation clear at every turn.

After Ilia/Rhea Silvia's violation, Livy laments that "neither gods nor men protected the mother herself or her children from the king's cruelty [crudelitate]," as her children are cast into the Tiber and she is "manacled and cast into prison" (1.4.4). Dionysius's account fleshes out this cruelty, citing various accounts of Ilia's fate. As Amulius refuses to believe the pleas of Ilia's innocence, in one account he concedes to spare her death at his daughter's behest—though not to spare her imprisonment, where she spends her life, liberated only upon the death of Amulius (DH 1.79.1-3). In another account, Amulius's anger rules the day, as he demands Ilia be tortured to death by rod—the punishment meted to defiled Vestals at the time (DH 1.78.5).[15] Regardless of the account, in each instance Rhea Silvia endures

---

15. DH notes that the current punishment for Vestals who fail to maintain their virginity is live burial (1.78.5).

suffering upon suffering not only as she bears her violation itself, but as both she and her children are punished for the violence done to her.

Rhea Silvia/Ilia in Ovid

In her article "Rape and the Founding of Rome," Julia Hemker writes,

> In the didactic treatise on *amor*, the *Ars Amatoria*, Ovid's narrator addresses his audience as "soldiers in arms" (*miles in arma venis* 1.36). According to him, love itself represents a kind of warfare (*militiae species amor est* 2.233) involving force, sieges, and carefully waged "campaigns." The relationship between the "conquests" of love and war in Roman history, however, points to a far different analysis of what attitudes forge the underlying connection between these two pursuits.[16]

While Hemker elaborates the connections between "love," conquest, and rape, particularly in terms of the Sabines narrative, these dynamics are seen as well in Ilia's tale of rape, which precedes it.

Though the *Ars Amatoria* does not reference Ilia by name, her memory is obliquely evoked as Ovid traces Augustus's lineage through the gods Mars and Caesar, who have girded him with arms (*arma*).[17] This connection between war and love, or more appropriately lust, in terms of Rhea Silvia/Ilia is more explicit in his treatments of her in the *Fasti*[18] and *Amores*.[19] Book 3 of the *Fasti*, Ovid's poetic Book of Days

16. Hemker, "Rape and the Founding of Rome," 41.
17. "Your father and the father of your country has girded you with arms. . . . Father Mars and father Caesar, vouchsafe him your presence as he goes; for one of you is, and one will be, a god" (Ovid, *Ars* 1.196–97, 203–4). Ovid also mentions Ilia in *Tristia* 2.257–60 (referencing Ennius). This connection between Mars, Augustus, and love is important for the reading of the Ovidian texts. As Augustus traces his lineage through Mars and Venus (Venus and the mortal Anchises parent Aeneas; Ilia is also a descendant of Aeneas, she and Mars parenting Romulus), they are also parents through an illicit affair of the god of love, Cupid. Referencing *Amores* 1.2.34–37, Cahoon emphasizes that "the introduction of elements from Roman triumphs into the conventional figure of love's warfare explicitly links *amor* and Rome in a striking new way. Like a Roman victor, Cupid subjugates and enslaves the conquered; Roman love demeans and enslaves the lover. Thus, the final lines of the poem ominously equate Caesar and Cupid" ("Bed as Battlefield," 295). Here, Cupid and Augustus are linked not only through their lineage but through their actions—actions that will resonate with Rhea Silvia's portrayals in the *Fasti* and *Amores*, where she captivates the god of war (*Fasti*) and then is destroyed in the aftermath of his "love" (*Amores*).
18. See esp. Stephen Hinds, "*Arma* in Ovid's *Fasti*, Part 1: Genre and Mannerism," *Arethusa* 25.1 (1992): 81–112; and his "*Arma* in Ovid's *Fasti*, Part 2: Genre, Romulean Rome and Augustan Ideology," *Arethusa* 25.1 (1992): 113–53.
19. See esp. Cahoon, "Bed as Battlefield."

explaining the Roman calendar, addresses Mars's own month of March. Ovid begins,

> Come, warlike Mars; set down your shield and spear for a short time, and loose your glistering locks from your helmet. Perhaps you may ask, "What has a poet to do with Mars?" . . . You see, yourself, fierce wars are waged by Minerva's hands. Is she for that the less free for noble arts? Follow the precedent of Pallas, take time to lay aside the lance. You will find something to do unarmed (*inermis*). Then, too, were you unarmed [*inermis*] when the Roman priestess captivated [*cepit*] you, that you might grant this city a great seed." (*Fasti* 3.1–3; 5–10)[20]

Rhea Silvia/Ilia has yet to be named, though is clearly marked through the words "Roman priestess." Anyone hearing or reading Ovid's words in the ancient world would know the story well, understanding that, while Mars may be laying aside his arms, he is not laying aside his violence. Indeed, *cepit* (*capio*), with its connotations of seizure, war, and imprisonment,[21] indicates that the machinations of war have not been left aside as Mars is taken captive by Ilia even as he intends to capture her.[22]

Ovid then turns to describe "Silvia the Vestal," who has gone "to fetch water to wash the holy things" (*Fasti* 3.11–12). Worn from her journey with the water vessel, she wearily sat by the river bank and "opened her bosom to catch the breezes, and composed her ruffled hair" (3.15–16). At peace, and thinking she is alone in this serene setting, Ilia falls asleep, and "[s]eductive slumber stealthily [*furtim*] stole [*obrepsit*] her conquered [*victis*] eyes" (3.19).[23] As Ovid applies the

---

20. Translation in consultation with, Ovid, *Fasti* (Frazer and Goold, LCL).
21. Lewis & Short, s.v. *capio*: "to take in hand, take hold of, lay hold of, take, seize, grasp; very frequently of arms, to take up arms, i.e. engage in war or battle; to take into possession, take captive, seize, make prisoner."
22. Cf. Hinds, "*Arma* in the *Fasti*, Part 1," 93: "For *Mars inermis*, as he succumbs to Silvia, the life of war yields temporarily to . . . the life of love" (cf. *Fasti* 3.8–10). While this may be a part of the story, his violence toward Rhea Silva and the militarization of the language of "love," seem to indicate that nothing is left behind but rather the life of war is infused into the life of love. Hinds does address some of the complications of this when Ovid again invokes Mars in 3.167–68, and, though Mars lays aside his helmet, he does not lay aside his spear as he is "invoked to promote peace," as Mars's "renunciation of *arma* in favour of *studia pacis* (3.173) is actually less than complete," illustrated further as he begins his renunciation by telling a story of *arma*—that of the Sabine women (99–103). Hinds's concern in this essay is primarily one of genre and the relationship between elegy and epic in the *Fasti*. See below in the discussion of Ovid's version of the Sabines narrative.

attributes of stealth and conquest to her "seductive slumber," these words more aptly describe the actions Mars is about to take, as this vision of Ilia "captivates" him. In quick succession we are told, "Mars saw her; the sight inspired him with desire [*cupit*], and his desire [*cupita*] was followed by possession [*potiturque*], but by his divine power he concealed his stolen joys [*furta fefellit ope*]" (*Fasti* 3.21–22). In these lines Ovid directly connects Mars's actions to Rhea Silvia's sleep through the words *furtim/furtum*, as both sleep and Mars secret her away.

Mars departs the scene as Ovid returns to Rhea Silvia, already pregnant and growing with Mars's progeny. She then speaks her vision predicting the births of Romulus and Remus, the attempt against them by Amulius, and their salvation by the shewolf. Ovid says little about her state beyond the physical, noting her "weakness" from the pregnancy (*languida*, 3.25) as she supports herself with a tree (3.26) and lifts her water jar with "feeble force" (*non firmis viribus*, 3.39). While Ovid primarily affords Ilia a physical description in the *Fasti*, he paints a painful portrait of her emotional state in the sixth elegy of his *Amores*.[24]

In the *Amores*, the personified Anio river, which flowed into the Tiber and provided much of the water in ancient Rome's aqueducts, was "charmed" (*placuit*) by Ilia, though, rather than in a relaxing repose as Mars found her, "she was disheveled, hair torn by nails, cheeks marked by them" as she "mourned both her uncle's crime [*nefas*] and Mars's offense [*delictaque*]." Acknowledging her harm by both man and god, she was found "wandering barefoot through deserted places" (*Amores* 3.6.45–50),[25] as

23. See Lewis & Short, s.vv. *furtim* and *obrepo*. Both words have connotations of stealth, though *furtim* seems to spill into the clandestine and private while *obrepo* indicates creeping up on and surprising.

24. Connors notes that in the *Fasti* Ovid "uses [Ilia's] dream to close off her point of view and demonstrate only her ignorance of what happened to her, while the audience can easily interpret the dream's symbolism" ("Ennius, Ovid and Representations of Ilia," 108). This strategy is in opposition to that which Ovid will use in the *Amores*. Ovid draws on Ennius, whose work is preserved in Cicero (*De Divinatione* 1.20.40–41), who also relays a dream of Ilia's, opening Ilia's consciousness rather than foreclosing it. See the discussion below of Ilia in the *Amores*.

25. This translation is in consultation with Ovid, *Amores*, trans. A. S. Kline, http://poetryin translation.com/PITBR/Latin/AmoresBkIII.htm#_Toc520536662; and Ovid, *Amores* (Showerman and Goold, LCL).

Anio saw her from his fierce, flowing rapids
and lifted from the waves his hollow mouth,
and said, "Why do you anxiously tread my banks,
Ilia, child of Laomedon's Troy?
Where has your splendor gone? Why do you roam alone,
with no white ribbon to bind your hair?
Why do you weep, marring your moist eyes with tears,
and why do you beat your bared breasts with frantic hand?
He has stone and iron in his heart
who can look indifferently at the tears on your tender face.
Ilia, allay your fears! My palace will open for you,
my waters will tend you. Ilia, allay your fears!
You will reign among a hundred nymphs or more:
for a hundred or more are held in my stream.
Don't reject [sperne] me so, I beg you, child of Troy:
you will have gifts greater than my promise."
He spoke. She cast her modest [modestos] eyes on the ground
And scattered a storm of tears on her tender breast.
Three times she struggled to flee [fugam], three times she resisted [resistit]
the water,
fear snatching her strength to run.
Then, at last, rending her hair with hostile hands,
she uttered with quivering mouth resounding words of shame [indigos]:
"O, if only my bones had been gathered in my father's tomb,
when they were able to be gathered as the bones of a virgin!
Why, as a Vestal, am I summoned to a wedding torch [taedas]
disgraced [turpis], and disowned [infitianda] by Ilium's hearth?
Why remain and be designated as an adulteress [adultera] by the pointing
crowd?
Let the face die that carries the mark [notet] of infamy [famosus] and shame
[pudor]!"
With this she placed her dress against her swollen eyes,
and released herself, ruined [perdita], into the swift waters.
The river placed his slippery hands under her breast,
they say, and shared with her the vow [iura] of the marriage bed [tori].
(Amores 3.6.51–82)

Through these lines, we see how, in Nita Krevans's words, "Ilia's
seduction brings her exile and loss."[26] Though Krevans is speaking of
Ilia's seduction by Mars, these words also reflect Ilia in the wake of
her seduction by the Anio. Ilia's exile and loss form the undercurrent

---

26. Nita Krevans, "Ilia's Dream: Ennius, Virgil, and the Mythology of Seduction," HSCP 95 (1993): 270.

of Ovid's picture of her in the *Amores*, where, in the aftershock of Amulius's crime and Mars's offense, Ilia is left isolated, enduring the consequences of their actions against her. In her moment of anguish, the river Anio takes advantage of her desperate state, seducing and sexualizing her as in her encounter with Mars, but it also provides an option, a reprieve, a way out—though one that would end her life.[27] Those who encounter Ilia's story are left with a visceral sense of the profound alienation, loss, and acute shame felt by her—an alienation and shame that convince her that suicide is a better option than life;[28] a loss so profound that she gives in to the life-ending seduction of the river, knowing that the events of her life have already given her death whether she remains alive or not.[29]

27. Connors notes the disjunction between Ilia's and Anio's perspectives: "from Ilia's point of view it is suicide . . . ; from Anio's point of view it is marriage" ("Ennius, Ovid and Representations of Ilia," 110).

28. Ibid., 100–111: "Like Lucretia (and note that Ovid in the *Fasti* pointedly juxtaposes Lucretia and Ilia/Rhea Silvia), Ovid's Ilia in Amores 3.6 commits suicide in the aftermath of rape in order to exert control over the interpretation of her sexual behavior, that is to prevent herself from being regarded as a woman who sought out scandal. Like Lucretia, Ovid's Ilia tries to avoid becoming a textbook example of illicit and scandalous sexual behavior," 111. (Of course, in many ways there is even more at stake for Rhea Silvia than for Lucretia, given her status as a Vestal.) But, despite Ilia's attempt to salvage her reputation, Ovid, in Connor's readings disallows this possibility. Connor turns to *Amores* 3.4.37–40 ("He is too rustic who is wounded by his wife's adultery, and does not sufficiently know the manners of the City, in which Mars's sons were not born without crime, Romulus, son of Ilia, Ilia's son Remus," *rusticus est nimium, quem laedit adultera coniunx, / et notos mores non satis Urbis habet, / in qua Martigenae non sunt sine crimine nati / Romulus Iliades Iliadesque Remus*), arguing that these lines imply that "Ilia's children Romulus and Remus were the result of her sexual misbehavior. . . . the poet-narrator has just turned his own gaze upon the text of Rome's origins and pointed to Ilia herself as an exemplar of sexual misconduct" (111). She continues, "[Ovid's] story of Ilia and her suicide calls attention to the power he as a poet exerts over her reputation. . . . Thus, Ennius and Ovid devise Ilia's perceptions of her rape by Mars in ways which call attention to their own processes of poetic production. These suggestions about poetic self-consciousness in representations of Ilia's point of view do not encourage one to read sympathy into Ennius' and Ovid's narratives of rape and its aftermath in the founding of Rome. On the contrary, the poets' literary exploitations of Ilia's point of view mirror the mythical exploitation of her powers of reproduction" (112).

Connor's points here are extremely important, as they call attention to the way that both the act of rape and its reproduction participate in the power dynamics inherent in sexual violence, though I still believe that Ovid's portrayal is more complicated than this. Though Ovid uses Ilia as an example of why a husband should show leniency toward his wife's adultery, his framing of Ilia here calls into question the nature of adultery itself. In the *Fasti*, it is a sleeping Ilia that Mars has forced himself upon and there is no tradition that makes Ilia complicit in her rape—they all name the act as a violent one, as one of force. Here, too, Mars is named as the father, and it is impossible to know if the "crime" to which Ovid refers is the rape of a freeborn woman of Rome, the rape of a Vestal, or adultery (a crime of which Mars himself is guilty). Ovid's representation of Ilia in the *Amores* is, in my read, a complex and sympathetic one, and one that, as with so many of his works, addresses multivalent themes, including those of Augustan culture and ideology.

29. Cahoon proposes that "the connections between love and conquest through the imagery of the

Conclusion

These stories of Rhea Silvia's rape by Mars highlight connections between divinity, deception, and violence embedded in Rome's origins—against Numitor and his family more generally, but particularly against his daughter Ilia. Regardless of whether Mars is believed to be the prime perpetrator in Rhea Silvia's rape, the language used by Livy, Dionysius, and Ovid to describe her violation is the language of battle and violence—language that associates these acts, irrespective of the actor, with Mars.[30] This connection of Mars both with Rhea Silvia and with the founding of the city becomes a particularly important one as Augustus refashions Rome in the wake of his defeat of Antony and rise to power. Augustus, through the Julian line, could trance his ancestry to Aeneas, thus to the goddess Venus, mother of Aeneas by Anchises. Rhea Silvia, as well, "belonged to the Trojan family of Aeneas and could therefore be incorporated into the family tree of Augustus"—hence her appellation of Ilia by the Augustan poets, that is, from Ilium/Troy. Therefore, Augustus could doubly claim divine origins through Rhea Silvia: once by way Aeneas, son of Venus and Anchises, ancestor of Rhea Silvia, and again through Romulus, Rhea Silvia's son by Mars, and ancestor to the Roman people.[31] Through these genealogies, Augustus not only could trace his ancestry back to the two most important figures for Rome's founding, Aeneas and Romulus, but was also able "to consolidate the story of his emergent Roman Empire into a clean genealogical line back to Mars and Venus."[32] But tracing this lineage through Mars and Venus, portrayed

Amores . . . suggest[s] that the theme of erotic warfare is not merely a witty exercise, but also and exposé of the competitive, violent, and destructive nature of *amor*, an exposé that calls into question fundamental Roman attitudes in both the public and the private spheres" ("Ennius, Ovid and Representations of Ilia," 294). In the story of Rhea Silvia in the *Amores*, Ovid shows the consequences of the "competitive, violent, and destructive nature of *amor*," as the violence perpetrated against Rhea Silvia by the god of war for the public good, that is, the birth of the founders of the city, compels her to enact her own self-destruction.

30. Livy 1.4.2: *vi compressa*; DH 1.77.1: βιάζεταί; 1.77.2: τὸν βιασάμενον, τοῦ βιασμοῦ; Ovid Fasti 3.10: *cepit*; 3.19, 22: *furtim*; 3.19: *obrepsit*; 3.22: *potiturque*; Amores 3.6.49: *nefas, delictaque*.
31. Paul Zanker, *The Power of Images in the Age of Augustus*, trans. Alan Shapiro (Ann Arbor: University of Michigan Press, 1988), 195.
32. Lopez, *Apostle to the Conquered*, 62.

side by side as Augustus's progenitors both on the pediment and in the cella of his temple to Mars Ultor, was not without its issues.[33] Mars and Venus, the spouse of Vulcan, were engaged in an adulterous relationship—something Ovid in particular poked at, given Augustus's strict Julian Laws on adultery.[34]

There is a resonance between Augustus as he traces his lineage through Mars and Venus and Mars and Rhea Silvia/Ilia—both pairings venturing into the realm of taboo. While the adulterous pairing of Mars and Venus represents a taboo in terms of Augustan sexuality laws, Rhea Silvia's rape signifies the ultimate sacred taboo:[35] not only is Rhea Silvia a citizen who is raped (an act that breaks the Julian Laws regulating sexuality), but the integrity of the Vestals, whose perpetual virginity ensures the integrity of the state, is broken through Mars's rape—but it is broken so that the city of Rome itself can be founded.[36] This will also be the last time this type of transgression will be permitted in relation to the Vestals—for other transgressions signal the penetrability of Rome itself.[37] Augustus's new sexual legislation also signifies the importance of Roman bodily integrity for the state, as well as the morality and piety it reflects, in his refounding and renewal of Rome. But of course this bodily integrity applies only to Rome and to Romans proper—others can be done with as seems fit.

---

33. Zanker, *Power of Images*, 195–96.
34. Ibid.: "Venus and Mars were then both ancestors of the Romans, though by different partners—something Ovid would turn into an ironic comment on the marriage legislation. Together Mars and Venus would watch over and protect their own. Mars guaranteed the Romans *virtus*, while Venus granted fertility and prosperity. The myth of the Julian family thus became the centerpiece of the new national myth. From now on the statue of the goddess of love would always stand beside that of the war god, even though this inevitably recalled the story of their adulterous affair in Greek mythology. But under Augustus this issue was skirted and the myth reinterpreted as prefiguring the destiny of the Julii as the chosen people of Mars.

   "Before the Battle of Actium Octavian had minted coins with his ancestress Venus holding the arms of Mars, a blatant reference to the erotic aspect of their relationship. But in the pediment of the Temple of Mars Ultor, she reflects her new role, dignified in a long garment and holding a scepter, standing beside the war god. In the temple cella her statue was also beside that of Mars (*Ultori iuncta*, says Ovid, Tristia 2.295, adding that her husband [Vulcan] had to wait outside the door). There indeed stood the statue of the fire god, in honor of Augustus for his establishment of the city fire department."
35. See Mary Douglas, *Purity and Danger: An Analysis of Concepts of Pollution and Taboo* (New York: Routledge, 2002).
36. See Holt N. Parker, "Why Were the Vestals Virgins? Or the Chastity of Women and the Safety of the Roman State," *American Journal of Philology* 175.4 (2004): 563–601.
37. See also "Tarpeia and the Sabines" and "Embodied Nations and Vestal Virgins" in this chapter.

While these complex dynamics will continue to play an important role in the subsequent narratives explored in this study, it is of significance here, as Davina Lopez rightly notes, that "the centrality of the violence against Ilia/Rhea, presented as what must occur for her to give birth to the founder(s) of Rome, should not be overlooked—this pivotal event in the divinely ordained story of Roman origins is a rape narrative."[38]

The Romans' Rape of the Sabines[39]

The next pivotal rape narrative in the history of Rome's foundation is the rape of the Sabine women, a tightly woven narrative of sexual and imperial conquest; a tale of rape, war, and colonization, as well as an aetiological tale of Roman marriage.[40] Studies of this story often focus solely on the rape of the women but, especially in the narratives of Livy, Dionysius of Halicarnassus, and Plutarch (though also important in Cicero's and Ovid's treatments respectively), the rape of the Sabine (and other) women[41] cannot be extricated from its broader story line of conquest. The story of the Sabine women is a story of what it means to be a wife, what it means to be a colony, and what it means to be Roman. These thematics will be crucial for looking at the gendering of conquest in Roman imperial ideology, as well as for looking at the connections between the rulers, rape, and relationships within the Genesis cosmogonies. This section begins by looking at the narratives of Livy, Dionysius of Halicarnassus, and Plutarch, as well as the short treatment by Cicero, in a comparative frame. Next, I turn to Ovid's two accounts of the rape of the Sabines, as their narrative strategies differ significantly from the other accounts.[42]

---

38. Lopez, *Apostle to the Conquered*, 61.
39. Translations in this section are also based on the LCL editions noted above and Plutarch, *Romulus* (Perrin, LCL), often with significant emendations.
40. See, e.g., Treggiari, *Roman Marriage*, 3–5; Gary B. Miles, "The First Roman Marriage and the Theft of the Sabine Women," in *Innovations of Antiquity*, ed. Ralph Hexter and Daniel Selden (New York: Routledge, 1992), 179; Emma Dench, *Romulus' Asylum: Roman Identities from the Age of Alexander to the Age of Hadrian* (New York: Oxford University Press, 2005), 20–25.
41. Throughout this study I will generally use the expression "the Sabine women" to signify all the women abducted by the Romans in this narrative, but often (depending on the version of the story) women from other neighboring towns are among the abducted women as well.
42. This analysis will, of course, be limited and will not be able to engage all of the complexities of honor and shame, gender, and violence that are present in the text. Rather, I will address and

Romulus's Plan and Seizure of the Sabine Women

Rome was a city of men—filled with rabble and ex-criminals. But though, as Livy puts it, "Rome was now strong enough to hold its own in war with any of the adjacent states . . . owing to the want of women a single generation was likely to see the end of its greatness, since it had neither prospect of posterity at home nor the right of intermarriage [*conubia*] with its neighbors" (Livy 1.9.1). This lack of women is the primary reason for the Romans' seizure and rape according to all of the sources, though several of them offer alternative motives as well. Cicero claims that, though the plan to entrap the women was "rather boorish" (*subagrestis*), it was one that "bore the mark of a great and foresighted [*longe providentis*] man" because it "secured the resources of his kingdom and people" (*muniendas opes regni ac populi*, *Rep.* 2.12). Cicero is the only one to explicitly call Romulus's plan to rape the women "boorish," but he seems to annul this sentiment in his subsequent praise of Romulus. While Livy, Dionysius, and Plutarch do not state any objections to the plan or make any comments as pointed as Cicero's, their narratives exhibit certain ambivalences regarding the Romans' actions as well.[43]

Dionysius initially states in his *Roman Antiquities* 2.30.1 that the nations surrounding Rome were not "friendly" (φίλιον) to them, and the Romans "desired to conciliate them by intermarriages [οἰκειώσασθι ταῦτα βουληθεὶς ἐπιγαμίας], which, in the opinion of the ancients, was the surest method of cementing friendships [φιλίας]" (DH 2.30.1). Later, in 2.31.1, he lists several different reasons that he attributes to other historians regarding the motivation for Romulus's actions. These include both a "scarcity of women" and simply "a pretext for war," but Dionysius favors the opinion that it was for "forcing an alliance with the neighboring cities, founded on friendship" (εἰς τὸ συνάψαι φιλότητα πρὸς τὰς πλησιοχώρους πόλεις ἀναγκαίαν, DH 2.31.1). But, despite these appeals, the neighboring cities "were not willing to unite [συνέλθοιεν]

---

highlight aspects and thematics in an effort to understand further the Genesis cosmogonies that lie at the heart of this study.

43. See Robert M. Ogilvie, *Commentary on Livy: Books 1–5* (Oxford: Clarendon, 1965), 65.

with the Romans, who were just getting settled together, and who neither were powerful by wealth nor displayed any brilliant works, but they would yield to force [βιασθεῖσαι] if no wantonness [ὕβρις] accompanied such compulsion" (DH 2.30.2).

Like Dionysius, Livy stresses Romulus's desire for alliance (*societatem*), but, again, this reason seems co-equal with the Romans' request for intermarriage (*conubiumpque*). On the advice of the senate, Romulus sends envoys to the neighboring nations (*gentes*) in an effort to establish these ties (Livy 1.9.2). The Romans appeal to their neighbors on two grounds: first, that "Rome's origins had been blessed by the gods and their manliness was not lacking" (*origini Romanae et deos adfuisse et non defuturam virtutem*); and, second, that because of their blessing and manliness their neighbors "should not be reluctant to mingle their blood and race with the Romans, who were as truly men as they were" (*ne gravarentur homines cum hominibus sanguinem ac genus miscer*, Livy 1.9.4.) But, according to Livy, the envoys did not receive a "friendly hearing" anywhere (*nusquam benigne legatio audita est*) and were rejected (*spernebant*). The neighboring peoples "feared" (*metuebant*) the bourgeoning power of the Romans, "both for themselves and their descendants." Adding insult to injury, Livy says that the Roman envoys "were frequently asked, on being dismissed, if they had opened a sanctuary for women as well as for men, for that was the only way they would obtain suitable wives" (Livy 1.9.5).

Plutarch also offers two possible motives for the seizure of the Sabine women. He states that "some say" Romulus, "being naturally fond of war [τῇ φύσει φιλοπόλεμον ὄντα], and being persuaded by sundry oracles, too, that it was the destiny [πέπρωται] of Rome to be nourished and increased by wars [πολέμοις] until it became the greatest of cities, thereby merely began unprovoked hostilities [βίας] against the Sabines; for he did not take many maidens [παρθένους], but thirty only, since what he wanted was war rather than marriages" (*Rom.* 14.2). Plutarch does not believe this explanation and says that Romulus, upon "seeing his city filling up at once with aliens, few of whom had wives, while the greater part of them, being a mixed rabble of needy and obscure persons, were looked down upon and expected to have no strong cohesion [συμμενεῖν]; and hoped to make the wrong [τὸ ἀδίκημα] an occasion for some sort of comingling [συγκράσεως] and political fellowship [κοινωνίας ἀρχήν] with the Sabines after their women had been tamed [ἡμερωσαμένοις]"[44] (Rom. 14.2). Again there is the implication that the Romans are not of good stock, but here the gloss is the narrator's and is not placed in the mouths of the neighboring communities, as in Livy.

Plutarch's reference to Romulus's actions as ἀδίκημα echoes some of the same negative sentiments seen in Cicero (Rep. 2.12), but these sentiments, as in Cicero, will be tempered by the rest of Plutarch's narrative frame. The impulse to temper this negative assessment can be seen already in an earlier reference in Romulus describing the event:

> For that the residents of Alba would not consent to give the fugitives the privilege of intermarriage with them, nor even receive them as fellow-citizens [πολίτας], is clear, in the first place, from the rape of the Sabine women, which was not a deed of wanton daring [ὕβρει τολμηθέν], but one of necessity [ἀνάγκην], owing to the lack of marriages by consent; for they certainly honored [ἐτίμησαν] the women beyond measure when they had ravaged them [ἁρπάσαντες]. (Rom. 9.2)

Here there are also echoes of Dionysius of Halicarnassus (DH 2.30.2) in Plutarch's insistence that the rape of the Sabines was not one of "wanton daring," but justifiable on the basis of the Romans' need for both women and political alliance.[45]

In order to secure both women and alliances with the neighboring peoples, Romulus concocts a plan to lure them to Rome under the guise of celebrating a festival in honor of Neptune, which he names the Consualia (Livy 1.9.6; DH 2.30; Rom. 14.3). Dionysius and Plutarch both state that it was the neighboring peoples' disregard for the Romans that "necessitated" Romulus's plan of abduction (DH 2.31.1–2; Rom.

---

44. LSJ, s.v. ἡμερόω: "tame, make tame. Of men also, civilize, humanize, tame by conquest, subdue." This is especially interesting given the intersections between the rape and Rome's colonial project in this narrative.

45. Plutarch will again deny the ὕβρις of Romulus's actions with the Sabine women in comparing him with Theseus (T&R 6.1–3). It seems likely that the constant need for justification of both Dionysius and Plutarch points to some uneasiness about the narrative on their parts.

9.2), but Livy is more specific, noting the reaction of Romulus and the Romans to their neighbors' refusals. Livy says the Romans found their neighbors' rejection "grievous," thus ensuring that "the matter was certain to end in violence [*vim*]" (Livy 1.9.6) and that Romulus "concealed his resentment" as he put his plan into action (Livy 1.9.6). While Dionysius also mentions the use of force (βιασθεῖσαι, DH 2.30.2), he—as well as Plutarch—consistently tempers the violence of Romulus and the Romans by saying that this "force" was without "wantonness" (ὕβρις) (DH 2.30.2; *Rom.* 9.2; 14.6).

While Plutarch simply states that "many people gathered" to see the games (*Rom.* 14.4)[46] and Dionysius states that "many strangers came with their wives and children to the festival" (DH 2.20.4),[47] Livy's narrative is more elaborate in describing the Romans' reception of their neighbors. He relates that the Romans used all of the resources at their disposal for the event in order to ensure excitement among their neighbors (Livy 1.9.7), and that many came, including those from Caenina, Crustumium, and Antemnae, because, in addition to attending the festival, they were "eager to see the new city" (1.9.8). The Sabines came as well "with all their people, including their children and wives" (1.9.9). Livy recounts that "they" (probably all who came and not just the Sabines) were "hospitably entertained [*invitati hospitaliter*] in every house, and when they had looked at the site of the city, its walls, and its numerous buildings, they marveled that Rome had so rapidly grown great" (1.9.9). So, despite their initial fear of Rome's power (1.9.5), Rome's neighbors were enticed enough by the festival and intrigued enough by the city to overcome, or at least set aside, their fears and accept the Romans' invitation. One can imagine, as well, that these fears were allayed by the Romans' hospitality, and, although Livy does not explicitly say it, the Romans' hospitality seems only a ruse given what follows.

During the "spectacle,"[48] which consisted of "sacrifices" and

---

46. Note that Plutarch names only the Sabines among the women who are ravaged in *Rom.* 14.5.
47. Dionysius's text seems to imply that more than just the Sabine women were ravished, but it is unclear from the text and is never explicitly stated.
48. Livy 1.9.10: *spectaculum*; DH 2.30.4 and *Rom.* 14.4: θεά

"games,"[49] and which Livy notes kept "people's eyes and thoughts . . . busy," Romulus gave a signal for "the preconcerted attack" (*ex composito orta vis*, Livy 1.9.10)—an attack that Plutarch names "an onslaught" (ἐπιχειρήσεως, *Rom.* 14.5)—and the virgins (*virgo*/παρθένος) were ravaged (*rapio*/ἁρπάζω) (Livy 1.9.10; *Rom.* 14.5-6).[50] Livy's earlier remark (1.9.6) that "the matter seemed certain to end in violence [*vim*]" is realized in his parallel usage of *vis* here.

Livy, Dionysius, and Plutarch all remark on the haphazard nature of the seizures. Livy says that after the signal, "the young Romans darted this way and that, to seize and carry off the virgins. In most cases these were seized by the men in whose path they chanced to be" (*iuventus Romana ad rapiendas virgines discurrit. Magna pars forte, in quem quaeque inciderat, raptae*, Livy 1.9.10–11).[51] Dionysius relates that the young men were ordered "to seize the virgins who had come to the spectacle, each group taking those they should first encounter" (ἁρπάζειν τὰς παρούσας ἐπὶ τὴν θέαν παρθένους, αἷς ἂν ἐπιτύχωσιν ἕκαστοι, DH 2.30.4) and that "when they saw the signal raised, turned to seizing the virgins" (ἐπιδὴ τὸ σύνθημα ἀρθὲν εἶδον τρέπονται πρὸς τὴν τῶν παρθένων ἁρπαγήν, DH 2.30.5). And Plutarch states this most simply, saying, "and when the signal was given, they drew their swords, rushed in with shouts and ravished away the daughters of the Sabines" (καὶ τοῦ σημείου γενομένου σπασάμενοι τὰ ξίφη καὶ μετὰ βοῆς ὁρμήσαντες ἥρπαζον τὰς θυγατέρας τῶν Σαβίνων, *Rom.* 14.5).

Each of the authors presents similar but varying accounts of the crowd's reactions in the midst of the commotion. Plutarch says that the

---

49. DH 2.30.4 and *Rom.* 14.4: θυσία and ἀγών; Livy and Cicero, "games" (ludus) only (Livy 1.9.6 and *Rep.* 2.12).
50. These terms are consistent throughout all four of the texts (Lewis & Short, s.v. *virgo*;/LSJ, s.v. παρθένος: maiden or virgin; Lewis & Short, s.v. *rapio*, "carry off by force; to seize, rob, ravish; to plunder, ravage, lay waste, take by assault, carry by force"; LSJ, s.v. ἁρπάζω, "seize, snatch away, carry off, be a robber, overpower, captivate, ravish, plunder"), though in these verses Plutarch refers to the women as "the daughters of the Sabines" (τὰς θυγατέρας τῶν Σαβίνων, *Rom.* 14.5).
51. Hemker ("Rape and the Founding of Rome," 42) notes that, in Livy's narrative, "Chance, *fors*, plays the greater role [than deliberate action], an idea which recurs throughout Livy's narrative. The men seize whichever women they come upon: *magna pars forte in quem quaeque inciderat raptae* (1.9.11). The 'accidental' nature of the planned seizure frees both Romulus and the men from any guilt by placing the blame on 'chance,' a nonhuman agency." This idea seems to connect to 1.9.4, where the Romans claim that Rome's "origin had been blessed with the favor of the Gods," and follows the textual through-line of the Romans' evading responsibility for their actions.

Romans "permitted and encouraged the men themselves to escape" (*Rom.* 14.5), and Dionysius reports that "straightaway the strangers were in an uproar and fled, suspecting some greater evil" (DH 2.30.5). Livy recounts that "the games broke up in a panic and the parents of the maidens fled sorrowing" and, reacting to the initial hospitality of the Romans (Livy 1.9.9), says that in addition "they charged the Romans with the crime of violating hospitality, and invoked the gods to whose solemn games they had come, deceived in violation of religion and honor" (*incusantes violate hospitii scelus deumque invocantes, cuius ad sollemne ludosque per fas ac fidem decepti venissent*, Livy 1.9.13).[52] It is this violation of hospitality, religion, and honor that sets the stage for the Roman marriage.

The First Roman Marriage

Though the subject is addressed at different points in each of the Sabines narratives, all three authors speak about marriage ritual and custom—rituals and customs inextricable from the violent actions in which they are embedded. Dionysius differs significantly from both Livy and Plutarch in that he appeals to the Greek past as justification in his narrative rather than using the story as a specifically Roman narrative to explain present-day customs. In Dionysius, Romulus relays that the seizure of women for marriage, "was an ancient Greek custom and that of all methods of contracting marriages for women it was the most distinguished" (DH 2.30.5), thereby justifying the Roman's use of abduction and force.

Livy specifically uses the story of the women's abduction to explain the origin of the wedding cry, "Thalassius." He says,

> Some, of exceptional beauty [*forma excellentes*], had been marked out for the chief senators, and were carried off [*raptae*] to their houses by

52. Cicero summarizes this whole episode in two brief sentences: "Respectable Sabine virgins had come to Rome on the festival of Consus to attend the yearly games which Romulus had inaugurated. On his orders they were seized and assigned in marriage to young men of the foremost families" (*Sabinas honesto ortas loco virgines, quae Romam ludorum gratia venissent, quos tum primum anniversarios in circo facere instituisset, Consualibus rapi iussit easque in familiarum amplissimarum matrimoniis collocavit*, Rep. 2.12).

plebeians to whom the office had been entrusted. One, who far excelled the rest in her figure and loveliness, was seized [*raptam*], the story relates, by the gang of a certain Thalassius. Being repeatedly asked for whom they were bearing her off [*ferrent*], they kept shouting that no one should violate her [*ne quis violaret violo*], for they were taking her to Thalassius, and this was the origin of the wedding-cry. (Livy 1.9.11–12)

Plutarch significantly elaborates what is found in Livy. As opposed to the "exceptionally beautiful" women being taken for the Senators, Plutarch says,

certain men of a meaner sort were dragging along a damsel who far surpassed the rest in beauty and stature; and when some men of superior rank met them and tried to rob them,[53] they cried out that they were conducting the girl to Talasius, a young man, but one of excellent repute. The other party, then, on hearing this, shouted and clapped their hands in approval, and some of them actually turned back and accompanied them, out of good will and favor to Talasius, shouting his name as they went along. Hence, indeed, down to the present time, Talasius is the nuptial cry of the Romans. (*Rom.* 15.1–2)

Plutarch continues, suggesting several other origins of the wedding cry: "Talasius was the word which Romulus gave as a signal for the rape [τῆς ἁρπαγῆς]. Therefore, all those who took the maidens [τὰς παρθένυος] away shouted 'Talasius!'" (*Rom.* 15.2–3). The most benign explanation, which Plutarch says is the opinion of most writers, is that "*talasia*" is an old Italian word for "spinning," and that after the war with the Sabines, "it was agreed that their women should perform no other tasks for their husbands than those which were connected with spinning." Therefore, the cry "Talasius!" was a "playful" one because "the woman was led home for no other task than that of spinning" (*Rom.* 15.3–5).

Plutarch also names the story as the origin of the tradition in which women are carried over the threshold into their new homes. New wives are carried over the threshold by their husbands as "the Sabine women were carried in by force [βιασθείσας] and did not go in of their own accord" (*Rom.* 15.5). Finally, Plutarch notes the story as a possible

---

53. Again, the struggle over a woman's body is about rivalry between the men.

origin for "the custom of parting the bride's hair with the head of a spear" as "a reminder that the first marriage was attended with combat [μάχης] and war [πολεμικῶς]" (*Rom.* 15.5).

Here the texts move from public to private, the realm of politics to the realm of the home and marriage, indeed the first Roman marriage. Beginning with the corporate act of deception and abduction, the story moves to intimate relationships where these dynamics play out one to one, where the hierarchy and power inherent in the ravishing of brides becomes the template for relationships between husbands and wives—as evidenced in the custom of carrying over the threshold. This is not the only aetiology of conquest contained in the narrative of the Sabines, but for now, it is important to highlight this shift from public to private and the ways in which the two intersect and implicate each other. As Livy notes, these customs serve as "a reminder that the first marriage was attended with combat and war"—and that these originary dynamics between the Romans and their women will form an ongoing template for Rome's relations with others.[54]

Romulus and His Justifications to the Abducted Women

The story of the Sabine women continues as Romulus (and in some

54. This connection between public and private will be an important theme throughout this study. See, e.g., Rex Stem, "The Exemplary Lessons of Livy's Romulus," *TAPA* 137.2 (2007): 435–71, who argues that Livy's Romulus is an exemplary figure for post-Actium Roman leadership: "When Livy challenges his readers to learn from the monument of history in *pref.* 10, he notably urges them to choose *exempla* both for themselves as individuals and for the state. Thus there is a private and public standard for judgment, and the reader is challenged to uphold that which advances both personal morality and the public good. These two goals can be expected to overlap and would ideally coincide, but the value of an exemplary figure becomes particularly instructive when these different demands come into competition, as they do in the case of Romulus. This study argues that Livy's characterization of Romulus demonstrates the lesson that the needs of the state should be understood as predominant, and hence that when the survival of the state is at risk, the preservation of the state inherently justifies the means necessary to do so" (439). For complexities of the relationship between public and private particularly in Livy, Stem cites Joseph B. Solodow, "Livy and the Story of Horatius, 1.24–26," *TAPA* 109 (1979): 251–68; Ann Vasaly, "Personality and Power: Livy's Depiction of the Appii Claudii in the First Pentad," *TAPA* 117 (1987): 203–26; Andrew Feldherr, *Spectacle and Society in Livy's History* (Berkeley: University of California Press, 1998); and Elizabeth Vandiver, "The Founding Mothers of Livy's Rome: The Sabine Women and Lucretia," in *The Eye Expanded: Life and the Arts in Greco-Roman Antiquity*, ed. F. B. Titchener and R. F. Moorton Jr. (Berkeley: University of California Press, 1999), 206–32. Additionally, while the binary of public and private often occurs along gender lines the reality of this is, as always, much more complex; see Mary T. Boatwright, "Women and Gender in the Forum Romanum," *TAPA* 141.1 (2011): 108 and 108n9.

cases the Roman men as a whole) address the newly abducted women. Dionysius's narrative is the only one in which Romulus orders the Roman men not to violate the women upon their seizure but "to guard their chastity through the night [φυλάττειν ἁγνὰς ἐκείνην τὴν νύκτα] and bring them to him the next day" (DH 2.30.4). When the "virgins" (παρθένων) are brought to Romulus, Dionysius says "he comforted [παραμυθησάμενος][55] them in their despair" (DH 2.30.5). Dionysius then states—using the same justification found in 2.30.1—that Romulus assured them "that they had been seized [ἁρπαγῆς], not out of wantonness [ὕβρει], but for the purpose of marriage; for he showed them [ἀποφαίνων] that this was an ancient Greek custom and that of all methods of contracting marriages for women it was the most illustrious [ἐπιφανέστατον], and he asked them to cherish [στέργειν] those whom Fate [τύχης] had given them for their husbands" (DH 2.30.5). Of particular interest is the word that Dionysius uses for "cherish" (στέργειν). It is a word that connotes affection in relationships laden with power differentials—parents and children, ruler and ruled, god and humans, city and colonies, masters and dogs—and can also signify both private and broader public sentiment.[56] Given the connotations of στέργειν, it seems that this sentiment of cherishing provides a link between the private marriage that has just been presented in Dionysius's text and the colonization to come. In addition, while Romulus's voice is clear and strong in articulating the women's situation, Dionysius says nothing of the women's reactions or feelings themselves, but only presents the actions and words of Romulus and the Romans in regard to them.

Livy's account finally relays something of the reaction of the women: "The stolen maidens [raptis] were no more hopeful of their plight [than their parents], nor less indignant." As in Dionysius, Livy's Romulus

55. LSJ, s.v. παραμυθέομαι: "speak soothingly, encourage, console, comfort, relieve, assuage, abate, soften down palliate, explain away, excuse, support, justify."
56. LSJ, s.v. στέργω: "love, feel affection, freq. of the mutual love of parents and children; of the love of the ruled people for a ruler; of the love of a tutelary god for the people; of a wheedling demagogue; of a city and her colonies; of the love of dogs for their master; less freq. of the love of husband and wife; seldom of sexual love; of a horse and mare; generally, to be fond of, show affection for; accept it gladly; to be content or satisfied, acquiesce; oblige, do me the favour; bear with; desire, entreat."

45

responds to the women; he "went among them and explained [*docebatque*][57] that the arrogance [*superbia*][58] of their parents had caused this deed, when they had refused their neighbors the right to intermarry" (Livy 1.9.14). Julie Hemker emphasizes Livy's use of the verb *doceo*,[59] highlighting that Romulus is "teaching" the women that their feelings are moot, because the abduction is actually the fault of their own parents and their *superbia* ("arrogance").[60] There are resonances between Romulus as portrayed by Livy and Dionysius as Dionysius's Romulus "shows by reasoning" or "gives evidence" (ἀποφαίνων) to the women that their capture is actually "illustrious" (ἐπιφανέστατον, DH 2.30.5), though these are two different types of justifications for the Roman's actions.

Livy's Romulus continues by telling the women that "nevertheless they should be wedded and become allies in all the possessions of the Romans [*in societate*[61] *fortunarum omnium*], in their citizenship [*civitatisque*] and, than which nothing is dearer [*carius*] to the human race, in their children [*liberum*]" (Livy 1.9.14). What may have been an allusion and foreshadowing by Dionysius in his use of the word στέργειν ("to cherish") is shown in Livy's use of *carius* here. Gary Miles argues that

> the most important basis of the couples' own alliance is through the *caritas* of their children. . . . [*Caritas* in Livy] is the source of the power that both children and the Roman homeland have to evoke strong sentimental attachments.[62] The *caritas* of children to their parents and that of Rome to its inhabitants are very similar—*caritas liberum* and *caritas patriae* are the only two kinds of *caritas* describe as "innate" [*ingenita*, 1.34.5; 8.7.8]—and, in fact, are closely associated.[63]

This connection is explicit as Livy juxtaposes matrimonial and societal

---

57. Lewis & Short, s.v. *doceo*: "to teach, instruct, inform, show, tell."
58. Lewis & Short, s.v. *superbia*: "loftiness, haughtiness, pride, arrogance."
59. Translated as "explained" in Livy 1.9.14.
60. Hemker, "Rape and the Founding of Rome," 42. Miles also notes that "Romulus's tone here seems to be as much admonitory as conciliatory" ("First Roman Marriage," 179).
61. Lewis & Short, s.v. *societas*: "fellowship, association, union, community."
62. See Miles, "First Roman Marriage," 194n51: "E.g. 8.7.18, 32.4; 40.9.3, 15.15 and 1.34.5; 5.42.1, 54.2, 3; 3.49.3, respectively."
63. Ibid., 179–80.

values (*matrimonio . . . societate . . . civitatisque*) and then embodies these values in the promise of "free children/citizens" (*liberum*) to come. Livy continues, "only let them [the women] soften [*mollirent*] their anger [*iras*], and give up their minds [*darent animos*] to those to whom Fate had given up their bodies [*fors corpora dedisset*]" (Livy 1.9.14–15). The verb translated as "give up" in both of these clauses, *do*, has additional connotations of "yielding, giving away, suffering for," as well as, in militaristic situations, "to yield or surrender."[64] Once again, the word chosen has an abundance of meaning that may point to both the blurring of boundaries between public and private and the connection between the Roman's seizure of the women and their militarism, just as previously with Livy's use of *caritas* and Dionysius's use of στέργειν discussed above.[65] As the women have "surrendered" their bodies through their seizure by the Roman men, so too they should "surrender" both their hearts and minds (*animus*) to the Roman household, social, and civic projects. Additionally, Livy's subsequent use of *fors* ("fate") in this section[66] parallels Dionysius's use of τύχη in 2.30.5, where Romulus asks the women "to cherish [στέργειν] those whom Fate [τύχης] had given them for their husbands" (DH 2.30.5) as a way once again to elide responsibility of the Roman's actions.[67]

Romulus continues to respond to the women, telling them, "Often from injury, affection grows, and they would find their husbands the kinder for this reason, that every man would earnestly endeavor not only to be a good husband, but also to appease [*expleat*] his wife for the fatherland and the parents she grieved" (Livy 1.9.15). Addressing these appeals of Romulus to the abducted women in Livy 1.9.14–15, Miles underscores that

marriage between husband and wife [is] a kind of microcosm of the

64. Lewis & Short, s.v. *do*.
65. See Robert Brown, "Livy's Sabine Women and the Ideal of *Concordia*," *TAPA* 125 (1995): 295, who sees in Livy's narrative a subordination of the political needs of the Romans to their biological ones. He cites the contrasting analysis of Miles, "First Roman Marriage," 165. See also Stem, "Exemplary Lessons," 439, quoted above.
66. Used also in Livy 1.9.11: "the young Romans darted this way and that, to seize and carry off the virgins. In most cases these were seized by the men in whose path they chanced to be" (*iuventus Romana ad rapiendas virgines discurrit. magna pars forte, in quem quaeque inciderat, raptae*, 1.9.10–11).
67. Again, see Hemker, "Rape and the Founding of Rome," 42.

THE RAPE OF EVE

political alliance between families and peoples that it is supposed to effect. It is an "alliance," a *societas*, just like that which the Romans sought unsuccessfully with the Sabines. It offers the same sharing of fortunes and above all sharing of community that the Romans and Sabines will ultimately agree to. It is precisely because it constitutes a kind of substitute for (as well as a means to) an alliance between states that Roman husbands can promise to satisfy their wives' desire for parents and for fatherland.[68]

But, as Miles alludes to in his use of the word *substitute*, this *societas* is meant to be a replacement, an entirely new arrangement for fatherland and family taken from the women by force. Given the deception, seizure, and violence that have marked the "alliance" between the Romans and their neighbors, it is worth wondering what kind of *societas* has actually been created.

Not only does Livy's Romulus attempt to appease the women, but "[h]is arguments were joined by the flattery [*blanditiae*] of the men, who justified their act by passion and love, the most effectual of all entreaties to a woman's nature"[69] (Livy 1.9.16). Miles argues that, with Livy's use of *blanditiae*, "the men's self-justification [for their actions] is essentially rhetorical" for nothing is known about "the men's actual feelings," but only that they appeal "to woman's nature as they perceive it." Miles continues, saying that the "men accommodate [the women's nature], but they do not share it. . . . At the most private, most intimate level of the relationship between Sabine bride and Roman groom there remains a note of reserve—at least on the part of the men—and distance";[70] that is, there is distance because the true feelings of the men are never shared or made known.

Miles offers two possible ways to read this scene. The first is that "the men as well the women are motivated by *cupiditas* and *amor*; then the whole distinction between stronger, more rational men and weaker, more passionate women that justifies the abduction and accounts for the women's transformation from captives into wives

68. Miles, "First Roman Marriage," 179.
69. *accedebant blanditiae virorum factum purgantium cupiditate atque amore, quae maxime ad muliebre ingenium efficacies preces sunt.*
70. Miles, "First Roman Marriage," 182–83.

dissolves. Men are revealed to be no more competent to govern rationally than are women. The implicit justification for their exploitation of women is exposed as spurious."[71] The second is that "the men may only have been feigning *cupiditas* and *amor*, their appeals merely rhetorical. . . . In this case, we must recognize that the men are compounding their original act of violence by an act of bad faith—they are, in fact, increasing the distance between themselves and their captives even as they seem to be bridging it."[72] Miles notes that "[t]here is much . . . to support this [second view],"[73] including (though unmentioned by Miles) the Romans' previous act of "bad faith," when they used the festival as a ruse to lure their neighbors to Rome in the first place. These appeals display both the coercion and the power designs of the bourgeoning Romans, giving credence to the distance between the men and women that Miles observes: the Romans are "real" men for whom the ends justify the means; and not only do they see domination as their destiny, but this distance signifies a real power differential between the men and the women, the Romans and the Sabines, and, as the story will show, between Rome and its colonies.[74]

The Wars of Colonization and the First Triumph

Just as the bonds between the Romans and the stolen women were compelled by force, so too will the bonds between the Romans and their neighbors be forged through force. Dionysius summarizes the situation before the battles, writing that when "the report of the seizure of virgins [τὴν ἁρπαγὴν τῶν παρθένων] and of their marriage [γάμους] was spread among the neighboring cities, some of these were angered at the proceeding itself" (DH 2.32.1). But, he relays, "others, considering the motive from which it sprang and the outcome to which it led, bore it with moderation" (DH 2.32.1), implying that some

71. Ibid., 185.
72. Ibid.
73. Ibid.
74. It is possible that the ambiguities in the text as well as the "distance" Miles highlights imply some nervousness and apprehension on Livy's part that the constant justifications by Dionysius and Plutarch may signify as well. See R. Brown, "Livy's Sabine Women," 298–99, on this portion of Livy and *blanditiae*.

considered the Romans' motives justifiable. Nevertheless, the incident did lead to "several wars . . . of small consequence" though the one with the Sabines was "great and difficult" (DH 2.32.1). Of course, all of the wars were "successful"—that is, were won by the Romans—just as "the oracles had foretold" (DH 2.32.1). Caenina, Antemnae, and Crustumerium were the first cities to wage war using "the seizure of virgins" [τὴν ἁρπαγὴν τῶν παρθένων] as a "pretext" (πρόφασιν), though, similarly to Livy 1.9.5,[75] Dionysius says, "but the truth was that they were displeased at the founding of Rome and at its great and rapid increase and felt that they ought not to permit this city to grow up as a common menace to all its neighbors" (DH 2.32.2).

While Livy does not refer to the seizure of the women as a pretext for the move against the Romans, as Dionysius does, in all three narratives the Romans' staging of the festival seems to operate as a pretext for the seizure of the women so that "alliances" may be forged—though for Rome the ruse is successful (i.e., they get both women and alliances) and for their neighbors it is not (they will lose the war). In Dionysius's framing of the bourgeoning wars against the Romans, the women are once again a means to an end for their families as well—the women are not the primary concern for their families but rather the growing power of Rome. This framing also highlights that the women are subjugated on all fronts, by Rome as well as by the men of their own countries—indeed they are secondary to the men's political concerns, a theme that runs throughout the Sabines narrative.

The other neighboring cities tried to appeal to the Sabines to lead the war against the Romans both because of their strength and because most of the abducted women (ἡρπασμένων) were Sabines (DH 2.32.3). This was to no avail, as the Sabines kept delaying their involvement; the cities, therefore, decided to make war on their own. The Caeninenses "rashly set out ahead of the others," and Romulus's army caught the enemy off guard and made himself the "master" (κύριος) of their newly established camp (DH 2.33.1–2). Before word of the defeat

---

75. "[T]hey feared [*metuebant*], both for themselves and their descendants, that great power [*molem*] which was then growing up in their midst. . . ."

reached their city, Romulus "overtook the city by onslaught," slaying their "king" (βασιλεύς) and "took away his arms" (DH 2.33.2). After Romulus had "conquered" (ἁλούσης) the Caeninenses, he ordered "the conquered" (τοὺς ἁλόντας) to hand over their weapons, and he took those children he wanted as "hostage" (ὁμηρείαν) (DH 2.34.1). Next Romulus marched upon the Antemanates, defeating them as well and treating the conquered (τοὺς ἁλόντας) in the same manner as the Caeninenses (DH 2.34.1).

With Romulus's first major conquest behind him, Dionysius tells the story of the first triumph and building of the temple to Jupiter. Having conquered the Caeninenses and Antemanates, Romulus returned with his army to Rome,

> carrying with him the spoils [λαφύρων] of those who had been slain in battle and the choicest part of the booty [ἀκροθίνια] as an offering to the gods; and offered many sacrifices [θυσίας] as well. [Romulus] himself came last in the procession [πομπῆς], clad in a purple robe and wearing a crown of laurel [δάφνῃ] upon his head, and . . . he rode in a chariot drawn by four horses.[76] The rest of the army . . . followed . . . praising the gods in songs of their fathers [πατρίοις] and honoring their general [ἡγεμόνα] in improvised verses. The citizens who met them with their wives and children lined each side of the road, rejoicing in their victory [νίκη] and welcoming [φιλοφροσύνην] them in every other way. (DH 2.34.1–2)

Additionally, an abundance of food and wine was offered to the Roman army.

> Such was the victorious [ἐπινίκιος] procession [πομπή], marked by the carrying of trophies [τροπαιοφόρος] and concluding with a sacrifice [θυσία], which the Romans call a triumph [θρίαμβον], as it was first instituted by Romulus. . . . After the procession [πομπήν] and the sacrifice [θυσίαν] Romulus built a small temple on the summit of the Capitoline hill to Jupiter whom the Romans call Feretrius. . . . In this temple he consecrated the spoils [σκῦλα] of the king of the Caeninenses, whom he had slain with his own hand. (DH 2.34.2–4)[77]

---

76. A quadriga.

77. See Mary Beard, *The Roman Triumph* (Cambridge, MA: Belknap Press of Harvard University Press, 2007), particularly 67–69, 73–74, on Romulus and the origin of the triumph. As she notes, "In many ways the triumph came to be seen as a marker of wider developments in Roman politics and society. So, for example, the increasingly far-flung peoples and places over which triumphs were celebrated represented a map of Roman imperial expansion and of the changing geopolitical

Romulus[78] then assembled the senate in an effort to figure out how "the conquered cities [τῶν κρατηθεισῶν πόλεων] should be treated" (DH 2.35.1) After receiving praise from the senators for his "safe and brilliant" actions and the "advantages that were likely to accrue from them . . . not only for the moment but for all future time" (DH 2.35.2), Romulus ordered "all of the women belonging to the races [γένους] of the Antemnates and of the Caeninenses who had been seized [ἡρπασμέναι]" to gather (DH 2.35.2). And, giving his readers the first hint of the women's reaction to their situation, Dionysius continues:

> And when they gathered, lamenting, throwing themselves at his feet [προκυλιόμεναι][79] and bewailing the fate [τύχας] of their fatherlands, he commanded them to stop their lamentations and be silent, then spoke to them as follows: "Your fathers and brothers and your entire cities deserve to suffer every severity for having preferred to our friendship [φιλίας] a war [πόλεμον] that was neither necessary nor honorable." (DH 2.35.2–3)

Again, Romulus justifies the Romans' violent actions on the victims of their violence (i.e., the perpetrators make themselves the victims).[80] In the Roman's eyes, or through their justification, their neighbors are the ones who instigate this violence, first by denying them women (DH 2.30.2) and second by going to war (DH 2.32.1–2). Romulus continues:

> "We, however, have resolved for many reasons to treat them with moderation; for we not only fear the vengeance of the gods, which ever threatens the arrogant [ὑπερόγχοις], and dread the ill-will of men, but we also are persuaded that mercy contributes not a little to alleviate the common ills of humankind, and we realize that we ourselves may one day stand in need of that of others. And we believe that to you, whose behavior

shape of the Roman world" (67). Also note that Romulus is wearing the triumphal laurel (δάφνη) here in his first victory.

78. Here Romulus is referred to as "the king" (βασιλεύς)—this is the first time Romulus is referred to as "king" in the Sabines narrative ("After the king had offered to the gods the sacrifices of thanksgiving and the first-fruits . . . ,"῾Ως δ᾽ ἀπέδωκε τοῖς θεοῖς ὁ βασιλεὺς τὰς χαριστηρίους θυσίας τε καὶ ἀπαρχάς)—in 2.34.2 he acts "with royal dignity" riding in the quadriga, but is not called "king" until this moment.

79. This comes from the word κυλίω and means to roll up or grovel—there is something reminiscent of the position of the defeated nations and others who take this position on coins and friezes.

80. This seems to be a regular strategy of violent perpetrators—whether as individuals or collectives. See Das, *Life and Words*, particularly 108–34, on this dynamic after the assassination of Indira Gandhi.

towards your husbands has thus far been blameless, this will be no small honor [τιμήν] and grace [χάριν]." (DH 2.35.3)

Here, again, Dionysius continues to use rhetoric in which the Romans blame their neighbors for responding to their actions, not acknowledging that the Romans themselves are the ones who initially instigated the violence. Romulus insists that their "mercy" (does he refer to his abduction of the women here? the conquest of their parents?) should be seen as an "honor" and "grace" to the women who have suffered abduction at the Romans' hands.

Refusing to acknowledge the suffering the Romans have caused, Dionysius's Romulus once again claims the role of the victim, ironically saying, "We suffer this offense of theirs, therefore, to go unpunished and take from your fellow citizens neither their liberty nor their possessions nor any other advantages they enjoy" (DH 2.35.4). This may be Romulus's most audacious claim. Dionysius has just told the story of the slaughter, pillage, and capture (including taking children hostage) of the Caeninenses and Antemnates, and here he claims that it is he who in fact has suffered. In addition, Dionysius has related the seizing and parading of "the spoils of those who had been slain in battle" and additional booty through the streets of Rome (DH 2.33.1–34.1). Far from being the victim, Romulus is displaying his role as victor and enacting this role by publicly humiliating those conquered through celebration and spectacle. How is the parading of booty and hostages a sign of retained possessions or the granting of liberty?

Once this triumphant spectacle has occurred Romulus returns to the women telling them that those defeated both "who desire to remain there [i.e., in their fatherlands] and to those who wish to change their abode, we grant full liberty to make their choice not only without danger but without fear of repenting." But he adds in a telling statement that shows the true nature of this new alliance

> to prevent their ever repeating their fault or finding an occasion to induce their cities to break off their alliance with us, the best means, we consider, and that which will at the same time conduce to the reputation and security of both, is for us to make those cities colonies [ἀποικίας] of Rome

and to send a sufficient number of our own people from here to inhabit them jointly with your fellow citizens. (DH 2.35.4)

So, as evidenced both by the triumph and Romulus's words to the women, there is no "full liberty" granted to Rome's neighbors beyond the "full liberty" associated with colonization. This good news, in turn, is supposed to alleviate any concerns of the women as well as indebt them to the Romans further, as Romulus exhorts: "Depart, therefore, with good courage; and redouble your love [ἀγαθήν] for your husbands, to whom your parents and brothers owe their preservation and your fatherlands their liberty" (DH 2.35.4).[81]

In the wake of Romulus's speech, according to Dionysius, "The women, hearing this, were greatly pleased, and shedding many tears of joy left the Forum" (DH 2.35.5). But we are left to wonder if this is a genuine reaction on the women's part and on what level it might be so. Are the women relieved that at least the wars are over and no more harm will be done? Have they come to genuine acceptance of their lot? Or are they just feigning relief in an attempt to pacify their captors?[82] There is no room for such questions in the text, as

81. See Clifford Ando, *Imperial Ideology and the Provincial Loyalty in the Roman Empire*, Classics and Contemporary Thought 6 (Berkeley: University of California Press, 2000), 299–300, whose discussion of Augustus's advice to Tiberius and the populace in his final papers (Dio 56.33.3) is eerily reminiscent of the dynamics here: Augustus "urged 'especially that they should not free too many slaves, lest they fill the city with an indiscriminate mob, and that they not enroll a great many to citizenship, in order that there be a substantial difference between themselves and their subjects.' By 'fill the city' Augustus intended 'fill the city with citizens descended from slaves,' since the children of freedmen were automatically enrolled among the citizen body. He therefore lumped slaves and foreign subjects together as a class of humanity that existed to be exploited for the profit and comfort of the citizens of Rome. He had made his priorities clear early in the *Res gestae* when he described his clemency in foreign wars: 'When foreign races could safely be spared, I preferred to preserve rather than exterminate them' [Res gestae 3.2]. The safety in question is that of the *res publica populi Romani*; the decision to spare or slaughter came only after considering the safety of one's own kind. Nor does the verb 'prefer' suggest that Augustus recognized his decision as a moral one: sparing the vanquished may have been an active good, and therefore deserving of commensurate gifts of aurum coronarium, but extermination had always been an option."

82. The dynamics of this are very complex, and, while the scope of this study limits the extent of addressing this, I would be remiss if I did not say a few words. The dynamics in any scenario such as this are very difficult to understand. Often, one thinks of things like Stockholm Syndrome, where hostages end up identifying with their captors, or, more prevalent in a country like the United States, women who return to their abusers (for example, see the #whyistayed #whyileft #howileft hashtags in the wake of the Ray Rice domestic violence episode)—though we do have instances of abductions spanning years and the complications surrounding this. Das also speaks about this dynamic in the wake of the partition of India (*Life and Words*, 18–37). Women were abducted, raped, became parts of other families, had children with other men, and then were

immediately "Romulus sent a colony [ἀποίκους] of three hundred men into each city, to whom these cities gave a third part of their lands to be divided among them by lot" (DH 2.35.5)—again, indicating that the Caeninenses and Antemnates did not, in fact, retain the full extent of their property—as he seemed to have promised earlier—and

> those of the Caeninenses and Antemnates who desired to transfer their households to Rome brought their wives together with their children, permitting them to retain their allotments of land and to carry with them all of their possessions they could get; and the king immediately enrolled them, numbering not less than three thousand, in the tribes and the *curiae*, so that the Romans had then for the first time six thousand foot in all upon the register. Thus Caenina and Antemnae, no inconsiderable cities, whose inhabitants were of Greek origin . . . after this war became Roman colonies [ἀποικίαι]." (DH 2.35.5–7)

After successfully installing Caenina and Antemnae as colonies, Romulus then sets his sights on "the Crustumerians who were better prepared than the armies of the other cities had been. After he had reduced them both in a pitched battle and a siege, although they had shown great bravery in the struggle, he did not think fit to punish them any further, but made this city also a Roman colony like the two former" (DH 2.36.1). With these defeats, "rumor spread to many cities of the general's valor in war and of his fairness to those conquered [κρατηθέντας], and many brave men joined him, bringing considerable troops and migrating [μετανισταμένας] with their whole households [πανοικία]. . . . Whole cities also submitted [παρεδίδοσον] to [Romulus], beginning with Medullia, and became Roman colonies [ἀποικίαι]" (DH 2.36.1–2). While Dionysius seems to spin Romulus's treatment of those the Romans warred with in a positive manner, given the slaughter, capture, and spoils seized it seems likely that the submission and

---

forced once again to return "home"—which once again stripped them of any control over their bodies. Especially in a situation like that of the Sabines—whether or not this is a "true" tale—for women during that time, protection came from family, through the male lineage. It is easy to make judgments that the women are being manipulated, suckered, by the Romans, and this may be true (it is very difficult to know with such little attention paid to their perspective by these male authors), and there should be no doubt that the Romans' actions of abduction are horrific, but, as a modern interpreter, I want to be careful that I do not infantilize the Sabine women, that I do not judge them and become a part of the same cycle that strips them of the complexity of their humanity and allows them to retain a measure of control over their bodily integrity.

migration of Rome's neighbors had less to do with Romulus's "valor" and "fairness" than with their fear of annihilation.[83]

Unlike Dionysius, Livy tells his readers that the abducted women were moved by Romulus's initial overtures toward them. Livy says, "The feelings [*animi*] of the ravished women [*raptis*] were already much softened [*mitigati*] at the very moment when the ravished women's parents [*raptarum parentes*] in mourning garb [*sordida veste*] and with tears [*lacrimisque*] and lamentations [*querellis*], were attempting to arouse their states to action" (Livy 1.10.1). It seems as if Romulus has "taught" the women well as they have complied with his initial request to "soften" their anger in 1.9.15,[84] but despite this, Rome's neighbors are primed for war, and they, too, will be "taught" by Rome.

As in Dionysius, the men of Caenina, Crustumium, and Antemnae, who also had "a share in the wrong [*iniuriae*]," decided to wage a "joint campaign" against the Romans, as they felt that "Tatius and the Sabines were procrastinating" and did not want to wait for them to wage war (Livy 1.10.2). But it seems that the Crustuminians and Antemnates themselves moved too slowly to "satisfy the burning anger [*ardore irque*] of the Caeninenses," and they attacked Rome on their own (Livy 1.10.3). Livy relates that "while [the Caeninenses] were dispersed and engaged in pillage, Romulus met them with his army and taught [*docet*] them, by easy victory, that anger is meaningless without strength [*vanam sine viribus iram esse*]" (Livy 1.10.4).

With Romulus's "easy victory" over the Caeninenses, Rome's neighbors are brought into a parallel process to their daughters in 1.9.14-15 and are "taught" by the Romans. In Livy 1.9.14, Romulus "teaches" (*docebatque*) the stolen maidens that it is "their parents' arrogance [*superbia*] that caused this deed"; that is, their parents' refusal to give the Romans their daughters led to their abduction (again, here the perpetrator fashions himself as the victim). Because the blame for their abduction lies with their parents, and additionally

83. Cf. DH 2.32.2: "but the truth was that they were displeased at the founding of Rome and at its great and rapid increase and felt that they ought not to permit this city to grow up as a common menace to all its neighbors."
84. Though in 1.9.15 Livy uses *mollirent* rather than *mitigati*.

because of all the benefits[85] the Romans will extend to them (fellowship/community/*societate*, citizenship/*civitatique* and free children/*liberum*), the women should "soften their anger" (*mollirent . . . iras*), which they in fact do. This softening of the women's anger occurs in inverse relation to the increasing anger of their menfolk—particularly the Caeninenses, who cannot contain their "burning rage" (*ardore iraque*). Accordingly, the men, too, are "taught" (*docet*) by the Romans through military devastation and death. The lesson is that there is no resisting the Romans—capitulate or be conquered—either way, the Romans are on top and in control.[86]

Romulus's teaching is made vividly clear as Livy describes the confrontation between the Caeninenses and the Romans: Romulus "broke their army and routed, and pursued [*persequitur*] it as it fled [*fusum*]; he slaughtered their king in battle and despoiled him;[87] once the foreign leader was slain, he captured [*capit*] their city at the first assault" (Livy 10.4). Livy does not narrate a full-scale triumph, as do Dionysius and Plutarch, though it is not altogether absent. Leading his "victorious army" (*exercitu vicotre*) back to Rome and "no less anxious to display his achievements than he had been great in doing them,"[88] Romulus "arranged the spoils [*spolia*] of the enemy's dead commander upon a frame, suitably fashioned for the purpose [i.e., a trophy], and carrying it himself, mounted the Capitol" (Livy 1.10.5). Romulus places this trophy by a sacred oak on the hill and as "he made his offering he marked out the limits of a temple to Jupiter, and bestowed a title upon him": Jupiter Feretrius (Livy 1.10.6). Romulus declares that this will be "a seat for the honorable spoils which the coming generations shall bring here in the time to come, following my example, when they have slain kings and commanders of the enemy. This was the origin of the first temple that was consecrated in Rome" (Livy 1.10.6-7). So,

85. I use this word purposefully to evoke the idea of benefaction.
86. See note 83 above regarding the complicated dynamics in terms of the women's relationship to the Romans. This complicated and compromised relationship also has parallels in the relationship between Rome and its colonies. See also Ando, *Imperial Ideology*, 299–300.
87. *regem in proelio obtruncat et spoliat.*
88. For this line, see Rev. Canon Roberts 1912 translation, http://www.perseus.tufts.edu/hopper/text?doc=Perseus:text:1999.02.0199:book=1:chapter=10. . . . *cum factis vir magnificus tum factorum ostentator haud minor. . . .*

while not giving as detailed an account of the triumph as Dionysius,[89] Livy specifically uses the Sabines story to explain the origin of Jupiter's temple on the Capitoline.[90]

While Romulus marched with his trophy and his army and dedicated land for the temple to Jupiter Feretrius, the Antemnates "seized the opportunity afforded by their absence, and made an assault upon their territory; but so swiftly was the Roman legion led against them that they, too, were taken by surprise while scattered about in the fields. The enemy were therefore routed at the first assault and shout—and their town was captured" (1.11.1-2). Unique to Livy's narrative is the notice that while "Romulus was celebrating his double victory, his wife [coniunx] Hersilia, beset with entreaties by the captive women [raptarum], begged him to forgive their parents and receive them into the state [civitatem accipiat]; which would, in that case, gain strength by harmony [coalescere concordia posse]. He readily granted her request" (Livy 1.11.2). With Hersilia's appeal to Romulus, Livy introduces the concept of concordia, or harmony, for the first time—an idea that, as Robert Brown emphasizes, is central to Livy's narrative.

To address the concept of concordia in Livy, Brown positions himself in relation to Miles, whom he reads as emphasizing "the complexity and ambiguity of Livy's narrative, seeing in it an ultimately self-defeating attempt to gloss over the inequality of Roman marriage," and rather sees in Livy "consistency and relative clarity of meaning," centered on the martial, social, and political ideal of concordia.[91] Brown

89. See DH 2.34.4.
90. Zanker discusses the new temples to Mars Ultor and Jupiter Tonans, as well as the rebuilding of Jupiter Feretrius. The new temples served to display the recaptured eagles and standards (Mars Ultor) and to commemorate victory over the Parthians (Jupiter Tonans) (Power of Images, 186–87). These acts, then, make this story—retold by both Dionysius and Livy during the time of Augustus—very intriguing, and provide another connection between these two "founders" of Rome in the building of temples to display their victories on the Capitoline. Though it is interesting that Dionysius has an aside in 2.34.3 after describing Romulus's first triumph where he says, "But in our day the triumph has become a very costly and ostentatious pageant, being attended with a theatrical pomp that is designed rather as a display of wealth than as the approbation of valor, and it has departed in every respect from its ancient simplicity." It is most likely that Dionysius is referring to the triumph of Pompey here, but he could be making a more general statement about "contemporary" triumphs. On Dionysius and the ostentatiousness of triumphs, see Beard, Roman Triumph, 67–68, 289.
91. R. Brown, "Livy's Sabine Women," 292, citing Miles, "First Roman Marriage." (See above

finds it particularly significant that Hersilia is the first in Livy's narrative to raise the concept of *concordia*.[92] He highlights that Livy "transfers the vision of the proposal from Romulus to Hersilia, who argues not just for mercy but for the incorporation of the defeated parents into a state, which, she says, will heal the breach by promoting harmony."[93] Brown continues:

> It is well known that the extension of citizen rights, especially *commercium, conubium,* and *migratio* (the right to acquire citizenship in a new state by change of residence), played a crucial role in the Roman assimilation of Italy.[94] As Plutarch says with reference to the present occasion: "Now this, more than anything else, was what gave increase to Rome: she always united and incorporated with herself those whom she conquered" (*Rom.* 16.5, tr. B. Perrin). But Plutarch gives the credit for this farsighted policy to Romulus.[95] Livy attributes it to a woman, and this is a remarkable fact. It is equally significant that Hersilia is the first person in Livy's history to articulate the concept of *concordia*—harmony among the diverse classes and interests of the citizenry—which is one of Livy's dearest political ideals.[96]

Brown further argues that Livy's innovation in making Hersilia central to the ideal of *concordia* helps

> to explain why he singles out the scarcity of women—*penuria mulierum*—as the reason for the seizure of the Sabines. Dionysius and Plutarch differ from Livy . . . in attributing to Romulus the political aim of alliance. I suggest that Livy wished to reserve for *Hersilia* the credit for initiating

discussion on Miles's work.) More generally on the Roman ideal of *concordia*, see Lobur, *Consensus, Concordia*.

92. R. Brown, "Livy's Sabine Women," 302. He also notes that, unless there is an unknown source on which Livy is relying, this intervention by Hersilia seems to be his innovation.

93. Ibid., 302.

94. Here Brown cites A. N. Sherwin-White, *The Roman Citizenship*, 2nd ed. (Oxford: Oxford University Press, 1973), 32–37, 108–16. It is important to note that Sherwin-White is dealing with the period of Roman history between the fourth century and the second century BCE, primarily using the works of Livy and Dionysius of Halicarnassus that are a part of this current study. It seems to me that the emphasis of Sherwin-Whight has little to do with the Sabines narrative, which I read to be much more a reflection of contemporary concerns mapped onto the primordial past and elucidating the complexity of relationships, both personal and political, in the bourgeoning Augustan empire.

95. Here, Plutarch is definitely covering a much wider swath of history in his comment, given that he is writing from the perspective of the early second century CE. Placing Sherwin-White and Plutarch together in making this point seems to be more disjunctive than helpful—it seems that the comparison would be more fruitful if made in conjunction with Dionysius of Halicarnassus, who is writing during the same period as Livy.

96. R. Brown, "Livy's Sabine Women," 302.

a policy of reconciliation with Rome's neighbors—not in order to slight Romulus, but to enhance the role of the women, who represent for Livy the spirit of forgiveness and harmony. Reading between the lines, we sense that Hersilia's insight arises from the success of her own marriage and that of the other Sabines, in which we may infer that a sense of injury has given way to affection, true to the prediction of Romulus (1.9.15). Romulus's promise of partnership [societas] and the men's affirmation of love have mollified the women, who in turn have given their minds as well as their bodies to their husbands, as he requested. Here, for Livy, are the makings of concordia, the spirit of mutual good will and cooperation—literally a concurrence of hearts—which transcends the functional notion of societas. And since the establishment of marital concord depended above all else on the acquiescence of the aggrieved women, so it is fitting that it should now be Hersilia, in the role of coniunx (1.11.2)—a word itself signifying union—who promotes the idea of political harmony; her valuable suggestion is, in fact, the fruit of the assiduous cultivation of the women's good will by Romulus and the Roman men.[97]

While Brown's reading of the text is cohesive, and particularly salient regarding the centrality of concordia in Livy's text, he nonetheless fails to address a number of points that add both ambiguity and complexity in terms of his interpretation. First, though Hersilia is referred to as coniunx ("wife") in this portion of the text, the women as a whole (which includes Hersilia) are referred to as raptarum, the "captive or ravished women"—they are not referred to as wives, they are still the abducted ones. Second, it is difficult to know if the women have been truly "mollified" by the Roman men's strategic and possibly disingenuous "cultivation of the women's goodwill" or not—or if the women's actions, rather than prompted by a spirit of forgiveness, are aimed at self-preservation.

Nonetheless Brown's emphasis and insight regarding the function of concordia are important, especially given the connection and overlap in Livy 1.11.2 between concordia in the marriage relationship and in the relationship between different states/peoples. But it is important to keep sight of the ambiguity found by Miles, particularly in terms of the inherent power differential between the Roman men and the

---

97. Ibid., 302–3.

raptarum—especially given that the "minds and bodies" of the women have been subsumed under the Roman ("given," maybe, but not necessarily given freely). It is possible, then, to read Hersilia's appeal to *concordia*, and by extension the women's as a whole, as an effort to curtail further loss of life as well as a means by which the women can secure their own protection in a society where a woman is often at risk if she is not under the care of a man.[98] This reading has an analog if the notion of *concordia* is extended to the neighboring peoples whom Romulus has slaughtered and pillaged—that is, for the nations, whose appeal to *concordia* may be an act of self-preservation as well. Finally, it is important to note that, while Romulus agrees to Hersilia's request, he does not honor her request (or his promise) completely and does so on his own terms, as the next portion of Livy's narrative shows. Romulus's act of partial acquiescence—and acquiescence made on his own terms—will have parallels in the ways in which he continues to implement his "foreign policy."

After Hersilia begs Romulus to "forgive their parents and receive them into the state," and Romulus "acquiesces" to her request, he then "set out to meet the Crustuminians, who were marching to attack him. They offered even less resistance for their spirits had been killed by the destruction of the other foreigners. Colonies were dispatched to both places, though many preferred to enroll for Crustumium on account of the fertility of its soil. On the other hand, many persons left Crustumium and came to live in Rome, chiefly parents and kinsmen of the captured women" (Livy 1.11.3–4). Despite Romulus's assurances to Hersilia to "forgive" and "receive," he immediately engages in war, and Livy tells the story of another people conquered and colonized. Even as Livy's text emphasizes the ideal of *concordia*, it is a *concordia* laced with power differentials and one based on violence. This pattern will continue in Livy's narrative as Romulus engages the Sabines.

Plutarch begins his story of Romulus's colonization by narrating that "the Sabines were a numerous and warlike people [πολεμικοί]"—which

---

98. See Miles, 169, on the protection of women.

is ironic given that their first act after the Romans' display of ill-will and violence was to send

> ambassadors [πρέσβεις ἀπέστειλαν] with reasonable and moderate demands, namely, that Romulus should give their maidens [τὰς κόρας αὐτοῖς] back to them, disavow his deed of violence [τὸ τῆς βίας ἔργον], and then, by persuasion and lawful means [νόμῳ], establish a friendly relationship between the two peoples [τοῖς γένεσι φιλίαν καὶ οἰκειότητα]. But Romulus would not give up the maidens and demanded that the Sabines engage in partnership [κοινωνίαν] with them, whereupon they all held long deliberations and made preparations [for war]. (*Rom.* 16.1–3)

Though Plutarch claims that the Sabines are a "warlike" people, they seem, at least here, to attempt diplomacy, in contrast to the Romans, who keep relying on violence and war to get their way.[99]

Plutarch continues that, unlike the Sabines, who were mired in deliberations and preparations for war, "Acron, king of the Caeninenses, a passionate man and skilled in war, had been suspicious of the shameless acts of Romulus from the beginning, and the plot concerning the women already done, regarded him as a danger to all and insufferable unless checked, at once rose up in arms and with a great force advanced against him" (*Rom.* 16.3). As in Livy 1.9.5[100] and Dionysius 2.32.2,[101] Acron is worried about the power wielded by the Romans, but unlike Dionysius in particular, the abduction of the women is not simply a "pretext" for war but part of the Romans' "insufferable" danger and violence. Romulus, then, marched out to meet Acron, and

> when they were face to face and had seen one another, they challenged each other to single combat before the battle, while their armies remained still. Romulus, then, after making a vow that if he should conquer [κρατήσειε] and overthrow [καταβάλοι] his adversary, he would carry home the man's armor and dedicate it in person to Jupiter, not only

99. Though Plutarch does acknowledge in 14.1 that "some say Romulus himself [was] naturally fond of war, and . . . that it was the destiny of Rome to be nourished and increased by wars. . . ."
100. "[T]hey feared [*metuebant*], both for themselves and their descendants, that great power [*molem*] which was then growing up in their midst."
101. "[B]ut the truth was that they were displeased at the founding of Rome and at its great and rapid increase and felt that they ought not to permit this city to grow up as a common menace [κοινὸν . . . κακόν] to all its neighbors."

conquered [κρατήσας] and overthrew [καταβάλλει] him, but also routed his army in the battle which followed and seized his city as well. To the ones captured [τοὺς ἐγκαταληφθέντας], however, he did no injury beyond ordering them to tear down their dwellings [οἰκίας] and follow him to Rome, where, they should be citizens [πολίτας] on equal terms with the rest. (*Rom.* 16.3–4)

After narrating the conquest of the Caeninenses, Plutarch, uniquely and explicitly, offers his understanding of this first Romulan victory, stating, "Indeed this, more than anything else, was what gave increase [ηὔξησε][102] to Rome: it always attached to itself and made its partner those whom it conquered [ἀεὶ προσποιοῦσαν[103] ἑαυτῇ καὶ συνέμουσαν[104] ὧν κρατήσειεν[105]]" (*Rom.* 16.5).[106] And this interjection is pivotal for understanding the dynamics of the story as a whole, highlighting Plutarch's continued argument that the abduction of the Sabine women was necessary in order to create alliances between Rome and its neighbors (cf. *Rom.* 14.2, 6; 16.2), thus forming the template for Rome's relationship with all those peoples who are gathered under its reach. But what is also clear from Plutarch's description of the Romans' battle with Acron and the Caeninenses is that this is an alliance predicated on military victory and dominance: before being made "equal" (ἴσοις) they are overwhelmed, slaughtered, made captive, and forced to destroy their homes and move to Rome, displaced from their homelands to live under the watchful eyes of the Romans.

Then, as in Dionysius, Plutarch narrates Romulus's enactment of the first triumph. In an interesting twist, Plutarch says that Romulus considered both gods and men when he contemplated

how he might perform his vow in a manner most acceptable to Jupiter and accompany the performance with a spectacle most pleasing to the citizens, [and] cut down a monstrous oak that grew in the camp, hewed

---

102. The word αὐξάνω can have the connotation of both an increase in power/strength or an increase in size.
103. LSJ, s.v. προσποιέω: "to make over to, or attach to; procure for oneself, take to oneself what does not belong."
104. LSJ, s.v. συννέμω "feed or tend together; make one's partner or associate."
105. LSJ, s.v. κρατέω: "strong, powerful; rule hold sway; be lord or master of, rule over, conquer, prevail; become master of, get possession of."
106. See the discussion above of Brown and his "Livy's Sabine Women," 302, where Brown notes that this "policy" is attributed to Hersilia in Livy versus Romulus in Plutarch.

it into the shape of a trophy [τρόπαιον], and fitted and fastened to it the armor of Acron, each piece in its due order. Then he himself, girding his raiment about him and wreathing his flowing locks with laurel [δάφνη], set the trophy [τρόπαιον] on his right shoulder, where it was held erect, and began a triumphal march [ἐβάδιζεν], leading off in a paean of victory [ἐξάρχων ἐπινικίου παιᾶνος] which his army sang as it followed under arms, and being received by the citizens with joyful amazement. This procession was the origin and model of all subsequent triumphs. (*Rom.* 16.5–6)

Here, just as Plutarch has used Romulus's battle with the Caeninenses as the originary moment that explains the Roman model of conquest, so too, this first triumph becomes the Roman template for the practice throughout the ages. Of particular note is Plutarch's association of the triumph with "spectacle," making sure that this ritual was not only a fitting tribute to the gods but an event that bonded the citizens of Rome and celebrated their power.[107]

Plutarch concludes this section with the alliance forged between Fidenae, Crustumerium, and Antemnae in an effort to take on the Romans. They, too, were defeated and "surrendered to Romulus their cities to be seized, their territory to be divided, and themselves to be transported to Rome. Romulus distributed among the citizens all the territory thus acquired, excepting that which belonged to the fathers of the ravished maidens; this he permitted its owners to keep for themselves" (*Rom.* 17.1). In this last line, Romulus seems to change the policy instituted with the Caeninenses, forcing them to destroy their homes and relocate to Rome.

Romulus's allowance that the fathers of the "ravished maidens" be allowed to keep their lands can be read in at least two ways. The first is that, by letting them keep their land, Romulus may be "admitting" on some level that his actions against the fathers of the women were wrong, though, of course, he is only admitting this to an extent, as he keeps the women for himself—and this is a wrong against the *fathers*, not the abducted women themselves. In this way Romulus trades the land for the women, though ultimately he is still in charge of both.

---

107. One wonders which of the newly conquered citizens might have attended the spectacle and how they might have perceived it. See Beard, *Roman Triumph*, 139–41, on the incorporation of conquered peoples into Roman culture through the triumph.

A second possibility is that the allowance to retain land is the means by which Romulus constructs a proper alliance with those whom he has forced to be kin through abduction and marriage, finally beginning to bring to fruition the alliances he has sought throughout the text—though alliances forged through manipulation, deceit, and war (cf. *Rom.* 14.2, 6; 16.2). Regardless of the reading, the end result remains that Romulus is the one in control of both the peoples and the lands, and his arrangement only extends to the fathers of the abducted women—not to others within those communities he has defeated and colonized.

Tarpeia and the Sabines

After Rome's defeat and colonization of its neighbors, the Sabines, according to Dionysius, "were distressed and blamed one another for not having crushed the power of the Romans while it was in its infancy" (DH 2.36.3)—now they were required to contend with a Rome that had grown exponentially in size and power due to its conquests. The Sabines were "determined, therefore, to make amends for their former mistake by sending out an army of respectable size" (DH 2.36.3). They assembled and voted for war and appointed Titus Tatius "to be their general" (DH 2.36.3). Dionysius tells his readers that, after the assembly, the Sabines returned to their home cities, where they prepared to war with Rome the following year" (DH 2.36.3).

At the same time, "Romulus was also was making the best preparations he could in his turn, realizing that he was to defend himself against a warlike people" (DH 2.37.1).[108] Dionysius tells his readers that, though the Sabines were prepared to go to war with the Romans in the spring, they, much like Caenina, Antemnae, and Crustumerium before them (DH 2.32.2, cf. Livy 1.9.5), nonetheless first sent "an embassy [ἀποστεῖλαι πρεσβείαν] to the enemy both to ask for the return of the women and to demand satisfaction for their seizure

---

108. Dionysius, like Plutarch, portrays the Sabines as warlike (DH 2.37.1 τὰ πολέμια; *Rom.* 16.1 πολεμικοί)—and as before, one wonders if it is supposed to be in contrast to the Romans, but if so, it seems quite an irony given the narrative thus far.

[ἁρπαγῆς], just so that they might seem [δοκῶσιν] to have undertaken the war from necessity [ἀνάγκην] when they failed to get justice [δικαίων], and they were sending the heralds [κήρυκας] for this purpose" (DH 2.37.2-3; cf. *Rom.* 16.1-3). Once again, though this time on the part of the Sabines, the women are used simply as a pretext to wage war. In addition, Dionysius's use of δοκῶσιν, meaning to "seem" or "pretend," implies a kind of deception on the part of the Sabines, with ἀνάγκην ("necessity") indicating a need for justification. Here, the cycle of deception, justification, and violence, initially started by the Romans, continues through the ongoing struggle for power, land, and the stolen women.

Despite the entreaties of the Sabines, Romulus would not return the women, saying that they "were not unwilling to live with their husbands [and] should be permitted to remain married to them [γεγαμηκόσι μένειν]; but he offered to grant the Sabines anything else they desired, provided they asked it as from friends [φίλων] and did not begin war" (DH 2.37.4). With these words, Romulus speaks for the women—their voices and true feelings about their circumstances and relationships with their husbands left unknown as his voice subsumes theirs. And, of course, the Sabines would never agree to Romulus's terms because their only desires are for their women and war, so the Romans and Sabines led out their two large armies.[109]

While neither Livy nor Plutarch narrates this exchange with the Sabines, at this juncture all three segue into the story of Tarpeia, the daughter of the citadel's commander,[110] and her betrayal of the Romans' citadel on the Capitol.[111] While both Dionysius and Plutarch qualify her as a virgin (παρθένος),[112] Livy implies that she is actually a Vestal, relating that she was bribed (*dolus*) by the Sabine general Tatius to let his army into the citadel when she was outside the walls

---

109. Dionysius gives the details that the Sabine army "consisted of twenty-five thousand soldiers on foot and almost a thousand on horse," while the Roman army had twenty thousand soldiers on foot and eight hundred on horse (2.37.4-5).
110. Livy 1.11.6; DH 2.38.2; *Rom.* 17.2.
111. Livy 1.11.5-9; *Rom.* 17.2-18.1. For detailed accounts and interpretations of the story, see Miles, "First Roman Marriage," 183-85; R. Brown, "Livy's Sabine Women," 303-6.
112. DH 2.38.2; *Rom.* 17.2.

getting water for a sacrifice (Livy 1.11.6).[113] Rather than depicting her being approached by Tatius, both Dionysius and Plutarch say that her betrayal of the citadel hinged upon her desire for the Sabines' golden arm bracelets and that she offered the citadel to the Sabines in exchange for them.[114]

In addition, each of the stories relates that, in the end, Tarpeia gives the Sabines the citadel and demands her payment: that which they wore on their arms. But instead of giving her their bracelets, they pelt her with their shields—which also hung on their arms, thereby following the letter, if not the spirit, of their agreement—crushing her to death.[115] Dionysius and Plutarch both give additional explanations for Tarpeia's motives. Dionysius offers one version where Tarpeia was actually trying to trick the Sabines with her plot, exploiting the

---

113. Livy 1.11.6: *Huius filiam virinem auro corrumpit Tatius ut armatos in arcem accipiat; aquam forte ea tum sacris extra moenia petitum ierat.* R. Brown ("First Roman Marriage," 305) "suspect[s] that Livy is hinting at a comparison between the Sabine bribery of Tarpeia and the Roman rape of the Sabines. Both are cases of deception (1.9.6, *dissimulans*, 1.9.13, *decepti*, 1.11.6, *dolus*). Both occur in a religious context (the Consualia and the ritual fetching of water by Tarpeia). Both involve the imposition of male control upon young virgins. Both evoke bitter condemnation from the aggrieved male parties (1.1.13, 1.12.4). . . . As an embodiment of internal disloyalty, Tarpeia nevertheless throws into sharper relief the extraordinary loyalty displayed by the Sabine women at the climax of the battle in the forum. Outsiders who have become Romans by force, they show a loyalty toward their husbands equal to that which they feel toward their parents and powerful enough to effect the union of the two peoples. Tarpeia is an antitype (Natalie Kampen, "Reliefs of the Basilica Aemilia: A Redating," *Klio* 73 [1991], 455)." While Brown cites Kampen here, Kampen's analysis is more nuanced and complicated. Discussing the Sabine and Tarpeia friezes in the Basilica Aemilia, she states, "The Julian laws of marriage, adultery and procreation provide an important element of the setting for the Basilica Aemilia frieze. The Sabine women's story is about the origins of marriage, about who may legitimately marry whom and about the correct conduct of women who are at the same time daughters, wives, and mothers. It fits well as a symbolic expression of the social concern with the relationship between classes which the Lex Julia on marriage regulates, and it addresses as well the relationship between Romans and their various Latin and foreign allies. The reliefs emphasize the need for controlled female sexuality in a society which must reproduce in order to endure but which regards the loyalty of women, symbolic outsiders, as problematic. Since the Sabine women do, in fact, perform as ideal Augustan women/allies and become insiders, they stand in contrast to the figure of Tarpeia. Her perfidy violates right conduct of daughters as well as virgins and married women. She exemplifies unregulated female conduct as inherently dangerous. She behaves like an outsider even though, like the Roman opponents of Augustus in the Civil War, she is more of an insider than the Sabines. . . . Her punishment, being crushed by men's weapons, contrasts with the Sabine women's later physical intervention between those weapons to stop the battle. On one level, the message of the two scenes is that behavior is transcendent, and essence, whether national or sexual, is mutable. On a more immediate level, the concern with the revival of traditional morality in the form of controlled female sexuality is well served by these two stories of women from Rome's earliest history" (455).

114. Though, of course, she is also bribed with gold in Livy; DH 2.38.3; *Rom.* 17.2.

115. Livy 1.11.8; DH 2.40.1; *Rom.* 17.4.

ambiguity of their agreement to take their shields rather than arm bracelets, and sent a dispatch to Romulus to let him know they were ripe for attack. But the messenger instead went to Tatius and told him of Tarpeia's betrayal (DH 2.39.1). Plutarch relays an additional explanation that Tarpeia was actually the daughter of Tatius and was "living under Romulus under compulsion and acted and suffered as she did at her father's behest" (*Rom.* 17.5). This explanation seems to imply that Tarpeia was one of the abducted women and that her father thought her better dead than defiled by the Romans.

While Plutarch does not believe the alternative story he recounts, Dionysius does, thus both presenting two different interpretations of the significance of the Tarpeian Rock. Dionysius says that Tarpeia was honored and that libations were poured for her at a yearly ritual, arguing that it is impossible to think the Romans would have honored her in this way had she actually been a traitor (DH 2.40.3). Plutarch, on the other hand, says the Tarpeian Rock was named as such to remember Tarpeia's treachery, betrayal, and treason and that this is the reason criminals are hurled to their death from it (*Rom.* 18.1). Plutarch's version of the Tarpeian Rock's legacy is the one that seems to hold true, as both he and Livy note the many individuals punished by death there throughout their histories.[116]

Of particular note in Livy's version of the Tarpeia story is her identification as a Vestal. Unlike the Vestal Rhea Silvia, whose violation brings forth the founding of Rome, Tarpeia typifies the treatment of Vestals who lose their "integrity." Indiscretions (including adultery) by the Vestals were linked with treason but with much higher stakes: as the Vestals signified the integrity of Rome, for example, its impenetrability by foreign forces, the penetrability of the Vestals signified outside threat.[117] While Tarpeia's penetrability was not sexual, it nonetheless precipitated the Sabines' penetration of Rome's

116. E.g. Livy 6.20.12; Plutarch, *Sulla* 1.4; Plutarch, *Coriolanus* 18.4.
117. On the Vestals, see Parker, "Why Were the Vestals Virgins?"; Robin Lorsch Wildfang, *Rome's Vestal Virgins: A Study of Rome's Vestal Priestesses in the Late Republic and Early Empire* (New York: Routledge, 2006); Sarolta A. Takács, *Vestal Virgins, Sibyls, and Matrons: Women in Roman Religion* (Austin: University of Texas Press, 2008). See also the discussion in "Mars's Rape of Rhea Silvia" and "Embodied Nations and Vestal Virgins" in this chapter.

boundaries. Thus, Tarpeia is marked as the quintessential traitor from whose rock all those who commit crimes will be hurled. She also provides an analogue to the Sabine women: the Sabine women act with concord in the aftermath of their penetration, buttressing the integrity not only of their men but of Rome itself. Tarpeia, on the other hand, acts alone (whether in Rome's favor or against it), without concord, opening Rome to penetrability from without, her acts leading not only to her death but to her infamy.[118]

The Intervention of the Sabine Women

After the Sabines gain control of the Roman citadel, the final war between the two peoples ensues. Each of the three authors narrates the battles of the Romans and Sabines in different ways, Plutarch's being the pithiest of the three, with Livy's and Dionysius's versions more extensive. Dionysius gives the most gruesome details and also differs substantially from the other two; he narrates several battles, with both sides suffering enough casualties that both the Roman and Sabine armies retreat from the battle lines, wondering if they should continue the battle or appeal for peace (DH 2.41–44). Plutarch also says that many battles were fought and that, in the last and most memorable one, Romulus was hit in the head by a rock and fell to the ground. With their leader fallen, the Romans retreated up the Palatine (*Rom.* 18.5). In Livy, the Romans retreat when their champion Hostius Hostilius (rather than Romulus) fell to the Sabine Mettius Curitus in hand-to-hand combat (Livy 1.12.2–3). At this point in the narrative,

---

118. David Konstan looks at book 1 of Livy in terms of the interplay of structure, stability, and the expansion of Rome ("Narrative and Ideology in Livy: Book 1," *ClAnt* 5.2 [1986]: 198–215). He reads the stories of the Sabines and Tarpeia particularly in terms of the tension between "lineal descent and matrimony," where internal boundaries of the community are met with external expansion. He reads Tarpeia's betrayal as "defy[ing] . . . the duty of a daughter," while the Sabine women are "taking up the cause of their Roman husbands" (he does also note the alternative version of Dionysius) (212–13). His overall thesis in the article is sound and quite compelling, but I think this reading of the Sabine women in particular is oversimplified. While the women's actions ultimately support the consolidation of Roman power, they do not simply indicate a capitulation to the cause of their Roman husbands, as the next section will elucidate—theirs is not an uncomplicated intervention. Nevertheless, Konstan's observations show the ways in which gender is integral to questions of stability, expansion, and, ultimately, potential penetrability (though this is not the focus of his investigation), highlighting the political tensions opened up through the story of Tarpeia.

Livy and Plutarch tell similar stories—Romulus, upon seeing his men retreat, prays to Jupiter for help. Livy relays this prayer in full: "Father of the Gods and men, hold back our enemy from this spot; take away the Romans' terror and stop their shameful flight!" Romulus then vows to build a temple on the spot to "Jupiter the Stayer" (Livy 1.12.5–6; cf. *Rom.* 18.6). The prayer moves the Romans and they once again begin to advance on the Sabines (Livy 1.12.7–10).

Then, in all three narratives, the Sabine women intervene in the battle scene. In Dionysius, this occurs during the "stalemate" between the Romans and the Sabines (DH 2.45.1). Hersilia and the stolen women come together without their husbands to forge a plan (DH 2.45.2). They bring this plan to the Senate and "[make] long pleas, begging to be permitted to go out to their relations and declaring that they had many excellent grounds for hoping to bring the two nations together and to establish friendship between them" (DH 2.45.3). The senate and king see this intervention as the "only solution" to their problem, so they agree to let the Sabine women broker their peace (DH 2.45.3–4). Dionysius's story, while seemingly complimentary of the Sabine women's initiative, implies that the best thing about this solution was that the Romans, fearing their defeat by the Sabines, would not be the ones brokering the peace; for "if they should have dealings with the Sabines for friendship, not one entertained to be met with moderation, not only for many other reasons, but chiefly because the proud and headstrong treat a rival who resorts to courting them, not with moderation, but with severity" (DH 2.44.3). In this way, the Romans would preserve their manliness by letting the women win the war for them.

Despite the way in which the Romans manipulate and use the actions of the ravished women, as Dionysius narrates it, the bold actions and initiatives of the women should not be diminished—as Livy and Plutarch demonstrate by making the actions of the women even bolder. In Livy's version, as in Dionysius's, Hersilia makes entreaties, though this time she directly appeals to her husband, Romulus. In contrast to Dionysius's version, these appeals occur after the Roman victories against the Caeninenses and the Antemnates (Livy 1.10.3–1.11.2). As discussed above, Hersilia had earlier begged Romulus "to forgive their parents and receive them into the state; which would in that case, gain strength by concord" (Livy 1.11.2).[119] Livy says that Romulus granted her request (Livy 1.11.2), but clearly his word was empty because, as discussed earlier, he then "set out to meet the Crustuminians" to defeat and colonize their lands (Livy 1.11.3–4), and then goes to war with the Sabines (Livy 1.12).

At this juncture in Livy and Plutarch, the Romans are in the midst of their war with the Sabines, Romulus taking the advantage with Jupiter at his side. The Sabine women and children then walk onto the battlefield. In Livy's version, the women actually enter an active battlefield, the men engaged in ongoing war:

> The Sabine women [mulieres], out of whose injury [iniuria] the war began, with loosened [passis] hair and torn [scissaque] garments, their feminine anxiety conquered by their misfortune [victo malis muliebri pavore], dared [ausae] to go among the flying missiles, and crossing the battlefield to part the hostile forces and dissolve their anger [dirimere iras], beseeching their fathers on this side, on that side their husbands, that father-in-law and son-in-law should not stain themselves with impious blood, nor pollute with parricide their suppliants' offspring, grandsons of one and free descendants [liberum progeniem] of the other. "If you loathe," they continued, "the relationship that unites you, the marriage-tie [conubii], turn your anger [iras] against us; we are the cause of war, the cause of wounds [vulnerum], and even death to both our husbands and parents. It will be better for us to perish than to live, without either of you, as widows or as orphans." (Livy 1.13.1–3)

Here Livy names the violence done to the Sabine women, a violence bound up with the violence they now feel forced to infiltrate. The women take the blame for the men's violence upon themselves as well as the blame for the war, wounds, and death it has wrought. In an effort to bring an end to their never-ending pain, they appeal to kinship ties between them. And though these ties were forged through force, they have linked their fathers, husbands, and children, who are now free

---

119. See the discussion of this passage and concordia in particular in the "The Wars of Colonization and the First Triumph" earlier in this chapter.

citizens of Rome. Kinship ties, therefore, have become ties to the state, and though established through deception and violence, now seem beyond dissolution. Because of this, in Livy's telling, the Sabine women would rather see their own destruction than find themselves caught in an unending cycle of violence between the men who lay claim to them.

In Plutarch's version, rather than entering an active battlefield, the women appear just before the battle is about to begin again, and he says that the men were stopped

by a sight that was terrible to behold and a spectacle [θέαμα] beyond description. The ravished [ἡρπασμέναι] daughters of the Sabines were seen rushing from every direction, with shouts and lamentations, through the armed men and the dead bodies, as if in a frenzy of possession, up to their husbands and their fathers, some carrying young children in their arms, some veiled in their disheveled hair, and all calling with the most endearing names now upon the Sabines and now upon the Romans. So then both armies were moved to compassion, and drew apart to give the women a place between the lines of battle; sorrow ran through all the ranks, and abundant pity was stirred by the sight of the women, and still more by their words, which began with argument and reproach, and ended with supplication and entreaty. "Where, pray, have we done you wrong or harm, that we must suffer in the past, and must suffer now still, such cruel evils? We were violently [βία] and lawlessly [παρανόμως] ravished away [ἡρπάσθημεν] by those by whom we are now possessed [ἐχόντων] but though thus ravished [ἁρπασθεῖσαι], we were neglected by our brothers and fathers and kinsmen until time had united us by the greatest force with those whom we had most hated, and made us now fear for those who had treated us with violence [βιασαμένων] and lawlessness [παρανομησάντων], when they go to battle, and mourn for them when they are slain. For you did not come to avenge us, while we were virgins [παρθένοις], from the wrong-doers, but now you would tear wives from their husbands and mothers from their children, and the help [βοήθειαν] with which you would rescue [βοηθοῦντες] us, miserable women which we are, is more lamentable than your former indifference and betrayal [προδοσία][120] of us. On the one hand, we were loved by these, on the other we are pitied by you. Even if you were fighting for other motives, you should stop for our sakes, having become fathers-in-law and grandfathers, and being made kin [οἰκείους]. If, however, the war is on our behalf, carry us off as spoils [κομίσασθε] with your sons-in-law and their children, and so restore to us our fathers and kindred [οἰκείος], but do not rob us of our

---

120. Here the Roman men are the "betrayers" rather than Tarpeia see *Rom.* 17.2, 3, 5.

children and husbands. Let us not, we beseech you, become prisoners of war [αἰχμάλωτοι] again." (*Rom.* 19.1–5)

Plutarch begins with the reactions of the men—something Livy will address minimally after the women's speech. It is hard to know if the men are moved because of their kinship ties, or if it is simply the "spectacle" of women—still referred to as the "ravaged women" here—and children on the battlefield, so outside of their allocated sphere. The women's long speech here is striking: they are clear about the violence done to them and clearly name not only the violence the men have done but the harm they have caused. Despite Plutarch's constant justifications of Romulus, in the mouths of the women, the men are directly blamed. As in Livy, here too the women appeal to the kinship ties of those involved in the war, but unlike in Livy there are no appeals to the Roman state. The women only appeal to the violence done to them, referring to themselves as "prisoners of war."

In comparison to both Livy and Plutarch, Dionysius's presentation of the women's intervention is short, and they seem to intervene at no risk to their lives. He simply states,

> [T]he women went out dressed in mourning, some of them also carrying their infant children. When they arrived in the camp of the Sabines, lamenting and falling at the feet of those they met, they aroused great compassion in all who saw them and none could refrain from tears. And when the councilors had been called together to receive them and the king had commanded them to state their reasons for coming, Hersilia, who had proposed the plan and was at the head of the embassy, delivered a long and sympathetic plea, begging them to grant peace to those who were interceding for their husbands and on whose account, she pointed out, the war had been undertaken. As to the terms, however, on which reconciliation should be made, she said the leaders, coming together by themselves, might settle them with a view to the advantage of both parties. (DH 2.45.5–6)

Dionysius's telling starkly contrasts with the other two. The women's bravery and boldness of speech are barely to be found—in fact, Dionysius simply states that Hersilia gave a speech and says little about it. The women never speak at all. There are no appeals to kinship ties or to the state. The reader is simply told that the women beg for peace and then negotiations are handed back over to the men.

The Brokered Peace

After the battlefield appeals made by the women, peace is finally brokered between the Romans and the Sabines. As Livy puts it, "Then the leaders came forward to make a treaty, and not only did they make peace but they made one people/community/state out of two [*civitatem unam ex duabus faciunt*]" (Livy 1.13.4). Plutarch alone mentions the Sabine women's actions after the initial peace is brokered wherein they

> carried food and drink to those that wanted, and carried the wounded to their homes for healing; here they also made it evident that they were mistresses of their own households [ἀρχούσας . . . αὐτὰς οἴκου], and that their husbands were attentive to them and showed them all honor with good will. (*Rom.* 19.6)

Because of these actions, "agreements were made that such women as wished to do so might continue to live with their husbands, exempt, as aforesaid, from all labor and all drudgery except spinning" (*Rom.* 19.7). In Plutarch, the women take continuing responsibility for the well-being of the war-torn men, cleaning up the real mess of war, and are subsequently returned to their proper realm. Capitalizing on the valor of the women's actions, the men once again regain control over the public realm of politics: all has returned to its "rightful" place.

All three continue the narrative by emphasizing the common kingship created between Romulus and the Sabine Tatius, but each also states that the city should retain the name of its founder;[121] that is, there is really only one founder and that is Romulus—thus, the city shall be called Rome. Livy names the reality of this "shared" state of affairs explicitly relating that "all power was transferred to Rome" (*imperium omne conferunt Romam*, Livy 1.13.4). And though all three of the texts note that the people of this new alliance will be called Quirites

121. DH 2.46.2; *Rom.* 19.7; cf. Livy 1.13.9.

(derived from the native city of Tatius, Cures), Dionysius qualifies this, noting that the appellation only applies to the people as a whole; individuals are still called "Romans" (DH 2.46.2), with Livy referring to the appellation as "a concession" (*daretur*, Livy 1.13.5). In these statements it is clear that, despite these new alliances, Romulus and the Romans are the real arbiters of power—there is still a differentiation between the conquerors and the conquered despite the rhetoric.

All three narratives also state that the Sabine women are honored by the naming of the thirty *curiae* (wards) after them, though both Dionysius and Plutarch question the reality of this: Dionysius, both because the *curiae* were named by Romulus before the war and because there were 527 women who formed the embassy and it would have been a dishonor to those whose names were not used (DH 2.27.4);[122] and Plutarch, simply because "this seems to be false, since many of them bear the names of places" (*Rom.* 20.2). Plutarch additionally mentions a host of other honors granted to the women, including "to give them the right of way when walking; not to utter any indecent word in the presence of a woman; that no man should be seen naked by them, or else that he be liable to prosecution before the judges of homicide; and that their children should wear a sort of necklace, the 'bulla,' so called from its shape, and a robe bordered with purple" (*Rom.* 20.3).

Plutarch alone follows this story with Romulus's founding of the Roman hearth-fire and the Vestal virgins who guard it (*Rom.* 22.1), then proceeds to discuss Romulus and his marriage laws. Plutarch notes that among these laws is "one of severity, which forbids a wife to leave her husband, but permits a husband to cast out his wife for using poisons, for substituting children, and for adultery" (*Rom.* 22.3). But he adds that if she is sent away for any other reason, half of his wealth will go to his wife and the other half consecrated to Ceres; "and whosoever puts away his wife, shall make a sacrifice to the gods of the lower world" (*Rom.* 22.3). Of note is that Plutarch follows the narrative of these early Roman battles with both the founding of the Vestals and marriage

---

122. Livy also mentions that there were more than thirty women, but this does not seem to cause him issue (1.13.6).

laws—two things that guard the integrity of Rome and guarantee its increase and empire.

Dionysius, too, discusses Romulus's marriage laws, but in an earlier portion of his text, laws that appear to be even more severe than those described by Plutarch. According to Dionysius, these laws decreed that, when husband and wife were married, they were to share in all possessions, but once the union was forged, there was no way to dissolve it (DH 2.25). Dionysius writes, "This law forced both the married women, having no other recourse or refuge, to conform themselves entirely to the temper of their husbands, and the husbands to rule [κρατεῖν] their wives as necessary and inseparable property [κτήματος]" (DH 2.25.4). If she was "modest" (σωφρονοῦσα) and "obedient" (πειθομένη) a wife could expect to be a mistress (κυρία) as her husband was lord, and to be included in inheritance should he die. But if she "failed [ἁμαρτάνουσα] the one wronged was her judge and entitled to decide the degree of her punishment" (DH 2.25.5–6). Other wrongs, like committing adultery and drinking wine, were judged by her kin along with her husband: Romulus allowed both of these to be penalized by death (DH 2.25.6). Throughout time, these offenses continued to be "met with merciless severity" (DH 2.25.7), but the "merits" of the law were great, as no marriages were dissolved during a 520-year span in Rome (DH 2.25.7). In both Dionysius and Plutarch, following the design created by the Romans' initial abduction of the women, all of the power dynamics of married life were controlled by the men (in much that same manner as the power in allegiance lies with the Romans).

Livy closes this portion of the story on the most optimistic note of the three narratives, when he declares, "Out of so sad a war suddenly came a joyful peace endearing [cariores] the Sabine women even more to their husbands and parents, and above all to Romulus himself." Once this peace was declared, "the two kings ruled [regnum duobus regibus fuit] not only jointly [commune] but in concord [concors]" (Livy 1.13.6–7). Livy ends his narrative with a direct connection between the earlier virtues of caritas and concordia that the Sabine women bring to their marriages and the relationship between the Romans and their newly formed state.[123] Through these virtues that undergird both private and public relationships, home life and society, "sad war" is clothed in care and harmony. But this concord, based on deceit and violence, is a fleeting one. For some years later, in the aftermath of the murder of king Tatius, Romulus will once again take sole control of Rome and reinstate a monarchy. (Livy 1.14; DH 2.51–52; *Rom.* 23)

Ovid and the Sabines

The Ovidian portrayals of the Sabines narrative bring the complex dynamics of these three other histories into sharp relief. While often Livy, Dionysius, and Plutarch attempt to hide, dismiss, or justify the underlying violence of the narrative, the ambivalence within their frame persists in leaking out. Ovid, on the other hand, in both the *Ars Amatoria* and the *Fasti*, seems to relish these complexities, showing both their irony and their horror. But with the Sabines, even more so than with Ilia/Rhea Silvia, he exhibits a darkly humorous and biting edge to bring these dynamics to the fore.

The *Ars Amatoria* flirts with connections between *amor* and *arma* (love and war), while the *Fasti* exploits connections between war and peace.[124] Ovid frames the *Ars* as a self-help book on how to attain a lover, addressing his readers as "soldiers in arms" (*miles in arma, Ars* 1.36), "love itself represent[ing] a kind of warfare [*militiae species amor*

---

123. Again, see both R. Brown, "Livy's Sabine Women"; and Miles, "First Roman Marriage," esp. 179–80, on *caritas*: "the most important basis of the couples' own alliance is through the *caritas* of their children. . . . [*Caritas* in Livy] is the source of the power that both children and the Roman homeland have to evoke strong sentimental attachments. The *caritas* of children to their parents and that of Rome to its inhabitants are very similar—*caritas liberum* and *caritas patriae* are the only two kinds of caritas described as 'innate' (*ingenita*, 1.34.5; 8.7.8)—and, in fact, are closely associated."

124. It is likely that the *Ars* contributed to Ovid's exile in 8 CE. See Genevieve Lively, *Ovid's Metamorphoses: A Reader's Guide* (London: Continuum, 2011), 3–6, for a pithy overview of Ovid's exile. Most of the information regarding his banishment comes from his work the *Tristia* 2.207, where he speaks of "a poem and a mistake"(*carmen et error*). Most scholars speculate that the poem is probably the *Ars Amatoria* and that the "mistake" may have been in relation to Augustus's granddaughter, Julia, who was exiled about the same time as Ovid. While the *Fasti* can be read as an exilic "corrective" to the *Ars* in certain ways, it too plays with the Augustan morality legislation, founding narratives, and, particularly in the stories addressed in this chapter, Roman marriage (see Andrew Feldherr, *Playing Gods: Ovid's Metamorphoses and the Politics of Fiction* (Princeton, NJ: Princeton University Press, 2010), 220.

est, 2.233] involving force, sieges, and carefully waged 'campaigns.'"[125] The *Fasti,* by contrast, chronicles the Roman calendar as an ode to Augustus and Rome (see *Fasti* 1.1–36), and, while Ovid's self-appointed task is to sing of "Caesar's altars and days" rather than "Caesar's wars" (*Fasti* 1.13–14), he cannot leave behind the topic of *arma* in his pursuit, which is no less fraught than that of the *Ars.* These themes are highlighted in Ovid's treatment of the Sabines story in both of these texts, the *Ars* featuring the women's abduction while the *Fasti* focuses on the Romans' womanless plight and later reconciliation.

The tale of the Sabines occurs in the middle of book 1 in the *Ars Amatoria,* as Ovid elucidates the best locales to find a lover. As a hunter knows where to stalk his prey, so, too, the would-be lover "must learn first which places young girls flock" (1.50).[126] Ovid suggests walks through Rome (1.67–88), the theater (1.89–228), the circus (1.135–70), triumphs (1.171–228), banquets (1.239–52), and the shore (1.253–62) as the best hunting grounds to snare a woman.[127] And, of course, the theater makes this list as the site where the first Roman men seized their wives.

125. Again, quoting Hemker, "Rape and the Founding of Rome," 41.
126. All translations are in consultation with http:// www.poetryintranslation.com/PITBR/Latin/ ArtofLoveBkI.htm#_Toc521049257 (A.S. Kline); and Ovid, *The Art of Love and Other Poems* (Mozley and Goold, LCL).
127. Each of the locations and Ovid's treatment of them are loaded with political overtones. The walks through Rome mention Pompey's Theater (Pompey's public theater, which was his public monument to celebrate is private exploits and where he displayed the images of personified nations, as women, he conquered; see Zanker, *Power of Images,* 24), the Portico of Octavia (built by Augustus for his sister and encircling the temples of Jupiter Stator and Juno Regina); the Portico of the Danaids in Apollo's temple on the Palatine (see Feldherr, *Playing Gods,* 86–87, on the Portico, its association with Actium, and the ambivalence of its interpretation by potential viewers). Adonis (god of beauty and desire, but also associated with the Hebrew Adoni and connected in Ovid's text to the Jews—who were more prevalent in Rome after Pompey's conquest of Jerusalem in 63 BCE), Isis's temple (in the *Ars* specifically connected with Jupiter's rape of Io), and finally the temple of Venus Genetrix and the courthouse (a possible reference to the Ovidian theme of Venus and Mars—Augustus's divine ancestors—and their adultery, which broke the Augustan adultery laws). The theater will be Ovid's site to tell the story of the Sabines who were ravaged by the Roman's ruse in the theater. In the circus, women will need to be comforted in the midst of the gladiatorial fights. The triumph gives Ovid an occasion to list the conquests of Augustus (not only does Ovid list his exploits, but refers to him as the *genitor patriaeque* [1.197] and foresees the apotheosis of Augustus [1.203–4]). The banquets call for public drunkenness and again Ovid invokes Venus (see Treggiari, *Roman Marriage,* 194, 209, 268–69, 360, 422–23, 461–62, on the morality of dinners, drinking, and adultery, social mores basically condemning all that Ovid advocates in this passage). Finally, Ovid reaches the shore—a place hearts are both enflamed and broken—the shrine of Diana Nemorensis is invoked here, referencing both Diana's eschewing of *amor* (love) and the shrine's location as a place "much resorted to by lovers" (Ovid, *Art of Love* [LCL], 30–31n1).

Ovid paints a bucolic picture of the theater scene, comparing the "rush[128] of cultivated ladies to the crowded games" with ants passing in processions, "carrying [their] accustomed grain" and bees in the woods and meadows "fly[ing] through the flowers and thyme" (*Ars* 1.93–97). It is the place "most fertile for your vows," where "you'll find one to love [*ames*], or one you can play [*ludere*] with, one to touch [*tangas*] just once, or one you wish to keep [*tenere velis*]" (1.90–92). But despite this bucolic and playful scene (for the men at least), Ovid frames this search as a "hunt" (*venare*, 1.89), calling the place "fatal for chaste modesty" (*casti . . . pudoris*, 1.100) as, "You first, Romulus, made the games disturbing, /when the raped [*rapta*] Sabines delighted unmarried men" (1.101–2).

Ovid again evokes the bucolic as he describes the ancient atmosphere of these Romulan games:

> Then no awnings hung from the marble theatre,
> the stage wasn't stained red with saffron perfumes:
> Then what the shady Palatine provided, leaves
> simply placed; the scene unadorned:
> The people sat on seats made of grass,
> With leaves, as they please, covering their unkempt hair [*hirsutas . . . comas*].[129] (*Ars* 1.103–8)

But this rustic scene quickly becomes disconcerting as:

> [The Romans] look about them,
> and each with his eyes noting the girl [*puellem*]
> he wanted, and greatly stirred in their silent heart [*pectore*].
> While, the Tuscan flautist offers wild measures,
> the dancer struck three times with feet the leveled floor,
> amongst the applause (applause was without manners then)
> the king gave the sign to assault their spoils.[130]
> (*Ars* 1.109–14)

With these lines, the theater changes from festive to frightening, and

---

128. Ovid seems to be playing with the full semantic range of *ruo*, meaning, "to rush down; to fall down, tumble down" but also to "go to ruin" (Lewis & Short, s.v. *ruo*).

129. Cf. the hair of Rhea Silvia in *Fasti* 3.16; *Amores* 3.6.48, 56, 71; the hair of the Sabine women in Livy 1.13.1 and Plutarch, *Rom*. 19.1.

130. *Rex populo praedae signa petita dedit*. Cf. *Rom*. 19.5, κομίζω.

Ovid names the transformation of the Sabine women from objects of the heart's desire to spoils.

As Ovid evokes the hunt at the start of the story, in his next lines the Romans embody this hunt as they "showed their souls" and "lustfully seized the maidens" who fearfully flee "as doves flee the eagle" and the "lamb flees the hostile wolf" (*Ars* 1.115–18). Instead of the orderly ants and fluttering bees, the women fearfully flee as prey from "the violent rushing [*ruentes*] of unvirtuous men" (1.119). Ovid then, in a powerful move unique among the Sabines narratives, unequivocally describes the reactions of the women to their seizure:[131]

> Now their fear was one, but not singularly was how their fear appeared:
> Some tear [*laniat*] their hair [*crines*]; some sit, out of their minds;
> one is despondently silent; another uselessly cries [*frustra vocat*] for her mom;
> this one wails [*queritur*], that one's numb; that one stays, this one runs [*fugit*]. (*Ars* 1.121–24)

Despite the shock and terror of the women, Ovid then seems to return to the perspective of the Roman men as "the ravished girls [*raptae . . . puellae*] were led away" and refers to them, in sharp contrast to the picture he has just painted, as "a joyful spoil [*genialis*[132] *praeda*]" (*Ars* 1.125). Not only this, but Ovid remarks that "many had the power to make fear [*timor*] itself becoming" (1.126). In these lines, Ovid exposes the deep disconnect between the perspective of the Sabine women and the Roman men, who see their fear as a "joyful spoil"—a disconnect so deep it is diametrically opposed.[133]

---

131. As with the portrait of Ilia in the *Amores*, discussed earlier, Ovid here brings the perspective of the women affected by this violent act to bear in his narrative. Of course, this is not without complication, as he narrates the events of the Roman men without critique, but it seems to me that his narration, in and of itself, does much to counteract the lauditory accounts of the Romulan perspective that frame (though at times unsuccessfully) the narratives of Livy, Dionysius of Halicarnassus, and Plutarch.
132. Lewis & Short, s.v. *genialis*, also, "the marriage bed or marriage couch"—a double entendre.
133. Hemker emphasizes, "At this point, Ovid's description, unlike Livy's, sympathetically conveys the horror of the situation. Whereas Livy had grouped the women all together with the single word *raptis*, Ovid describes the painful reaction to each individual victim. A simile (117–19) compares the women's fear to that of timid doves fleeing eagles, or a young lamb fleeing wolves. These comparisons overtly challenge the validity of the men's actions by emphasizing the helplessness of those hunted by an overwhelming, violent predator. From the narrator's perspective, the erotic 'hunt' awards him with delightful *commoda*, but from the women's perspective, the hunt

Ovid continues to expose the divide between the Sabine women and Roman men as he states, "If any resisted [*repugnarat*] too much, and refused her companion," she would be "taken [*sublatam*][134] on his lustful breast the man carry[ing] her off himself" (*Ars* 1.127–28). Then, clearly oblivious to her feeling of fear and violation, he would say to her, "Why corrupt your tender [*teneros*] eyes [*ocellos*][135] with tears [*lacrimis*]? / As your father is to your mother, that I will be to you" (*Ars* 1.129–30). With these lines from the anonymous Roman ravisher, Ovid concludes the story of the Sabines in the *Ars*, but he ends with an aside that recalls the juxtaposition between *arma* and *amo,r* as the narrator speaks directly to Romulus and then to reader:

> You, Romulus, alone, knew what was suitable to give to soldiers:
> So if you confer such a favor on me, a soldier I will be.
> Certainly, by solemn custom from that time the theatres,
> even now, remain dangerous for the beautiful [*formosis*].
> (*Ars* 1.131–34)

If women, beautiful in the wake of violent seizure, are the favors—or spoils—that are incurred in the army of Romulus, then the narrator is ready to enlist. But the narrator also warns that this "originary" act

endangers and violates them, making them into the men's sexual "spoil" (*genialis praeda* 125)" ("Rape and the Founding of Rome," 45).

Cf. Richlin's critique of Hemker's perspective ("Reading Ovid's Rapes," 168): "Remarkably, a recent critic sees this passage as a strong antirape statement by Ovid. The premise of the argument is that the *praeceptor* is so obviously wrongheaded that the reader sees the falsity of all he says, as if the whole poem were in quotation marks and the quotation marks nullified the content. Yet Hemker simultaneously argues that Ovid's description 'sympathetically conveys the horror of the situation'; she singles out the climactic vignette of the women in flight as showing 'the women's perspective.'

Such a reading blurs the content; the women's fear is displayed only to make them more attractive. We have this myth, too, in comedies and action romances (squeaky voice: 'Put me down!'); it is part of the plot. Likewise, for the Sabine women, there is really nothing to be worried about, because they are getting married. Their fears are cute, and the whole thing is a joke. Again the text uses women's fear as its substance. There are indeed quotation marks around the text, the marks that tell the reader 'this is amusing'; but they act not to attach the content but to palm it off."

Both Hemker and Richlin point to the complexity of Ovid's presentation of the story as he both subverts and reifies Roman norms of gender, violence, and sexuality, readings varying depending on one's perspective. As Alison Sharrock notes, the *Ars* "both oppose[s] and partake[s] in the norms of Roman masculinity" ("Gender and Sexuality," in *The Cambridge Companion to Ovid*, ed. Philip Hardie [Cambridge: Cambridge University Press, 2002], 102).

134. Lewis & Short, s.v. *tollo*: "to take up, lift up; but also to get, beget a child; take away, carry off, make away with; to kill, destroy, ruin." Again, Ovid pushes the full semantic range of the word here.

135. Lewis & Short, s.v. *ocellus*, "little eye, eyelet"—this is a term of endearment.

of violence has forever made the theater a dangerous place, despite its
bucolic façade, for women who hazard to go.

The tale of the Sabines in the *Fasti* recounts the story that occurs
before and after the abduction sequence found in the *Ars*, the two
together complementing each other and completing the narrative. The
story ushers in the date of March 1, Kalends, the poet asking Mars "why
women [*matronae*] keep your feast, you who are apt to be served by
men [*virilibus*]" (*Fasti* 3.169–70).[136] Before answering, Mars responds to
the poet's requests at the opening of book 3[137] and "laying aside his
helmet, but keeping his throwing spear in his right hand," responds
saying,

> Now I am a god used to warfare, invoked
> In the study of peace, and I march into new camps,
> I am not reluctant of the undertaking: I delight to take part as well,
> Lest Minerva think such power is hers alone.
> Learn what you seek, laboring poet of Latin days,
> And inscribe my words in your heart's memory. (*Fasti* 3.173–78)[138]

While Mars lays aside his helmet, he keeps his (phallic) spear as he
"studies peace," alluding not only to the entangled relationship
between war and peace in Rome's past and present but to the violence
at the heart of the story he is about to tell. While the poet wonders
why it is women who serve him at his feast rather than warriors, it will
be evident from the Sabines story that, while men make war, women
are needed both to sustain and to disrupt it. Therefore, Mars must
keep his spear, a weapon wielded to secure women for the Romans,
ensuring both the assimilation of new peoples into the Roman fold and
continuing generations of warriors to take up his arms.

Mars begins his explanation of why women keep his feast day with

---

136. As, of course, it is generally men who serve the god of war on the battlefield.
137. *Fasti* 3.1–3, 5–8: "Come, warlike Mars; lay down your shield and spear for a little while, and loose
your glistering locks from your helmet. Perhaps you may ask, What has a poet to do with Mars? . . .
You see, yourself, fierce wars are waged by Minerva's hands. Is she for that the less free for noble
arts? Follow the precedent of Pallas, take time to lay aside the lance. You will find something to
do unarmed."
138. This whole opening to the Kalends of March reflects the opening of book 3 (3.1–3, 5–8): Mars
removes his helmet, though he does not lay down his spear, trades the study of war for peace, and
follows Minerva's example.

the Romans' humble beginnings but emphasizes that these humble beginnings already reflected the potential for the city's greatness. This dynamic is seen in Mars's description of Romulus:

If you ask where my son's palace was,
See there, that house made of straw and reeds.
He snatched [capiebat][139] the gifts of peaceful sleep on straw,
Yet from that bed he sprang to the stars.[140] (Fasti 3.183–86)

Though his palace was but a hut, Romulus would be made a god. But this metamorphosis would not be possible without Mars's intervention, as he relates the sad and dejected state of the Roman men:

Already the Roman's name reached beyond his city,
Though he had neither wife nor father-in-law.
Wealthy neighbors spurned [spernebant] poor sons-in-law,
And hardly believed I was the author [auctor] of their blood.
It hurt the Romans that they lived in stables,
Grazed sheep, and had a few acres of wasteland.
Winged creatures and wild beasts each mate with their own kind,
And even a snake has some female with which to breed;
Rights of intermarriage [connubia] are afforded to distant peoples:
Yet none wished to marry the Romans. (Fasti 3.187–96)

Mars "grieved" this state of affairs and afforded Romulus his warring disposition instructing him, "Do away with prayers, arms [arma] will grant what you seek!" (Fasti 3.197–98).

Mars skips the story of Romulus's plot to deceive the Romans' neighbors and the seizure of the Sabine women, but Mars's instructions to Romulus, that is, to give up prayers and take up arms, have a correspondence in the Sabine men's accusations against the Romans in Livy 1.9.13, where "they charged the Romans with the crime of violating hospitality, and invoked the gods to whose solemn games they had come, deceived in violation of religion and honor."[141] While

---

139. Lewis & Short, s.v. capio: "take hold of, lay hold of, take, seize, take into possession, take captive, hold prisoner."
140. Romulus's apotheosis.
141. incusantes violate hospitii scelus deumque invocantes, cuius ad sollemne ludosque per fas ac fidem decepti venissent.

Romulus has shown piety to his god and father by following his words and taking up his arms, in using these weapons against his neighbors and deceiving them in the name of the god Consus, Romulus has at the same time left behind piety and violated hospitality, religion, and honor—and most of all he has violated the women. As these violations occur in the name of Consus, Mars will leave for Consus to tell the story of Romulus's plot and the abduction of the Sabines, and Mars will continue with the war and the women who intervene (*Fasti* 3.199–200).[142]

Mars names the complicated kinship relationships that have resulted from Romulus's plan, briefly addressing the war: "Then a father-in-law first waged war on his daughter's husband.[143] / And now the raped [*raptae*] women also possessed the name 'mother' [*matrum*]" (*Fasti* 3.202–3). As the war "dragged on," Mars turns his tale to the women, gathered in Juno's temple, among whom, "my daughter-in-law dared to speak" (*Fasti* 3.204–6). Then Ovid imagines Hersilia's (who remains unnamed—her identifying feature her relationship to Mars) speech, as, according to Mars, she appeals to the gathered women:

> Oh, all you ravished women [*raptae*] (we have that in common)
> We can no longer delay our duties.
> The battle continues, but choose for which of the two parties you will pray to the gods:
> Your armed husbands [*coniunx*] on this side, your armed fathers [*pater*] on the other.
> The question is whether you're prepared to be widows or orphans:
> I will give you courageous and dutiful counsel. (*Fasti* 3.207–12)

Hersilia appeals to the women on the basis of their shared experience of the past (their abduction) as well as the shared threat to their futures (becoming widows and/or orphans).[144] Here, the women are

142. Ovid never writes this portion of the *Fasti*.
143. This is an oblique allusion to the civil wars, referring to the fact that Julius Caesar's daughter, Julia, was Pompey's wife (Ovid, *Fasti* [LCL],134n.b.); noting more generally this connection, see, e.g., Hemker, "Rape and the Founding of Rome," 41–47; Cahoon, "Bed as Battlefield," 298–99. See also chapter 2 of this study.
144. Rather than using *raptae* to describe the ravished women and collapsing them into a single entity from the "outside," that is, by the Romans or narrators, here it is used by "insiders" to define their shared experience.

the ones who enact proper piety, the piety that Romulus and the Romans have left behind in their deception and war waging.

In the *Fasti*'s telling of the Sabines story thus far, the virtues of *virtus* and *pietas* are portrayed along gender lines—Romulus and the Romans following the *virtus* of Mars with the Sabine women embodying the ideal of *pietas*. *Virtus* and *pietas* are two of the four virtues Augustus inscribed on the shield in his new senate house, the Curia Iulia.[145] *Virtus* was particularly associated with "manly valor on the battlefield"[146] and was a "competitive virtue" that included "the notion of self-aggrandizement."[147] *Pietas*, on the other hand, functioned as its "'cooperative' counterweight, representing the time-honored Roman ideal of social responsibility, which includes a broad spectrum of obligations to family, country, and gods. . . . [P]ietas . . . is a quality or a bond that cannot function without reciprocity. It requires the unselfish effort of all for the common good."[148] Just as in Livy's portrayal of the Sabine women and *concordia*, the Sabine women in the *Fasti*—"outsider" women, forced to become "insiders" through violence—are the ones left with the responsibility not only for their own well-being but for the well-being of their children, fathers, husbands, and ultimately the state: they are the ones responsible for tending to "the common good." Here, Ovid evokes the tension between these two virtues and elicits questions about how *virtus* and *pietas* function together, what constitutes reciprocity, and who is included within the idea of "the common good."

Hersilia gives her counsel to the women, and, though Mars does not relay her words, he describes the ensuing actions of the women who "loosened their hair and clothed their bodies in sad funeral garb" (*Fasti* 3.213–14). Here the women use the "rhetorical" tools at their disposal, that is, their bodies, as Ovid quickly segues to the battle scene, where "Already the armies stood, preparing for death by sword, / Already the

---

145. Karl Galinsky, *Augustan Culture: An Interpretive Introduction* (Princeton, NJ: Princeton University Press, 1996), 80–88; the other two virtues are *clementia* and *iustitia*.
146. Ibid., 84.
147. Ibid., 86.
148. Ibid., 86–88.

trumpet was about to give the battle sign" (*Fasti* 3.215–16). Into this scene of impending carnage

> the ravished women [*raptae*] came between father and husband,
> Bearing their babies at their breasts, the precious [*cara*] pledges of love [*pignora*].[149]
> When, with streaming hair, they reached the middle of the field,
> They fell to their knees, kneeling on the ground [*in terram posito procubuere genu*],
> And, as if they understood, the grandchildren with alluring cries [*blando clamore nepotes*],[150]
> Stretched out their small arms to their grandfathers:
> Those who could, called to their grandfather, seen for the first time,
> And those who could scarcely speak yet, were urged to try. (*Fasti* 3.217–24)

The women, dressed for their own funerals, or for that of their kin,[151] disrupt the battle arrays, falling on the field, children and grandchildren calling out to the men poised for battle. The blandishments and *caritas* used by the men in Livy to persuade the women are here used by the children in an attempt to stop the violence.

The impact of the women's intervention is swift as the "weapons and wills of the warriors [*viris*] fall" (*Fasti* 3.225). The warriors then "set aside" (*remotis*) their swords, just as earlier Mars "laid aside" (*posita*) his helmet, freeing their hands so father-in-law and son-in-law could grasp one another, so fathers could hold daughters in their arms. Grandfathers' shields now bear grandchildren rather than protecting from the weapons of war (*Fasti* 3.225–28). Because of their intervening actions, the Sabine mothers

> have the duty, no light one,
> to celebrate the first day, my Kalends,
> Either because in boldly facing unsheathed blades,
> by their tears, they ended these wars of Mars
> Or because Ilia happily became a mother by me,
> Mothers are the guardians of the rites on my day. (*Fasti* 3.229–34)

149. Lewis & Short, s.v. *pignus*: only used to refer to family members (i.e., "children, parents, brothers and sisters, relatives as pledges of love") after Augustan period.
150. Cf. Livy 1.9.16.
151. Cf. DH 2.45.5.

After discussing the story of the Sabine women at length, Mars, almost as an aside, mentions that it may not be their actions at all but those of Ilia that require mothers to celebrate Mars's Kalends. With this invocation of Ilia, Ovid brings Mars's month full circle, as he returns to his introduction to March, recalling Ilia's rape and connecting the kinship between Mars, Ilia, Romulus, and the Sabine women.

Steven Hinds highlights a further connection between the celebration of his month, the Sabine women and the figure of the "unarmed" Mars. Regarding *Fasti* 3.229-32, Hinds notes, "On his own [Mars's] explanation (he offers a second, shorter one in the following couplet [3.233.234]), women worship Mars on the Kalends because of their *ending* of *Martia bella* ["wars of Mars"]. What is paradoxically celebrated on the god's first day is the *negation* of his usual power—in favour of the more peaceful, more elegiac Mars *inermis* ["unarmed"] specifically desiderated in the book's preface."[152] The "second, shorter explanation offered by Mars in 3.233 for his worship by women on the Matronalia [i.e., the rape of Ilia] also returns us to Mars *inermis*—as characterized earlier in the book in the Ilia/Silvia episode (3.9 ff.: *tum quoque inermis eras, cum* . . .)."[153] While Hinds reads Mars's negation of power in these lines as paradoxical, I read it as more ironical. In the Ilia episode it is the poet who suggests that Mars find something to do "unarmed,"[154] and Mars has yet to lay aside his weapons as the poet narrates his violent encounter with Ilia (his weapons are only laid aside at the Sabines episode in *Fasti* 3.173-78). Though he does not use external implements of war, he nonetheless wields his body as a weapon against Ilia—he is not "unarmed." This irony holds in the Sabines story as well. As Mars lays aside his helmet, he still holds his (phallic) spear (*Fasti* 3.171-72); though he claims to study peace (*Fasti* 3.173-74), he encourages his son to give up prayers and take up arms (*Fasti* 3.198). After Romulus follows these instructions from Mars, abducts the women, and wages war, the women not only are

152. Hinds, "*Arma* in the *Fasti*, Part 1," 105. See *Fasti* 3.8-9 and the discussion of this verse in "Rhea Silvia in Ovid" in this chapter.
153. Hinds, "*Arma* in the *Fasti*, Part 1," 105n28.
154. Indicated by Hinds's use of "desiderated," though not stated.

forced to take up the *pietas* he has abandoned in service of the welfare of both home and state, but do so by entering the battlefield. Far from embracing an unarmed state, Mars's weapons—whether material, bodily, or rhetorical—exert themselves upon Ilia, Romulus, the Romans, the Sabine women, and the Sabine men. Ultimately, it is those who have had Mars's violence thrust upon them who have the duty to honor him on Kalends.

Lucretia and Verginia

Often linked together (as Livy notes even within his narrative)[155] the stories of Lucretia[156] and Verginia[157] provide important counterpoints to the stories of both Rhea Silvia and the Sabines, though just as politically charged. In the story of Ilia, rape is justified—though it breaks the taboo of Vestal virginity—because through it the founders of Rome are born. Rape is again justified in the story of the Sabines as they become conduits for the continuance and expansion of Rome.[158] The tales of Lucretia and Verginia, on the other hand, represent the rape of insiders and illustrate Roman concerns for women's chastity. In these two stories, rape is viewed as a mark of shame, and both women, one by her own hand and the other by her father's, will lose their lives rather than live in its wake.

Lucretia's story occurs in the midst of a military campaign at the end of the monarchy. Resentment for the royal family already building from their exploitation of the people,[159] Lucretia's tale begins with the

155. Livy 3.44.1.
156. Livy 1.57–60. The translation of the Lucretia story is that of Benjamin Oliver Foster, Livy, *The History of Rome, Book 1* (LCL), with some emendations; *Fasti* 2.685–852; DH 4.64–85.
157. Livy 3.44–48. The translation of the Verginia story is that of Benjamin Oliver Foster, Livy, *The History of Rome, Book 3* (LCL), with some emendations.
158. This is a somewhat oversimplified portrayal. As in the thorough treatment of the Ilia and Sabines stories in the previous section, there are many ambivalent dynamics at play both within their framing by the authors and in shared plot lines of the stories themselves. These ambivalences come to the fore particularly in the Ovidian readings of the stories, as Ovid exploits these ambivalences in an effort to highlight the violence they portray. While especially Livy's, Dionysius's, and Plutarch's tellings attempt in many ways to elide this ambivalence, they often fail at the task.
159. Livy 1.57; *Fasti* 2.684–710; DH 4.64.1. See James A. Arieti, "Rape and Livy's View of Roman History," in *Rape in Antiquity: Sexual Violence in the Greek and Roman Worlds*, ed. Susan Deacy and Karen F. Pierce (London: Gerald Duckworth, 2002), 212.

king's son Sextus Tarquinius, who is in the middle of a siege against Ardea. Bored one evening, Sextus and other noble Roman officers sit around dining and drinking when conversation turns to the virtues of their wives.[160] As they hotly debated whose wife was best, Tarquinius Collatinus boasted of his wife and suggested the drinking party go to his own Lucretia and the other wives in that moment, as surprising them unexpected would be the quickest way to prove his point.[161]

Upon their arrival, the daughters-in-law of the king were found dining in luxury, in leisure with friends. Lucretia, though it was late, was discovered quite differently, spinning wool with her maids, thus the "prize of this contest in womanly virtues fell to Lucretia" (Livy 1.57.9).[162] Lucretia then invites the party to dinner, where "Sextus Tarquinius was seized with a wicked desire to defile Lucretia by force; not only her beauty, but her observed chastity as well, provoked him." Then all return to the military camp (1.57.10–11).[163]

Several days later, unknown to Collatinus, Sextus returns to Lucretia's home. He is welcomed to dinner, then shown to a guest room. When the household is asleep, he draws his sword and goes to the unsuspecting Lucretia. Holding her down, his hand on her breast, he says to her, "Be still, Lucretia! I am Sextus Tarquinius. My sword is in my hand. Utter a sound, and you die" (Livy 1.58.1–2).[164] He pleads with her to bed him, declaring love, making threats and offering prayers, but Lucretia will not be moved, even under threat of death.[165] As a last resort, Tarquin threatens her with "disgrace," saying he would kill her and "when she was dead he would kill his slave and lay him naked by her side, that she might be said to have been put to death in adultery with a man of base condition. At this dreadful prospect her resolute modesty was vanquished, as if with force, by his victorious lust; and

160. Livy 1.57.4–7; *Fasti* 2.721–31; cf. DH 4.64.2.
161. Livy 1.57.7–8; *Fasti* 2.731–35.
162. Cf. *Fasti* 2.736–60; cf. DH 4.64.4. As Arieti notes, "The very fact that she is spinning is symbolic of her virtue, for wool-making is a ritual symbol of marriage; Roman brides carried a spindle and wool during their weddings" ("Rape and Livy's View," 213). Cf. the Sabines narrative on spinning and honor (Plutarch, *Rom.* 15.3–5; 19.7).
163. See *Fasti* 2.761–83; cf. DH 4.64.4.
164. See *Fasti* 2.784–96; DH 4.64.4–65.1.
165. Livy 1.58.3–4; *Fasti* 2.797–806.

Tarquinius departed, exulting in his conquest of a woman's honor" (1.58.4–5).[166]

Lucretia, "grieving at her great disaster," sent messages to her father and husband that something had happened, and that they should come to her quickly, each bringing a trusted companion. Her father, Spurius Lucretius brought Publius Valerius, while Collatinus brought Lucius Junius Brutus. They found Lucretia, "sitting sadly in her chamber" (1.58.5–6).[167] As they enter, Lucretia's eyes well, her husband asking if all is well." She replies,

> Far from it; for what can be well with a woman when she has lost her honour? The print of a strange man, Collatinus, is in your bed. Yet my body only has been violated; my heart is guiltless, as death shall be my witness. But pledge your right hands and your words that the adulterer shall not go unpunished. Sextus Tarquinius is he that last night returned hostility for hospitality, and brought ruin on me, and on himself no less—if you are men—when he worked his pleasure with me. (1.58.7–8)[168]

Unlike Romulus's Romans, who are justified for violating hospitality and honor in their violent quest for foreign wives,[169] Sextus is condemned for violating a Roman woman's honor.

The four men pledge to uphold her honor and assure her "by diverting the blame from her who was forced to the author of the fault [*auctorem delicit*].[170] They tell her it is the mind that sins, not the body, and that where purpose has been wanting there is no guilt" (1.58.9).[171]

---

166. See *Fasti* 2.807–11; DH 4.65.1–66.1. Jennifer A. Glancy notes, "Typically unexamined is Lucretia's horror at the prospect of sex with a slave. The story codifies a primitive horror at the thought of a freeborn woman's body joined carnally to a slave's body, and attitude toward the purity of the freeborn woman that exceeds the bounds of the moral to become a fear of pollution by what is defined as base. According to ancient mores, the conditioning of the freeborn woman should lead her to recoil physically from such pollution. The purity of the matron's body requires complete dissociation from what is ignoble. Even the appearance of sexual union with an enslaved man would taint that purity" (*Corporeal Knowledge: Early Christian Bodies* [New York: Oxford University Press, 2010], 69).

167. See *Fasti* 2.811–17; cf. DH 4.66.1, in Dionysius's version Lucretia goes to her father's house.

168. See *Fasti* 2.817–28; cf. DH 4.66.1–67.1.

169. See Livy 1.9.13, where: "they charged the Romans with the crime of violating hospitality, and invoked the gods to whose solemn games they had come, deceived in violation of religion and honor" (*incusantes violate hospitii scelus deumque invocantes, cuius ad sollemne ludosque per fas ac fidem decepti venissent*).

170. Cf. Livy 1.4.2, where Mars is the "author" of Rhea's Silvia's "fault" (*auctor culpae*).

171. See *Fasti* 2.829.

She answers their assurances saying, "It is for you to determine what is due to him; for my own part, though I acquit myself of the sin, I do not absolve myself from the punishment; nor hereafter shall any shameless [*inpudica*] woman live through the example of Lucretia." And taking a knife concealed by her dress, "she plunged it into her heart, and sinking forward upon the wound, died as she fell" (1.58.10–11).[172]

As her father and husband lament, Brutus pulls the knife from Lucretia's wound, "and holding it up, dripping with gore," vows to avenge her wrong and pursue not only Sextus but his father, the king, and his entire family to ensure that neither them or any other will be king of Rome (Livy 1.59.1).[173] Thus, with Lucretia's violation, death, and promise of retribution, her story instigates the end of the monarchy in Rome and the beginning of the Republic (1.59–60).[174]

As Lucretia's rape leads to the end of the monarchy, Verginia's attempted rape will lead to the end of the Decemvirate and restoration of the consulship.[175] Livy begins his tale of attempted rape calling it an "outrage . . . inspired by lust and was no less shocking in its consequences than that which had led, through the rape and the death of Lucretia, to the expulsion of the Tarquinii" (Livy 3.44.1). At this point in Rome's history, the "patrician and plebian orders were engaged in savage class warfare," and Appius Claudius, head of the Decemvirate was "charged with publishing the law [which] threatened the newly won representation of the plebs in the political hierarchy," further inflaming the war between the classes.[176] Verginia, the daughter of the centurion Lucius Verginius, was betrothed to "the former tribune Lucius Icilius, an active man of proven courage in the cause of the plebeians" (3.44.2). Livy describes Verginia as "exceedingly beautiful" (3.44.4), and Appius Claudius "was seized with desire to ravish the plebeian virgin" (3.44.2). Appius, "crazed with love [*amore*], attempted to seduce [*perlicere adortus*] her with money and promises [*pretio ac spe*],

172. See *Fasti* 2.830–34; DH 4.67.1.
173. See *Fasti* 2.835–44; cf. DH 4.67.4; 4.70.1–5.
174. See *Fasti* 2.844–52; DH 4.71–85.
175. See Arieti, "Rape and Livy's View," 214–16; Dixon, *Reading Roman Women*, 46–47.
176. Dixon, *Reading Roman Women*, 46–47.

but when he saw that he was impeded by modesty [*pudore*], he turned to cruel and tyrannical violence [*ad crudelem superbamque vim animum convertit*]" (3.44.4).

In order to possess his heart's desire, Appius tasks one of his dependents (*cliens*), Marcus Claudius, to claim her as his slave.[177] Upon entering the Forum to attend school, Marcus approached and grabbed Verginia, naming her as "the daughter of his bond-woman and a slave herself" (3.44.5–6). He commanded her to come with him—and, if she hesitated, threatened "to drag her away by force [*vi abstracturum*]." Verginia was "stupefied with terror, and her nurse cried out to draw a crowd. Her nurse called out the names of both her father and her betrothed, well known to and popular with the people, and they supported Verginia against Marcus's claims. Marcus stated that he would "proceed lawfully, and not by force," summoning Verginia to court—the tribunal presided over by Appius (3.44.7–9). The trial is postponed in the absence of Verginia's father, but when it resumes, after many machinations by Appius to prevent his presence (3.44.9–47.1), Verginius goes with Verginia to the Forum and pleads his case to the people. But, Livy notes, "the women who attended [the proceedings] were more moving than any words, as they wept in silence" (3.47.1–3).

Appius, witnessing the appeals of both Verginius and the weeping women, "hardened his heart [*obstinato animo*]—so violent with the madness, as it may more truly be called than love, that had overthrown his reason [*tanta vis amentiae verius quam amoris mentem turbaverat*]" convenes the tribunal (3.47.4–5). Of course, Appius judges in favor of Marcus Claudius. The crowd, initially frozen in shocked silence, wails and laments as Marcus begins to lead Verginia away. As his daughter is led away, Verginius, shaking his fist at Appius, cries, "It was to Icilius, Appius, not you that I betrothed my daughter; and it was for wedlock, not dishonor, that I brought her up. Would you have men imitate the beasts of the field and the forest in promiscuous gratification of their

---

177. Again, note Glancy, *Corporeal Knowledge*, 69. While differently figured, it is interesting that the intersections between slavery and purity occur here as well.

lust?[178] Whether these people propose to tolerate such conduct I do not know: I cannot believe that those who have arms will endure it" (3.47.6–7).

Appius, "crazed with lust," demands both silence and the transfer of Verginia to her "master." As he screamed these words the crowd parted, leaving Verginia unprotected and "prey to villainy" (3.47.8–48.3). Seeing no other alternative, Verginius apologizes to Appius for his behavior and respectfully requests to have a moment in private with his daughter and her nurse in an effort to know why he has been "falsely called a father" (3.48.4). Appius honors his request, and Verginius moves with Verginia toward the vending booths. Then "snatching a knife from the butcher, he exclaimed, 'Thus, my daughter, in the only way I can, do I assert your freedom!' He then stabbed her to the heart, and, looking back to the tribunal, cried, 'It is you, Appius, and your life I devote to destruction with this blood!'" (3.48.5).

Appius orders Verginius seized, but Verginius, who made a path by wielding his knife, was protected by the crowd. Verginia's betrothed and uncle lifted the body for all to see with the matrons crying, "Was it on these terms that children were brought into the world? Were these the rewards of chastity [pudicitiae]?" (3.48.5–8). Livy adds that the women also voiced "other complaints as are prompted at a time like this by a woman's anguish, and are so much the more pitiful as their weakness [imbecillo animo] makes them the more subject [subicit] to grief. The men, and especially Icilius, spoke only of the tribunician power, of the right of appeal to the people which had been taken from them, and of their resentment at the nation's wrongs" (3.48.8–9). With these lines, the voices of the women—like the voice of Verginia which never utters a word—are subsumed by the voice of men and their political posturing; and the violence done to Verginia, to which these crying voices respond, fades from view.

Miles Lavan observes, "Throughout the Roman historiographical tradition, unrestrained lust and sexual violence are symbols of tyranny. In Livy, for example, the rape of Lucretia by Tarquinius

178. Cf. *Ars.* 1.115–19.

Superbus and the attempted rape of Verginia by Appius Claudius are the concrete signs that excessive power has corrupted the kings and the decemvirate respectively."[179] Yet in the stories of Rhea and the Sabines, lust and sexual violence symbolize not tyranny but the founding and flourishing of Rome. While rape brings honor and citizenship to the Sabines, it only spells shame and death for Lucretia and Verginia; while sexual violence and chastity are unproblematic for "outsiders,"[180] they are lethal for "insiders." The presence of rape in all of these stories extends their pivotal importance not just as signifiers of profound moments of Rome's decline, but also crucial moments for its increase. What does remain consistent throughout all of the narratives is that women and the violence they suffer are of less concern to the men than the future of the state.

Conclusion: Founding, Refounding, and the Renewal of Rome

These myths of Rome's beginnings form an important narrative arc, each connecting and intersecting through their use of gender roles, sexual violence, and war to tell the story of Rome's founding, a founding that upholds the "logic" of male control and power. The narratives also have continuing significance, not just in literature that spans the time of the Roman Empire, but in its visual program, material culture, and later within private, rather than more public works. Not only are these works used to remember and celebrate the origins of Rome; they also serve to signify the investments of particular eras, using these narratives as a way to connect contemporary concerns with Rome's beginning itself.

One such public monument that uses, in this case several of, the stories presented is the frieze of the Basilica Aemilia. The frieze can most likely be dated to 14 BCE, commissioned as part of the basilica's

179. Myles Lavan, *Slaves to Rome: Paradigms of Empire in Roman Culture* (New York: Cambridge University Press, 2013), 150.
180. I would argue that Ilia's status as a Vestal gives her a type of "outsider" status as well, but again, her rape lies in the realm of the taboo and is moot if she has been raped by a god. It is important to note, though, that in some traditions Rhea Silvia is condemned to death. See discussion below on the Vestals.

restoration after a fire in the Forum. While the Aemilius family undertook this restoration, it was financed by Augustus himself.[181] As noted by Fred Albertson, the frieze illustrated a "popularized" and "recently formulated view of Romulus, a view fostered by both Julius Caesar and Octavian and linked to current interest in the etiology of Roman cults and festivals."[182] Additionally, Donald Strong emphasizes that the scenes not only reflect the founding narratives of the city itself but are linked to the "Augustan revival, when the myths of Rome's foundation became a central theme of political propaganda."[183] Among the smaller extant fragments, one probably depicts either Mars and Rhea Silvia or Romulus, Remus, and the she-wolf,[184] another possibly representing Romulus's and Remus's abandonment on the banks of the Tiber.[185] Four larger scenes are more easily identified: Romulus and Remus departing Alba Longa for Rome; the construction of Rome's walls; the Consualia and abduction of the Sabine women by the Romans; Romulus and Acron in hand-to-hand combat and the *spolia optima*; and the death of Tarpeia.[186]

Figures 1–8 are photographs taken by the author at the Roman Forum in Rome, Italy. Figure 1 shows a panel of the rape of the Sabines, with figures 2–6 showing details of the panel. Figure 7 is a panel of the death of Tarpeia, and figure 8 shows a detail.

181. The Basilica Aemelia was originally built in 170s BCE, with several restorations occurring between this time and the Forum fire. There is some controversy surrounding the dating of the Basilica Aemelia frieze. On the 14 BCE dating, see Donald Emrys Strong, *Roman Art* (Harmondsworth: Penguin Books, 1988), 78–79; Diana E. E. Kleiner, *Roman Sculpture* (New Haven: Yale University Press, 1992), 88–89; Natalie Kampen, "The Muted Other," *Art Journal* 47.1 (1988): 15–19; Kampen, "Reliefs of the Basilica Aemilia: A Redating," *Klio* 73 (1991): 448–58; cf. Boatwright, "Women and Gender," 124–25. For arguments for earlier dating, see Fred C. Albertson, "The Basilica Aemilia Frieze: Religion and Politics in Late Republican Rome," *Latomus* 49.4 (1990): 801–15.
182. Albertson, "Basilica Aemilia Frieze," 802. While Albertson's dating of the frieze is technically earlier than his emphasis on its import for Julius Caesar and Octavian, his statement holds even more weight with the 14 BCE date.
183. Strong, *Roman Art*, 78.
184. Alberston, "Basilica Aemilia Frieze," 806: "One small fragment depicts the lower portion of two surprised shepherds; based on comparable representations, this fragment would have belonged to a scene illustrating either the encounter of Mars and Rhea Silvia or the discovery of the twins nursed by the she-wolf."
185. ibid. This scene has an analogue "to that painted on the wall of a contemporary tomb on the Esquiline."
186. Ibid., 807; Kampen, "Reliefs of the Basilica Aemilia," 449–50.

Figure 1.

Figure 2.

Figure 3.

Figure 4.

Figure 5.

Figure 6.

Figure 7.

Figure 8.

Both Natalie Kampen and Mary Boatwright stress the importance of the Basilica Aemilia frieze in the male-oriented space of the Forum, particularly given the dearth of women depicted in the era's state-funded sculptural program (save deities and personifications).[187] Kampen links the frieze to Augustus's "policy on moral conduct, especially concerning family and sexuality,"[188] specifically connecting the scenes of the Sabine women and Tarpeia to the *Lex Iulia de maritandis ordinibus* (which regulated intermarriage between upper and lower classes) and the *Lex Iulia de adulteriis coercendia* (which made women's adultery a public crime).[189] Additionally, "sanctions applied to the unmarried and childless," which encouraged reproduction, date to this period.[190] The *Lex Juliae*, regulating marriage, adultery, and procreation relate to both the story of the Sabines and Tarpeia:

> The Sabine women's story is about the origins of marriage, about who may legitimately marry whom and about the correct conduct of women who are at the same time daughters, wives and mothers.[191] It fits well as a symbolic expression of the social concern with the relationship between classes which the Lex Julia on marriage regulates, and it addresses as well the relationship between Romans and their various Latin and foreign allies. The reliefs emphasize the need for controlled female sexuality in a society which must reproduce in order to endure but which regards the loyalty of women, symbolic outsiders, as problematic. Since the Sabine women do, in fact, perform as ideal Augustan women/allies and become insiders, they stand in contrast to the figure of Tarpeia. Her perfidy violates right conduct of daughters as well as virgins and married women. She exemplifies unregulated female conduct as inherently dangerous. She behaves like an outsider even though, like the Roman opponents of Augustus in the Civil War, she is more of an insider than the Sabines. . . . [T]he concern with the revival of traditional morality in the form of controlled female sexuality is well served by these two stories of women from Rome's earliest history.[192]

Here, Kampen illustrates the way in which Augustus not only appeals to the early myths of Rome's founding as a part of his more general

---

187. Kampen, "Reliefs of the Basilica Aemilia," 450–51; Boatwright, "Women and Gender," 124. This dearth of women is particularly true of the Forum but applies throughout Rome as well. Notable exceptions to the Ara Pacis, a few reliefs with Vestals, the Ravenna relief, the Nerva Forum Minerva frieze, and the public statues of Octavia and Livia granted by Augustus in 35 BCE, and an additional one granted to Livia by the Senate in 9 BCE.
188. Kampen, "Reliefs of the Basilica Aemilia," 448.
189. Ibid., 453.
190. Ibid.
191. See Ariadne Staples, *From Good Goddess to Vestal Virgins: Sex and Category in Roman Religion* (London: Routledge, 1998), 74–80, on the Sabine women and Roman marriage.
192. Kampen, "Reliefs of the Basilica Aemilia," 455.

renewal project, but also shows in particular how the stories of the Sabines and Tarpeia connect with his program of sexual regulations—laws, which, by keeping men and women in their proper place and in proper relationship, keep the city strong.

Kampen is also clear that this regulation is not simply a negotiation of the private lives of men and women. The civil wars of Julius Caesar's era extending through Actium created instability within Roman society, including marriage and family life. "[P]erceptions of female sexuality as uncontrolled and capable of creating social chaos emerge repeatedly in this period, as in the issue of upper class prostitution and adultery or the blame placed on women for childlessness, divorce, abortion, and even political interference."[193] These dynamics of instability were seen not only within Roman society as a whole but within the ruling family itself, ultimately tearing it apart—for it was Cleopatra, the foreign woman, consort of both Julius Caesar and Octavian's brother-in-law and rival Antony, whom Augustus blamed for the war.[194] Just as in the Sabines and Tarpeia narratives, relationships between individual men and women were also about broader relationships between Rome and those it had conquered, about what correct relationships were and about who was in charge.[195] Given the instability of Rome both internally and externally during the period of the civil wars, it is no wonder that Livy stresses *concordia* in his telling of the Sabines narrative.[196]

Not only, then, do these founding narratives provide a way to consolidate imperial ideology during Augustus's rise to power, but they also provide a template for the wider investments and workings of the

---

193. Ibid., 453.
194. Although it is a rhetorical example, see Cassius Dio's treatment of Actium and in particular Octavian's address to the troops before the battle in *Rom. Hist.* 50.24.3–4 where he says, "For we who are Romans and rulers of the greatest and best part of the world should be despised and trampled by an Egyptian woman is unworthy of our fathers, who destroyed Pyrrhus, Philip, Perseus, and Antiochus, who displaced the Numantians and the Carthaginians, who massacred the Cimbri and the Ambrones; it is also unworthy of ourselves, who have subjugated the Gauls, conquered the Pannonians, advanced as far as the Ister, crossed the Rhine, and crossed to Britain." See also Hemker, "Rape and the Founding of Rome," 41–47, for the connection between the Sabines narrative, the civil wars, and Actium.
195. Dench, *Romulus' Asylum*, 23–25.
196. On Augustus and *concordia*, see Lobur, *Consensus, Concordia*, 90–93.

empire. The ancient connection between microcosm and macrocosm, body and state,[197] allowed for the model of marriage to be extended to the wider field of Rome's relationships with its colonies. As Emma Dench shows, much in these Augustan retellings of the founding narratives is based on how to incorporate diverse and disparate peoples into the empire of Rome. But these narratives show that it is not just about incorporation and assimilation; it is about Rome's strength and power—its control.[198]

These narratives of assimilation and control also play out in the story of the triumph, another important aetiology that appears in the tale of the Sabine women. The triumph "was perceived in antiquity to be a prime means of characterizing a specifically Roman way of enacting power in conjunction with the display of the conquered."[199] By re-presenting and reenacting the victory on the battlefield, the triumph allowed those in Rome to participate symbolically in this victory.[200] In addition to the display of power proclaimed by the ritual, Mary Beard notes the significance of the triumph for incorporating new peoples into the Roman power structure—exactly the work that this first triumph embedded into the Sabines narrative enacts. She observes, "Just as the ceremony itself was no less the beginning of peace than it was the culmination of war, so the victims were both the humiliated and defeated enemies of Rome and at the same time new participants, in whatever role, in the Roman imperial order. The triumph was a key moment in the process by which the enemy became Roman."[201] The totality of this work—of conquest, victory. and incorporation—is borne out in the Sabines narratives of rape, which marks Rome's earliest beginnings.

Beard is also careful to note in her study,

---

197. For the dynamics of macrocosm/microcosm, see Bruno Centrone, "Platonism and Pythagoreanism in the Early Empire," in *The Cambridge History of Greek and Roman Political Thought*, ed. Christopher Rowe and Malcolm Schofield (Cambridge: Cambridge University Press, 2000), 559–84; and, in the same volume, Malcolm Schofield, "Epicurean and Stoic Political Thought," 435–56. See also Dale B. Martin, *The Corinthian Body* (New Haven: Yale University Press, 1999).
198. Dench, *Romulus' Asylum*, 23.
199. Ibid., 76.
200. Beard, *Roman Triumph*, 32.
201. Ibid., 140.

Modern historians, who often have a great deal invested in an image of ancient Rome as an almost uniquely cruel and blood thirsty society, have generally been reluctant to read the myths of Roman violence (whether in the arena, on the battlefield, or in the triumphal procession) as anything other than a direct reflection of the acts of violence at which they appear to hint. But often, as here, there is a good case for seeing the bloodshed more as part of a pattern of menacing discourse than of regular practice.[202]

Whether a matter of reality or rhetoric, Rome's subject peoples are kept in line and forced into a mandated concord through a consistent threat and message of retaliation if they do not bend to Rome's will—just like those who attempted to fight Romulus in an effort to wrest their stolen women from Rome's grip.

Just as the triumph was used both to establish and consolidate Roman identity throughout the time of Rome's rule, narratives such as those of Ilia and the Sabines played an ongoing role in symbolizing Roman values and identity. As noted earlier, Plutarch's narratives date to the end of the last decade of the first century CE or the beginning of the second, but they are just one example of the continued interest in these myths of Rome's founding, which extends well into the second century and beyond. Fred Albertson, in his extensive study of Mars and Rhea Silvia imagery states that

a large number of examples of the encounter [between Mars and Rhea Silvia] suddenly appear in the Hadrianic and early Antonine periods. The renewed popularity of the motif is clearly linked to the construction in Rome of the Temple of Venus Felix and Roma Aeterna, the first cult established in the city to the goddess Roma. It seems that only under Hadrian does the scene of Mars and Rhea Silvia take on one of permanent national significance, linked to the overriding theme of "eternity" [aeternitas]—Rome's divinely favored origins, its predestined rise to greatness, and the continuation of this power. This is supported by an analysis of all the examples surviving from the period ca. A.D. 120 to 280, where a clear chronological pattern is revealed. With one or perhaps two exceptions, all extant examples fall into three periods: the reign of Hadrian and the early reign of Antoninus Pius; the first three decades of the 3rd century A.D.; and the middle of the 3rd century A.D. Each of these periods corresponds to times of attempted political and cultural

202. Ibid., 31.

rejuvenation [renouatio], when the legends surrounding Rome's foundation were employed to reassert in the minds of the Roman people the idea of preordination, of their city's destiny to rule the world, and of its continued greatness. . . . The scene thus enjoys sporadic periods of popularity during the Empire, generated by imperial political programs focusing on renouatio and aeternitas and stimulated by the celebration of important anniversaries of the founding of Rome. Scenes depicting the rape of Rhea Silvia by Mars, unlike the more universal she-wolf and twins, are linked directly and unequivocally to the origins of the city, and the concept of divine favor and ordained greatness inherent in the stories of those origins.[203]

Albertson also notes the movement of the image during the second century from "state art to the private realm. It occurs most notably in a funerary context," linking it to "the common theme of eternity," which accounts for the motif's "apparent popularity outside of Rome which begins . . . in the 2nd century A.D., especially on the Rhine and Danube frontiers."[204]

During this period, there is also a resurgence of the iconography of the rape of the Sabine women. In Antonia Holden's study of the abduction of the Sabine women on late antique contorniate medallions (medallions that commemorate "games and entertainments at the circus"), she notes that the prototype for these coins was a medallion issued during the reign of Antoninus Pius "between 141 and 144 C.E., in connection with the ninth centenary of Rome" and also as a commemoration "for the deceased empress Faustina the Elder, who appears on its obverse."[205] The reverse, which contains the image of the abduction of the Sabine women and the legend "SABINAE," is set in the Circus Maximus in Rome "by means of the inclusion of turning posts."[206] This addition of the turning posts, the first of its kind in relation to numismatic evidence portraying the abduction of the Sabines, is significant in Holden's opinion because she believes it represents "a theatrical reenactment of the narrative . . . though

203. Albertson, Mars and Rhea Silvia, 11.
204. Ibid., 12.
205. Antonia Holden, "The Abduction of the Sabine Women in Context: The Iconography on Late Antique Contorniate Medallions," AJA 112.1 (2008), 122, 125.
206. Ibid., 125.

evidence for Sabine plays before the second half of the fourth century C.E. is somewhat controversial."[207] Regardless, Holden speculates that the reemergence of this type in the Antonine medallion, in conjunction with Antoninus Pius's promotion of *concordia* ("a theme that was the centerpiece of Antonine social policies") and "the inclusion of Sabine plays in the jubilee games would have provided an appropriate commemoration of the foundation of the Roman race and a fitting homage to an empress who was promoted as an exemplum of devoted mother and wife, just as were the Sabine women."[208] In addition, there are two extant examples of the rape of the Sabines on funerary monuments with other scenes of Rome's founding, dating to the second century CE.[209] As with the appearance of Rhea Silvia on private funerary monuments symbolizing eternity, it is possible that the inclusion of the Sabines signifies the ideal of *concordia* in the private realm.

Through these examples, we can see how these stories of relationships between men, women, and marriage serve not only as ideals for individuals but as a microcosm of the imperial relationship between Rome and its conquered states, Rome and its nations. While those such as Ilia and the Sabine women may be seen as exemplars, as embodiments of eternity, *concordia*, and piety—both for individuals and for Rome as a whole—this does not change or mask the fact that these women of Rome's past are the objects of a system of domination whereby some benefit by the violence done to others. As noted by Beard earlier, a rhetoric of violence, in these cases sexual violence, does not necessarily reflect the reality of it. But whether reality or rhetoric, this violence is wielded as a tool to keep certain people(s) subject to others, to enforce a state of *concordia* or benefaction with Rome—and it is always clear who holds the power.

207. Ibid., 126, 127.
208. Ibid., 129.
209. Francesco Scoppola, ed., *Palazzo Altemps Guide* (Milan: Electa, 2012), 28–29.

Embodied Nations and Vestal Virgins

The rhetoric of rape, conquest, and the domination of male over female plays a larger role in the ideological constructs of the Roman Empire beyond their associations with Rome's founding narratives. While the scope of this study prevents a full treatment of the topic, attention to corollaries between Rome's empire-wide visual program used to represent the geography of its territories and the counterpoint to this, represented by the Vestals, is crucial for understanding the gendered construction of conquest. Here, I begin with a short overview of the use of female personifications of the nations in public sculptural programs, then contrast the function of these nations with that of the Vestals to show the ways in which conceptions of women and penetrability directly relate to ideas of Roman dominance and conquest.

Simulacra Gentium, Images of the Nations

Personifications of lands and cities were a staple of Greek visual culture, generally portrayed as females, and could be used in either "celebratory or friendly" or "domineering and hostile" manners.[210] These personifications were sometimes displayed alone and at other times as groups; they were used as a way to visually represent different geographic areas. Rome drew upon this visual motif for centuries, but during the late Republic, and becoming much more popular during the Augustan era, these images begin to change, taking on new connotations, especially "a newly self-conscious Roman imperialism."[211] By combining Greek personifications of territories with the visual optics of triumph, whether actual triumphs or depictions of them, the objects of Rome's conquest began to be portrayed in a more literal manner as captive, female personifications.[212] These images did

---

210. Ann L. Kuttner, *Dynasty and Empire in the Age of Augustus: The Case of the Boscoreale Cups* (Berkeley: University of California Press, 1995), 73–74. For a complete overview, see Kuttner's chapter 3, "The Peoples of the Empire," 69–93; see also Ando, *Imperial Ideology*, 287.

211. Kuttner, *Dynasty and Empire*, 73.

212. Ibid., 78–79: "This is where Roman formulations of corporate entities differ from the Greek. The Romans were not, or at least never thought of themselves as, members of a body of equals: they *dominated* a corporate body of clients and possessions. They belonged to a corporate body as

not replace images of conquered men, which also proliferated throughout the empire, but were used in addition to them, generally portraying these figures more "realistically" than their "idealistic" Greek counterparts.[213] Often these figures were crafted with the "attributes" of the people they reflected and were dressed in traditional clothing, though oftentimes with the women wearing male dress.[214]

One of the first major installations of a grouping of personified nations was displayed in Pompey's theater, where he exhibited statues of fourteen nations he conquered.[215] It seems likely that this display provided a template for groupings erected by Augustus, particularly in the Portico of the Nations built in his forum.[216] Although there is no archaeological evidence today for the Portico of the Nations, it is referred to by name in Servius's commentary on the *Aeneid* (8.720–23), in Pliny's *Natural History* (36.39), and in Velleius (2.39.2), and remains important for thinking about visual representations of geography during Augustus's reign, especially due to its location in the forum of Augustus.[217] It is likely that the Portico of the Nations was fashioned as a caryatid porch with individual nations conquered by or under the rule of Rome in place of the Caryae women.[218] This formation

heads of empire, not as one of a number of states equal in a *symmachia*. And the occasion where Roman audiences of the Republic were most accustomed to seeing a collection of images depicting a number of peoples and places was the triumph: the procession celebrating one individual's victories, explaining and praising them by means of painting of cities taken, images of cities and rivers, strings of actual captives led to symbolize the defeat of their entire peoples." See also Ando, *Imperial Ideology*, 287–89.

213. Kuttner, *Dynasty and Empire*, 79; Ando, *Imperial Ideology*, 287–89.
214. Kuttner, *Dynasty and Empire*, 79. On representations of nations, particularly in the triumph, see Beard, *Roman Triumph*, chapter 5, "The Art of Representation," 143–86.
215. Pliny, *Nat. Hist.* 36.39; Suetonius, *Nero* 46; Pluarch, *Pompey* 45; Ando, *Imperial Ideology*, 298; Kuttner, *Dynasty and Empire*, 79; Kleiner, *Roman Sculpture*, 42; I. M. Ferris, *Enemies of Rome: Barbarians through Roman Eyes* (Stroud: Sutton, 2000), 30; Joseph Geiger, *The First Hall of Fame: A Study of the Statues in the Forum Augustum*, Mnemosyne Supplements 295 (Leiden: Brill, 2008), 102; Claude Nicolet, *Space, Geography, and Politics in the Early Roman Empire*, trans. Hélène Leclerc (Ann Arbor: University of Michigan Press, 1990), 38.
216. R. R. R. Smith, "*Simulacra Gentium*: The *Ethne* from the Sebasteion at Aphrodisias," *Journal of Roman Studies* 78 (1988): 72; Kuttner, *Dynasty and Empire*, 80, 83; Ferris, *Enemies of Rome*, 30; Ando, *Imperial Ideology*, 297–98; cf. Geiger, *First Hall of Fame*, 102.
217. Smith, "*Simulacra Gentium*," 72; Kuttner, *Dynasty and Empire*, 80–81.
218. Kutter, *Dynasty and Empire*, 83; Ferris, *Enemies of Rome*, 31. Ferris says that the use of caryatids by Augustus was "a choice of image that as well as being linked to classical Athens could also have directly alluded to the original story of the capture and exiling of the women of Caryae. In the

seems particularly likely due to Augustus's use of defeated Parthians as caryatids in his reconstruction of the Basilica Aemilia in 14 BCE.[219] While the evidence of Augustus's Portico is only found in textual sources, there are other statues, monuments, and artifacts that confirm Augustus's employment of *simulacra gentium*, that is, images of the nations, including the pedestal of the altar of the Ara Pacis,[220] the cuirass of the Prima Porta statue,[221] and the personifications used as part of Augustus's funeral procession.[222] At Augustus's funeral,

> The procession's use of triumphal art and its passage through a triumphal arch continued to emphasize a strictly Roman imperialist attitude toward those provinces added to the empire in the Augustan age, in a martial fashion befitting the man who, in his own words, "had extended the borders of all those provinces of the Roman people adjacent to which were nations that did not obey our empire (*Res Gestae* 26.1)."[223]

The procession, then, embodied the wide variety of influences from Greek personification to the visual art of Roman triumph as a way to represent visually not only the worldwide geography of Rome but its hegemonic power—a visual representation that also would have been reflected in a monument such as Augustus's Portico of the Nations, with its location in his forum.

While, again, archaeological evidence does not remain of the *simulacra gentium* displayed in Augustus's forum, this type of display survives in the extant panels of the temple of Hadrian, built by

light of the known and attested Augustan practice of demanding women hostages to secure the future good behaviour of their defeated tribes, the choice of the caryatid image seems apposite."

219. Kleiner, *Roman Sculpture*, 90, 284; Kuttner, *Dynasty and Empire*, 83; Ferris, *Enemies of Rome*, 31.

220. Smith, "*Simulacra Gentium*," 72–73; Kuttner, *Dynasty and Empire*, 88. The frieze, of while little is extant today, seems to contain images of all those under Roman rule, figured as female and in the traditional dress of their countries.

221. Kuttner, *Dynasty and Empire*, 84; Zanker, *Power of Images*, 188–92. Both Gallia and Hispania are represented as personified nations, along with an image of a defeated Parthian. The cuirass seems to be "a visual paraphrase of the boast in *Res gestae* 28–29" (Kuttner, *Dynasty and Empire*, 84).

222. Dio, 56.34.3; Smith, "*Simulacra Gentium*," 74–75; Ando, *Imperial Ideology*, 298; Nicolet, *Space, Geography, and Politics*, 180. For other Augustan monuments and artifacts containing personifications, see Kuttner, *Dynasty and Empire*, chapter 3, "The Peoples of the Empire." In addition, as Ando observes, "Augustus provided a literary and supremely public complement to these Roman monuments in his *Res gestae*" (*Imperial Ideology*, 298), where, among other achievements, Augustus lists "the foreign activities, the conquests, and the victories or diplomatic achievements that constitute the explanation and the justification of the initial formula for the conquest of the *orbis terrarium*" (Nicolet, *Space, Geography, and Politics*, 17). See also *Res Gestae* 26–33.

223. Ando, *Imperial Ideology*, 298.

Hadrian's adopted son and successor Antoninus Pius, and in a probable quotation of the Augustan Portico.[224] The nations displayed seem to reflect coins issued during Hadrian's reign that contained twenty-four images of personified nations on their reverse (figs. 9, 10).[225] As no conquests took place during the reign of Hadrian, the display of nations in the temple is generally seen as a more benign monument representing a visual geography of the empire under Hadrian's reign.[226] In addition to these personifications, there are other panels that display arms used by nations other than Rome (fig. 9).[227] It is hypothesized that these were mounted between the panels of the nations, though some dispute this on the basis of their size and shape.[228] If this hypothesis is correct, though, one wonders how benign a configuration this was if the nations are interspersed with weapons of war.

The third major portico, of which there is also archaeological evidence, is one that lies outside the city of Rome. Commissioned in Aphrodisias by a family who found favor with the Julio-Claudian line, the Sebasteion was built to honor Augustus and his family, the building project beginning around 20 CE and being completed about 60 CE.[229] Two porticoes in the complex held a wide variety of panels whose themes ranged from Roman emperors to mythological scenes to personified nations.[230] Images such as "Augustus over Land and Sea," reflect the words of Augustus's Acts, the *Res Gestae* 3, where Augustus says, "I waged wars on land and on sea, against internal and external foes, throughout the whole world and as victor. . . ."[231] Other images present mythological stories such as Leda and the Swan,[232] while yet

---

224. Kleiner, *Roman Sculpture*, 283; Ferris, *Enemies of Rome*, 83–84.

225. Jocelyn M. C. Toynbee, *The Hadrianic School: A Chapter in the History of Greek Art* (London: Cambridge University Press, 1934), esp. 152–59; Kleiner, *Roman Sculpture*, 284.

226. Kleiner, *Roman Sculpture*, 283, 284; Ferris, *Enemies of Rome*, 84: "Under Hadrian the empire was consolidated with no new conquests being undertaken, hence the gallery of personifications could have been designed to be understood as a gathering of the provinces of the empire presided over by the benevolent figure of the emperor whose cautious and wise stewardship had helped guarantee an era of general peace and prosperity."

227. Kleiner, *Roman Sculpture*, 284; Ferris, *Enemies of Rome*, 84.

228. Kleiner, *Roman Sculpture*, 284–85; Ferris, *Enemies of Rome*, 84.

229. R. R. R. Smith, "Imperial Reliefs from the Sebasteion at Aphrodisias," *Journal of Roman Studies* 77 (1987): 90; Ando, *Imperial Ideology*, 311–12; Ferris, *Enemies of Rome*, 55.

230. Smith, "Imperial Reliefs"; idem, "*Simulacra Gentium*"; Kleiner, *Roman Sculpture*, 158–61.

others show the emperor being crowned in victory over a bound, female captive (fig. 11).[233]

Figure 9. *Ethnos* (embodied nation) and Trophy panel from the Temple of Hadrian. Capitoline Museum, Rome, Italy. Photo by the author.

231. Sarolta A. Takács translator, in Werner Eck, *The Age of Augustus,* 2nd ed. (Malden, MA: Blackwell, 2007); Smith, "Imperial Portraits," 104–6.
232. Smith, "Imperial Reliefs," 97. Other mythological panels include "Demeter and Triptolemus, Bellerophon and Pegasus, Orestes at Delphi, Meleager and the boar, Centarus and Lapiths, Achilles and Thetic, Achilles and Penthesilea, Ajax and Cassandra; Apollo appears three times, twices with different Muses, once with the Delphic Pythia; Dionysus is shown five times, twice as a child for rearing by nymphs and satyrs, and in three different postures of drunkenness; and Heracles, the classic Greek hero, appears six times, with Prometheus, Telephus, Nessus and Deianira, the Hesperides (?), and once drunk."
233. Smith, "Imperial Reliefs," 112–15; see 101–32 for other portraits of imperial figures with captives, including "Augustus with Nike and Trophy," "Germanicus with Captive," "Claudius and Britannia," "Nero and Armenia," and "Unfinished Imperator (Tiberius?) with Captive."

Figure 10. *Ethnos* (embodied nation) panel from the Temple of Hadrian. Capitoline Museum, Rome, Italy. Photo by the author.

Figure 11. Imperator with Roman People or Senate, Trophy and Bound Captive.
Sebasteion, Aphrodisias, Turkey. Photo by the author.

Each of these two porticoes, north and south, contained an upper
and lower story and depicted different yet connected themes: the
"south portico had emperors and gods above, Greek mythology below,"
while the "north portico had allegories (and probably emperors) above,
the series of *ethnē* ["nations" or "peoples"] below."[234] There were

probably about fifty personified nations that encompassed the lower level of the north portico, of which sixteen are at least partially extant: thirteen *ethnē* and three islands.[235] These personified nations, like those in Augustus's Portico, provided a visual geography of the empire, though here it seems that the nations represented encompassed lands falling under the purview and administration of the Roman Empire, rather than simply those conquered (or claimed to be conquered) by Augustus.[236] Nonetheless, these personifications, represented by both inscription and ethnic dress, continued to follow the pattern of Roman personification, wedding the Greek style to elements of triumphal art.

Two of the most striking panels connected to the personifications of the nations on the north portico are those found on the south portico portraying Claudius and Britannia (fig. 12)[237] and Nero and Armenia (figs. 13, 14).[238] In these two panels, the conqueror and the conquered are held within the same frame. Nero holds a dead or dying Armenia, breasts bared, while he towers above her, his knee thrust into her back. Claudius, too, towers over the captive Britannia, pinning her with his knee and pulling her head back by her hair, and exposes her bared breast, his arm raised above her poised to strike. These two images uniquely bring together the realism of triumphal captives, the

234. Smith, "*Simulacra Gentium*," 51.
235. Ibid., 53, 57; cf. Ando, *Imperial Ideology*, 312, citing Smith, "*Simulacra Gentium*," 59: "But the artists at Aphrodisias did not mindlessly replicate Roman originals. In his publication of the statuary R. R. R. Smith made the important observation that the 'iconography of the surviving ethnos and island reliefs . . . [does] not stress the iconography of defeat." Yet the people of Aphrodisias and the artists who crafted the Sebasteum knew full well the appearance of Roman *simulacra*: a triumphal relief celebrating the conquest of Britain depicts Claudius in heroic garb, weapon raised, threatening to strike a suppliant native. The artist of the *ethnos* gallery and his patron evidently divided the world into two categories. The Britons, then the object of Roman campaigns, were not yet members of the civilized world. But the other reliefs clearly indicate a choice not to celebrate Augustan conquest as such, but rather to depict the other members of the political universe of which Aphrodisias and all the East were now a part." See also Hal Taussig, "Melancholy, Colonialism, and Complicity: Complicating Counterimperial Readings of Aphrodisias's Sebasteion," in *Text, Image, and Christians in the Graeco-Roman World: A Festschrift in Honor of David Lee Balch*, ed. Aliou Cissé Niang and Carolyn Osiek (Eugene, OR: Pickwick, 2012), 280–95.
236. Smith, "*Simulacra Gentium*," 57–58.
237. Smith, "Imperial Reliefs," 115–17; Ferris, *Enemies of Rome*, 55–58; Lopez, *Apostle to the Conquered*, 43–45.
238. Smith, "Imperial Reliefs," 117–20.

female personification of nations, and the moment of conquest into one image.

Figure 12. Claudius and Britannia. Sebasteion, Aphrodisias, Turkey. Photo by the author.

Figure 13. Nero and Armenia. Sebasteion, Aphrodisias, Turkey. Photo by the author.

Figure 14. Nero and Armenia. Detail, Sebasteion, Aphrodisias, Turkey. Photo by the author.

While the image of Nero and Armenia is horrific in its depiction of a dead or dying Armenia, the image of Britannia, clearly alive and pictured in the midst of her assault by Claudius, seems even more so. Britannia embodies the pain and submission that were a part of Roman military conquest and freezes the moment before the final blow, when defeat is inevitable. The highly sexualized imagery of this scene has deep resonances with the words that Tacitus gives to the general Calgacus in his speech rousing the troops as they prepare for their final battles with Agricola. As Britannia stands on the precipice of defeat, Calgacus cries,[239]

> Rapists [*raptores*] of the world, now that the earth betrays their encompassing devastation, they ransack the sea. If the enemy is rich, they are greedy; if poor, they encircle them. Neither east nor west has satisfied them—they alone covet equally want and wealth. To rob, slaughter and rape [*rapere*] they give the false name of empire; they make desolation, they call it peace. Children and kin are by nature each one's dearest [*carissimos*] possessions. They are snatched [*auferuntur*] from us by conscription to be slaves elsewhere: our wives and sisters, even if they escape the enemy's wantonness [*libidinem*], are violated in the name of friendship and hospitality [*amicorum atque hospitum*]. Our goods and fortunes go for tribute; our lands and harvests in requisitions of grain; our hands and bodies themselves are shattered through clearing forest and swamp in the midst of insult and lash. Those born into slavery are sold once and for all and moreover are fed by their masters, but Britannia pays for her enslavement daily and feeds the enslavers. And as in the household the newest among the slaves is a mockery to his fellow-slaves, so in a world long used to slavery, we, the newest and most worthless, are marked out for destruction. (*Agricola* 30.4–31.3)[240]

This text also holds deep resonances with the characterizations of the Romans in the Sabines narratives and Calgacus's characterization of them, though rather than the idealized version of the rape, conquest, and colonization of the Sabines' story, here the effects of that story are articulated by the conquered.[241] Both of these stories connect rape and conquest; both reflect the use of lands and peoples to satisfy Rome's own ends; both reflect the ways in which peace is infused with war; and both name children and kin as dearest possessions—but only if these children and kin are Roman, otherwise their lives are naught. And lest we think the charge of rape is simply metaphorical, we need only turn to the practices of the Roman army, particularly illustrated in Britannia by the story of Boudica, queen of the Iceni, who

---

239. Lopez, *Apostle to the Conquered*, 109–10; Ferris, *Enemies of Rome*, 57–58.
240. Translation in consultation with Lopez, *Apostle to the conquered*, 109; and Tacitus, *Agricola* (LCL).
241. Obviously, this is a rhetorical speech from the pen of Tacitus, but it nonetheless reflects a starkly different yet utterly similar picture to that of the Sabines.

dared to rebel against Rome and whose daughters were captured and raped by the Roman army in response.[242] But, of course, the practice of rape in warfare was not reserved just for Britannia or those who rebelled against Rome, but was perpetrated on many who inhabited the frontlines of Roman expansion.[243]

In these monuments and texts there is a clear connection between the sexualized logic of conquest as seen both in the Sabines narratives and in the images of the personified nations. These are the penetrable female counterparts to Rome's manly conquest. While the situation in Rome's provinces was not as cut-and-dried as Tacitus's depiction of Britannia—many noncitizens within the empire also reaped the benefits of their position in the empire—we can assume that attitudes toward Rome ranged from condemnation to consent, accommodation to assimilation, resentment to rebellion. Nonetheless, Tacitus's words surely reflect the sentiments of some and clearly draw together both the textual and visual rhetoric of Roman conquest.

Vestals Virgins and Penetrable Nations

While the connection between the Vestal virgins and the personified nations may not seem obvious, nor was it been expressly conscious on the Romans' part, these two groups form a very tight point and counterpoint: the Vestal virgins, symbolizing the integrity of Rome,

---

242. Tacitus, *Annals* 14; Cassius Dio, 62; David Mattingly, *An Imperial Possession: Britain in the Roman Empire 54 BC–AD 409* (New York: Allen Lane, 2006), 106–13; Lavan, *Slaves to Rome*, 147–54; Eric Adler, "Boudica's Speeches in Tacitus and Dio," *CW* 101.2 (2008): 173–95.

243. William V. Harris, *War and Imperialism in Republican Rome 327–70 B.C.* (Oxford: Clarendon, 1979), 52–53: "It was of course commonplace in Roman as in much other ancient warfare for prisoners to be enslaved (women and children included), for women prisoners to be raped [citing Polybius 10.18.19.3–5 and 21.38.2], and for booty to be gathered in the most ruthless fashion." See also C. R. Whittaker, *Rome and Its Frontiers: The Dynamics of Empire* (New York: Routledge, 2004), 120–38; Angelos Chaniotis, *War in the Hellenistic World: A Social and Cultural History* (Malden, MA: Blackwell, 2005), see esp. chapter 6, "The Gender of War: Masculine Warriors, Defenseless Women, and Beyond," 102–14; Joshua Levithan, *Roman Siege Warfare* (Ann Arbor: University of Michigan Press, 2013), 205–27, here 216: "After the pillaging of the most obvious targets, prisoners were rounded up. Every person in the stormed city became a prisoner without rights and could be kept or sold as a slave. Although the sources are rarely as explicit as Tacitus was about the sexual aspect of the sack of Cremona, it seems clear that any sack included rape. 'Without any respect for age or for status they added rape to murder and murder to rape. Aged men and decrepit old women, who were worthless as booty, were dragged off to make sport for them. If some grown girl or a handsome boy fell into their clutches, they would be torn to pieces in the struggle for possession, while the plunderers were left to cut each other's throats' (Tacitus *Hist.* 3.33)."

the chaste counterpart to the penetrable nations. The Vestals, sacred keepers of Rome's hearth-fire, signified the impenetrability of Rome through their virginity. Each as an individual and all together collectively, they signified the integrity of the Roman people. This connection between the bodily integrity of the Vestals and of Rome is most clearly shown through the correspondence between threats to Rome and charges of loss of virginity brought against a Vestal.[244] The historical evidence seems to indicate a high likelihood that many of these charges were fabricated, as Rome needed a reason or justification for the audacity of an outsider who attempted to penetrate the Roman state. The punishment for this crime was being buried alive.[245] As Ariadne Staples writes,

> A Vestal's virginity was indispensable for the political well-being of Rome. But . . . the loss of her virginity was equally indispensable for the political well-being of Rome. A single lapse by a single priestess threatened the very existence of the state. In such an event the only way to restore the *status quo* was to rid the state of the offending Vestal in the manner described by Plutarch [i.e., burial alive, Plutarch, *Numitor*, 10]. The flip-side of this was that when the political stability of the state was under threat the possibility that a Vestal might have been unchaste provided a convenient mechanism for averting the threat. Virginity was an indispensable requirement for a Vestal because the potential loss of that virginity was every bit as vital for the welfare of the polity as virginity itself.[246]

Part of the reason the Vestals could relate to the state in this manner was because of the peculiar legal status they carried, unique within the Roman citizenry. Upon becoming a Vestal, a woman cut all ties with her *paterfamilias,* including automatic rights to inherit and bequeath.[247] Vestals were accorded the right to have a will, and thus could leave their wealth to those of their choosing, and their former families could do the same, but not without a written will.[248] If a written will was not

244. See esp. Parker, "Why Were the Vestals Virgins?"
245. See Wildfang, *Rome's Vestal Virgins,* 57–61.
246. Staples, *From Good Goddess to Vestal Virgins,* 135; see also Parker, "Why Were the Vestals Virgins?," 568, 574.
247. Staples, *From Good Goddess to Vestal Virgins,* 138–45; Takács, *Vestal Virgins,* 81–83; Parker, "Why Were the Vestals Virgins?," 572–74; Wildfang, *Rome's Vestal Virgins,* 37–74.
248. Wildfang, *Rome's Vestal Virgins,* 64–67; Parker, "Why Were the Vestals Virgins?," 573–74.

in place at the time of death, the Vestal's wealth would be transferred directly to the state.[249]

There are many scholarly debates concerning the liminal status of the Vestals, and also many theories that try to explain it.[250] But, given the evidence surrounding the Vestals' status, what seems to make the most sense is that, upon cutting all family ties and becoming a Vestal, a woman was transferred from her birth family not to no family at all but to the Roman family, the *patriae*. This change is seen in the way in which Vestals' virginity "enabled them to remain members of the Roman state's civic structure while at the same time placing them outside the state's family cult structure. This peculiar status enabled them to represent the Roman state as a whole."[251] A hallmark of this change can be seen most clearly in the aforementioned inheritance laws, where as Robin Lorsch Wildfang observes,

> The state inherited the estate of an intestate Vestal, because it stepped into the vacuum created by the necessities of the Vestals' peculiar status and fulfilled the function of the *familia* for the Vestals. Thus, the same principle that operated when an ordinary individual died intestate also operated here. The state functioned in the *locus familiae* for the Vestals, inheriting their estates, if they died intestate.[252]

Additionally, the Vestal's "[f]reedom from *patria potestas* . . . did not bring independence to the Vestal. She stood in dependence to the *pontifex maximus*, who could exact corporal punishment, and the judgment of the college of pontiffs in cases of a Vestal's failure in upholding her chastity."[253] So, while no longer under the authority of her biological father, she was under the authority of a male representative of the state.

The public institution of the Vestals gained increasing importance

249. Ibid.
250. One of the earliest theories was that of Mary Beard, "The Sexual Status of Vestal Virgins," *Journal of Roman Studies* 70 (1980): 12–27, surrounding the "male-ness" of the Vestals. She somewhat changed her argument in her subsequent "Re-Reading (Vestal) Virginity," in *Women in Antiquity: New Assessments*, ed. Richard Hawley and Barbara Levick (London: Routledge, 1995), 166–77. See also, Parker, "Why Were the Vestals Virgins?"
251. Wildfang, *Rome's Vestal Virgins*, 55; see also, 37.
252. Ibid., 67.
253. Takács, *Vestal Virgins*, 82; Wildfang, *Rome's Vestal Virgins*, 55–57.

under the reign of Augustus. They led the procession to meet him upon his return from Actium and also were ordered, according to the *Res Gestae*, to make yearly sacrifices with the magistrates and priests at the Ara Pacis—these acts connecting the safety of the emperor and his family with that of the state (*Res Gestae* 12).[254] Most importantly, Augustus became *pontifex maximus* in 12 BCE (*Res Gestae* 10), moving the shrine of Vesta to his house on the Palatine, his house hearth and the state hearth physically linked as one (ibid.). In addition, Augustus was decreed "Father of the Fatherland" (*Pater Patriae*) by the Senate in 2 BCE (*Res Gestae* 35), which made him not only the male authority in charge of the Vestals as *pontifex maximus*, but also their "father," as they represented the Roman state and people.

On the one hand, particularly given their new status afforded by Augustus, the Vestals were both part of the Roman family and guardians of it, their intact virginity ensuring the impenetrability of Rome. On the other hand, the Augustan period was also the time in which *simulacra gentes* grew in popularity in public art: these were the nations penetrable by Roman power. Just as the penetration of the Sabine wives leads to the penetration and annexation of their lands by the fatherland, so too did these *simulacra gentes* symbolize Rome's penetrability of, and power over, the nations. The Vestals then become the inverse of the *simulacra gentes* as graphically illustrated in the Claudius and Britannia panel, the Vestals symbolizing the purity and integrity of the Roman state versus the penetrability and serviceability of the nations in its empire.

What is most striking in this configuration is that the control and regulation of women's bodies *within* the state symbolize the integrity of Rome, while the images of subdued and violated women—particularly images like that of Armenia and Britannia—symbolize the way in which Rome's power extends to its territories. This regulation of Roman integrity is also seen in the paternalism of the Augustan morality laws, particularly those that regulate the sexuality and reproductivity of the women who will continue to help the empire flourish. What remains

254. Wildfang, *Rome's Vestal Virgins*, 100–101.

the domain of men is the *vis* necessary to keep these "women" under control.

Conclusion

Throughout this chapter I have traced the function of rape in terms of its use in retellings of the beginnings of Rome, weaving them with broader issues of the Roman imperial ideology of rape and conquest, particularly as employed in the Augustan era. Whether a matter of reality or rhetoric, Rome's subject peoples are kept in line and forced into a mandated concord through a consistent threat and message of retaliation if they do not bend to Rome's will—just like those who attempted to fight Romulus in an effort to wrest their stolen women from Rome's grip. The tales of the rape of Ilia/Rhea Silvia, the rape of the Sabines, the rape of Lucretia, and the attempted rape of Verginia bear directly upon the visual program of monuments such as the Basilica Aemelia, Augustus's Portico of the Nations, and the Sebasteion at Aphrodisias. The paradigms laid out in these sources are reflected in Augustus's morality legislation and the regulations of the Vestal—both constructs regulating sexuality to ensure Rome's integrity and prosperity. Through these texts—written, visual, and regulatory—the connection between the ways in which the control and regulation of women's bodies within the state symbolize Rome's integrity as well as the ways in which subdued and violated women account for the extension of Rome's power are brought into sharp relief.

This dynamic, the totality of which is most clearly articulated in the story of the Sabines, where violence, victory, and the traitorous Vestal are woven together in its tale of rape and conquest, lays the foundation for the study to follow. Chapter 2 builds on this foundation and brings it into Ovid's mythic realm of the *Metamorphoses*. As Ovid exploited the fissures and ambivalences within Rome's founding narratives, he brings these strategies into his *Metamorphoses* in an effort not only to tell an entertaining tale of fiction and fantasy but also to comment on the Augustan culture in which he lives.

2

"One loves, the other flees . . ."

In Ovid's *Metamorphoses* we return to narratives of rape, but these are the rapes of gods who found the world rather than the rapes of men who found Rome. Weaving together epic and elegy, comedy and tragedy, and drawing on a myriad of influences from Homer to Vergil, Callimachus to Ennius as well as a range of other mythological sources, Ovid's *Metamorphoses* is a highly complex narrative that defies genre.[1] The poem covers a vast expanse of time from primordial beginnings to the "present day," that is, the reign of Augustus. It is likely that the *Metamorphoses* was finished, or nearly so, when Ovid was banished to Tomis in 8 CE by the emperor.[2] Though there is much speculation as to the reason for Ovid's banishment, the details are largely unknown.[3] Whatever may have raised the ire of Augustus, these speculations have

---

1. See particularly, Brooks Otis's appendix "On the Sources Used by Ovid," in his *Ovid as an Epic Poet*, 2nd ed. (Cambridge: Cambridge University Press, 1970), 375–423; Philip Hardie, *Ovid's Poetics of Illusion* (Cambridge: Cambridge University Press, 2002), 10–22; Lee Fratantuono, *Madness Transformed: A Reading of Ovid's* Metamorphoses (Lanham, MD: Lexington Books, 2011), xv.
2. Fratantuono believes that the *Metamorphoses* was already in circulation at this point (*Madness Transformed*, xvii), while Genevieve Lively argues that it remained unfinished (*Ovid's* Metamorphoses: *A Reader's Guide*, 3.
3. Again, see Lively, *Ovid's* Metamorphoses: *A Reader's Guide*, 3–6 for a pithy overview of Ovid's exile. Most of the information regarding Ovid's banishment comes from his work the *Tristia* 2.207, where he speaks of "a poem and a mistake" (*carmen et error*).

led later interpreters to paint Ovid's work in a variety of pro- or anti- (and in-between) Augustan manners.[4] It is a testament to the complexity of his thought and work that interpretations expressing both pro- and anti-Augustan slants in Ovid's writings are so easily argued.[5] Despite these differing viewpoints, what cannot be contested is the Augustan context in which Ovid consciously places the *Metamorphoses*.

This broader Augustan context, as well the conscious framing of the poem with Augustus himself in books 1 and 15, provides fertile ground for interpreters to raise a variety of questions concerning the relationship between metamorphosis and identity in Augustan Rome. These questions range from the eternity to the mutability of Rome;[6] to the relationship between the divine and human, particularly in terms of the apotheosis of Julius Caesar and the divine framing of Augustus;[7] to social status in Augustus's Rome;[8] to constructions of gender[9]—questions also explored in the study of the Roman narratives in chapter 1. These types of questions will again anchor the investigations pursued in this chapter, exploring the multivalent possibilities layered into Ovid's work, which not only address the Augustan context but extend into broader inquiries elicited by this cultural milieu.

This chapter begins by looking at the story of Daphne and Phoebus/

4. See, e.g., P. J. Davis, "Ovid's *Amores*: A Political Reading," *CP* 94.2 (1999): 431–39, esp. nn1–11. See also Davis, *Ovid and Augustus: A Political Reading of Ovid's Erotic Poems* (London: Duckworth, 2006); Karl Galinsky, "Ovid's Metamorphoses and Augustan Cultural Thematics," in *Ovidian Transformations: Essays on the Metamorphoses and Its Reception*, ed. Philip Hardie, Alessandro Barchiesi, and Stephen Hinds, Supplementary Vol. 23 (Cambridge: Cambridge Philological Society), 103–11; Niall Rudd, *Lines of Enquiry: Studies in Latin Poetry* (Cambridge: Cambridge University Press, 1976), 1–31.
5. See, e.g., Duncan F. Kennedy, "'Augustan' and 'Anti-Augustan': Reflections on Terms of Reference," in *Roman Poetry and Propaganda in the Age of Augustus*, ed. Anton Powell (London: Bristol Classical Press, 1992), 26–38; Alison Sharrock, "Ovid and the Politics of Reading," *MD* 33 (1997): 97–122; and Andrew Feldherr, *Playing Gods*, who rely on postmodern, poststructuralist, and reader-response methods to discuss these complexities.
6. See, e.g., Karl Galinsky, *Ovid's* Metamorphoses: *An Introduction to the Basic Aspects* (Berkeley: University of California Press, 1975).
7. See, e.g., D. C. Feeney, *Gods in Epic: Poets and Critics of the Classical Tradition* (New York: Oxford University Press, 1991), 188–249.
8. See, e.g., Feldherr, *Playing Gods*, 60–122.
9. See, e.g., Patricia B. Salzman-Mitchell, *A Web of Fantasies: Gaze, Image, and Gender in Ovid's* Metamorphoses (Columbus: Ohio State University Press, 2005).

Apollo,[10] a possible intertext of the rape of Eve stories in the Genesis cosmogonies,[11] and one of the fifty-odd stories of rape and attempted rape that occur in the poem.[12] After analyzing this narrative, the rest of the chapter explores the story of Daphne in the wider context of book 1 while also looking toward other pertinent stories in the work as a whole to elucidate broader themes of gender, violence, and the Augustan milieu of the work. Ovid's narrative is so complex in its interwoven stories that this chapter explores only some of the hundreds of possible connections that could be made. The strands pulled from this vast web are used to connect the narratives explored in the previous chapter with those that are to come.

Python, Apollo, and Daphne

After the creation narratives that constitute approximately the first two thirds of book 1, the poem quickly moves to Apollo's defeat of Python.[13] Tightly woven with the Daphne and Apollo episode, the story

10. The appellations of Phoebus and Apollo are used interchangeably throughout this chapter.
11. Pearson, "She Became a Tree," 413–15; and Karen L. King, "Ridicule and Rape, Rule and Rebellion," in *Gnosticism and the Early Christian World: In Honor of James M. Robinson*, ed. James E. Goehring, Charles W. Hedrick, and Jack T. Sanders (Sonoma, CA: Polebridge, 1990), 3–24. Cf. Ursula Ulrike Kaiser, *Die Hypostase der Archonten (Nag-Hammadi-Codex, II,4): Neu herausgegeben, übersetzt und erklärt*, Texte und Untersuchungen zur Geschichte der altchristlichen Literatur 156 (Berlin: de Gruyter, 2006), 228.
12. Leo Curran, "Rape and Rape Victims," 263–64. Curran's is the classic article on rape in the *Metamorphoses*. There are many readings of these rapes from the dismissive and indifferent to those that take Ovid to task. One of the most interesting and compelling is that of Lynn Enterline, *The Rhetoric of the Body from Ovid to Shakespeare* (Cambridge: Cambridge University Press, 2000), 33, who uses Louis Althusser's notion of interpellation in conjunction with a reading of Caenis's story (*Met.* 12.176–209). Enterline writes, "Caenis, ravished by Neptune, might be a fitting spokeswoman for many of the poem's victims. Bid to choose what she wishes in payment for having been raped, Caenis responds by seeking the only way out: 'Grant me that I not be a woman' ('mihi da, femina ne sim,' 12.202). Caenis' request strikes my ear, at least, as an epitome of Althusser's notion of 'internal distance.' For him, internal distance 'presupposes a retreat' or 'internal distantiation' from the ideology to which a text 'alludes and with which it is constantly fed.' In its blunt conformation with the conditions of being a woman in the poem, 'Mihi da, femina ne sim' makes us understand 'in some sense from the inside . . . the very ideology' of sexual difference which the Metamorphoses also deploys. Such a claim—that in the Metamorphoses, rape is represented as the call that interpellates the female subject as 'femina'—suggests to me that Ovid's text . . . is more a critique of the systematic violence and subordination embedded in patriarchal culture than mere repletion or perpetuation of it," (quoting Louis Althusser, *Lenin and Philosophy*, trans. Ben Brewster [New York: Monthly Review Press, 1971], 222).
13. I return to the Apollo and Python story when exploring its connections to Jupiter and his slaying of the Giants, but it is important to note that the story of Apollo and Python, with Apollo restoring order in the face of Pythian chaos, is often connected to Octavian's victory at Actium—and it is, of course, the Actium Apollo who helped Augustus to triumph. See, e.g., John F. Miller, *Apollo,*

of Apollo and Python follows the second creation account in book 1, describing the state of the world when "the earth, muddy because of the recent flood, grew hot from the heat of the high celestial sun, it brought forth innumerable species; some were the ancient forms, restored; and some were monsters, newly created" (1.434-37).[14] One of these monsters brought forth from earth was Python (1.438).[15] This gargantuan serpent, "a terror to the newly fashioned humans" (1.439), was slain by Apollo, though it took one thousand arrows to defeat him—almost every one he had (1.443). Here, as Apollo enters the narrative,[16] his "first act is one of destruction."[17] And although Apollo succeeds in killing Python, it is only after using one thousand arrows and nearly emptying his quiver. As Frederick Ahl observes, "Either the serpent's size is especially great or Phoebus' archery leaves something to be desired."[18] This act of conquest, both grand and humorous, ushers

Augustus, and the Poets (New York: Cambridge University Press, 2009), 340–43; W. S. M. Nicoll, "Cupid, Apollo, and Daphne (Ovid, Met. 1.452ff)," CQ 30.1 (1980): 174–82—but cf. Miller's, "Ovid and Augustan Apollo," Hermathena 177/178 (2004/2005): 171, where he notes that "Nicoll's suggestion that the [Apollo and Python] myth was already an Augustan topos is not backed up by sufficient evidence." But Miller, in this piece, explores many other tenable connections. The connections between Apollo and Augustus will also be explored in subsequent sections.

14. *ergo ubi diluvio tellus lutulenta recenti / solibus aetheriis altoque recanduit aestu, / edidit innumeras species; partimque figuras / rettulit antiquas, partim nova monstra creavit.* All translations are my own in consultation with Ovid, Met. (LCL); Ovid, The Metamorphoses, trans. Charles Martin (New York: W. W. Norton, 2004); and www.perseus.tufts.edu.

15. Frederick Ahl notes that Python's "sexuality, like that of other snakes in the Metamorphoses, is ambiguous. It is *masculine* when Ovid calls it by its name but feminine when he refers to it generically, as a snake" (*Metaformations: Soundplay and Wordplay in Ovid and Other Classical Poets* [Ithaca, NY: Cornell University Press, 1985], 125).

16. Phoebus = Apollo. "Phoebus" does make brief appearances at both 1.11 and 1.338 simply as the sun, but this narrative series is the first time that Phoebus strays from his set course across the skies and enters into the unfolding drama of the earth. In the Apollo-Python-Daphne narrative Apollo is almost exclusively referred to as "Phoebus" (1.451, 452, 463, 490, 553), with the exception of 1.454, where he is the "Delian," and 1.473, where he is called "Apollo" for the only time in this segment of narratives. He is only given this name, where the "destroyer," is destroyed by Cupid's arrow (1.473; Ahl notes the pun between "Apollo" and ἀπόλλυμι, the first extant usage found in Aeschylus, Agamemnon 1080–82 (*Metaformations*, 129, 131); see also Miller, Apollo, Augustus, and the Poets, 340, who also on 340n23 cites Euripides Phaethon 224–26 [Diggle], and Plato, Cratylus 405d–e). The use of the appellation Phoebus almost exclusively sets up the juxtaposition between the desires of Phoebus and the one he pursues, who desires to be like his sister Phoebe, that is, Daphne.

17. Ahl, Metaformations, 126.

18. Ibid.; see also Stephen Michael Wheeler, Narrative Dynamics in Ovid's Metamorphoses (Tübingen: Gunter Narr, 2000), 55: "One need not take the hyperbole at face value, but it certainly smacks of epic parody." See also Miller, Apollo, Augustus, and the Poets, 340. Here is one of the many instances where multiple readings are possible: is the reader to take this seriously or humorously?

in the new post-flood order, positioning Apollo as the paternal protector of humanity.[19]

Apollo, worried that his great deed will go unremembered, institutes the Pythian Games in honor of his conquest (*perdomitae*) of the serpent (1.445–47). The youths who were "victorious [*vicerat*] with hand, foot, or wheel," in these games "captured [*capiebat*] an oak wreath as reward [*honorem*]," because, Ovid says, the "laurel [*laurus*] did not yet exist, so Phoebus crowned his temples, his handsome flowing hair, with any tree anywhere" (1.448–51).[20] This statement paves the way for the aetiological narrative of Daphne and the laurel that follows, a story connected to Apollo and Python through the use of bow and arrow.[21]

The story begins, saying, "The first love [*primus amor*] of Phoebus was Daphne, daughter of Peneus," though this "was no ignorant accident [*fors ignara*] through which he yielded [*dedit*] but because of Cupid's savage anger [*saeva Cupidinis ira*]" (1.452–53). As in the cases of Rhea Silvia, the Sabines, Lucretia, and Verginia, it is far from clear what type of "love" this is, but in contrast to the case of the Sabines, Ovid does not pretend that this is a "love" of "chance" or "fortune" (*fors*), but names it as a part of the malicious scheming of Cupid.[22] Cupid's wrath is incurred as the "Delian" Apollo, arrogant (*superbus*)[23] from

19. Fratantuono notes the Augustan undertones of the Apollo-Python narrative, as Python emerges from the muddy waters associated with Egypt and the Nile (*Madness Transformed*, 16–17). As Apollonian Octavian has defeated the "monstrous" Cleopatra and Antony at Actium, saving humanity (cf. the Priene calendar inscription where Augustus was "sent as a savior both to us and our descendants, so that he might end war and order all things"), so too does Apollo defeat the monstrous Python.
20. Romulus, too, will "wreath his flowing locks with laurel" (δάφνῃ δὲ ἐστέψατο τὴν κεφαλὴν κομῶσαν) when he celebrates his triumph in Plutarch, *Rom.* 16.5.
21. See Ahl on this connection, particularly in terms of Apollo and Cupid (*Metaformations*, 127, 130–31). For ancient sources for the Daphne and Apollo text, see Otis, *Ovid as an Epic Poet*, 378–88; Mary E. Barnard, *The Myth of Apollo and Daphne from Ovid to Quevedo: Love, Agon, and the Grotesque* (Durham, NC: Duke University Press, 1987), 14–17, 21–22; Peter E. Knox, "In Pursuit of Daphne," *TAPA* 120 (1990): 183–202, 385–86, esp. 188–90; and Fratantuono, *Madness Transformed*, 17–20, 28–29nn41–48. Ovid's changes to the traditional Daphne story are complex, as with the text as a whole, weaving together Callimachus, Vergil, and other traditional Greek sources, to make complex meaning as well as to fit the episode into the overall flow of his narrative.
22. Livy 1.9.11, 15 uses *fors* to describe how the women end up with their husbands; cf. Dionysius of Halicarnassus, *Ant. rom.* 2.30.4–5, τύχη. There seems to be an awareness here in the Ovidian texts, as in many of his others, that to call this "love" is ironic, and that the whole scene—regardless of the perspectives that flow through the narrative—is one framed by malintent.
23. This is the same charge that Livy's Romulus levels against the Sabine parents, that is, "arrogance" (*superbia*) who refuse the Romans the right to intermarry, thus forcing the Romans' violent response (Livy 1.9.14).

his recent victory over Python, sees Cupid "bending his sinew-strung bow" and taunts him, saying, "What, wanton boy, are you doing with manly [fortibus] weapons of war [armis]? That one suits our shoulders, which furnish faithful wounds to beasts and enemies [hostis], and not long ago overthrew with countless arrows the protuberant Python whose pestilential paunch pressed many acres. Content yourself with inflaming the insignificant fires of love [amores] with your torch [face], not claiming our glories!" (1.456–62).

Cupid responds to Apollo's arrogance by retorting, "You may pierce [figat] all things, Phoebus, but my bow will pierce you: as all living creatures are less than gods, so is your glory less than mine!" Cupid then draws two arrows from his quiver "with differing effect: one causing flight [fugat], the other love [amorem]. The one that induces love is sharp, gold with gleaming tip; the one that causes flight [fugat] is blunt with lead beneath its shaft [harundine]"—the leaden arrow Cupid "thrusts" (fixit) into Daphne and the golden one "penetrates" (traiecta) Apollo (1.463–73). Ahl again humorously notes, "Phoebus is less triumphantly successful when he mocks [Cupid's] prowess as an archer than when he challenges and kills Python."[24] But even so Cupid's victory over Pheobus may be more successful than Phoebus's over Python, as Cupid needs only one arrow per victim, while Phoebus requires one thousand.

Here the text makes clear its earlier assertion that it was the anger of Cupid—in response to Apollo's arrogance—and not chance that caused Apollo's obsession with Daphne. Rather than being the piercing archer, Apollo, along with Daphne, is penetrated by Cupid's arrow and subjected to his game of "love."[25] The confrontation between Cupid and Apollo contains echoes of the confrontations between Amulius and Numitor as well as between Romulus and the neighboring cities: the dispute here is solely between Apollo and Cupid, but Daphne, like

24. Ahl, Metaformations, 130.
25. Though this is not made explicit by Ovid in this particular tale, Ovid's other works display a consciousness of both the association of Augustus with Apollo and with Cupid, his relation through his descent from Venus. It makes for interesting intra-family dynamics for these two to be at odds—though, given the relationship between Augustus and Antony, possibly a reflective one.

Rhea Silvia and the Sabine women, becomes a pawn, a mediator, and a casualty in the men's dispute. And as with Amulius and the Roman men, Cupid's act is predicated on a desire for retribution, a bruised ego, and the need to display power.[26]

After Apollo and Daphne are hit with Cupid's arrows, Ovid's narrator states, "Immediately one [i.e., Apollo] loves [*amat*], and the other [i.e., Daphne] flees [*fugit*] love's name [*nomen amantis*]" (1.473–74), then relays that Daphne flees:

> delighting in the refuge of the woods and the hides of wild beasts she snared, emulating unmarried Phoebe. A fillet restrained her unfurled hair. Many assailed her, but she shunned their assaults, free from men and unwilling to endure them, roamed the remote woods, untroubled by Hymen or Amor, or whatever marriage might be. Her father often said "Daughter, you owe me a son-in-law," and her father often said "Daughter, you owe me grandsons." But, detesting the wedding torch as if it were a crime she would blush red with shame over her fair mouth and face, and holding fast her father's neck with fawning arms, would say "Precious father, let me be as I am forever," she said, "delighting in virginity! Diana's father gave this to her." He, indeed, yielded to her, but that beauty of yours, forbids your desire, and your form resists your prayer. (1.475–89)[27]

Though the flow of the narrative seems to imply that Cupid's arrow is the cause of Daphne's fleeing and flight through the woods, the text is somewhat ambiguous. We are left to wonder if Cupid's arrow caused not only her flight from Apollo but from all men, or if this flight was already a part of Daphne's character, if she dedicated herself to Diana (Phoebe) before Cupid penetrates her with his arrow or after. Regardless, Daphne seems to have an entire life before fleeing Apollo's

26. While the details of Lucretia's and Verginia's stories do not fit quite as closely, similar dynamics in regard to both power and gender are present, and here, too, Lucretia is the casualty in a dispute that is not hers.

27. *silvarum latebris captivarumque ferarum / exuviis gaudens innuptaeque aemula Phoebes: / vitta coercebat positos sine lege capillos. / multi illam petiere, illa aversata petentes / inpatiens expersque viri nemora avia lustrat / nec, quid Hymen, quid Amor, quid sint conubia curat. / saepe pater dixit: "generum mihi, filia, debes," / saepe pater dixit: "debes mihi, nata, nepotes" ; / illa velut crimen taedas exosa iugales / pulchra verecundo suffuderat ora rubore / inque patris blandis haerens cervice lacertis / "da mihi perpetua, genitor carissime," dixit / "virginitate frui! Dedit hoc pater ante Dianae." / ille quidem obsequitur, se te decor iste quod optas / esse vetat, votoque tuo tua forma repugnat.*

pursuits. While eventually fleeing Phoebus, it is Phoebe whom Daphne herself pursues: hunting, roaming, and running.

The story is clear that Daphne shuns not only men but marriage itself, emphasizing the connection between the self-contained, self-directed state of virginity/maidenhood and contrasting it to the state of marriage. It is "unmarried [*innuptaeque*] Phoebe" whom Daphne emulates; she is "untroubled by Hymen or Amor, or whatever marriage [*conubia*] might be"; she "detested the wedding torch as a crime." Even as her father elicits her shame by claiming that a son-in-law and children are something she "owes" (*debes*) him, she uses her feminine wiles (*blandis*)[28] to persuade him to "let me be as I am forever . . . delighting in virginity." She lays it on thick, appealing to her father's sense of self, as she coyly adds, "Diana's father [Jupiter] gave this to her," implying that if he grants Daphne virginity, as Jupiter to his daughter Diana, Peneus can emulate the king of the gods. Though Daphne uses the tools at her disposal to gain what she wants, this passage further illustrates the role and control that men, and fathers, have over women. As raised in the previous chapter, much of the protection guaranteed to women is granted through the paternal male influence—whether father or husband. Here, too, it is no different, as Daphne appeals to her father to retain her autonomous, virginal state, needing his permission to authorize her aspirations.[29]

Though Peneus yields to Daphne's desire, the narrator, speaking directly to Daphne, tells her that Peneus's concession is actually

28. Here this is used is more typical fashion (i.e., by a woman) in contrast to the blandishments employed by the Romans to cajole the Sabine women in Livy 1.9.16.
29. Carlin A. Barton nuances her reading of this passage in a different manner, framing Daphne's blush as a "deliberate" one, "making her father play her game" (*Roman Honor: The Fire in the Bones* [Berkeley: University of California Press, 2001], 267–68). Barton sees Daphne as exploiting the honor–shame relationship in the face of her "antisocial" behavior as a way to maintain her autonomy, feeding this into a larger discussion of the "deliberate blush." While this is certainly a possible reading of the text, it seems to me that this blush is elicited as much by Peneus's push for grandchildren as by the simple manipulation of her father. And again, I think it is important to contrast the Romans' use of blandishments against the Sabine women with those of Daphne—the Romans use these "feminine wiles" as a way to appease those who, at least at this point in their narrative, no longer have the right to self-determination and bodily integrity in any manner, those who have been taken against their will. But Daphne employs them in order to maintain her bodily integrity and right to self-determination, but she needs to do this with the permission of her father so that she remains under his protection, that is, in relationship with him, despite her decision to maintain her virginal status.

meaningless: "your beauty . . . forbids your desire, and your form resists your prayer."[30] While this line explicitly foreshadows Daphne's coming fate, her fate is also elicited by her desire itself. Her first request from her father, "let me be as I am forever," will necessitate a second request as Apollo pursues her. Although her first wish is indeed granted, it is not granted in the form she expects. Through her transformation, Daphne will become stagnant, rooted, and unchanging, but while she remains in human form, she will run.

Despite the fact that Daphne has dedicated herself (with her father's permission) to Phoebe, Phoebe's brother Phoebus "loves [amat] her on sight [visaeque]," and he desires (cupit) that which Daphne has shunned—marriage (conubia). As he desires and hopes for Daphne, "his own oracles deceive him." And just as fire overtakes that which grows, transforming it, so too "the god was morphed [abiit] by flames," burning Phoebus's heart and "feeding his fruitless love [amorem] with hope" (1.490–96). Phoebus loves Daphne "on sight [visaeque]"; his gaze dissects her body,[31] taking it apart piece by piece and trying to remake it in his own image. He gazes (spectat) at her hair as it lingers on her neck and wonders what it might look like done up (1.497–98). He "sees [videt] her eyes sparkling like the flames of stars; he sees her mouth, where seeing [vidisse] does not satiate. He praises her fingers, hands, and arms, exposed to her shoulder; what is concealed he considers better" (1.498–502). Daphne is changed from a whole into parts, pieces that are not only consumed as they are, but imagined transformed in an effort to quench Apollo's own lust.[32] But Apollo's praises do not have

30. Here, the text makes clear that Daphne is at fault, or at least her beauty is, for Apollo's pursuit—not Apollo's own lust and actions—a very typical example of victim blaming. As Curran notes, "Beauty is dangerous. The victim's beauty . . . is an invitation to and a justification for rape" ("Rape and Rape Victims," 274).
31. See Enterline, *Rhetoric of the Body,* 99; Hardie, *Ovid's Poetics of Illusion,* 46; Salzman-Mitchell, *Web of Fantasies,* 29–31. As Charles Segal observes, "the female body in the *Metamorphoses* is characterized by its status as a visual object, its passivity, its appropriation by the male libidinal imagination, and its role as a vessel to be 'filled'" ("Ovid's Metamorphic Bodies: Art, Gender, and Violence in the 'Metamorphoses,'" *Arion* 5.3 [1998]: 23).
32. See Curran, "Rape and Rape Victims," 277: "The identification of rape and dehumanization is intimate and virtually immediate [with] Daphne, where the heroine begins to lose her humanity as soon as the chase begins. As Daphne runs from Apollo, the effect of the wind on her fluttering clothing and streaming hair corresponds closely to what the wind will do to the branches and leaves of the tree she is to become."

the desired effect, as Daphne does not return his gaze[33] but "flees [*fugit*] more swiftly than the fleeting breeze, and does not stay [*resistit*] when his words recall [*revocantis*][34] her" (1.502–3).

As Daphne flees, Apollo begins a long-winded diatribe directed toward her, trying to hold and restrain Daphne with his words since his body cannot catch her. He begs her to still and assures her that he is "not an enemy [*hostis*] pursuing [*insequor*] her." With language that strongly echoes the pursuit of the Sabine women in the *Ars Amatoria*, Apollo tells Daphne that, while prey flee their predators, he is chasing her because of love (*amor*), so she should not fear him.[35] But Apollo's own metaphor seems to mark his actions as belonging to the predatory. He then laments his misery (*miserum*), fearing that his pursuit will cause her to fall, marking (*notent*) her body, her legs in particular (1.504–9). He pleads, saying, "restrain [*moderatius*] yourself . . . cease your flight," and tells her if she will do this, "I will restrain [*moderatius*] my pursuit," as if Daphne's slowing will create a reciprocal response in Apollo's pursuit (1.510–11).

Apollo, becoming exasperated, asks her to "inquire whom it is you pleasure," though her pleasures and desires clearly fall outside the realm of Apollo's inquiry. Apollo declares that he is "not a mountain-man, nor a herdsman [*pastor*], nor a wild keeper of cattle and flocks" (1.512–14). But despite—or maybe because of—these assurances, Daphne still runs, and Apollo resorts to hurling insults, displaying the same arrogance he showed to Cupid earlier: "You are ignorant [*nescis*], thoughtless girl, you are ignorant [*nescis*] from whom you flee [*fugia*],

---

33. Salzman-Mitchell points out this detail, emphasizing that, while Daphne becomes a "spectacle" for Apollo, she "never looks back" (*Web of Fantasies*, 30).

34. Lewis & Short, s.v. *revoco* "call back, recall, draw or fetch back, burn back, bring back, restore, withhold, restrain, bring, induce, persuade, apply, reduce, refer, recall, revoke, retract, cancel, call again, summon anew."

35. *Ars* 1.115–19: "They leapt forth right away, showing their souls with their shouts, and, with hands, lustfully seized the virgins. As crowds of fearful doves flee the eagle, as the new-born lamb flees the hostile wolf: so they feared the violent rushing of unvirtuous men" (*Protinus exiliunt, animum clamore fatentes, / Virginibus cupidas iniciuntque manus. / Ut fugiunt aquilas, timidissima turba, columbae, / Ut fugit invisos agna novella lupos: / Sic illae timuere viro sine more ruentes*). *Met.* 1.504–7: "I am not an enemy pursuing you! Nymph, stay! As a lamb flees the wolf, as a deer the lion, as a dove flees with trembling feathers from the eagle, everything flees its enemies" (*non insequor hostis; / nympha, mane! Sic agna lupum, sic cerva lupum, sic cerva leonem, / sic aquilam penna fugiunt trepidante columbae, / hostes quaeque suos*").

that is why you flee [*fugis*] from *me*" (1.514–15). Then, as if she should be honored by his pursuit and belittling of her, Phoebus tells her just who this "me" is:

> Delphi is my land, and Claros and Tenedos; Patara serves [*servit*] me as king [*regia*]. Jupiter is my father [*genitor*]. Through me what was, what is, and what will be, are revealed. Through me strings harmonize in song. My arrow is sure, still a surer arrow has wounded [*vulnera*] my vacant breast! Medicine is my invention; the whole world calls me the aid-bringer [*opifer*]; herbs are subject [*subiecta*] to my power [*potentia*]! (1.515–22)

But, despite his greatness and the power he wields, Apollo ends his speech by bemoaning, "Ai me, but love cannot be healed by herbs, nor can the arts that benefit others benefit their master [*domino*]!" (1.523–24).[36]

Apollo "would have said more, but fearful [*timido*] the daughter of Peneus continued her course, fleeing [*fugit*], even now lovely to see [*visa*], leaving him with words unfinished" (1.525–26). Daphne's persistent loveliness in flight is envisioned as, "The winds bared her body, the turning breezes met her, trembling her clothes, and the light airs drove her streaming hair behind her, her form [*forma*] enhanced and augmented [*auctaque*][37] by flight [*fuga*]" (1.524–30). And in contrast to Daphne's pleas to her father, or the Romans' pleas to the Sabine women,[38] "the young god could no longer waste time on further blandishments [*blanditias*], and instructed [*monebat*] by love [*amor*][39] itself, he chased [*sequitur*] her letting his feet loose" (1.530–32).

Now becoming the predators he contrasted himself with earlier, Apollo pursues Daphne as an animal engaged in the hunt: "As a Gaul's dog sees [*vidit*] a rabbit in an empty field, it assaults its prey [*praedam*][40]

---

36. See Miller, *Apollo, Augustus, and the Poets*, 345–46, 353, 362–67, on Apollo's failure to heal himself—a theme throughout the *Metamorphoses*.
37. The word *autaque* accounts for both "enhanced" and "augmented"—the first transformation of her form.
38. Again, note Livy 1.9.16, and *Met.* 1.485. Here, just as Apollo is less effective with the arrow than Cupid, it seems that the god of poetry is less effective with his words than Daphne—he cannot woo her, so he turns to force.
39. This could also be read as a personification of the god Amor.
40. Lewis & Short, s.v. *praeda*: property taken in war, booty, spoil, plunder, pillage; an animal, bird, or the like, caught or killed in the chase; prey, game; in general, booty, spoil, gain, profit.

on foot, but the rabbit seeks safety: he, just about to fasten on her, now, even now, he trusts he has her, his muzzle extended, pressing her soles, while she waivers as to whether she's seized [*conprensus*], tears away from his bites, escaping the brush of his mouth. And so the god and the maiden [*virgo*]: he quickened by hope, she by fear [*timore*]" (1.533–39). Again resonant with the story of the Sabine women, Daphne is not simply prey but the spoils of war, Apollo's spoil (*praedam*),[41] his due prize in his battle for Daphne's affections—just as the laurel she will become will be the prize for conquerors both in games and on the field of battle.[42]

Apollo's pursuit continues, as he, "aided by wings of love [*amoris*], denied her rest and, bending over and threatening [*inminet*][43] her fleeing [*fugacis*] back, exhaled on the hair strewn on her neck" (1.540–42). At this point, the text once again returns to relay Daphne's perspective. The narrator describes Daphne as her body begins to give way to Apollo's pursuit: "Her strength consumed, she turned pale, overcome by fatigue of her flight [*fugae*]." In a final attempt to save herself, Daphne's voice is heard for the last time. Upon "seeing [*spectans*] Peneus's waves" Daphne cries out, "'Help me, father! If your rivers hold divine power [*numen*] change [*muta*] me, destroy [*perde*] this form [*figuram*] that gives too much pleasure!'" (1.543–47). Daphne blames neither Cupid's arrow nor Apollo's aggressive pursuit for her fate, but rather her own form and figure. The pleasure that this form may give to Daphne herself—through her running, hunting, and devotion to Phoebe—remains unmentioned, the destruction of her body is the only path through which she can imagine reprieve. But despite her transformation, she will still remain the object of Apollo's pleasure.

Daphne's transformation happens almost instantaneously: "Her

41. The Sabine women are referred to as "a joyful spoil" (*genialis praeda*) in *Ars* 1.125.
42. In a decisive blurring between the private and public realms, here, Apollo's private lust becomes a very public symbol for all to see. Hardie, *Ovid's Poetics of Illusion,* 37: "In the story of Apollo and Daphne in Metamorphoses 1 Ovid offers a kind of aetiology for [the] coupling of the power structures of the elegiac and imperial worlds, at the moment when Apollo lays claim to the laurel as the only available means of possessing the hard-hearted girl, and simultaneously prophesies that the laurel's presence will be enjoyed by Roman generals and by Augustus himself."
43. The word *inminet* accounts for both "bending over" and "threatening."

prayer was barely done when a heavy torpor seized [*occupat*] her limbs, slim bark[44] encircles her supple trunk, her hair turns to leaves, her arms grow to boughs, her feet so swift a moment ago are fixed in reluctant roots, her mouth enclosed by the tree's top. Her luster alone remains" (1.548–52). Each of the parts carved out through Apollo's gaze, piece by piece, become a tree. Throughout the narrative, Daphne has only spoken twice—the rest of the time the narrator is the one revealing her inner thoughts—and in both instances it is a prayer that ultimately leads to metamorphosis. In the first prayer, ironically, Daphne asks her father to remain "the same," unchanging, and she is turned into a fugitive; while in the second prayer, in which she again asks to remain "the same," she is transformed into an immovable tree.

This transformation, so complete that Daphne's luster is all that is left of her, fails to quench Apollo's lust. The poem tells us that despite her transformation "Phoebus loves [*amat*] her." And in this new form, rooted to the ground with no way to escape, Apollo is finally granted the outcome he has sought: "placing his hand on the trunk, he feels her breast still trembling beneath new bark. He hugs the boughs as human limbs, and surrenders his mouth to wood"[45] (1.548–56). As Apollo molests her new form, a form in which she cannot flee, we are told, "But even the wood recoils from his kisses" (1.556). It is difficult to know if this is a remnant of Daphne, still shrinking from Apollo while ensconced in her new form, or merely a projection, as the text has emphasized the completeness of her transformation.[46] What is clear is that, through Daphne's prayer, Apollo's desire is finally fulfilled—she remains still for him, her ignorance of him enlightened, and now he

---

44. "slim bark" = *tenui libro*. The phrase *tenuis liber* is one of many places in the Apollo and Daphne cycle that point to another double meaning to the work: Apollo is the god of poetry, and this story is also about poetry and literature (cf. the double meanings of *notent* [1.509] and *lingo* [1.556], for example). See, e.g., Joseph Farrell, "The Ovidian Corpus: Poetic Body and Poetic Text," in Hardie et al., *Ovidian Transformations*, 113–36; for a complex and nuanced reading of this see Enterline, *Rhetoric of the Body*, 31–32, and her chapter 2, "Body and Voice in the Metamorphoses," 39–90.

45. "wood" = *ligno*, also a "writing tablet" (Lewis & Short).

46. Here and below at 1.566–67, where Daphne "nods her head," the text can also be read as an utter dissociation after her experience with the predator Apollo. Though she is there, she is not there; her actions are automatic and disconnected from her inner self and desires. Cf. Curran, "Rape and Rape Victims," 277: "After her transformation, Daphne as tree is an . . . analog of a victim so profoundly traumatized by her experience that she has take refuge in a catatonic withdrawal from all human involvement, passively acted upon by her environment and by other persons."

can finally force her to experience him as he experiences himself. At the same time she is also saved: for if there is nothing of her left in this changed form, she has indeed escaped him, her wish fulfilled—but at what cost?

At last Apollo, here referred to simply as "the god," says to the transformed Daphne who can no longer flee his words, "Though you are not able to be my bride [coniunx], you will certainly be my tree! Laurel, you will forever embrace [habebunt] my hair, my lyre, my quiver. You will attend the Roman generals when joyful voices sing their triumph [triumphum], and beholding the long Capitol processions [pompas]. You will stand before Augustus's thresholds [postibus/fores], a faithful guardian, and keep watch over the crown of oak between. And as my head is youthful with its unshorn hair, you, too, will also bear the honor of everlasting leaves" (1.557-65).

In the final lines of Daphne's story, Apollo, having finally captured the object of his desire, "had finally finished"—for once he is silent (1.556). But this silence is laden, for as Apollo's gaze has objectified Daphne's human body, so too has she, in the form of a tree, become Apollo's object to use: she will be made to embrace him as she adorns his body and possessions, forced to do that which she fled while in human form. And she will not only honor Apollo's victory at her own expense, but honor all victories that occur at the expense of others[47] —she is the captive who symbolizes the triumph of the victor.[48]

---

47. Christopher Francese convincingly argues that "honor" is one of the main themes connecting the Python-Apollo-Daphne cycle, though he reads a much more positive valence to the text than my own reading ("Daphne, Honor, and Aetiological Action in Ovid's 'Metamorphoses,'" CW 97.2 [2004]: 153-57). He notes that the cycle explores "honor from various angles—Greek, Roman, athletic, religious, military, political—culminating in an elegant compliment to Augustus," highlighting the "glamour of Greek athletics, the majesty of Roman triumph, the dignity of Apolline cult and art, and the imposing presence of Augustus" (156). I would argue that, while it explores these aspects, the portrait painted by Ovid is much more complex, also highlighting the arrogant struggle over honor between Apollo and Cupid and the ways in which this struggle for honor produces casualties, namely, Daphne. This cycle shows a larger ambivalence about the relationship between honor, victory, and triumph—that for one to "win" others necessarily have to lose, that often one's honor is gained at the expense of others. See also Adrian S. Hollis, "Ovid, Metamorphoses 1.445ff.: Apollo, Daphne, and the Pythian Crown," ZPE 112 (1996): 69-73.

48. Much like the captives who are paraded during the triumph, Daphne, held captive by both her new form and Apollo will be forced to march through the streets remembering Apollo's victory. Here, Daphne is emblematic of what Hardie refers to as "absent presences," see Hardie, Ovid's Poetics of Illusion, 1-29. On the laurel's association with triumphs, see Beard, Roman Triumph, 52, 246-47.

Through her transformation, Daphne's humanity has literally been constrained by her form. In order to hold on to that which she holds most dear, she needs to give up everything else that she is. But despite this transformation, she is still circumscribed by her would-be rapist who continues to frame her meaning in relation to himself as she "appears" to "nod . . . in assent" to the "honor" Apollo has bestowed (1.566-67). After her transformation the narrator can only guess what Daphne is feeling—and can only speculate if any part of the human Daphne, who once ran through the woods, remains.

Intra- and Intertextual Connections

This section situates the story of Apollo and Daphne in the broader context of book 1 of the *Metamorphoses*, giving attention both to the narratives that precede and to those that follow Ovid's accounts of Apollo and Python and Apollo and Daphne. In addition, this section seeks to place the *Metamorphoses* within its broader Augustan milieu, connecting this context further with the Daphne and Apollo story itself. As noted in the introduction to this chapter, the *Metamorphoses* is a tightly woven text, each scene seamlessly leading to the next and each containing a myriad of intra- and intertextual references and allusions. Once again, my goal is not exhaustively to explore the entirety of the associations and interpretations within the text but to follow several strands that are relevant for the later analysis of the three cosmogonies at the center of this study.

The Creation of the World

Ovid begins his poem with the world as chaos: an "unwrought, orderless mass" of "the disconnected seeds of discordant [*discordia*] elements heaped together" (1.5-9). And though earth, water, and air existed, they were in perpetual flux, "no form remained the same" (1.16)[49]—prefiguring the perpetual flux of the bodies to follow, as has already been stated in the poem's first lines ("My soul drives me to

---

49. *nulli sua forma manebat.*

speak of bodies changed into new forms," 1.1–2).[50] From this chaos, "god, or a good-willed nature, redeemed this strife" (1.21), "separating earth from heavens and waters from earth" (1.22).[51] The god's, or nature's, "care" (1.48) in ordering continues throughout lines 1.23–88, but the chaos from which the "world creator" (*mundi fabricator*, 1.57) formed it always lurked around the corners. This lurking chaos can be seen in the poem's description of the movement of the air. For, though the world creator did not "allow the air to scatter unbounded, even now, with each ruling their own region, their gales controlled, they are scarcely kept from tearing the world to pieces: such is the discord between brothers" (1.57–60).[52]

Genevieve Lively characterizes this Ovidian world as a "chaosmos," which she observes would have had particular resonance in the era in which Ovid wrote his poem. She states,

> After years of conflict, culminating in the chaos and bloody fratricide of civil war, Augustus had only relatively recently restored Rome and its warring citizens to order and harmony, establishing peace and a new Augustan "cosmos." Ovid's description of a fratricidal conflict between the winds threatening to tear apart the new world order (1.58– 60) adds a political subtext to his Creation story. Here, Ovid reminds his readers that the new Augustan peace in itself is inherently fragile and that the world might return to chaos and conflict at any time.[53]

Not only does this "fratricidal conflict" point toward the recent war between Octavian and Antony, but it also resonates with Rome's own founding in the conflict between Romulus and Remus and Romulus's eventual murder of his brother.[54] Through both of these fratricidal connections, the beginnings of the world in the *Metamorphoses* elicit

50. *in nova fert animus mutates dicere formas corpora.* Even in these first lines, the juxtaposition of *animus* and *corpora* seems to resonate with the poem's ongoing question of the relationship between form and self and the ways in which they reflect and refract one another, the conjunctions and disjunctions between them.
51. *nam caelo terras et terries abscidit undas.*
52. *His quoque non passim mundi fabricator habendum aera permisit; vix nunc obsistitur illis, cum sua quisque regat diverso flamina tractu, quin lanient mundum; tanta est discordia fratrum.*
53. Lively, *Ovid's Metamorphoses: A Reader's Guide*, 17.
54. Fratantuono, *Madness Transformed*, 8, citing Franz Bömer, *P. Ovidius Naso Metamorphosen: Kommentar I–III* (Heidelberg: Winter, 1976) and William S. Anderson, *Ovid's Metamorphoses: Books 1-5* (Norman: University of Oklahoma Press, 1997). See Livy 1.7.1–3; DH 1.87–88; Plutarch, *Rom.* 9.4–10.2.

both the founding and refounding of Rome. This close juxtaposition of order and chaos, creation and conflict will continue throughout the *Metamorphoses* and flow through the creation narrative with the next scene: the advent of humans.[55]

To bring order to the chaotic world, each element of the newly formed world is assigned its own space—element, animal, and god alike (1.69–75). But then an element transgressing those assigned spheres is introduced: "an animal more sacred . . . more fit for lofty understanding and able to have dominion over all the rest was still missing: then human was born" (1.76-78).[56] Speculating on the origins of this new being, the narrator then wonders if the "artisan" (*opifex*) who was "source of this better world" (*mundi melioris origo*, 1.79) "created humans out of its own divine seed or if the new earth, freshly separated from the high heavens, retained some seed of its celestial kin, so that Prometheus, mixing it with the rains, formed it in the image of the gods who govern all" (1.78-83).[57] Humans were the first creatures to transgress and have dominion over the separate spheres of the earth, the first to stand upright, and thus the first animals who could look toward the heavens and to the gods,[58] rather than solely to

55. In her study of Roman honor, Carlin Barton notes the dissonance and complexities of holding these seeming contradictory aspects within the human as she reflects on the connection between honor and shame in ancient Rome: "When we read that Brutus and Torquatus slew their sons or that Aeneas left behind his beloved Dido, we want to imagine Brutus and Torquatus as men of conscience bravely and dutifully following a code that dictated that fathers should be severe to their sons, and that Aeneas was dutifully bowing to the will of the gods rather than pursuing his own selfish desires. We do not want to think that the very point of these stories is the terrible choice, the anguish of a father having to follow a code that conflicted with a father's intense feelings for a child, or the agony of a man whose duty to the gods conflicted with this commitment to the woman whom he loves. We do not want the double-bind to be 'real.' We do not want irresolvable paradoxes to be at the heart of our spiritual lives. We want the choice to be clear. . . . But the person of honor, the person with a sense of shame, in ancient Rome had to be willingly frustrated, somewhat ineffectual, and not completely in control. The honorable man and woman in ancient Rome continually experienced and tolerated a high degree of discomfort and disorganization; they were ashamed in avoidance of greater shame. There could be no resolution to this paradox" (*Roman Honor*, 272).

56. *sanctius his animal mentisque capacius altae deerat adhuc et quod dominari in cetera posset: natus homo est.*

57. *sive hunc divino semine fecit ... sive recens tellus seductaque nuper ab alto aether cognate retinebat semina caeli. quam satus Iapeto, mixtam pluvialibus undis, finxit in effigiem moderantum cuncta deorum.*

58. See Lively, *Ovid's* Metamorphoses: A Reader's Guide, 17–18: "The potential nature of the relationship between man and the gods is left ambiguous here (as it will be throughout the poem), but there is one clue as to the intended bound. Ovid distinguishes man from the other animals as 'holier' (*sanctius*—1.76), suggesting that a key role to be played by man on earth is the worship of the gods in heaven: man is the only animal who literally and figuratively 'looks up to' the gods. Moreover,

the earth: as creatures composed of earth and heaven they could look to both. Ovid concludes this section by reiterating this metamorphosis: "the earth, so recently unwrought and without likeness, was transformed by putting on the forms of humans"[59] (1.84–88).[60]

The Four Ages

As the earth itself transforms into human beings, the actions of human beings also transform the earth. These transformations are reflected in the four ages: the Golden, Silver, Bronze, and Iron. The first age,

it is this tripartite hierarch—god, man, beast—which will be transgressed in and by the stories of metamorphosis to come."

59. *sic, modo quae fuerat rudis et sine imagine, tellus induit ignotas hominum conversa figuras.*

60. There are many resonances, both thematic and textual, with the Genesis 1–8 narrative both in this section and with the flood that follows. Though Genesis begins with the creation of the world by God (Gen 1:1) and the *Metamorphoses* starts in chaos (*Met.* 1.7), both begin in a state of undifferentiated formlessness (Gen 1:2; *Met.* 1.7–20). Next God (or, according to *Met.* 1.21, "a good-willed nature") separates land from sky and sea from earth (Gen 1:6–10; *Met.* 1.22–23). The earth and seas are filled with life, and the heavens with the lights of the sky (Gen 1:11–25; *Met.* 1.69–75). Then, as the pinnacle of creation, a creature to rule over the earth is fashioned (*facio* in both Ovid and the Vulgate; cf. Gen 2:7, 18): the human, made in the image of god and containing some of the stuff of god (whether through seed, breath, or the simple fact that god created all that is material). Humans are created to have "dominion" (Gen 1:26 LXX ἀρχέτωσαν; Vulg. *praesit*; *Met.* 1.77 *dominari*; Vulg.) over the earth and are made in the image and likeness of God (Gen 1:26 LXX εἰκόνα, ὁμοίωσιν; Vulg. *imaginem, similitudinem*; *Met.* 1.83 *effigiem*—or from "divine seed" 1.78). The earth is a paradise (Gen 2:16; *Met.* 1.89–112, "The Golden Age"). But, eventually, humanity leaves this state of perfect peace (Gen 3:14–4:16; *Met.* 1.113–50). The world was a place of giants (Gen 6:4; *Met.* 1.151–55) and was filled with violence, corruption, and evil (Gen 6:5, 11–12; *Met.* 1.127–62). The God of Genesis and Jupiter of the *Metamorphoses* both decide it is time to bring humanity—and all living things—to an end (Gen 6:6–7, 13; *Met.* 1.182–89, 240–41). To accomplish this both decide to create a flood (Gen 6:17; *Met.* 1.260–61). But in each of these stories, one couple who is just and pious (Gen 6:9 LXX δίκαιος, τέλειος; Vulg. *iustus atque perfectus*; *Met.* 322–23, 327, *amantior aequi, metuentior . . . deorum; innocuos, cultores numinis*) is spared through the use of a boat (Gen 6:14–16; *Met.* 1.319). Then, finally, these two couples repopulate the earth (Gen 8:16–19; *Met.* 1.381–415). The *Metamorphoses* and Genesis have been interpreted together as early as Lactantius, advisor to Constantine, and throughout the ages have been interpreted in light of works such as Milton's *Paradise Lost*.

There is much textual work to be done on concurrent readings of Genesis and the *Metamorphoses* to establish if there is a continuous interpretational tradition of the two texts and how early it may have started. Both Lester K. Born ("Ovid and Allegory," *Speculum* 9.4 [1934]: 262–379) and Neil Wright ("Creation and Recreation: Medieval Responses to *Metamorphoses* 1.5–88," in Hardie et al., *Ovidian Transformations*, 68–84) note the lack of secondary literature exploring these connections between Augustine and the medieval period, but Born quotes Rudolph Schevill's study, *Ovid and the Renascence in Spain* (Berkeley: University of California Publications, 1913), 6, who says, "No evidence of any systematic study of the works of Ovid during the early centuries of the Christian era has hitherto been found. It is not likely that he was ever wholly forgotten, but it seems that the reading of his poetry, chiefly the *Metamorphoses*, was of a very casual character, and limited to a few students of the classics, widely scattered over Europe" (Born, 362). For later uses, see both Born and Wright, and particularly in terms of *Paradise Lost*, see Mandy Green, *Milton's Ovidian Eve* (Burlington, VT: Ashgate, 2009).

the Golden, was marked by unprecedented peace. It was an age of justice, where each one knew and kept their place; an age unmarred by war or violence against one another or against the animals or earth: the earth was in perpetual spring (1.89–112). The second age was the Silver. This age was marked by the casting of Saturn to Tartaros and the rise of Jupiter's rule. The Silver race (*proles*) was less than gold and greater than bronze and brought with it the four seasons, the building of houses, the planting of seeds, and the subjugation of animals to work the earth (1.112–24). The earth transitioned to the third age with the Bronze race, "fiercer in nature and more prone to savage war, but not yet impious" (1.125–27).[61]

The final age was that of Iron, an age marked by evil (*peioris*), when "decency, truth and fidelity fled; and deceit, deception, schemes, and violence, and depraved love of possession took their place" (1.128–31).[62] The things of the earth, iron and "more injurious" (*nocentius*) gold, were used to conquer it:

> [W]ar appeared . . . bloodied hands strike one another with clattering arms. Men live by plunder; guest was not protected from host, nor father-in-law from son-in-law; with brothers, too, there was rarely regard. Husband longed for the destruction of wife, and she her husband; and horrific stepmothers mix lurid poisons, and sons seek inheritance before their time. Piety lay vanquished, and virgin Astraea[63] the last of the gods abandons the blood-stained earth. (1.142–50)[64]

In Ovid's initial portrayal of the human-inhabited earth, he presents an ordered world, though one shaped by humans rather than the creator god or nature. Humans' time on earth begins with the Golden Age, a time of peace and harmony between all of earth's creatures as well as between these creatures and the earth itself—as humans live in peace, so too does everything else. The Golden Age slowly devolves with each

---

61. *saevior ingeniis et ad horrida promptior arma, non scelerata tamen.*
62. *fugere pudor verumque fidesque; in quorum subiere locum fraudesque dolusque insidiaeque et vis et amor sceleratus habendi.*
63. Goddess of justice.
64. *prodit bellum . . . / sanguineaque manu crepitantia concutit arma. / Vivitur ex rapto: non hospes ab hospite tutus, / non socer a genero; fratrum quoque gratia rara est. / Inminet exitio vir coniugis, illa mariti; / lurida terribiles miscent aconita novercae; / filius ante diem patrios inquirit in annos: / victa iacet pietas, et virgo caede madentis / ultima caelestum terras Astraea reliquit.*

successive generation transforming the earth into a place of chaos, filled with violence, plunder, conquest, greed, and exploitation.[65]

Ovid again alludes to fraternal discord ("with brothers, too, there was rarely regard"), first found in the description of the winds in 1.145, recalling both the Romulus and Remus episode, foundational to the Rome's origin myths,[66] and the civil wars. In addition, Ovid's line, "Men lived by plunder [*rapio*]: guest was not protected from host, nor father-in-law from son-in-law," which directly precedes the reference to fratricide in 1.145, may provide an allusion to the foundational Sabine narrative, where Rome's neighbors are deceived with the Romans' scheme to abduct (*rapio*) their women, causing war between father-in-law and son-in-law, ultimately ending in the Romans' possession of both their women and their lands—"deceit, deception, scheming, violence, and depraved love of possession" all the attributes of the Iron Age (1.130–31). Not only do these lines evoke the Sabine narratives, but they allude to the civil wars as well. As commentators note, Ovid's telling of the Sabines narrative in the *Fasti* contains an oblique allusion to the civil wars when it comments that it "was the first time that a father warred upon his son-in-law" (*tum primum generis intulit arma soccer*, *Fasti* 3.202), referring to the fact that Caesar's daughter, Julia, was Pompey's wife.[67] This allusion in the *Fasti* adds additional support to Ovid's use of the Sabines intertext here, illustrating the multivalent referents embedded within the *Metamorphoses*.

Civil war erupts in Rome again in the fraternal battles of Octavian and Antony, and Ovid's description of the Iron Age elicits the chaos of war and violence in the period before the Augustan era. But his comment extends it further if turned toward the Augustan era's depiction as a new Golden Age.[68] While Ovid's Iron Age is a reversal

---

65. For the intertextual antecedents from which Ovid crafts his narrative of the four ages, see Fratantuono, *Madness Transformed*, 9–10.
66. Ibid., 10.
67. Ovid, *Fasti* (LCL), 134n.b.; noting more generally this connection see, e.g., Hemker, "Rape and the Founding of Rome," 41–47; Cahoon, "Bed as Battlefield," 298–99.
68. On the Golden Age of Augustus, see Galinsky, *Augustan Culture*, 90–101; Zanker, *Power of Images*, 167–92.

of his Golden, bringing to fruition those things whose absence marks the age of Gold,[69] there are also intra- and intertextual echoes that link the Iron Age with the current Augustan Golden Age. Denis Feeney observes,

> If Caesar, for example, is Saturn, and Augustus is Jupiter [i.e., father and son], then we must now be in the Iron, and not the Golden, Age.[70] Augustus is indeed a great lawgiver, as befits an inhabitant of the Iron Age (15.833); we learnt early in the first book that in the Golden Age men lived without need of laws (1.89–93). The current era is never labeled Golden in the *Metamorphoses*, although it is in other parts of Ovid's work.[71]

Several of the references where Ovid does directly "label" the Golden Age of Augustus are found in the *Ars Amatoria*. Ovid's first reference in the *Ars* seems to draw on the irony of this appellation: "Now is truly an age of gold: with gold comes much honor, with gold love is obtained" (*Ars* 2.277–78).[72] His second reference occurs in book 3 of the *Ars,* where he writes, "Before there was raw simplicity, but now Rome is golden and possesses the vast wealth of the conquered world" (*Ars* 3.112–13). In these lines, gold is connected with the ability to purchase honor and seduce, with the trappings of empire. Ovid evokes these images in the *Metamorphoses* when he remarks that iron and "more injurious" gold would be used to conquer and remake the world (1.141). In these Ovidian lines, gold no longer represents the Golden Age, but is instead a tool of Iron—an age of war, conquest, and posturing. In these passages, Ovid draws on the paradoxes inherent in the Golden Age of the *Pax Romana*, where war brings peace, honor can be obtained through wealth rather than acts, and the elevation of some is predicated on the subjugation of others.[73]

---

69. See Galinsky, *Augustan Culture*, 99–100: "The Golden Age is characterized not by positive aspects of its own, but by the absence of contemporary practices, greed and war in particular" (100). See also Lively, *Ovid's* Metamorphoses: *A Reader's Guide*, 18.

70. Augustus is linked to Jupiter through both the defeat of the Giants, and particularly in the Palatine Hill metaphor in *Met.* 1.163–205.

71. Feeney, *Gods in Epic*, 221, "*Ars* 2.277; 3.113. It need hardly be said that these references in the *Ars* are not straight-faced.

72. *Aurea sunt vere nunc saecula: plurimus auro / Venit honos: auro conciliator amor.* Cf. Lively, *Ovid's* Metamorphoses: *A Reader's Guide*, 19; Davis, *Ovid and Augustus*, 29–30.

73. It is important to realize that these are oversimplified tropes but are those that represent the streamlined ideology of both the mythological and visual programs of the era; see chapter 1.

Significantly, as explored in the previous chapter, much of Augustus's program for the Golden Age was predicated on a return to the past, an appeal to origins and aetiologies.[74] The whole of the *Metamorphoses* mimics this impulse, as Ovid, too, appeals to origins and aetiologies, but to different ends. Instead of using these in an effort to create stability, he uses them as a sign of mutability, a way to show the ever-shifting and changing reality that not only led up to but continued to mark the Augustan era. As Galinsky notes, "In the Republic, the late Republic in particular, the eternity of Rome was presented as a call to action—it was the Romans' duty to make their city everlasting. In Augustan times, this emphasis receded and the eternity of Rome appears as a god-given reality."[75] But Ovid not only stresses Rome's change through growth, as Vergil does in the *Aeneid*, but "associates Rome with the fallen cities of the past (15.426-430). Troy, Sparta, Mycenae, Thebes and Athens have grown and passed away, and so will Rome."[76] With Ovid's pen the Golden Age of Augustus becomes alloyed with Iron—the age Ovid frames using Augustus's own foundational myths: Romulus and Remus, the Sabines, and Actium—and the very foundations that provide stability to the Augustan myth are transformed into symbols of mutability by Ovid.

The Defeat of the Giants

The description of the devolution through the four ages is followed

---

Galinsky notes that the Golden Age during the reign of Augustus "comes to connote a social order rather than a paradisiac state" (*Augustan Culture*, 93). He reads these passages in the *Ars* in terms of this outlook—the past is simplistic, crude, and slothful, while the "present" is based on taste and culture with echoes of the Vergilian virtue of labor (99–100). These attributes are certainly part of the complexities of the age, but, in my view, this seems to be an overly optimistic reading of Ovid.

74. Galinsky, *Augustan Culture*, 98–99; Zanker, *Power of Images*, 167–298.
75. Galinsky, *Ovid's* Metamorphoses, 43.
76. Ibid., 44, citing *Aeneid* 3.374ff and *Met*. 15.434 on the growth of Rome. Galinsky also contrasts Rome's fate in the *Metamorphoses* with Ovid's own self-proclaimed fate: "At the end of Book 15, Ovid makes an even more pointed comment on the transience of Rome by contrasting it with the permanence of his own name. In this epilogue, which is full of echoes of Horace's triumphant ode on his own poetic fame, Ovid, unlike Horace, does not equate the eternity of Rome with his own. He is polite enough to say that his work will be read wherever Rome's power extends over the conquered earth, but it is he, and not Rome, who will have permanence" (15.875–76). During his time, Ovid's closing remarks were probably viewed by many as hubris, but in many ways ended up being prophetic.

by another episode with Augustan allusions: the defeat of the giants. Though this consists of a few scant lines (1.151–62), it was unnecessary for Ovid to elaborate the myth since the "battle between the gods and giants would have been over-familiar to Ovid's Roman audience as an allegory for the recent civil war, with Jupiter's inevitable victory and restoration of order here, seen as an obvious . . . parallel for Augustus."[77] The short gigantomachy provides a thematic segue between Ovid's continuing allusions to the civil war in the description of the Iron Age, and the identification of Jupiter and Augustus in the scene that follows.[78]

The short gigantomachy packs an additional punch in the analysis of Stephen Michael Wheeler and John Miller, who argue for a connection between Ovid's narrative of the giants, Apollo's slaying of Python, and the battle at Actium.[79] While Wheeler observes, "Narratively speaking, Apollo's triumph over the forces of chaos repeats the gigantomachy,"[80] Miller's detailed textual analysis extends this observation, specifically highlighting the connections between Ovid's story of the giants and that of Apollo and Python. First, both the giants episode (1.151–62) and the Python episode (1.438–49) are composed of twelve lines each. The first three verses of each focus on "the threatening monstrosity—the Giants piling up mountains to attack heaven (1.151–53), huge Python [having just emerged from the 'chaotic' mud][81] dominating the mountain and frightening the people (1.438–40)."[82] Second, the

---

77. Lively, *Ovid's Metamorphoses: A Reader's Guide*, 19. In the ellipses of the quotation is a parenthetical note that this association between Jupiter and Augustus would be seen as "unequivocally positive." While this is certainly one possible way to read this association, I do not believe it is the only way, as the flexibility of Ovid's text readily opens a variety of interpretations. Lively also mentions that "the sub-genre of gigantomachy with its reputation as the dullest of dull epic, was unpopular among Augustan poets aspiring to a sophisticated Callimachean aesthetic: Ovid even jokes in his *Amores* (2.11–20) that, once upon a time, he had started to write a gigantomachy but had stopped when he realized that it just wasn't 'sexy' enough and that this was not the sort of poetry that would ever get a girl into bed with him" (ibid., 19–20). See also Alison Sharrock, *Seduction and Repetition in Ovid's Ars Amatoria 2* (Oxford: Clarendon, 1994), 115–16; cf. Galinsky, who says, "there is no reason we should not take Ovid's statement [regarding the writing of a gigantomachy in the *Amores*] at face value" (*Ovid's* Metamorphoses, 25).

78. On the connection between the civil war and gigantomachy, see Feeney, *Gods in Epic*, 297; Philip R. Hardie, *Virgil's Aeneid: Cosmos and Imperium* (Oxford: Oxford University Press, 1986), 381; Miller, *Apollo, Augustus, and the Poets*, 68, 301–7, and esp. 334, 336, 340 in conjunction with *Met.* 1.151–62.

79. Wheeler, *Narrative Dynamics*, 55; and Miller, *Apollo, Augustus, and the Poets*, 338–43.

80. Wheeler, *Narrative Dynamics*, 55.

81. See Lively, *Ovid's* Metamorphoses: A Reader's Guide, 25.

147

"Omnipotent Father," that is, Jupiter, "launched his thunderbolts, shattering Olympus, and struck down Mount Pelion from underlying Mount Ossa" (1.154–55), just as Phoebus, "crush[ed Python] with a thousand arrows" (1.442–44).[83] Third, in these accounts, "Ovid puts the gory aftermath of both combats on display: 'Earth is overspread with much blood' of the Giants (1.157 *perfusam multo . . . sanguine Terram*); 'poison spread forth through the dark wounds' of Python (1.444 *effuso per vulnera nigra veneno*)."[84] Here, "Apollo clearly follows in his father's footsteps as a creator of order."[85] The two episodes are finally linked by respectively ending "with negatively purposed memorials, in one case the victims' parent (Earth/Terra) wanting to avoid neglect of her children's memory (1.159), in the latter instance the divine archer intent on staving off oblivion of his own epic deed (1.445)."[86]

Through several intertextual allusions within Propertius and the *Aeneid*, Miller establishes connections between Ovid's Apollo and Python narrative and the battle of Actium.[87] He then shows how resonances between the Apollo and Python episode and Actium are also recalled through its pairing with Apollo and Daphne. As Apollo triumphs over the chaotic forces of the Egypt-created Python (1.422–26),[88] which threaten the *populisque* (1.439), so too Augustus triumphs over the chaotic forces of Cleopatran Egypt and Antony, which threaten the Roman *populi*, with the aid of Apollo.[89] After Apollo defeats Python, the aetiological narrative of the laurel follows, Apollo's personal symbol conquest and victory,[90] which becomes a universal

---

82. Miller, *Apollo, Augustus, and the Poets*, 340.
83. See both Wheeler, *Narrative Dynamics*, 55; and Miller, *Apollo, Augustus, and the Poets*, 340.
84. Again, Wheeler, *Narrative Dynamics*, 55; and Miller, *Apollo, Augustus, and the Poets*, 340; quotation is from Miller.
85. Wheeler, *Narrative Dynamics*, 55.
86. Miller, *Apollo, Augustus, and the Poets*, 340.
87. See intertextual analysis with Propertius 4.6, in Miller, *Apollo, Augustus, and the Poets*, 340–41; *Aeneid* 3.280, Miller, 341; *Aeneid* 6.69-70, Miller, 341–42; and *Aeneid* 3.75, 9, Miller, 342–43.
88. The laurel replaces the oak, which is also a symbol of the civic crown, given to Romans who save fellow citizens' lives in battle. The oak will be guarded and watched over by the laurel at the doors of Augustus's home on the Palatine—now that it has been created (1.562–63); see Fratantuono, *Madness Transformed*, 17; and Hollis, "Ovid, Metamorphoses 1.445ff.," 69–73.
89. See Eck, *Age of Augustus*, 43.
90. See Fratantuono, *Madneww Transformed*, 17; Zanker, *Power of Images*, 49–50, 92–94.

one, and the symbol of conquest and victory presented to Octavian as he celebrated his triumph over Cleopatra and Antony in Rome.[91]

Lycaon and the Olympian Palatine

With the giants defeated, Earth/Terra "soaked in their streaming blood, birthed the warm gore with life, and lest no memory of her descendants remain, she transformed it to human form" (1.157–60).[92] These new beings of transformed earth and gore "despised the gods, they were cruel, greedy for slaughter, and violent" (1.161–62)[93] —displaying the same characteristics as the humans of the Iron Age and embodying the violence that originally transformed the giants into earth and gore. It is these characteristics through which Ovid transitions into the story of Lycaon—and all of humanity's —punishment by Jupiter.

Lycaon's actions—exemplifying the impiety, cruelty, and violence of the humans/giant-humans of the Iron Age—are directed against Jupiter, but at this point in the narrative Ovid has only mentioned Lycaon's "filthy feast" (1.165) and Jupiter's "vast rage" (*ingentes . . . iras*, 1.166) at his recollection of it. In fact, Lycaon's meal of human flesh (1.226–29) and attempt on Jupiter's life (1.224–25) will not be mentioned until later in the tale, the reader/hearer unaware at this juncture of exactly what Lycaon has done. As Jupiter recollects his encounter with Lycaon, he immediately convenes a council (*conciliumque*) of the gods, who respond to his summons without delay (1.167).

---

91. Mary Beard relays this account from Pliny, *Nat. Hist.* 15.136–37: "Toward the end of his long account of the laurel and its various uses, Pliny tells the story of an unusual laurel grove at the imperial villa known as 'The Hennery' (*Ad Gallinas*), just outside Rome. It had been planted from the sprig of laurel held in the beak of a white hen that had been dropped by an eagle into the lap of the unsuspecting Livia, just after her betrothal to Octavian. It was obviously an omen of their future greatness. So the soothsayers (*haruspices*) ordered that the bird and any future brood should be carefully preserved—hence the name of the villa—and that the laurel should be planted. It successfully took root, and when Octavian triumphed in 29 BCE he wore a wreath and carried in his hand a branch after the triumphal ceremony and calling the resulting trees by the name of the emperor or prince concerned. A veritable Julio-Claudian memorial grove" (*Roman Triumph*, 287).

92. *perfusam multo natorum sanguine Terram immaduisse ferunt calidumque animasse cruorem et, ne nulla suae stirpis monimenta manerent, in faciem vertisse hominum.*

93. *contemptrix superum saevaeque avidissima caedis et violenta fuit.*

As the council is called, the *Metamorphoses* presents its first overt references to Augustus. These occur as Ovid describes the dwelling place of the gods:

> There is a lofty road, evident when the heavens are clear, called the Milky Way, distinguished by its dazzling brightness. This is the way the gods take to the royal dwelling of the great Thunderer. To the right and left, the courts of noble gods are filled with throngs, doors flung wide. (The plebeian gods dwell in a different place.) In this neighborhood the distinguished and mighty deities place their household gods. This is the place which, if I were afforded the audacity to say it, I would not fear to declare the Palatine of mighty heaven. (1.168–76)[94]

As Feeney observes, this is a "bold inversion of the expected terms of comparison, as the seat of divine government is compared to the residence of Augustus."[95] Just as each element, creature, and god has been assigned to their specific place in the order of things, so too, each class of gods is assigned to a social organization that mimics that of Rome: Jupiter Tonans's *domus* ("dwelling") mirrors that of Augustus;[96] while the atria of the noble gods are thronged, the lower gods live elsewhere, as the plebs; and the distinguished gods, the *clari* (i.e., Roman aristocrats) even set up shines for their own penates ("household gods").[97] Both Miller and Feeney note the "precise" nature of the correlation given that "Augustus held senate meetings in the library attached to his temple of Apollo on the Palatine, which was itself intimately linked with his residence."[98] This correlation between

---

94. *Est via sublimis, caelo manifesta sereno; / lacteal nomen habet, candore notabilis ipso. / hac iter est superis ad magni tecta Tonantis / regalemque domum: dextra laevaque deorum / atria nobilium valvis celebrantur apertis. / plebs habitat diversa locis: hac parte potentes / caelicolae clarique suos posuere penates; / hic locus est, quem, si verbis audacia detur, / haud timeam magni dixisse Palatia caeli.*

95. Feeney, *Gods in Epic*, 199.

96. Augustus built a temple of Jupiter Tonanas on the Capitoline after being "miraculously spared when a lightning bolt grazed him and struck the salve lighting the way for him" during his campaign against the Cantabri (Zanker, *Power of Images*, 108). Miller notes this connection and asserts that it "retrospectively imparts Augustan meaning to Jupiter shattering the Giants with his thunderbolt just previously" (*Apollo, Augustus, and the Poets*, 151–55). Miller continues with an extended analysis of Ovid's displacement of the Palatine Apollo with the Capitoline Jupiter Tonanas (already a source of controversy for rivaling the Capitoline Jupiter and corresponding temple)—"no less a part of the poet's audacia" than linking Olympus with the Palatine itself (336). See also Zanker, *Power of Images*, 186–87. This is the type of social organization that Galinsky emphasizes is a hallmark of the Golden Age of Augustus (*Augustan Culture*, 95).

97. See Miller, *Apollo, Augustus, and the Poets*, 334; Lively, *Ovid's* Metamorphoses: *A Reader's Guide*, 20–21.

Jupiter's council and the Roman Senate continues as the narrative proceeds.

Jupiter addresses the council, pronouncing that he has never been "more anxious for the sovereignty of the world" (1.182) and advising, "wherever Nereus[99] fills the world with sound, the human race must be destroyed" (1.187–88). Jupiter then speaks of the necessity of saving some—"the uncorrupted"—from Nereus's flood, that is, the demigods, rustic deities, nymphs, fauns, satyrs, and the mountain spirits. But these, too, are threatened by the scourge of humans. Alluding to the tale of Lycaon still to come, Jupiter asks how these other creatures will remain safe when humans, like the fierce Lycaon, have the audacity to "concoct a plot against me," the one who "wields the thunderbolt and who has and rules you?" (1.196–97).[100]

The connection between Jupiter's council and the Roman senate is vivid as Ovid describes the scene of the proceeding: "All clamored, and with burning zeal demanded the one who dared such infamy. As when impious hands were raging to extinguish the name of Rome with Caesar's blood, the human race was thunderstruck with an approaching terror of great ruin. Nor is the piety of your subjects, Augustus, less pleasing to you than Jove" (1.199–205).[101] This passage contains one of the four instances in which Ovid invokes the name of Augustus, the second occurring within the Apollo and Daphne narrative of book 1 (1.561) and the other two occurring in close proximity in book 15 (15.860 and 15.869), the final book of the *Metamorphoses*.[102] The location of these references at the beginning and end of the work form an *inclusio*, serving as a way to frame the entire

98. "Precise" is Miller's word (*Apollo, Augustus, and the Poets*, 335); the quotation is Feeney's (*Gods in Epic*, 119). Both authors note Suetonius, *Aug.* 29.3.
99. A sea god, son of Oceanus and Tethys, father of the Nereids.
100. *cum mihi, qui fulmen, qui vos habeoque regoque, struxerit insidias notus feritate Lycaon?*
101. *Confremuere omnes studiisque ardentibus ausum talia deposcunt: sic, cum manus inpia saevit sanguine Caesareo Romanum exstinguere nomen, attonitum tantae subito terrore ruinae humanum genus est totusque perhorruit orbis; nec tibi grata minus pietas, Auguste, tuorum quam fuit illa Iovi.*
102. The nominal Augustus is used adjectively in 6.73, the Pallas and Arachne narrative in relation to Jove and the gods; in 9.270, the apotheosis of Hercules—he becomes *august*; and in 15.145, by Pythagoras referring to his own words as "Delphic."

poem in the terms Ovid sets out in the proem: to sing an unbroken narrative "from the beginning of the world to my times" (1.4).

This first use of Augustus's name is unique in that it is an apostrophe, addressed to the princeps himself. As Miller notes, the "simile and address to the Princeps extend the Jovian compliment in the idea of *Palatia caeli* [Palatine of heaven]. Roman loyalty to Augustus in the wake of a foiled assassination attempt is fitting subject for a tribute, amplified here by sustained hyperbole: the conspirators were keen 'to extinguish Rome's name by shedding Caesar's blood'; in response, 'the human race was thunderstruck with sudden terror of such great ruination and the entire world shuddered' (1.200–203)."[103] The loyalty of the Romans to Augustus is then mirrored in the council's complete assent to Jupiter's actions after he tells his tale of the attempt on his own life by Lycaon (1.244–45).[104]

These comparisons are revisited in the final set of Augustan verses at the end of the *Metamorphoses*. This last portion of the poem leads with the apotheosis of Julius Caesar, "a god in his own city" (*in urbe sua deus est*, 15.746), and a list of his accomplishments (15.746–48, 752–58). Ovid emphasizes that the greatest of these acts was fathering Augustus and this, in particular, is what made Caesar a god (15.750–51, 759–61).[105] The text is clear that Caesar's deeds were not the primary reason for his divinization but rather the necessity of Augustus's own divinity: "So

---

103. Miller, *Apollo, Augustus, and the Poets*, 337, where he also links this to *Aen.* 1.148–52 and Horace *Od.* 1.21.14. Regarding whether the assassination attempt referred to Julius Caesar or to Augustus, see Feeney, *Gods in Epic*, 199 and, whom both Miller and Feeney cite, Otto Stein Due, *Changing Forms: Studies in the Metamorphoses of Ovid* (Copenhagen: Museum Tusculanum Press, 1974), 71–72. Due was the first to suggest that Ovid was referring to the 23 BCE plot against Augustus by Fannius Caepio and his co-conspirators. Feeney (199n41) also cites D. L. Thompson ("The Meeting of the Roman Senate on the Palatine," *AJA* 85 [1981]: 339), saying, "The correspondence of the simile is very close indeed if Thompson is right in suggesting that Senate meeting in Apollo Palatinus began in 23 BCE, with Augustus' convalescence from his near-fatal illness; for it may then have been in the temple of Apollo that the news was announced of the attempt on Augustus' life by Caepio and Murena." Fratantuono (*Madness Transformed*, 27n28) wonders why both Caesar and Augustus cannot be invoked by the passage. Especially given the ambiguities of the poem as a whole, there is no reason to think that this is not the case.

104. Feeney (*Gods in Epic*, 199n41) notes L. P. Wilkinson, *Ovid Recalled* (Cambridge: Cambridge University Press, 1955), 195; and Ahl, *Metaformations*, 79, on the parallels between Jupiter's council and senatorial procedure.

105. Of course, Augustus has been adopted by Julius Caesar; Caesar is not his biological father.

that his son might not be born of mortal seed, Caesar must be made a god" (15.760–61).[106]

Ovid then leaves Julius Caesar and moves to the acts of Augustus himself, though not yet naming him:

> Why should I count for you the barbarian lands or races between the oceans? Whatever habitable land the earth holds will be his, and the sea will also be his slave! When peace has been bestowed to the lands, he will turn his sensibility to civil matters and, as a just executer, give laws. By his own example he will govern morals, and looking forward to future times and coming generations, he will appoint his son, child of his pure wife, to bear both his name and his cares. (15.829–37)[107]

Feeney notes that 15.832–34 has been associated with phrases from Augustus's *Res Gestae*, and, though there are issues with anachronism, he thinks it likely that "the final version of the inscription contains language already familiar from the official self-presentation of the princeps."[108] So, although Augustus is not named, it is likely that it is his own voice that makes an appearance here, further grounding associations from the "real world" into the world of the poem.[109]

The climax of this section occurs at 15.858, returning to the comparison of Jupiter and Augustus found in book 1 and once again invoking him by name:

> Jupiter rules the citadels of the heavens and the three-fold kingdoms of the world, but the earth is subject to Augustus: both are father and leader. Gods, I pray you, companions of Aeneas, before whom sword and fire yield, and you native gods of Italy, Quirinus, sire of our city, and Gradivus, sire of unconquerable Quirinus, and Vesta, who holds a sacred place among Caesar's household gods, and with Caesarean Vesta, you Phoebus of the household, and Jupiter, who holds the Tarpeian citadel on high, and every other whom it is lawful and pious for the poet to address. May that day be delayed and later than our time, when the life of Augustus

---

106. *ne foret hic igitur mortali semine cretus, ille deus faciendus erat.*
107. *quid tibi barbariam gentesque ab utroque iacentes / oceano numerem? quodcunque habitabile tellus / sustnet, huius erit: pontus quoque serviet illi! / Pace data terri animum ad civilia vertet / iura suum legesque ferret iustissimus auctor / exemploque suo mores reget inque future / temporis aetatem venturorumque nepotum / prospiciens prolem sancta de coniuge natam / ferre simul monemque suum curasque iubebit.*
108. Feeney, *Gods in Epic*, 73–74; quotation from 74n26.
109. Ibid., 74.

leaves the world he rules and is added to heaven, and removed from our presence, keep our prayers!" (15.858–70)[110]

After once again juxtaposing Jupiter and Augustus, Ovid invokes the founding deities of Rome. He begins by naming Romulus, the *genitor* ("sire") of the city, and Mars, the *genitor* ("sire") of Romulus. Next, he names Vesta, goddess of Rome's hearth and the one who secures the inviolability of the city, who is intimately connected with Romulus and Mars through the myth of Rhea Silvia, the Vestal whose rape by Mars produced Rome's founder. Vesta is also connected to the founding myths through the Vestal Tarpeia. Tarpeia, then, completes Ovid's round by linking Jupiter back to these founding myths through connecting the location of his temple with the Tarpeian Citadel—Tarpeia, the Citadel, and Jupiter's temple being integral parts of the Sabine narrative. As explored in chapter 1, the importance of this cycle of deities is expressed in the Basilica Aemilia frieze in the Roman Forum: the two small fragments probably depicting either Mars's rape of Rhea Silvia or the twins nursed by the she-wolf with the other showing Romulus's and Remus's abandonment at the Tiber; and the larger fragments showing Romulus and Remus leaving Alba Longa for Rome; the building of Rome's walls, the Consualia and the rape of the Sabines, Romulus's hand-to-hand combat with Acron and the *spolia opima* (connecting the scene to Jupiter), and the punishment of the Tarpeia[111] —the deities invoked here in Ovid's text.

These connections are further emphasized as Ovid names Vesta and Apollo among Augustus's household gods. This pairing of Vesta and Apollo is significant on two levels. First, Apollo is the deity who secured the victory of Octavian over Antony at Actium, thus ushering in both the peace and dominance of Rome. Second is the location of Apollo's

---

110. *Iuppiter arces / temperat aetherias et mundi regna triformis, / terra sub Augusto est; pater est et rector uterque. / di, precor, Aeneae comites, quibus ensis et ignis / cesserunt, dique Indigetes genitorque Quirine / urbis et invicti genitor Gradive Quirini / Vestaque Caesarea tu, Phoebe domestice, Vesta, / quique tenes altus Tarpeias Iuppiter arces, / quosque alios vati fas appellare piumque est: / tarda sit illa dies et nostro serior aevo, / qua caput Augustum, quem temperat, orbe relicto / accedat caelo faveatque precantibus absens!*

111. Albertson () argues for a dating of the frieze between 55 and 34 BCE ("Basilica Aemilia Frieze"). For arguments for the alternate dating of the frieze to 14 BCE, see Kampen, "Reliefs of the Basilica Aemilia," See chapter 1 of this study.

temple on the Palatine, attached directly to Augustus's residence—and linked to book 1 through the Jupiter's council and the Roman senate[112]—and the relocation of Vesta's shrine to Augustus's house on the Palatine after he was elected *pontifex maximus* in 12 BCE, connecting both deities to the *domus* of Augustus. As Beard, John North and Simon Price note, with the relocation of Vesta's shrine, "the public hearth of the state, with its associations of the success of the Roman empire, had been fused with the private hearth of Augustus. The emperor (and the emperor's house) could now be claimed to stand for the state."[113] The same holds true for the relocation of the senate—even if only temporary—to the temple of Apollo on the Palatine, physically connecting the Senate House with Augustus's home.

Both Feeney and Miller point to the continued blurring of public and private realms during the Augustan Age, illustrated here in Ovid's naming of the state deities Vesta and Apollo as "household gods."[114] Feeney argues that this blurring extends to the other gods in the passage as well: specifically, Mars and Jupiter. He notes that in *Augustus* 29.1, Suetonius "chooses Mars Ultor, Apollo Palatinus, and Jupiter Tonans for special mention," and raises the question as to whether the Jupiter associated with the Tarpeian Citadel should actually be associated with Augustus's new temple to Jupiter Tonans rather than the temple of Jupiter Optimus Maximus, the latter temple having been usurped when the "Sibylline books [were] removed from his [i.e., Jupiter Optimus Maximus's] care and entrusted to Augustus' Apollo Palatinus, [and] the elaborate ceremonials which inaugurated and terminated the military expeditions of Rome were now staged before Augustus' Mars Ultor."[115]

Furthermore, the first names invoked by Ovid are Aeneas and Romulus, through whom Augustus traced his own divine lineage to

---

112. See the discussion of this above.

113. Mary Beard, John North, and Simon Price, *Religions of Rome*, vol. 1, *A History* (New York: Cambridge University Press, 1998), 191; see 188–92 on Augustus, *pontifex maximus*, and Vesta.

114. Miller, *Apollo, Augustus, and the Poets*, 369; Feeney, *Gods in Epic*, 215–16.

115. Feeney, *Gods in Epic*, 216–17. Regardless of which Jupiter is being invoked, it does not change the associations with Tarpeia and the Sabines narrative, as stated earlier—here again, Ovid's text opens rather than forecloses meanings.

Venus and Mars.[116] The prominence of these two figures in Augustan mythology is well attested to by their positions in places such as Augustus's forum[117] and their juxtaposition on the reliefs at the front of the Ara Pacis.[118] As Zanker highlights, Aeneas is the paradigm of *pietas*, as he rescues both the Penates (housed in the temple of Vesta "as guarantors of Rome's safety") and his father, in Augustus's new mythology, while Romulus, the first to conquer, dedicate *spolia opima*, and triumph, becomes the paradigm of *virtus*[119]—*pietas* and *virtus* Rome's two primary virtues.[120] As *pietas* is a "cooperative" virtue connected to "social responsibility" and "obligations to family, country, and gods,"[121] *virtus* is linked with "manly valor on the battle field," hence the corresponding word *victoria*, or victory.

Octavian embodies this in his triumph over Cleopatra and Antony, by "achiev[ing] military *virtus*, which he will continue to exercise against foreign peoples as the imperator of the Roman state."[122] But *virtus* was also associated with "moral effort" and a quality of the great statesmen of the age including Marius, Caesar, and Pompey—those whose acts served Rome.[123] With the external and internal, military and moral, aspects of *virtus*, Galinsky notes there is "a significant moral corollary to [Rome's ongoing] mission [of foreign conquest] and its underlying military *virtus*."[124] This corollary is the Augustan moral legislation, the *Leges Juliae*, or Julian Laws, specifically those regulating marriages of the senatorial and equestrian orders.

This legislation was "aimed particularly at the governing classes," because "the Roman ruling class was also ruling an empire;" and if the Roman people were to be viewed as "the imperial civilizers of the

116. Zanker, *Power of Images*, 195.
117. Ibid., 201; fig. 149, p. 194. Aeneas and Romulus mirror Venus and Mars (in addition to the statues, Mars, Venus, and Romulus are all featured on the temple of Mars Ultor's pediment—as well as Fortuna and Roma).
118. Ibid., 203.
119. Ibid., 201–3.
120. Galinsky, *Augustan Culture*, 84 (citing Propertius 3.22.21–22).
121. Ibid., 86.
122. Ibid., 84.
123. Ibid., citing Donald Earl, *The Moral and Political Tradition of Rome* (London: Thames & Hudson, 1967) 21.
124. Galinsky, *Augustan Culture*, 84.

world," Augustus had "to make the ruling classes of Rome and Italy into a morally superior people."[125] Through this moral legislation, Roman law, in many ways took the role of the *paterfamilias*, transferring the jurisdiction of marriage, adultery, and rape to the state.[126] This idea of Roman law as *paterfamilias* is represented by the statue of the quadriga, the horse-drawn carriage of the victor,[127] dedicated to Augustus by the senate and inscribed with the title *Pater Patriae* ("Father of the Fatherland") along with a list of his conquests.[128] This statue sat in the center of Augustus's forum, surrounded by the images of Aeneas, Romulus, and the temple of Mars Ultor.[129] This title, in conjunction with the privatizing of the public sphere through state worship (i.e., the movement of the Vestals and Penates to the Palatine, Augustus becoming *pontifex maximus*, and so on) and the publicizing of the private sphere through the *Leges Juliae*, exemplifies the wider construct of this slippage between public and private illustrated by this section of the *Metamorphoses*.

Again, this slippage between public and private also extends to figures of Venus and Mars. As mentioned in chapter 1, several passages in the *Amores* emphasize the adulterous relationship, contrary to the Julian moral legislation, of Mars and Venus[130]—a story that occurs in *Met.* 4.167–89 as well, and makes Vulcan, rather than Mars and Venus, look the fool. Ovid evokes the *Leges Juliae* legislation in the *Amores* again when he frames the birth of Romulus and Remus as Mars's "crime" (*crimine*) against Ilia.[131]

125. Ibid., 132–33.
126. Ibid., 130. See also the discussion in chapter 1.
127. See DH 2.34.1–2, where Romulus "carrying with him the spoils [λαφύρων] of those who had been slain in battle and the choicest part of the booty [ἀκροθίνια] as an offering to the gods; and offered many sacrifices [θυσίας] as well. [Romulus] himself came last in the procession [πομπῆς], clad in a purple robe and wearing a crown of laurel [δάφνη] upon his head, and . . . he rode in a chariot drawn by four horses.[127] The rest of the army . . . followed . . . praising the gods in songs of their fathers [πατρίοις] and honoring their general [ἡγεμόνα] in improvised verses. The citizens who met them with their wives and children lined each side of the road, rejoicing in their victory [νίκη] and welcoming [φιλοφροσύνην] them in every other way."
128. Zanker, *Power of Images*, 129, 2 BCE; *Res Gestae* 35.
129. Galinsky, *Augustan Culture*, 133; Zanker, *Power of Images*, 214.
130. Davis, "Ovid's Amores," 442–43. See *Amores* 1.8, 2.5, 2.9, and 1.2 and 3.9 for the familial relationship between Cupid and Augustus (Cupid was the "love child" of Mars and Venus's adulterous affair). See also Sharrock, "Ovid and the Politics of Reading," and her *Seduction and Repetition*.
131. Both Davis ("Ovid's Amores," 444) and Zanker (*Power of Images*, 195) note the use of "Ilia" by the

Emphasizing the more "positive" aspects of these new laws, Ovid directly links Augustus to his moral legislation in 15.832–37, where he says, "When peace [*pace*] has been afforded to the lands, he will turn his sensibility to civil law and justly promote it. By his own example he will direct morals and, looking forward to future times and coming generations, he will appoint his son, child of his pure wife, to bear both his name and his cares."[132] Here the connection between worldwide and internal *pax* ("peace") is made explicit—the *pax* in the world creating an opportunity for law and justice—and peace—in Rome itself. Augustus will be the exemplar for the morality of both nation and imperium, with his son, the child of this moral man, and his *sancta* ("holy") wife, Livia, also being examples of Roman virtue.[133]

Finally, of import is the way in which these passages underscore the slippage between and metamorphosis of man to god. In book 1, Ovid links Augustus with both Jupiter and Apollo, associations that extend through this portion of book 15. In book 15, though, the emphasis is not simply on Augustus's divine associations but on his divine origins. Here, all of the divine ancestors of the Julian line and Rome itself are invoked, and Caesar's apotheosis is based on the fact that Augustus is his son. While Augustus is still alive, and has yet to rise to the heavens, the fact that he will do so is not in question—and neither is his divinity. As the gods become human through their actions, so too humans (at least an ordained few) can become gods.

With these links established, I want to conclude with some of Miller's observations on the less complimentary implications of the initial analogy between Jupiter and Augustus found in book 1. As Miller observes,

> The gods at the council are toadies who instantly register their agreement with the king. They all clamor for Lycaon's punishment (1.199–200) before

Augustan poets rather than Rhea Silvia, linking her to Ilium, that is, Troy, and belonging to the Trojan family of Aeneas.

132. *Pace data terries animum ad civilia vertet / iura suum legesque ferret iustissimus auctor / exemploque suo mores reget inque futuri / temporis aetatem venturorumque nepotum / prospiciens prolem sancta de coniuge natam / ferre simul nomenque suum curasque iubebit.*

133. Fergus Millar reads this portion of book 15 as being marked by "an overt loyalism" ("Ovid and the *Domus Augusta*: Rome Seen from Tomoi," *Journal of Roman Studies* 83 [1990]: 6–9; quotation from 9).

hearing any particulars of the case—of course the malefactor has already paid the penalty. When Jove reiterates the need to wipe out "conspiratorial" humanity (1.242 *iurasse*), the councilors are divided only between approving shouts that inflame the angry king still more and adulatory applause (1.244-45). . . . The Ovidian proceeding is clearly a sham from the start, convened by irate Jupiter (1.166), who then totally dominates the stage. . . . The angry fixation on Lycaon also creates the impression that Jupiter is destroying all mankind as revenge upon a single heinous mortal.[134] Some readers may distinguish between the irascible tyrant Jupiter surrounded by sycophants and Augustus the glorious chief resident of the Palatine to whose side Romans rallied at a critical juncture. . . . Others will take the Augustan similes and Jovian actions to be interdependent, finding it difficult not to see something of the increasingly autocratic Augustus in the ill-humored *pater omnipotens* who dominates the poem's first narrative sequence.[135]

The Transformation of Lycaon, the Flood, and Deucalion and Pyrrha

The first "true" metamorphosis of the poem occurs as Lycaon is punished by Jupiter for his deeds—a punishment Jupiter has already doled out by the time he convenes the council.[136] The text connects Lycaon's cannibalistic feast (1.226-29—which the reader is hearing about for the first time now) and his attempt on Jupiter's life (1.224-25) directly to his impiety (1.220-21).[137] In response, Jupiter uses his thunderbolt to "overturn [his] house upon its household gods" (*everti tecta penates*, 1.230-31) and Lycaon "flees in terror" (*territus . . . fugit*, 1.232).[138] As he flees, his outer form begins to reflect his inner impulses: "His mouth itself gathers foam, and with his accustomed lust for slaughter turns against the flocks, delighting still in blood. His clothes change to tufts of hair, his arms to legs. He is made a wolf and yet keeps

---

134. Jupiter says, "One house has perished, but not only one deserves to be destroyed," *occidit una domus, se non domus una perire digna fuit* (1.240-41).

135. Miller, *Apollo, Augustus, and the Poets*, 337-38.

136. For a creative and informative reading on *Met.* 1.163-245 comparing the punishment of Lycaon and the council of the gods to the changing Roman system under Augustus, see K. Balsley, "Truthseeking and Truthmaking in Ovid's *Metamorphoses* 1.163-245," *Law and Literature* 23.1 (2011): 48-70.

137. Lycaon "mocks the pious prayers" (*inridet . . . pia vota*) of those worshiping Jupiter. The founding of the worship sites at Mount Lycaeus to Jupiter and his son Mercury are attributed to Lycaon (Fratantuono, *Madness Transformed*, 13; see also 27nn31-32).

138. Like Daphne, though for very different reasons, Lycaon flees from the gods.

a vestige of his former form. There is the same grey hair, the same fierce face, the same shining eyes, the same feral image" (1.234–39).[139] Of note here, in this first of the *Metamorphoses*'s transformations, is the connection between the inner person and the person's outer transformed form. Who a person is and what characterizes that person is elicited as the slipperiness between animal, plant, human, and god flows throughout Ovid's tales of metamorphosis, asking larger questions about identity in the ever-changing Roman context.[140] These are the same types of questions that emerge as the lines between human and divine are blurred in the climax of book 15, which begins with Caesar's own transformation from human to god through his apotheosis.

While the gods approve of Jupiter's plan to destroy the human race through flood, they are also "pained by the prospective loss of the human race" (1.246). Of central concern is the loss of piety—a loss of piety exemplified by Lycaon—as they ask, "Who would bring incense to our altars?"(*quis sit laturus in aras tura*, 1.248–49). Jupiter then assures them "not to be alarmed (for the rest will be in his care), for he would procure them another race of wonderful origin, unlike the first people" (1.250–52).[141] In these lines, the gods seem to be concerned only with being worshiped, with their own self-aggrandizement, which the humans bolster through their piety. Lycaon's actions, however, will cause the pious and impious alike to perish. But clearly, at least for

---

139. *colligit os rabiem solitaeque cupidine caedis / vertitur in pecudes et nunc quoque sanguine gaudet. / in villos abeunt vestes, in crura lacerti: / fit lupus et veteris servat vestigial formae; / canities eadem est, eadem violentia vultus, / idem oculi lucent, eadem feritatis imago est.*

140. See C. Segal, "Ovid's Metamorphic Bodies," 12: "By choosing metamorphosis as a theme, Ovid focuses on the moments when stable forms and familiar norms dissolve in order to tap creative, if necessarily disorderly, energies that are usually kept beneath the surface, under the control of political, social, and symbolic systems that insist on coherence and order"; and 32: "Metamorphosis is in itself anxiety-provoking, and Ovid's choice of his poem's subject probably has something to do with the individual's sense of losing autonomy and control as Augustus's regime became more authoritarian. As the center of power seems increasingly remote, the abrupt transformation of one's life by sudden, arbitrary violence seems more possible, and orientation seems more difficult in an ever-expanding bureaucratic and autocratic government. Metamorphosis is the fantasy projection of such concerns into a distant mythical realm; and the violation of personal, physical boundaries serves as an especially intense form of these anxieties about one's control of one's movements in a larger world. This explanation . . . of course can only be partial and in any case speculative."

141. *talia quaerentes (sibi enim fore cetera curae) rex superum trepidare vetat subolemque priori dissimilem populo promittit origine mira.*

Jupiter, these humans are replaceable and, hopefully, the new beings that emerge will display proper piety toward the gods.[142]

As the deluge comes, it effects a reversal of the ordered beginnings of the universe, and nothing is in its proper place: water is where land should be, dolphins swim in the woods, wolf and sheep swim with each other in the water (1.293–310). After the world has been destroyed by flood, most have been "seized by the water [and] those whom it has spared, are slowly conquered through a lack of food" (1.311–12).[143] The only humans spared from both the flood and famine are Deucalion and his wife Pyrrha, surviving on a small raft that found its way to Mount Parnassus—the only spot of land left (1.314–19). Unlike the impious Lycaon and others of the Iron Age, their first act on dry land was to worship "the Corycian nymphs[144] and the mountain deities, the prophetic Themis, who at that time kept the oracles" (1.320–21).[145] This piousness is reflected in the subsequent description of Deucalion and Pyrrha: "There was no better man than he, none who loved justice more, nor a woman who revered the gods more than she" (1.322–23).[146] Jupiter, finding them "both innocent and worshipers of the divine" (1.324),[147] ends the deluge with the sounding of Triton's shell, and calls back the waters from all the shores where Phoebus casts his light (1.328–46).[148]

Deucalion laments that he and his wife are the only two humans left upon the earth, and wishes he had the skills of his father, Prometheus,

---

142. On the importance of *pietas* under Augustus, see Zanker, *Power of Images,* 102–10; and Galinsky, *Augustan Culture,* 86–88.

143. *maxima pars unda rapitur; quibus unda pepercit, illos longa domant inopi ieiunia victu.*

144. Both the Corycian nymphs and Pan are associated with the Corycian cave on Mount Parnassus. Pan will figure into the last round of stories in book 1.

145. *Corycidas nymphas et numina montis adorant fatidicamque Themin, quae tunc oracle tenebat.*

146. *non illo melior quisquam nec amantior aequi vir fuit aut illa metuentior ulla deorum.*

147. Fratantuono notes the irony that these are the two *best* humans on earth because they are the *only* two humans on earth (*Madness Transformed,* 14–15). He also observes that "Jupiter had decided to spare the world an attack from his thunderbolts, out of fear that the whole universe might go up in flames; now Pyrrha, whose name in Greek means 'fir,' will be the mother of a reborn race of men. The implication is that the new generation will not match Jupiter's expectation of improvement in humanity." Even if this is indeed the case, Deucalion and Pyrrha do seem to live up to expectations in terms of their piety toward the gods—one of the primary laments regarding the Iron Race and Lycaon. In this manner, as the parents of the new human race, it seems they have lived up to the desires of the gods.

148. This is the first mention of Phoebus in the *Metamorphoses.*

so that he could "pour the breath of life into molded earth!" (1.348-64).[149] After their laments, the couple decides to "pray to heavenly authority and seek aid through the sacred oracles" (1.367-68). They go to Cephisus's stream and sprinkle water on their heads and clothes; then they "turned their steps to the sacred shrine of the goddess" (1.369-73). "When they had reached the temple steps, they both fell prostrate, prone on the earth, and with trembling lips kissed the icy stones and said, 'If the gods are softened by prayers of the just, if the rage of the gods is appeased, tell us, Themis, by what art our ruined race might be restored, and bring aid, most merciful, to this flooded affair!'" (1.375-80).[150]

Their pious prayers indeed "moved" (*mota*) the goddess, and she gives them this oracle: "Leave the temple, and with veiled heads and loosened robes throw the bones of your great mother behind your back!" (1.381-83).[151] In yet another act of Roman piety, Deucalion and Pyrrha are told to veil their heads—one of the foremost symbols of Augustan piety.[152] They are initially confused by the oracle's message answering their prayers, and Pyrrha does not want to offend the goddess, but at the same time she does not want to desecrate her mother's bones by throwing them and offend her ghost. Finally, Deucalion deciphers that the oracle is referring to Mother Earth, and her bones are its stones. Though they doubt this could possibly be the correct interpretation, they enact it anyway, veiling their heads, loosening their robes, and tossing the stones behind them. And, indeed, the stones change into human form, those the man throws becoming men, and those the woman throws becoming women. From these beginnings "come the hardness of our race and our endurance of labor; and we give evidence of the origin of which we are born" (1.384-99).[153]

---

149. Lively notes the humor of this scene, which highlights the sexual naivety of Deucalion and Pyrrha: "the most obvious way in which Deucalion might set about repopulating the world would to become a *father* himself" (*Ovid's* Metamorphoses: A Reader's Guide, 25). Cf. the initial creation of humanity in 1.74-88, where Prometheus is named as one of the possible creators of humanity.

150. *ut templi tetigere gradus, procumbit uterque pronus humi gelidoque pavens dedit oscula saxo atque ita "si precibus" dixderunt "numina iustis dic, Themi, qua generis damnum reparabile nostril arte sit, et mersis fer opem, mitissima, rebus!"*

151. *discedite templo et velate caput cinctasque resolvite vestes ossaque post tergum magnae iactate parentis!*

152. Zanker, *Power of Images*, 126-29.

Then the earth, of it's own accord, produces animals, and it is from these that Python is born—returning us in book 1 to the story of Apollo and Daphne.

Io and Syrinx

The story of Apollo and Python immediately precedes the story of Daphne, and the stories Io and Syrinx follow it in quick succession, completing book 1. As Apollo's pursuit transforms Daphne, the story of Daphne turns into that of Apollo's father, Jupiter, or more specifically the story of Io, who will be the next victim of Jupiter's violence. The story of Io and Jupiter begins as Daphne's father, the river Peneus, sits on his throne in his home (*domus*) located in the innermost chambers of the mighty stream, and gives laws (*iura*) to his waters and water nymphs (1.569–76). As his streams assemble, they are unsure whether to "congratulate or console" Daphne's father (1.577–78), pointing to an internal acknowledgment of the ambivalence of Daphne's story: should the honor bestowed upon Daphne by Apollo be celebrated or should the proper response to her transformation be one of grief?[154] As all of the waters arrive, there is one that remains absent. This is Inachus, who weeps and laments in his cave for his own lost daughter, Io: "He does not know whether she still lives or is with the shades. But since he cannot find her anywhere, he believes that she is nowhere, and his soul fears worse" (1.583–87).

And it seems Inachus's soul is justified in its fear: Jupiter has just seen Io returning from her father's stream and has become enamored. He says to her:

> "O maiden [*virgo*], deserving of Jove, who will make some man—I know not who!—happy when you share his marriage bed [*factura toro*]. Seek the shade of the deep woods,"—and he pointed out the shady woods—"while it is hot and the sun is at the zenith of its orbit. But if you fear to enter the retreat of wild beasts alone, guarded by a god, you can enter the solitary woods in safety. Nor am I of the common gods, but I am he

---

153. *inde genus durum sumus experiensque laborum et documenta damus qua simus origine nati.*
154. Curran points out that this scene, though, is all about Peneus: "The rivers of Thessaly, instead of lamenting the fate of Daphne, are worried about her father" ("Rape and Rape Victims," 271).

who holds heaven's scepter in his mighty hand, I am he who casts the capricious thunderbolt—do not flee [*fuge*] me!"—for she was already in flight [*fugiebat*]. (1.588–97)

Already Io's story bears resemblance to Daphne's: the god becomes obsessed with Io on "sight" (*video*, 1.490 // 1.588); the scene is set in "the woods" (*nemus*, 1.479 // 1.590, 593),[155] the haunt of "wild beasts" (*fera*, 1.475 // 1.592).[156] Furthermore, like Daphne, Io has less to fear from the wild beasts of the woods pursuing their prey than from the godly "beasts" who pursue "their" maidens (1.504-7, 533-36 // 1.593). And in their pursuits, both Apollo and Jupiter list their accolades, as if these should justify their actions (1.504-24 // 1.594-96), but nonetheless both Daphne and Io flee (1.502, 30 // 1.596).[157]

Unlike Daphne, Jupiter catches Io in her human form. As Io flees, Jupiter causes a "swelling mist" to fill the land, obscuring her view, and "seizes the fleeing girl and he rapes her" (*tenuitque fugam rapuitque pudorem*, 1.598-99). At the same time, Juno looks down upon the land of Argos, and the same mist that obscures Io's vision obscures her own.[158] Juno, though, is familiar with her husband's "deceit" (*furta*) and believes Jupiter is the author of this mist, remarking, "I am mistaken or I am being betrayed" (*aut ego fallor aut ego laedor*, 1.600-608). Juno then heads to earth, dispersing the mist, but Jupiter, having anticipated his wife's arrival, "turned Inachus's daughter into a glistening heifer" (1.608-10). Like Daphne, Io, in her new form, "[e]ven as a cow, is beautiful" (*bos quoque formose est*, 1.611).

Juno, feigning ignorance, asks Jupiter from where the cow has come, and Jupiter lies, saying she sprang from the earth, just as the other creatures in the second creation. Juno, knowing this is a lie, asks for the cow as a gift. Jupiter, now caught in his lie, wonders what to do:

---

155. The Daphne story uses *silva* also at 1.474. See Hugh Parry, "Ovid's *Metamorphoses*: Violence in a Pastoral Landscape," *TAPA* 95 (1964): 268–82.

156. Though Daphne wears their hides rather than fears them.

157. John Heath quips, "Jupiter has not learned form Apollo's example that an intended victim of rape is not impressed by the attacker's pedigree and professional station" ("Diana's Understanding of Ovid's 'Metamorphoses,'" *CJ* 86.3 [1991]: 235).

158. Salzman-Mitchell makes the point that here only Jupiter's male gaze is "penetrating"; neither Io nor Juno can see through the mist, though Juno wonders what her husband it up to (*Web of Fantasies*, 24).

"Shame urges he give her up, but love dissuades him" (*Pudor est, qui suadeat illinc, hinc dissuadet Amor*, 1.612–19). If not for his deception, "Love would have been victorious over shame" (*victus Pudor esset Amore*, 1.619), but, fearful he would be caught over such an "inconsequential gift" as a cow, he relinquishes Io to Juno (1.620–22). With Apollo before, as well as Mars and the Romans, it is questionable exactly what type of love Jupiter holds for Io given his treatment of her—especially as he has now transformed her into something "inconsequential" enough to warrant her release to Juno. But, though Juno's "rival" (*paelice*, i.e., Jupiter's kept mistress or concubine)[159] has been given over to her, she is still anxious about the possibility of further deceit (*fuit anxia furti*, 1.622) by Jupiter, and places Io under the surveillance of the many-eyed Argus (1.623–29).

Several connections are of note in the narrative to this point. The last time Jupiter was a central character in book 1 was in the story of Lycaon and the council of the gods, where he sought the destruction of the human race—those of the Iron Age marked by a lack of "decency, truth and fidelity" (*pudor verumque fidesque*, 1.129) and filled with "deceit, deception, schemes, and violence and depraved love of possession" (*fraudesque dolusqe insidiaeque et vis et amor sceleratus habendi*, 1.130–31). Additionally, Ovid says that in the Iron Age, "Men live by *rapto*" (1.144)—taking, seizing, and violating whatever they wished. Ironically, these attributes of Iron Age humanity, which Jupiter sought to erase with his flood, only recur in book 1 in relation to *his* actions: *pudor* is used when he rapes Io (1.600), as he literally "plunders" her "modesty" or "honor" (*rapuitque pudorem*), and then twice more in reference to his reaction when caught in the act by Juno[160]—not in reaction to his treatment of Io, whom he claims to love (1.618, 619). The word *mentior* (1.615), the opposite of *verum*, marks his lying words to his wife, who knows "the truth" (*veri*, 1.614).;[161] Jupiter also displays a lack of *fides* as he deceives his wife and takes a *paelex* (1.621). Jupiter's *fraudis*, *dolus*, and *insidiae*[162] are seen in his

---

159. See Lewis & Short, s.v. *paelex*.
160. These are the only three other uses of the word in book 1.
161. This is the only occurrence of *mentior* in book 1.

deceit (*furtum*, 1.622) and lies (*mentior*, 1.615), while his *vis*[163] and *amor scleratus*[164] *habendi* are shown through his *rapio* (1.600)—the two additional instances of *rapio* in book 1 refer to the effects of Jupiter's deluge upon land, animals, and humans as they are violently seized by the waters (1.287, 311).

There is further irony in the fact that Jupiter, likened to Augustus and his *domus* to that of the Palatine, is in violation of the *Leges Juliae*—just as were Augustus's divine ancestors, Venus and Mars. Here, Jupiter has clearly committed adultery against his wife and rape against a virgin of rank (her father being a river god). In the previous episode, Apollo violated these same laws with Daphne. As Miller observes, "In contemporary Roman terms, Phoebus would uphold the Julian *lex de maritandis ordinibus*, which the Princeps promulgated to encourage marriage and procreation. Yet as a would-be rapist threatening violence to an unmarried woman the god would aim to violate another piece of Augustus' moral legislation, the *lex Iulia de adulteriis*."[165] These texts, with their violations and conquests, which both evoke victory whether in war (1.560-61)[166] or in love (1.619),[167] exhibit the same themes and connections between rape, war, and conquest that are found in the story of the Sabines. Overall, the Jupiter of the Io narrative (and in many ways his son Apollo in the Daphne narrative as well) sanctions the very characteristics that his own flood sought to destroy.[168]

---

162. The words *fraudis* and *dolus* occur only in 1.130 in book 1; the only other instance of *insidiae* in book 1 is in 1.198 in relation to Lycaon, paradigm of Iron Age values.
163. The word *vis* occurs in varied contexts and meanings throughout book 1, though two instances are in relation to Jupiter, the first in 1.278, where he tells the rivers, "Pour forth your force," regarding the flood, and the second in 1.305 referring to the "force" of Jupiter's thunderbolt.
164. This is the only occurrence of *scelero* in book 1.
165. Miller, *Apollo, Augustus, and the Poets*, 344, citing Treggiari, *Roman Marriage*, 60–80. Miller also notes, "In *Met.* I Apollo occupies an ethical stage between the ideal of the faithful married couple embodied by the humans Deucalion and Pyrrha (esp. 1.351-62) and the unabashed divine adulterer Jupiter, who summarily rapes the nymph Io (1.600) after a perverse come-on that calls her both a virgin worthy of himself and a woman who will make someone happy in her marriage couch/in marriage with her (1.589-90)" (344n35).
166. "You [Daphne] will attend the Roman generals when joyful voices sing their triumph, and behold the long Capitol processions."
167. Where if not for Jupiter's deception, "Love would have been victorious over shame."
168. This is highly ironic, as Jupiter and Apollo are also the two who restore "order" to the world by vanquishing the giants and Python, respectively.

Jupiter's actions continue to reverberate, as Io is held captive both by the watchful eyes of Argus and by her bovine form. Argus's eyes remain on her at all times, and though he allows her to graze during the day, at night Argus "confined her and tied a shameful fetter around her neck" (1.625–31).[169] Her confinement and fettering—whether by gaze or bond—by Argus mirror the confinement and fettering of her human self within her bovine body:

> She fed on tree fronds and bitter herbs, and instead of a bed she lay upon the earth, not always having grass—wretched thing—and drinks water from a muddy stream. When she wished to stretch beseeching arms to Argus, she had no arms with which to stretch; and when she tried to lament, a moo came from her mouth—she feared [*pertimuitque*] the sound, and was struck with terror [*exterrita*] at her own voice. And she came to Inachus's bank where she used to play, but when she saw her gaping mouth and newly sprouted horns in the waters, she fled [*refugit*] in terror [*pertimuit*] of herself. (1.632–41)

In these lines, the psychological effects of Io's rape play out in what Andrew Feldherr astutely calls her "self-alienation"[170] from her Jupiter-fashioned form. The ramifications for Io provide a counterpoint and corollary to the repercussions experienced by Daphne after Apollo's attempted rape. While the narrative provides an exacting account of Io's experience of "self-alienation" as she struggles to make sense of the split between her inner and outer worlds, the text remains silent on the internal workings of Daphne after her transformation. While some read the laurel's shrinking from Apollo's kisses and shaking of its leaves as a sign of Daphne's continuing presence or sentience in her changed form, the text conspicuously leaves this ambiguous. Whether she is there or not, Daphne is entirely dissociated from her previous existence, her transformation leaving little but her luster. Io's transformation, on the other hand, leaves her human consciousness entirely intact, as she is forced to reckon with

---

169. On Argus's gaze, see Feldherr, *Playing Gods*, 17–18; see also Salzman-Mitchell, *Web of Fantasies*, 25, on Argus's eyes as a "surrogate" for Juno's gaze.
170. Feldherr, *Playing Gods*, 17.

the horror of juxtaposing her human nature with her confinement, fearing the bovine form she has become.[171]

This horror continues as Io encounters her family in her new form. She follows her sisters and father around, but to no avail. While they pet and admire her, feeding her grass, she tries to reveal her identity by licking her father's hand and trying to kiss it (1.642–46). But, the poem says, "She could not hold back her tears, and, if only words would come, she would have spoken, she would say her name and ask for aid and tell of her misfortune. With her hoof she fashioned in the dust, written marks instead of words and described the sad details of her body transformed" (1.647–50).[172] After all other attempts to make her identity known fail, Io engages in the only human gesture her bovine body can enact: writing.[173] This is the act that finally bridges the inner Io with the outer world and allows her identity to be revealed.

Upon her father's recognition, he cries, "Alas, woe is me!" and "clinging to the wailing heifer's horns and snowy neck," he exclaims again, "Alas, woe is me! Are you the daughter I have sought through all the earth? Undiscovered you were an easier sorrow than found. You are silent, and give back nothing in return for our words; but from your breast you draw deep sighs, and all that you are able to say to my words is moo!" (1.651–57).[174] Feldherr draws attention to the fact that "Io" holds a double meaning here: it is not only Io's name, thus signifying her identity, but is also the Greek for "alas." This "alas" is appropriate, considering Io's current form, and is also translated into the Latin through Inachus's lament, "*me miserum!*" Inachus's words are "not just the acknowledgment of her identity but a kind of sympathy

---

171. Feldherr highlights both the humor and the horror of this episode (*Playing Gods*, 16–20), though which or what combination the text elicits in the reader depends on what experiences the reader brings. This is "the kind of humor we have already seen to depend on an inability to penetrate Io's form" (ibid., 20).

172. *nec retinet lacrimas et, si modo verba sequantur, / oret opem nomenque suum casusque loquatur; / littera pro verbis, quam pes in pulvere duxit, / corporis indicium mutati triste peregit.*

173. See Feldherr, *Playing Gods*, 19, who cites C. Santini, "Segni grafici e metamorfosi," in *Ovidio da Roma all'Europa*, ed. I. Gallo and P. Esposito, Quaderni del dipartimento di scienze dell'antichità, Università di studi di Salerno 20 (Naples: Arte tipographica, 1998), 37–54.

174. "*me miserum!*" *excalmat pater Inachus inque gementis / cornibus et nivea pendens cervice iuvencae / "me miserum!" ingeminate; / "tune es quaesita per omnes nata mihi terras? tu non inventa reperta / luctus eras levior! retices nec mutua nostris / dicta refers, alto tantum suspiria ducis / pectore, quodque unum potes, ad mea verba remugis!"*

that literally makes him the vehicle for her voice." In addition, his words "convey Inachus's own emotional response to the discovery": while "Inachus intends *me miserum* to represent his own suffering . . . in context the *me* is Io."

But Philip Hardie, in a correspondence with Feldherr points to another possible "transformation" that occurs in this reading—"one of gender, for Inachus's *me* is grammatically masculine."[175] This reversal allows for a competing reading that suggests that Inachus's lament has less to do with sympathy for Io than pity for himself. This reading parallels Jupiter's shame when he is caught by Juno (1.618–619) and has resonances with Apollo's projections of himself onto the form of Daphne—in each case their only concern is themselves, there is no concern regarding the effects of their actions on others; in each case, the pain of the actual sufferer is usurped by the men around her, who include her perpetrators.[176]

Inachus's investment in his self-pity seems to bear out as his speech continues: "But I, in ignorance, was arranging a bridal bed [*thalamus*] and marriage torch [*taedasque*] for you, and had hope, first for a son-in-law, second for grandchildren. Now from the herd I must find you a husband, and now from the herd I must find your young. Not even by death am I allowed to end my anguish. Indeed it is baneful to be a god, for the door of death is closed, and our affliction is stretched endlessly in eternity" (1.658–63). This speech makes clear that Inachus, "far from empathizing with Io's misfortune . . . is interested only in what his daughter's new form means for him. Like any demigod—or Roman father—on the make, he had hoped to advance his status through his daughter's marriage. Now, however, the opposite will be the case: his son-in-law will be a bull, and his grandchildren cattle."[177] It is, of course, the high-status Jupiter whose machinations have created this predicament: Jupiter's rape and resulting cover-up have robbed Io,

---

175. Feldherr, *Playing Gods*, 19.
176. A similar impulse is found as the rivers are unsure whether to "congratulate or console" Daphne's father.
177. Feldherr, *Playing Gods*, 20. Grandchildren are also a major concern of Peneus when Daphne begins to follow the path of Diana; see *Met.* 1.481–82.

"the virgin" no longer, of the "marriage bed" (*torus*) he foretold would "make some man happy" (1.589-90) and ruined the "marriage bed" (*thalamus*, 1.658) of Inachus's dreams. And while Daphne eschewed the "wedding torch" as a "crime" (*crimen taedas*, 1.483), Io will be denied it (*taedasque*, 1.658) because of Jupiter's crime—and with their subsequent transformations, both Apollo and Inachus will lament.[178]

In the midst of Inachus's lament, the ever-watchful Argus "drove his daughter off and tore her from her father, withdrawing her to remote pastures" (1.664-66).[179] Argus then seats himself on a mountain so he can see her from all sides. And Jupiter, "no longer able to bear the great misfortune of Io" (1.668-69),[180] calls upon his son Mercury to slay Argus. Mercury agrees and transforms himself into a shepherd (*pastor*) to fool him.[181] While leading his sheep, Mercury plays his reed-pipe (*avena*), and, when Argus hears the sound, he invites the "shepherd"—whom he does not recognize—to sit. Argus's failure of recognition will lead to his slaughter, just as Lycaon's failure to recognize Mercury's father, Jupiter, leads to Lycaon's transformation and the destruction of the world in the deluge (1.220-43).[182]

Mercury and Argus while away the hours in conversation, and then Mercury, "by making music on his reed-pipe tries to conquer those watchful eyes" (1.676-84).[183] Argus "battles" (*pugnat*) his urge for sleep, and, while some of his eyes succumb to slumber, others remain watching. Fighting his slumber, he then asks Mercury how the reed-pipe—"for the reed-pipe was recently discovered"[184]—came to be (1.685-88). With these words, Mercury begins the tale of Pan and Syrinx, a rustic transformation of the tale of Apollo and Daphne.[185]

The story of Syrinx begins in much the same manner as Daphne's:

178. As Apollo says to the transformed Daphne, "Though you are not able to be my bride, you will certainly be my tree!" (1.557-58).
179. *submovet . . . ereptamque patri diversa in pascua natam abstrahit.*
180. *Nec . . . mala tanta Phoronidos ultra ferre potest.* It seems as if Jupiter wants to end the horror he has created for Io for *himself*—what she feels does not seem to be at issue.
181. A terrible thing for a god, according to Apollo, "*non ego sum pastor*" (1.513).
182. Apollo also worried about Daphne's failure to recognize him as he pursued her (1.504-24).
183. *iunctisque canendo vincere harundinibus servantia lumina temptat.*
184. *namque reperta fistula nuper erat.*
185. Feldherr calls it the "rustic modulation" of the Apollo and Daphne story (*Playing Gods*, 25).

she, too, is a nymph (1.472, 505, 506 // 1.691), devoted to Diana (1.476, 486–87 // 1.694–95), often pursued (1.507, 532 // 1.692) and then fleeing (1.474, 503, 526 // 1.701), shunning suitors (1.478 // 1.692); her name in Greek, like Daphne's, bears the weight of her transformation to come.[186] Mercury weaves his tale, telling Argus, "When she girded herself in the custom of Diana, she could deceive and be imagined as Latona's daughter, if not for her bow of horn, which wasn't golden as hers. But even so she was mistaken for the goddess" (1.695–98). It is this confusion over Syrinx's identity, another failure of recognition (i.e., that Syrinx is not Diana, just as Mercury is not a shepherd and Jupiter is not a mere mortal), which ushers in her transformation. Mercury continues his tale, as Pan sees Syrinx for the first time on Mount Lycaeus—harking back to the beginnings of book 1, as this is the eponymous mountain of Lycaon and also the site of Jupiter's slaughter of the giants.[187] But Mercury's voice falls away as the narrator continues the tale, alluding to the fact that Argus has fallen asleep and Mercury has seized the moment to slay him.[188] In Mercury's absence, the narrator relays that

> the nymph, rejecting his prayers, fled through the wilderness [avia][189] until she came to Ladon's peaceful and sandy stream; how when the waters hindered her passage, she beseeched her liquid-sister nymphs to change her;[190] and how Pan, believing he had now captured [prensam] Syrinx, instead of the nymph's body held swampy reeds; and while he

186. The word σύριγξ is Greek for "reed-pipe," as δάφνη is the Greek for "laurel." Both *harundo* (1.684) and *fistula* (1.688) are Latin equivalents of σύριγξ.

187. For the giants, see 1.151–62; and for Lycaon, 1.210–43. In legend, Lycaon is also the founder of Mercury's worship site at Cyellene, as noted above. Mount Lycaeus is also associated with Pan.

188. See Feldherr's brilliant analysis of this episode and the way it enfolds multiple layers of meaning and strategies of reading both for this narrative unit and the *Metamorphoses* as a whole (*Playing Gods*, 22–26).

189. Cf. *avia* and Daphne, 1.479.

190. Fratantuono notes the complex web of textual connections between Syrinx and the Daphne story, and the continued intertextualities with book 1 as a whole: Syrinx "was an Arcadian, and, like the Arcadian Daphne, a devotee of Diana. Like Virgil's Venus in disguise, Syrinx was mistaken for Diana (1.696–698). The return to Arcadia also brings back full circle to Lycaon and his crimes; Pan sees the virgin huntress returning from Mount Lycaeus. Syrinx runs to the streams of Ladon, the sometime father of Daphne, thus further reinforcing the ring composition wherein Ovid has brilliantly changed the story of the Arcadian Daphne into his own (Thessalian) creation and reminded us of the change by balancing her tale with that of the Arcadian Syrinx, who seeks salvation at Ladon" (*Madness Transformed*, 22). He also notes, "In another nice touch, at the waters of Ladon Ovid has Syrinx invoke her 'liquid sisters' (704 *liquidas orasse sorores*) to save her from Pan's advances, precisely because Ladon is not her father but Daphne's" (30n57).

sighed, his breath stirring in the reeds produced a low, lamenting sound. Taken captive [*captum*] by the new art of this sweet voice, the god said, "At least this union I will have with you." And so the pipes of disparate reeds, bound and joined between with wax, held the name of his beloved. (1.701–12)

Like Daphne before her, Syrinx sees her only means of escape from Pan to be through transformation (*muto*, 1.547 // 1.707); and as with Apollo and Daphne, Pan is able to grasp Syrinx only after she has been transformed to something wholly other than what she was before.[191] Though her transformation leaves her pledge to Diana intact, it has now made it possible for Pan to use her as his instrument—unable to flee from his grasp as he plays the pipes that are now his: like Mars and Ilia in the Fasti,[192] that which has "taken him captive" has become the captured. Just as Apollo, denied the marriage he sought (1.557), would have Daphne "forever embrace" him and all that he held dear (1.557–59), so too Pan would always "hold the name of his beloved" (1.712) as he held his pipes.[193]

The narrative then returns to Mercury's slaughter of the sleeping Argus. Juno, upon seeing his death-filled eyes, "set them on the feathers of her bird," and "immediately she burned with rage, and did not defer it. She cast her horrific fury before the eyes and soul of the Grecian mistress, and in her breast plunged a blinding prod, and she drove her to flee [*profugam*] in terror [*terruit*] across the entire world. At last, Nile, you allowed her rest from her immeasurable exertion" (1.722–28). Still in her bovine form, Io falls upon the banks of the Nile, so exhausted she only has the strength to throw back her head. And

191. Curran highlights the other versions of the Syrinx myth, observing, "Syrinx is . . . a seasoned veteran, who seems to have made a career out of evading rapists. In all previous encounters, she escapes with both virginity and humanity intact; with Pan she salvages virginity only at the cost of her humanity" ("Rape and Rape Victims," 266).
192. Ovid, *Fasti* 3.9–10, *capio*.
193. In book 11, the stories of Apollo and Pan will again be intertwined as they enter into a playing contest in the midst of the story of Midas. Pan, playing his pipes boasts to the nymphs that his playing is better than Apollo's, and a contest ensues with Pan on his pipes and the laurel-adorned Apollo (11.165) on his lyre. Though the mountain-god Tmolus judges in favor of Apollo, Midas declares this judgment an injustice. Apollo overhears his words and transforms Midas's ears into those of an ass (11.146–93). In another possible political allusion, Midas had just been saved from his touch of gold by the god Bacchus, the patron of Antony, against whom the Actium Apollo won the contest over Rome for Octavian.

with "moans and tears and mournful moos she seemed to sing her grief to Jove and to beseech him end her misfortune" (1.729-33).[194] Upon hearing Io's lament, Jupiter embraces his wife's (*coniugis*) neck and asks her to end Io's punishment (*poenas*), pleading, "Lay aside your fear of the future; she will never cause you pain again," and then swore this oath upon the Styx (1.735-37).

Of course, Jupiter's oath is specific: while Juno need not worry about Io in the future, this will not be Jupiter's last indiscretion.[195] Juno's wrath is mollified (*lenita*), at least for the moment, and Io begins her transformation back to human form. "Her features return to their prior form, and she is fashioned into what she was before" (1.738-39).[196] Ovid's words are specific here—it is her features and form that return to their former state. She is not what she was. After all that Io has endured, it is impossible to think she would, or could, return to her former self unchanged. Her internal transformation is borne out in the text, as her hair, horns, and hooves resume their human shape. Though she now stands upright on two legs she "still feared speaking, lest like a cow she moo, and timidly attempts to regain her speech" (1.739-46).[197] The story ends: "Today she is worshipped as a goddess and celebrated by the linen-clad crowd" (1.747).[198]

The Io, Syrinx, and Daphne stories are all marked by sexual violence,

---

194. *et gemitu et lacrimis et luctisono mugitu / cum Iove visa queri finemque orare malorum.*
195. Jupiter also rapes Callisto (2.401-507), Europa (2.833-3.7), Semele (3.253-315), and becomes obsessed with Ganymede, whom he forcibly kidnaps and forces into servitude (10.155-61).
196. *vultus capit illa priores / fitque, quod ante fuit.*
197. *metuitque loqui, ne more iuvencae / mugiat, et timide verba intermissa retemptat.*
198. *nunc dea linigera colitur celeberrima turba.* Io as a goddess is identified with Isis, one of whose symbols was the cow (the horns representing the crescent moons). The final scene of book 1 ends with a dispute between Io and Jupiter's son, Epaphus, and Clymene and Apollo's son, Phaëthon, regarding Phaëthon's parentage (1.748-79). While Apollo's son will ultimately triumph over Io's in this dispute (just as the Actium Apollo triumphs over Cleopatran Isis), the acknowledgment of Phaëthon's father ultimately leads to his demise (2.1-328). See Ahl, *Metaformations*, 148:

"Io, [Ovid] tells us, is now worshiped by the 'linen-wearing people' as a very celebrated goddess. These people are, of course, the Egyptians, and the goddess Io is worshiped in the same way as Isis. Io's connections with writing and . . . with music remind us that in some accounts Isis was the daughter of Mercury—who discovered writing and music (Plutarch, *Isis and Osiris* 3) and who has a very special role in Ovid's Io story.

"Once we see Io as Isi, the other figures in the narrative tend to metamorphose themselves about her. [Argus], who watches over her like a dog begins to look a little like the Egyptian 'dog' deity, Anubis. Mercury, who releases her by killing [Argus], has some of the characteristics of the Egyptian Thot, with whom he is regularly identified."

the loss of voice—in their new forms they are literally unable to speak—and the transformation of the body to something other than human.[199] These three are also "known" by their names—Daphne will become the laurel; Syrinx will become the reeds; and Io will become the "alas." Each of them in their transformation, will also be used by others: Daphne will reflect Apollo's victory and adorn him; Syrinx will be forever held and played by Pan; and Io's "alas" will be used by her lamenting father and justify her treatment in Juno's hands.

With the many similarities in these stories, there are also differences. Io's story diverges significantly; she is the only one who retains her humanity and has it restored—though the text never describes the impact of her self-alienation on her reinstated form. It is difficult to imagine her journey from raped to captive, fugitive to revered, a course with similarities to the one traveled by the Sabine women. And, like Rhea Silvia, the Sabine women, and Lucretia, for Daphne, Io, and Syrinx lust is justified in the name of love, while the power plays of men and gods are enacted on their bodies.

Conclusion

In book 1 of the *Metamorphoses*, as Ovid establishes the creation and order of the earth, he also exposes the character and machinations of the gods. Though at times they seem to promote order and justice, more often the gods are prone to outbursts of violence, scheming, and lust. In this way, they enact the very characteristics for which they critique the humans of the Iron Age: Jupiter justifies the extinction of all life on the basis of Lycaon's actions, and his passion for Io justifies his violence, scheming, and dishonoring of both Io and Juno. Juno's own wrath multiplies the tragedy brought on Io by her husband. Apollo's hubris allows him to mock Cupid, whose own ire ultimately turns on Daphne, making her an unwitting third party in their dispute.

199. Enterline, *Rhetoric of the Body*, 17, speaking of the literary tradition of Medusa: "I have found that whether the female voice is imagined to speak or to fall silent, it wields a telling (if unpredictable) power." I think this is also evident in the Daphne-Io-Syrinx cycle—whether they are speaking or, in the case of these three, forced into silence, their stories continue to speak and to say volumes about who they are and what they have endured.

Apollo's lust then forces Daphne into something wholly other in order to have any hope at self-determination and remain as she is—and even so, she is unable to evade Apollo's arms. Mercury wields the sword against Argus at his father's behest, he too, a pawn in Juno's retribution against her philandering husband. And Syrinx, suffering the same fate as Daphne, is the fixation of a lustful Pan, her only escape to ultimately turn into his instrument.

But, as many commentators note, there is also humor in these tales, or at least a ridiculousness in the sense that they produce ridicule. Jupiter's wrath and reaction to Lycaon are so hyperbolic they become absurd. Apollo, so puffed up and worried about his celebrity that he picks a fight with Cupid, gets caught in Cupid's game and desperately pursues what he cannot grasp—first with "feminine" blandishments, then name calling, and finally listing his mighty accolades (which fail him with the fleeing Daphne). In the end, when he finally catches her in her changed form, he is left to canoodle with a tree! And then there is Jupiter—the cheating husband, caught by his wrathful wife, whose marital problems are hung out for all to see. Finally, there is Pan, who is so dense he cannot tell the difference between Diana and her disciple.

These characterizations, both the base and the jocular, become more complex as Ovidian associations between the gods and Augustus accumulate, another set of connections becoming possible when the narrative is viewed through an Augustan lens. For example, the new world order established by the gods after the flood is one of dominance predicated on violence and deception (the slaying of Python, the near rape of Daphne, the rape and transformation of Io, the deception of Juno by Jove, the near rape of Syrinx, and finally the death of Argus at the hand of Mercury at Jove's behest). Just as with the founding myths of Rome, this order is predicated on sexual violence and domination. Mars and Romulus (at least by the poem's end in book 15) are the gods who instigate this founding aetiology of Rome through their own rapes—and the ones who continuously renew the Augustan regime and frame the apotheosis of the Julian line. With these stories and observations, the lines between divine and human, past and present, fantasy and reality become more and more blurred, constantly collapsing upon, elaborating, and weaving with one another.

This fluidity can also be seen in the changing nature of identity during Augustus's reign. There was fluidity and flux not only within Roman society itself but also between Rome and its colonies. What is particularly interesting is the way in which violence, metamorphosis, and identity formation are combined, particularly in the last third of book 1, where rape triggers this transformation. This type of violence marks a person both physically (as with Apollo's worries regarding the *notas* on Daphne's legs as she flees him) and psychologically. In the three rape narratives in book 1, this sexual violence enacts complete transformation: one was one thing and becomes wholly other. This is the same type of transformation enacted on the Sabine women, as their rapes turn them into wives then mothers, thus Romans. Though not always brought about specifically through sexual violence, violent transformation is also important in terms of conquest more generally—as the conquered lose their identity in the midst of colonization (like the Sabines and the Romans' other neighbors) and can even be extended the invitation to be transformed into Romans.[200]

Also to be noted in these stories of transformation, the boundaries between the realms of the public and private collapse. "Leonard Barken observes that Ovid in the *Metamorphoses* 'dissolves great public facts into private stories.'"[201] This has already been seen in instances like the Apollo and Daphne story, where Apollo's public triumphal laurel is framed by his private pursuit of Daphne. But this configuration becomes more complicated as the text transforms—or evokes the "real-world" transformation of—public gods like Apollo and Vesta into Augustus's household gods. This blurring of public and private is also seen in instances where Ovid plays with and alludes to moral legislation such as the *Leges Juliae,* which, as illustrated above, conflate the realms of the public and private, with Augustus fashioned as the paternal, moral exemplar from which the state extends.

---

200. Beard, *Roman Triumph*, 139–42.
201. Miles, *Apollo, Augustus, and the Poets*, 348, citing, Leonard Barken, *Gods Made Flesh* (New Haven: Yale University Press, 1986), 85, 226.

Daphne, at least in her human form, provides a foil for this logic. Though ultimately appealing to the will of her father, she shuns his wishes, his desire for son-in-law and grandchildren, and pursues her life, "untroubled by Hymen or Amor, or whatever marriage might be" (1.480), "detest[ing] the wedding torch as if it were a crime" (1.483). As Apollo conformed to the *Leges Juliae* in pursuing an advantageous marriage—though his attempt to assault Daphne broke them—Daphne, too, flouts them as she shuns her divine suitor. Here, Daphne's actions enact a reversal of the prevailing patriarchal order. And, although, in her transformed state, she will be used as a symbol of the prevailing order, she will never truly be a part of it.

3

"And they lusted after her . . ."

The Rape of Eve and the Violation of the Rulers

The rape of Eve narratives in the Genesis elaborations of the Secret Revelation of John, the Reality of the Rulers, and On the Origin of the World present a story that both mimics and critiques the Roman narratives of rape.[1] The rape of Eve as found in each of these three texts

---

1. What I refer here to as "the rape of Eve," is not always translated as such. Designated by the Coptic ϫⲱϨⲙ in all three of the Genesis cosmogonies (including all four manuscripts of SRJ), meaning "to defile, pollute," it corresponds to a range of Greek words (see Crum, 797b–798a) including, μιαίνω: "stain, sully, taint, defile"; μολύνω: "stain, sully, defile"; ἐκφύρω: "mix, spoil, defile"; διαφθείρω: "destroy, ruin, corrupt"; ῥυπόω: "make foul and filthy, befoul"; σπιλόω: "stain, soil"; μωμητός: "to be blamed, bringing disgrace"; ἀκάθαρτος: "uncleansed, foul, unpurified, morally unclean, impure"; βεβηλόω: "profane, pollute, defile"; ἀνόσιος: "unholy, profane"; μῶμος: "blame, reproach, disgrace"; μιαρός: "stained, defiled, polluted, abominable, foul," all within a similar semantic range (see LSJ for Greek). In both Reality of the Rulers and On the Origin of the World, this defilement is accompanied by the rulers "casting" (ⲛⲟⲩϫⲉ) their "sperm" (σπέρμα) into Eve (RoR 89.22–23; OnOrig 117.2–4).Unlike much of the earlier scholarship on Rhea Silvia, the Sabines, and Ovidian works, scholars have tended to refer to the rulers defilement of Eve as "rape." Often, these rape scenes are referred to as the "seduction of Eve," alluding to the wider trope of Eve's seduction by the serpent in the Hebrew Bible, intertestamental, rabbinic, and other Jewish and Christian sources (see Stroumsa, *Another Seed,* 18–70, for many of these). While many secondary sources do speak of the "seduction of Eve" as the overall trope and then specifically refer to the passages in the Secret Revelation of John, the Reality of the Rulers, and On the Origin of the World SRJ as "rape," this is not always the case. For example, see Robert M. Price, "Amorous Archons in Eden and Corinth," *Journal of Unification Studies* 2 (1998): 30, who refers to SRJ's version as "the seduction of Eve," and to the versions in RoR and OnOrig as the "attempted rape," because the spiritual Eve is not actually raped as she splits from the material Eve. In reference to RoR 89.17–28,

179

contains elements that resonate with the stories of Ilia, the Sabines, Lucretia, and Verginia;[2] with the story of Daphne;[3] and with the stories of the nations. In this chapter, after a brief description of each text with an eye always on Eve, I show not only the pivotal significance of the pericope in terms of each text's larger narrative but begin to render a comparative analysis between the other Roman myths and histories engaged earlier in this study and the rape of Eve texts.[4]

Stroumsa says, "In this text, the authorities are simply said to have fallen in love with the spiritual Eve (89:11); in a way, they were 'seduced' by her"; in relation to OnOrig 117.2ff. he refers to the "rapist" ruler (43) and continues to refer to her violation as a "rape" (44–45).

Given the framing of Eve's rape in SRJ, RoR, and OnOrig, while it does relate to this wider trope of Eve's seduction (though labeling it a "seduction" is questionable in some of the other primary sources as well), there is no reason to categorize this in any way as a seduction rather than a rape—in each of the three texts the Chief Ruler (sometimes with others) defiles her, and there is no indication on the part of any of the manuscripts that she is in any way a willing participant or has been seduced: this is a violent act on the part of ruler(s). Second, it is true that the spiritual Eve is not raped in the texts, but her material counterpart clearly is—saying that this is not a rape is dismissive both of the violence perpetrated by the rulers and authorities in these texts and of the violation of the material Eve. As shown throughout this study, the texts do not dismiss the violence of the rulers' and authorities' rape of Eve. Given this, while there are important textual connections between those narratives of "seduction" and "rape," these acts need to be distinctly named by contemporary commentators in an effort not only to clarify the content of the narrative but also to understand the power and gender dynamics on which these acts are based. On issues of translating "rape," particularly in classics, see Packman, "Call It Rape."

2. See Lillie, "Rape of Eve"; cf. Lewis, *Introduction to "Gnosticism,"* 142–45.
3. See Pearson, "She Became a Tree"; and King, "Ridicule and Rape."
4. While AJ, John, RoR, and OnOrig all share similar plot lines, their complex differences are vast. For some classic synoptic comparison, source-critical analysis, as well as analysis of the rape of Eve texts, see Michel Tardieu, *Trois mythes gnostiques: Adam, Éros et les animaux d'Égypte dan un écrit de Nag Hammadi (II, 5)* (Paris: Études Augustiniennes, 1974), who compares OnOrig with RoR. He proposes that Eve's "sex with the devil" (36), (i.e., the rape of Eve) as a "new myth" to explain Adam's expulsion from Eden (194n269), but see the comparative analysis of Stroumsa cited below. Tardieu (104, 129–31, 206) mainly sees the rape of Eve in terms of the fall of humanity (a view not shared by this study), and, though he addresses a vast amount of mythology, he has not looked toward either the Ovidian or Roman sources that share these features. Bernard Barc charts the synoptic relationship between RoR, SRJ, and OnOrig (*L'Hypostase des Archontes: Traité gnostique sur l'origine de l'homme du monde et des archontes,* Bibliothèque Copte de Nag Hammadi, Section "Textes" 5 [Louvain: Peeters, 1980], 7–14), specifically addressing the rape of Eve, but he labels this "The Origin of Cain and Abel" (13, 92–101). Like Tardieu, he associates the rape with the fall of humanity, seeing the spiritual woman as the key component in salvation, connecting her raising of Adam with the "resurrection of the dead" (93). Louis Painchaud compares a wide range of texts from Aristotle to the Gospel of Matthew, with some interest in RoR, and OnOrig (*L'Écrit sans titre: Traité sur l'origine du monde (NHC II, 5 et XIII, 2 et Brit. Lib. Or. 4926 [1])* [Québec: Presses de l'Université Laval, 1995], 29–121, 219–525; with RoR, see 410–22). See specifically 419–22 on the rape of Eve, where Painchaud reads, as do Tardieu and Barc, the rape as a "fall" that sullies humanity. See, in particular, Stroumsa, *Another Seed,* chapter 2, "The Archons as Seducers," 35–70; he compares the rape of Eve in SRJ, RoR, and OnOrig with a variety of Enochic, rabbinic, and early Christian literatures. Stroumsa relies heavily on "gnostic" categories, which, I believe, fail to account specifically for the political dimensions of the text but for others as well. His comparative work, however, is invaluable for both this study and future study of the rape of Eve story. As will be evident throughout this chapter, I read the Secret Revelation of John, the Reality of the Rulers, and On the Origin of the World SRJquite differently than these four scholars, but, nonetheless,

These are texts that do not hesitate to speak about rape. But, even so, it is still shocking that these narratives never shy away from the cruelty and power dynamics embedded in the Roman myths, histories, semiotics, and gendered ideologies of sexual violence and conquest, and boldly name them as such. The violence of the rulers in these three retellings of Genesis is addressed head-on—the narratives do not allow the rulers' violence to have the final word, nor do they allow those who have experienced such violence to be labeled as mere victims. The violence done to Eve is never glossed over or denied, but Eve's story does not end in shame or suicide. She goes on to love her partner, Adam, and to birth the heir(s) to salvation through that love.

The Rape of Eve in the Secret Revelation of John[5]

The Secret Revelation of John, found in four extant manuscripts,[6] is framed as a teaching dialogue between the Savior and John, son of Zebedee. The Savior begins his teaching by describing God—also called "Father of all things," "the holy One," "the invisible Spirit," among other titles—in a primarily apophatic manner. Next, the Savior narrates the proliferation of the divine realm through God's contemplation and thought, God's thought (ἔννοια) becoming a thing[7] and beginning a proliferation of divine beings. Each successive generation of beings emanated from a male and female pair acting in concert with their partner and with permission of God, exemplifying the collective harmony of the divine realm.

Wisdom, one of these emanations, had a thought (ⲙⲉⲉⲩⲉ) on her own and without the consent of the invisible Spirit or her partner. With

---

their close and insightful readings have been invaluable for this study. This analysis will continue through chapters 4 and 5.

5. For a thorough analysis of the Secret Revelation of John, see King, *Secret Revelation of John.* I use her translation (pp. 26-81) with minor alterations throughout. See also the text and translation in Michael M. Waldstein and Frederik Wisse, eds., *The Apocryphon of John: Synopsis of Nag Hammadi Codices II,1; III,1 and IV,1 with BG 8502.2,* NHMS 33 (Leiden: Brill, 1995). Any retranslations here have been in consultation with their Coptic text. In addition, see Tardieu, *Trois mythes.*

6. There are four extant manuscripts of the Secret Revelation of John—the Berlin Codex (BG) and Nag Hammadi Codices II, III, and IV. Where relevant, specific manuscripts will be cited on their own, or with parallels—these citations will generally occur in the footnotes and simply noted SRJ in the body of the text.

7. SRJ BG 27.4-5 // III 7.12 // II 4.26-27 // IV 7.1-2.

this she broke the harmony of the divine realm, and her powerful thought became a thing—but this thing was different from what came before and was created in ignorance: it had the form of lion and a serpent with eyes of fire.[8] Her offspring, Yaldabaoth, the Chief Ruler,[9] copulated with madness (ἀπόνοια), which was inside him, and created his own realm with the power given to him by his mother, Wisdom.[10] He also created attendant authorities, powers, and angels—his world a deficient reflection of the divine realm, based not on harmony and concord but in ignorance, jealousy, deception, and desire.[11]

Yaldabaoth, emboldened by the glory and power of the light of his Mother, becomes Lord (II, ϫοειc) over // Christ (BG, χριστός) to his creation[12] and declares, "I am a jealous god and there is no other god besides me!"[13] Wisdom became disturbed upon hearing this and became aware of her deficient creation—created alone, without her partner or the divine realm. Realizing what she has done, Wisdom repents for her actions and is reembraced by the divine realm. Upon her repentance, a voice sounds from heaven, and Yaldabaoth and his attendants hear it and see an image on the waters. They then plot with one another, saying, "Let us create a human in the image of God and according to our likeness, so that his image may enlighten us."[14]

Following Genesis, Yaldabaoth and his minions decide to create a human in the image of God, which they saw in the waters, and their own likeness, hoping that the human's power will enlighten them.

---

8. SRJ BG 37.19–38.1: ⲉⲁϥϣⲱⲡⲉ ⲙ̄ⲡ̄ⲧⲩⲡⲟⲥ ⲛ̄ⲕⲉⲉⲓⲛⲉ ⲉϥⲟ ⲛ̄ⲣⲁ ⲛ̄ⲣⲟϥ ⲁⲩⲱ ⲛ̄ⲣⲟ ⲙⲙⲟⲩⲉⲓ ⲛⲉϥ<ⲃⲁⲗ ⲛ̄>ⲉ̄ⲩⲣ̄ ⲟⲩⲟⲓⲛ ⲉⲛ̄ ⲟⲩⲕⲱⲣⲧ̄ // III 14.9–12 // II 10.8–11: ⲁϥϣⲱⲡⲉ ⲛ̄ⲟⲩⲧⲩⲡⲟⲥ ⲉϥϭⲃⲃⲓⲁⲉⲓⲧ ⲛ̄ⲁⲣⲁⲕⲱⲛ ⲛ̄ⲣⲟ ⲙⲙⲟⲩⲉⲓ ⲛⲉϥⲃⲁⲗ ⲇⲉ ⲛⲉⲩⲟ ⲛ̄ⲑⲉ ⲛ̄ⲛⲓⲕⲱⲣⲧ̄ ⲛ̄ⲣ̄ⲃⲃⲣⲏϭⲉ ⲉⲩϯ ⲟⲩⲟⲉⲓⲛ.
9. Yaldabaoth and the Chief Ruler are used interchangeably to talk about this being.
10. Drawing on the Prologue of John's Gospel, the Secret Revelation of John enacts a stark reversal of the description of Logos in terms of the Chief Ruler saying, "When the light [ⲟⲩⲟⲉⲓⲛ] mixed [ⲧⲱⲣ] with the darkness [ⲕⲁⲕⲉ], it caused the darkness [ⲕⲁⲕⲉ] to shine [ⲣ̄ ⲟⲩⲟⲉⲓⲛ], but when the darkness [ⲕⲁⲕⲉ] mixed [ⲧⲱⲣ] with the light [ⲟⲩⲟⲉⲓⲛ], it darkened [ⲅⲧⲙ̄ⲧⲙ̄] the light [ⲟⲩⲟⲉⲓⲛ], so that it became neither light [ⲟⲩⲟⲉⲓⲛ] nor dark [ⲕⲁⲕⲉ] but it was weak [ϣⲟⲛⲉ]." Highlighting the Coptic in John 1:5, the resonances between these two "And the light [ⲟⲩⲟⲓⲛ] shines [ⲣⲟⲩⲟⲓⲛ] in the darkness [ⲕⲁⲕⲉ] and the darkness [ⲕⲁⲕⲉ] did not attain [ⲧⲁⲣⲟ] it."
11. On Yaldabaoth's creation, see SRJ BG 38.19–44.15 // III 16.4–18.25 // II 10.23–13.9 // IV 17.1–20.24.
12. SRJ II 12.6 // IV 19.4; BG 42.19.
13. SRJ BG 44.14–15 // II 13.8–9 // IV 20.22–24. Cf. Exod 20:5; 34:14; Deut 5:6–7; 32:39; Isa 45:5–6; 46:9; Joel 2:27.
14. SRJ II 15.2–4: ⲁⲙⲏⲉⲓⲛⲉ ⲛ̄ⲧⲛ̄ⲧⲁⲙⲓⲟ ⲛ̄ⲟⲩⲣⲱⲙⲉ ⲕⲁⲧⲁ ⲑⲉⲓⲕⲱⲛ ⲙ̄ⲡⲛⲟⲩⲧⲉ ⲁⲩⲱ ⲕⲁⲧⲁ ⲡⲛⲉⲓⲛⲉ ϫⲉⲕⲁⲁⲥ ⲁⲣⲉⲧⲉϥ `ϩⲓⲕⲱⲛ ⲛⲁϣⲱⲡⲉ ⲛⲁⲛ ⲛ̄ⲟⲩⲟⲉⲓⲛ. // IV 23.16–20 // BG 48.11–14. Cf. Gen 1:26.

The seven authorities of Yaldabaoth create out of their powers, and in doing so inadvertently give these powers to their human creation, i.e. Adam. After Adam's creation, the divine realm intervenes and tricks the Chief Ruler into transferring his Mother's power to Adam by breathing into Adam's face. This transfer of power with this breath incites the jealousy of the authorities and powers as they realize that not only have they given Adam their power, but also that Adam is wiser than they. In their jealousy they "picked him up and threw him down into the lowest part of all matter [ὕλη]."[15]

The Father (BG // III)/Mother-Father (II // IV) once again intervenes on behalf of the human, sending the Insight[16] of Light so that the rulers, powers, and authorities might not gain power over Adam's (soul-full and perceptive) body.[17] The introduction of the Insight of Light begins to turn the text toward Eve as Insight exhibits many of Eve's attributes from the Hebrew Bible: Insight is sent to Adam as a helper (SRJ, βοηθός;[18] Gen 2:18; 2:20 LXX) and is also called Life (SRJ, ζωή;[19] Gen 3:20 LXX). Insight is also the one who "labors for the whole creation by toiling with [Adam] (cf. Gen 3:13),[20] by setting him right in his own perfect temple,[21] and by teaching him about the descent of his deficiency and instructing him about his ascent."[22] Beyond these connections with the biblical Eve, Insight is also described as the good

15. SRJ BG 51.1–55.13 // III 23.19–26.25 // II 19.15–21.13 // 29.24–32.26.
16. In an effort to acknowledge that those encountering these texts in the ancient world would not have simply thought of these as names but rather as personifications of the concepts these words represent, I have opted to use English translation for all personifications. (Cf. Frances T. Fallon, *The Enthronement of Sabaoth: Jewish Elements in Gnostic Creation Myths*, NHS 10 [Leiden: Brill, 1978], 6–7n7.) Additionally, to emphasize the connections within the range of -*noia* (mind) names used, I have opted to use Insight to translate Epinoia and Foresight for Pronoia. While other translations are more widely used, particularly Reflection for Epinoia and Providence for Pronoia (and highlight other important aspects of the semantic range of the Greek), the English obscures certain relationships between these words that the Greek does not.
17. SRJ BG 52.2–53.8 // II 19.34–20.17; Father BG // III and Mother-Father II // IV; "soul-full and perceptive," uniquely in II 20.14.
18. SRJ BG 53.6 // III 25.8 // II 20.17.
19. SRJ BG 53.9 // III 25.11 // II 20.19 // IV 31.16.
20. SRJ BG 53.11–12 // III 25.12–13 // II 20.19–20 // 31.16–17.
21. Cf. 1 Cor 3:16: "Do you not know that you are God's temple and the God's Spirit dwells in you?"; 1 Cor 3:17: "If anyone destroys God's temple, God will destroy that person. For God's temple is holy, and you are that temple."; 1 Cor 6:19: "Or do you not know that your body is a temple of the Holy Spirit within you, which you have from God, and that you are not your own?"
22. SRJ BG 53.4–17 // III 20.15–23; II 20.22–23, "by teaching him about the descent of his seed."

Spirit²³ and the tree whom the rulers call "the knowledge of good and evil,"²⁴ sent by the Father/Mother-Father as a correction for Wisdom's deficiency²⁵ and hidden inside of Adam so that the rulers "might not know her."²⁶

Those who create Adam again realize he is superior to them and decide to mix fire, earth, water, and flame, creating a disturbance (ⲁⲩⲧⲟⲣⲧⲣ̅), "enclos[ing] him in the shadow of death," making "another form from earth, water, fire, and spirit, a thing from matter, which is the ignorance of the darkness, desire, and their counterfeit spirit. This is the tomb of the molded body with which the robbers clothed the human, the chain of forgetfulness."²⁷ The Chief Ruler then places Adam in paradise.²⁸ In what is perhaps the clearest articulation of how the Secret Revelation of John views the rulers, the manuscripts go on to describe paradise, the rulers, and their Tree of Life. "For their delight [τρυφή] is bitter and their beauty²⁹ is lawless. Their delight [τρυφή] is a deception and their tree is iniquity (II, impiety).³⁰ Their fruit is an incurable poison and their promise is death to him. Their tree which they planted is the Tree of Life." The Savior tells John that he will explain this to him and "teach you all about the mystery of their life. It is their counterfeit spirit which dwells in them, whose purpose is to make him wander so that he does not know his perfection. That tree is of this sort: Its root is bitter. Its branches are shadows of death. Its leaves are hate and deception. Its fragrance is an ointment/anointment

23. SRJ BG 53.5; III 25.6, the Father "sent his Spirit"; II 20.14–16, the Mother-Father sent a helper, "through his beneficent Spirit."
24. SRJ BG 57.8–19 // III 28.6–15.
25. SRJ II uniquely calls Wisdom the "Wisdom of Insight" (II 9.25), so Wisdom is of Insight and Insight then comes to help Wisdom.
26. On both "being a correction for Wisdom's deficiency" and "hidden in Adam," see BG 53.18–54.4 // III 25.17–23 // II 20.25–28.
27. SRJ BG 51.1–55.13 // III 23.19–26.25 // II 19.15–21.13 // 29.24–32.26.
28. Cf. Gen 2:8. Here SRJ plays on the original Greek meaning of paradise and in particular the LXX's translation of Eden (עדן meaning "delight") as τρυφή. BG // III notes that the Chief Ruler says of paradise, "'It is a delight for him' but really [said this] so that he might deceive him (Adam)" (BG 55.19–56.3 // III 27.4–8). See King also on the play between τρυφή and τροφή, the Greek for food (Secret Revelation of John, 103–4, 131–32, 186–87).
29. The instance in this section and its parallels are the only time the verb ⲥⲁ/ⲉ is used in the entire text.
30. Cf. Gen 3:6.

of evil. And its fruit is the desire for death. Its seed drinks from darkness. The dwelling place of those who taste it is Hades."[31]

The Savior then returns to Adam's story as Insight hides herself within Adam. At this point, following Genesis 2:21–22, Adam's bodily integrity is violated by the Chief Ruler (as Eve's will be) in an effort to extract the Insight of Life from within him.[32] Through this extraction the Chief Ruler attempts to take this divine power from Adam for himself, but the text tells us that Insight is "ungraspable" (ⲁⲧⲧⲁϩⲟ) and adds, "Although the dark pursued (ⲡⲏⲧ ⲛ̄ⲥⲱⲥ) her, it did not lay hold (ⲧⲁϩⲟⲥ) of her."[33] Even so, Yaldabaoth does manage to bring a part of Adam's power from him through making a molded form in the shape of a woman—in II this woman is specifically made according to the image of Insight—who again intervenes on behalf of the divine realm.[34]

As soon as Adam sees the molded woman beside him,[35] Insight, "uncovering the shroud/veil which had been on his understanding," causes Adam to become "sober from the drunkenness of darkness."[36] Adam knows this woman as his essence (BG 60.4, οὐσία), co-essence (III 30.4, συνουσία), likeness (II 23.9, ⲉⲓⲛⲉ), and partner (IV 36.1, ϣⲃⲣⲉⲓⲛⲉ)[37]

---

31. SRJ BG 55.19–57.7 // III 27.4–28.6 // II 21.16–22.2 // IV 33.1–34.5. II is very similar in tone, but with a few variants: "But I, I will teach [ⲧⲥⲁⲃⲱ] you all what the mystery [μυστήριον] of their life [ⲱⲛϩ] is, the plan they made with each other, the likeness [ⲉⲓⲛⲉ] of their spirit [πνεῦμα]. Its root [ⲛⲟⲩⲛⲉ] is bitter and its branches [κλάδος] are deaths [ⲙⲟⲩ]. Its shade/shadow [ϩⲟⲓⲃⲉⲥ] is hate and deception [ἀπάτη] dwells in its leaves. And its blossom is the anointment [ⲧⲱϩⲥ̄] of evil. And its fruit is death [ⲙⲟⲩ], and desire [ἐπιθυμία] is its seed [σπέρμα], and it blossoms from the darkness. The dwelling place of those who taste from it is Hades, and the dark is their resting [ⲙ̄ⲧⲟⲛ] place" (II 21.26–22.2).

32. Karen L. King, "Reading Sex and Gender in the *Secret Revelation of John*," *JECS* 19.4 (2011): 522. Cf. King, "The Book of Norea, Daughter of Eve," in *Searching the Scriptures*, vol. 2, *A Feminist Commentary*, ed. Elisabeth Schüssler Fiorenza (New York: Crossroad, 1994), 70, on the "surgical violation of Adam" in RoR.

33. SRJ BG 59.6–12 // III 29.12–17 // II 22.28–32 // IV 35.14. Note the parallelism between Insight's attribute of ungraspability, ⲁⲧⲧⲁϩⲟ, and the Chief Ruler's inability to "lay hold," ⲧⲁϩⲟⲥ, of her. Cf. John 1:5: ⲁⲩⲱ ⲡⲟⲩⲟⲓⲛ ϥⲣⲟⲩⲟⲓⲛ ϩⲙ ⲡⲕⲁⲕⲉ ⲁⲩⲱ ⲙⲡⲉ ⲡⲕⲁⲕⲉ ⲧⲁϩⲟϥ. This portion of text also has parallels to the story of Daphne and Apollo, as Apollo pursues Daphne (*insequor* = ⲡⲏⲧ ⲛ̄ⲥⲱⲥ = διώκω) and he cannot grasp or catch her (*Met.* 1.473–544).

34. SRJ BG 59.12–15 // III 29.18–20 // II 22.32–36 // IV 35.14–19. See King, *Secret Revelation of John*, 104–5, on Adam, Insight, and the creation of Eve.

35. SRJ II 23.4–6 // IV 35.25–28 specifically states that when "Adam saw the woman beside him . . . enlightened Insight appeared." Insight's precise relationship to the woman in BG is more ambiguous—a trend that continues throughout that manuscript.

36. SRJ BG 59.20–60.2 // III 30.1–3 // II 23.5–8 // IV 35.26–31.

37. Cf. Gen 2:19 LXX: "Let us make him a helper according to him" (ποιήσωμεν αὐτῷ βοηθὸν κατ᾽αὐτόν); and Gen 2:20: "but for Adam there was not found a helper like him" (τῷ δὲ Αδαμ οὐχ εὑρέθη βοηθὸς ὅμοιος αὐτῷ).

and quoting Genesis 2:23–24 says, "Now this is bone from by bone and flesh from my flesh. Because of this, man will leave his father and his mother and will cling to his wife, and from two they will become a single flesh."[38] BG explains the meaning of this quotation, saying, "For the Mother's partner [σύνζυγος] will be sent forth and she will be set right. Because of this, Adam named her the mother of all the living[39] by the authority of the exalted height and the revelation" (BG 60.12–18).

While BG clearly draws a connection between Adam and Eve's sexual union (i.e., "become a single flesh")[40] and the restoration of Wisdom and her partner, Codices II and IV are even more explicit about this connection. They explain "a single flesh" by saying, "For his partner [ϣⲃⲣ̄ ⲛ̄ⲍⲱⲧⲣ̄][41] will be sent to him and he will leave his father and his mother. It is our sister Wisdom who came down in innocence in order that she might correct her deficiency. Because of this she was called Life, the mother of the living by Foresight of the authority of heaven"—"and by Insight who appeared to him" (IV 36.18–20 only)—"and through her they tasted the perfect knowledge" (II 23.14–26). In these two manuscripts, the figures of Eve, Insight, Wisdom, and Life overlap,[42] moving in and around one another, with each connected to Foresight and forming a tight constellation of divine figures working with and for humanity under the reign of the rulers.[43] In this way, the partnership between Adam and Eve is therefore a display of Wisdom's own involvement in the transformation of Yaldabaoth's world. Foresight honors Wisdom's role in this transformative process by calling her Life, mother of the living, just as Insight was called in BG 53.9. Wisdom is no longer associated with the death-dealing Yaldabaoth, but with the forces of life that connect the divine and human realms.

Next the manuscripts of SRJ present two slightly different stories in which the actors differ, though the outcomes are the same. In BG,

38. SRJ BG 60.5–11 // III 30.5–10 // II 23.10–14 // IV 36.2–8.
39. Gen 3:20.
40. See King, *Secret Revelation of John*, 127–28; King, "Reading Sex," 525–26, 525n3.
41. In both cases here, it is his partner and not his woman/wife.
42. See King, *Secret Revelation of John*, 106, 248–49.
43. See King, "Reading Sex," 527–30.

Insight appears in the form of an eagle from the tree and teaches "him to eat of knowledge so that he might remember his perfection for both were in a fallen state of ignorance" (BG 61.1–7).[44] Codex II, by contrast, says that it was actually the Savior, speaking here in the first person, rather than Insight, who appears in the form of an eagle "on the Tree of Knowledge, which is the Insight from the pure, enlightened Foresight, so that I might teach them and awaken them from the depth of the sleep. For they were both in a fallen state and they knew their nakedness. Insight appeared to them as light, awakening their thought" (II 21.26–33). Here again, Codex II emphasizes the connections between Insight and Foresight, but now pulls the Savior into this constellation of interwoven entities. While Codex II adds the Savior to the story, in both II and BG Adam and Eve are found to be in a "fallen state," and it is the work of Insight (or Insight/the Savior) to awaken them from this condition. Through Insight's teaching they awaken and what has been extracted from Adam through bodily violation is then reintegrated later through the "eating" (BG) and "tasting" of knowledge.[45]

As Adam and Eve awaken and remember because of Insight's teaching, Yaldabaoth knows (ⲉⲓⲙⲉ)[46] that they have withdrawn from him; that is, Yaldabaoth "knows" that Adam and Eve have changed and withdrawn because of the knowledge and insight they have gained.[47] In BG and Codex III Yaldabaoth curses Adam and Eve for their withdrawal,[48] whereas in Codices II and IV he does not simply curse Adam and Eve but "curses his earth."[49] Then BG and III state that,

44. Here the text seems to be speaking of Insight particularly teaching Adam to "eat of knowledge," though it seems that "both" are in a fallen state of ignorance. Insight and Eve are fairly conflated in this portion of BG, so it is difficult to know if this is what prompts the text to speak predominantly of Adam's need to eat and enlightenment, or if there is something else occurring given the "both" in BG 61.6. The reconstruction of III 30.17–21 uses the plural "they" at each of the points in which BG uses the singular "he/him."
45. SRJ BG 60.19–61.4 // III 30.17–19 // II 23.25–31 // IV 36.19–29. In II it is through Foresight/Pronoia that they "taste" knowledge, and the Savior who teaches them "in the form of an eagle on the Tree of Knowledge, which is the Insight/Epinoia from the Foresight/Pronoia of pure light." Here Insight and Foresight are inextricably linked.
46. SRJ BG 61.8 // III 30.22 // II 23.35 // IV 37.4—all four manuscripts use the verb ⲉⲓⲙⲉ.
47. SRJ BG 61.8–9 // III 30.23 // II 23.36 // IV 37.5–6—all four manuscripts use "they," indicating that both Adam and Eve withdraw from Yaldabaoth.
48. SRJ BG 61.9–10 // III 30.23 (reconstructed in III).

after the curse, Yaldabaoth "adds concerning the female that the male should rule [p̄ ϫoϵιc] over her[50] for he does not understand [cooyn an] the mystery [μυστήριον] which came from the design of the Holy Height."[51] Codices II and IV are not quite as clear, given the difficulty with the antecedents for the various "he's": "*He* found the female preparing herself for the male [i.e., Adam]. *He* was lord [ϫoϵιc] over her, for *he* did not understand [cooyn an] the mystery [μυστήριον] which had come from the holy design."[52] Despite the various "he's," in II and IV, it is clearly Yaldabaoth who finds Eve preparing herself for Adam ["the male"]. It is, however, not entirely apparent if it is Adam or Yaldabaoth who is "lord over her," not understanding the "holy design." Given the context, and what is to come, it seems likely that these manuscripts are implying that Yaldabaoth is lord over Eve because he did not understand the mystery, rather than Adam, particularly given that II and IV say that Yaldabaoth "showed his angels his ignorance which is in him," but the text is open to interpretation.[53] At this juncture BG and III note, "they [presumably his angels] were afraid to curse him and to reveal his ignorance."[54] Even with these ambiguities, two points are made clear across all four of the SRJ manuscripts: first, the position of the male as lord over the female is not part of the divine plan, and, second, Yaldabaoth's creation of this hierarchy reveals his ignorance.

After cursing Adam and Eve and decreeing a hierarchy between them, Yaldabaoth casts them out of paradise. The Chief Ruler then sees "the virgin" (πάρθενος) standing beside Adam,[55] II and IV adding he saw that "the living [ⲱⲛ̅ϩ] enlightened [oyϵin] Insight appeared in her."[56] Upon seeing her, Yaldabaoth was filled with "ignorance"

---

49. SRJ II 23.37 // IV 37.6.
50. Gen 3:17: "And your refuge with be with your man and he will be lord of you" (καὶ πρὸς τὸν ἄνδρα σου ἡ ἀποστροφή σου, καὶ αὐτός σου κυριεύσει).
51. SRJ BG 61.10–15 // III 30.24–31.1. See King, *Secret Revelation of John*, 106, who calls this "the strongest overt critic of patriarchy in ancient literature."
52. SRJ II 23.37–24.3 // IV 37.7–11.
53. SRJ II 24.5–6 // IV 37.12–14.
54. SRJ BG 61.16–18 // III 31.2–3.
55. SRJ BG 62.3–4 // III 31.6–7 // II 24.8–10 // IV 37.17–19.
56. SRJ II 24.10–11 // IV 37.19–21.

(ⲙⲛ̄ⲧⲁⲧⲥⲟⲟⲩⲛ)[57] and "senselessness" (ⲙⲛ̄ⲧⲁⲑⲏⲧ),[58] "desiring to raise up a seed in her."[59] Codices II and IV add that, when "Foresight of all things knew [ⲉⲓⲙⲉ], she sent some beings and they snatched [ⲧⲱⲣⲡ][60] Life from Eve"[61]—the spiritual aspect of Eve splitting and leaving her body before being raped by the Chief Ruler.

All four of the manuscripts then simply state that the Chief Ruler defiled (ⲭⲁϩⲙⲉⲥ)[62] Eve.[63] The rulers Cain and Abel are born from the Chief Ruler's rape, implying that Yaldabaoth did not rape her once but many times.[64] These two rulers, born from the Chief Ruler's act of rape, are then "set over the authorities [ἀρχή] so that they might rule [ἄρχειν] over the tomb [ⲙϩⲁⲟⲩ/σπήλαιον] [i.e., bodies[65]]."[66] Not only does the Chief Ruler's rape bring his children as rulers to rule humanity, but it brings about the act of marital intercourse (συνουσία γάμος)—presumably for the male to rule the female—which has continued "up to the present day" (BG 63.1-4). Codices II, III, and IV closely parallel BG but do not qualify the intercourse (συνουσία II and IV/συνουσιασμός III) as "marital," though συνουσία itself has

---

57. SRJ III 31.8 // II 24.12 // IV 37.23.

58. SRJ BG 62.6.

59. SRJ BG 62.6-7 // III 31.8-9.

60. This is the same word (ⲧⲱⲣⲡ) that is used in Acts 8:39 when "the Spirit of the Lord *snatched* Philip away," and in Rev 12:5 where the child of the woman "who is to rule the nations . . . was *snatched* away and taken to God and to his throne."

61. Codex II 24.13-15 // IV 37.23-26. BG and III alone of the four SRJ manuscripts and the stories of the rape of Eve as told by Reality of the Rulers and On the Origin of the World do not have some spiritual part of Eve split from the material Eve. This may be in part because BG and III are more ambiguous regarding the exact relationship between Insight and Eve, never indicating whether they inhabit the same being, unlike the complex weaving of the two in II and IV. BG and III simply note that Insight lifts the shroud and Adam becomes sober, then she teaches from the tree—the text remains unclear regarding the exact relationship between Insight and Eve. See below for the discussion on this splitting in RoR and OnOrig.

62. Again see Crum, 797b-798a.

63. SRJ BG 62.8 // III 31.10 // II 24.15-16 // IV 37.27-28.

64. SRJ BG 62.8-20 // III 31.10-20 // II 24.16-25 // IV 37.28-38.11. Cf. Gen 4:1-2: "Now Adam knew [ידע; γινώσκω] his woman/wife Eve, and she conceived and bore Cain, saying, 'I have acquired a man with the Lord [יהוה; LXX God, θεός].' Next she bore his brother Abel." See the discussion of this in both the RoR section of this chapter as well as chapter 4.

   See also Stroumsa, *Another Seed,* 38: Yaldabaoth "begot from her two sons, Elohim and Jahwe—'And these he called with the names Cain and Abel, with a view to deceive' (II 24:8-25). In other words, he gave them these names in order to conceal their archontic nature."

65. Cf. SRJ BG 55.10-13 // III 26.20-23 // II 21.9-13 // IV 32.22-25. BG: "This is the tomb of the form of the body with which they clothed the human as the bond of matter." III // II // IV: "This is the tomb of the form of the body with which the robbers had clothed the human, the bond of forgetfulness. And he became a mortal human."

66. SRJ BG 63.10-12 // III 32.4-6 // II 24.32-34 // IV 38.21-24.

connotations of social connections and ties.[67] Regardless of whether "intercourse" is framed as specifically "marital" or not, each of the four SRJ manuscripts speaks of a physical relationship that is based on hierarchy and physical violation. Codices II and IV continue, saying that the Chief Ruler "planted [xⲱ] a seed [σπορά] of desire [ἐπιθυμία] in her who belongs to Adam,"[68] while BG and III state that this "desire [ἐπιθυμία] for seed [σπορά]" was planted in Adam himself.[69] Whether this desire resides in Adam or Eve, the Chief Ruler has planted it for the purpose of creating bodies through both intercourse with his "counterfeit spirit"—bodies that he and his children, his authorities, and his powers, can rule.[70]

---

67. SRJ II 24.26–27 // IV 38.12–15 // III 31.21–23. See LSJ, s.v. συνουσία.

68. SRJ II 24.28–29 // IV 38.16–17.

69. SRJ BG 63.5–6 // III 31.23–24. Stroumsa reads this as indicating that "Eve became sexually attractive to Adam only after her seduction by the demiurge" (*Another Seed*, 35). I, instead, read with King that their sexual relationship is already indicated. See SRJ BG 60.3–11 // III 30.3–10 // II 23.9–11 // IV 36.1–3, where Adam knows the woman as his essence (BG 60.4, οὐσία), co-essence (III 30.4, συνουσία), likeness (II 23.9 ⲉⲓⲛⲉ), and partner (IV 36.1 ϭⲃⲣ̄ⲉⲓⲛⲉ), and declares, "Indeed you are bone of my bones; and flesh of my flesh. Therefore the man will leave his father and his mother and he will cleave to his woman and they will both become one flesh" (cf. Gen 2:23–24). See discussion of Adam and Eve's sexual union and the birth of Seth below.

70. SRJ BG 63.5–9 // III 31.23–32.3 // II 24.29–31 // 38.17–21. In an earlier episode (not presented in this study until now), the savior is explaining to John that the commandment from the rulers was to not eat of "the knowledge of good and evil," which is Insight, but that this is indeed what the savior has influenced them to do (BG 57.8–58.1 // II 22.4–9). John then asks the savior if it was not the serpent that taught them (variously Adam, Eve, or both—see below), and the Savior answers that the serpent taught about the seed of desire, pollution, and destruction because these are useful to the serpent, but they disobeyed him (again, see variants below) (BG 58.2–10 // II 22.9–18). As King notes, "It is on the basis of these two passages [i.e., BG 58.2–10 // II 22.9–18 and BG 63.1–9 // II 24.26–31] that most interpreters read *SRJ* as rejecting sexual intercourse" ("Reading Sex," 525). In the course of this study, I am arguing, in agreement with King (in certain ways), that SRJ does not reject sexual intercourse as such, but particular dynamics and constructs of intercourse. The connections between these two passages in SRJ are significant, and the episode with the serpent parallels Yaldabaoth's "planting of desire" in relationship to his rape of Eve:

II 22.12–18 // IV 34.16–25: "The serpent [ⲅⲟϥ] taught them to eat from a wicked seed [σπορά] of desire [ἐπιθυμία] which brings destruction so that he [Adam] might be useful to him. And he knew that he was disobedient to him because of the light of Insight which exists within him, which made him more correct in this thinking than the Chief Ruler."

II 24.15–16; 24.26–31 // IV 37.27–28; 38.13–21: "And the Chief Ruler defiled [xⲁⲣ̄ⲙⲉⲥ] her. . . . Now up to the present day intercourse has continued from the Chief Ruler. And he sowed [xⲱ] a seed [σπορά] of desire [ἐπιθυμία] in her who belongs to Adam. And he set up through intercourse the likeness of the bodies and he supplied them from his counterfeit spirit."

BG 58.4–10: "The serpent [ⲅⲟϥ] taught her about the seed [σπορά] of desire [ἐπιθυμία], defilement [ⲥⲱⲱϥ] and destruction because they are useful to him. And he knew that she would not obey him because she is wiser than he."

BG 62.8; 63.1–9: "He defiled [xⲁⲣⲙⲉⲥ] her. . . . Up to the present day, marital intercourse came about from the Chief Ruler. He sowed [xⲟ] in Adam a desire [ἐπιθυμία] for seed [σπορά] which gave birth to a likeness from their counterfeit spirit from this essence (desire)."

III 28.20–25: "The serpent [ⲅⲟϥ] appeared to them because the seed [σπορά] of desire [ἐπιθυμία]

Yaldabaoth's act of sexual aggression is then sharply contrasted through the descriptions of Adam's union with Eve. Codices II and IV relate that, when Adam "knew [ⲙ̅ⲙⲉ] the likeness [ⲉⲓⲛⲉ] of his own Foreknowledge [πρόγνωσις], he begot the likeness [ⲉⲓⲛⲉ] of the Child of the Human; he called him Seth following the way of generation [ϫⲡⲟ] in the [upper] realms [αἰών]."[71] In BG, the birth of Seth occurs after

which is the defilement [ⲥⲟⲟϥ] of destruction, so that he might be useful to him. He knew that he was disobedient to him because he was wiser than he."

III 31.10; 31.21–32.3: "And he defiled [ϫⲱⲣⲙ̅] her. . . . Up to the present day, intercourse continues and remains from the Chief Ruler. And he planted [ϫⲟ] in Adam a seed [σπορά] of desire [ἐπιθυμία] so that through this essence they gave birth to their likeness through their counterfeit spirit."

Although the actors occur in different configurations (In II // IV "they" are taught by the serpent, though it seems that the "seed of desire" is connected particularly to Adam, while the "seed of desire" is connected with Eve after her rape; in BG the serpent teaches "her" [which Wisse and Waldenstein infer to mean Insight-Life, but could be referring to Eve because of her connection with this portion of Genesis] about the "seed of desire," and Eve again in whom this seed is sown by Yaldabaoth after her rape; in III "they" are both taught that the "seed is desire which is defilement" by the serpent throughout this passage, and then it is Adam in whom the "seed of desire" is planted after Yaldabaoth's rape of Eve. Additionally, in the serpent passage, Wisse and Waldenstein read the "he's" that follow in terms of Yaldabaoth, while King reads them as referring to the serpent, ϩⲟϥ being grammatically masculine), each of the pairs contains a sowing or teaching of the "seed of desire" by Yaldabaoth, with BG and III also adding defilement to the serpent episode, thus further paralleling the two (although ⲥⲱⲱϥ is used in the serpent episode of both while ϫⲱⲣⲙ is used in Yaldabaoth's rape of Eve, these two words contain the same semantic range, have been used interchangeably in identical verses in different Coptic Hebrew Bible manuscripts, and often translate identical Greek words; see Crum). Significantly, the serpent and Yaldabaoth are also not only within the text itself, but through the constellation of signifiers associated with Yaldabaoth. BG 37.20–21 // III 15.11 describes Yaldabaoth as having "the face of a serpent [ϩⲟϥ] and the face of a lion," and II 10.9 describes him as "a lion-faced dragon [δράκων]."

71. SRJ II 24.35–25.2 // IV 38.25–30. For the direct parallelism between the proliferation between the divine realm and Adam-Eve-Seth, see BG 34.19–35.5: "And from Foreknowledge [ⲛϣⲟⲣⲡ ⲛ̅ⲥⲟⲟⲅⲛ] and the perfect [τέλειος] Mind [νοῦς], through God, through the good will of the great invisible Spirit and the good will of the Self-Generated [came] the perfect, true Human, the original one to be revealed. He was Adam"; III 12.24–13.4: "From the Foreknowledge [ⲛϣⲟⲣⲡ ⲛ̅ⲥⲟⲟⲅⲛ] of the perfect [τέλειος] Mind [νοῦς], through the gift and good will of the great invisible Spirit, in the presence of the Self-Generated, the perfect [τέλειος], true, holy Human, the original one who was revealed—he was named Adamas"; III 8.28–34: "And from the Foreknowledge [πρόγνωσις] of the perfect [τέλειος] Mind [νοῦς], through the revelation of the desire of the invisible Spirit and the desire of the Self-Generated, the perfect [τέλειος] Human, the original revelation and the truth—the one whom the invisible Spirit called Pigera-Adamas." This seems to follow Gen 4:25; 5:1–3: "Adam knew his wife again, and she bore a son and named him Seth, for she said, 'God has appointed for me another child instead of Abel, because Cain killed him. . . .' This is the list of the descendants of Adam. When God created humankind, he made them in the likeness of God. Male and female he created them, and he blessed them and named them 'Humankind' when they were created. When Adam had lived one hundred thirty years, he became the father of a son in his likeness, according to his image, and named him Seth." See the discussion in the RoR section of this chapter and chapter 4.

Of additional note here, particularly in the Adam-Eve-Seth construct, is the heteronormative construct of procreation embodied here. Though this construct is complicated, especially in the divine realm (though to some extent with Adam and Eve as well), by the complex gender

Adam "knew [ⲥⲟⲩⲱⲛ] his essence [οὐσία] which is like [ⲉⲓⲛⲉ] him" (BG 63.12-13), while III says, "He knew [ⲥⲟⲩⲛ̄] his own lawlessness [ἀνομία]" (III 32.6-7).[72] Initially this "lawlessness" may seem a negative trait, especially as the only other place lawlessness/ἀνομία/ἄνομος occurs is in relation to the rulers.[73] But, in a text that places a premium on knowing and being able to see reality for what it is, it is possible that Adam's ability to recognize and see his lawlessness—as compared to the ignorant rulers—is what gives him the capacity to engage in a mutual sexual relationship with his partner "according to the generation which is above among the realms" (III 32.8-9 // BG 63.14-16).[74]

So, despite the desire that the Chief Ruler planted, Adam and Eve's sexual relationship is based not on this desire but on their recognition of one another as partners. This is further illustrated in the double entendre embedded in the verb "to know" (ⲙ̄ⲙⲉ;[75] ⲥⲟⲩⲱⲛ[76])—Adam not only has sex with his partner,[77] but, unlike Yaldabaoth, he actually *knows* her. The awakening and knowledge connected to—and connecting—Adam and Eve through the presence of Insight, their eating of knowledge, and their union occurs in stark relief to the ignorance, folly, desire, and defiling of Yaldabaoth. BG's specific connection of Yaldabaoth's rape of Eve with "marital intercourse" seems to indicate a difference between the hierarchical sexual relationship established by Yaldabaoth and defined by marriage compared with the relationship between Adam and Eve. Though this difference is not named as such, it is illustrated, as Yaldabaoth's rape

---

configurations present, heteronormativity still in many ways undergirds the Adam-Eve relationship. Cf. King, "Reading Sex," 526n25, 528, 531.

72. Cf. Gen 4:25; 5:3: "Adam knew [יָדַע; γινώσκω] his woman/wife, and she bore a son and named him Seth, saying, "God [אֱלֹהִים; θεός] has provided me another seed [זֶרַע אַחֵר; σπέρμα ἕτερον] in place of Abel for Cain killed him"; "When Adam had lived one hundred thirty years (LXX: two hundred thirty years), he begot a son in his likeness [דְּמוּתוֹ; ἰδέα], according to his image [צֶלֶם; εἰκών] and named him Seth."

73. SRJ BG 56.5 // III 27.10 // II 21.20 // IV 33.6.

74. It is, of course, also possible that this was a scribal error.

75. SRJ II 24.35 // IV 38.25.

76. SRJ BG 63.12.

77. Again, see King, *Secret Revelation of John*, 127–28; King, "Reading Sex," 525–26, 525n3.

of Eve and the subsequent birth of Cain and Abel is contrasted with the sexual union of Adam and Eve and the birth of Seth.

Rather than Yaldabaoth's construct of marriage SRJ connects Adam and Eve's procreation and the proliferation within the divine realms. Just as beings flow out from the Father-Mother-Unity, these offspring, created with permission from the Father-Mother-Unity and in conjunction with one's partner—that is, out of the concord of the divine community—so it is with Adam and Eve. Eve literally comes out of Adam, who is made in the image of God and is endowed with the power of the Mother (i.e., power from the divine realm) through the breath of Yaldabaoth "following the holy design."[78] Then the Mother-Father's Spirit,[79] Eve/the Insight of Light/Life, is sent to Adam from the divine realms as a helper because the Mother-Father "is a merciful benefactor. He had mercy on the Mother's power that had been taken from the Chief Ruler so that they might not find power over the body."[80] In these ways, the material Adam and Eve fall into the lineage of those created in the divine realm.[81] Their place in this lineage is further emphasized when all four manuscripts state that the Chief Ruler did not understand "the holy design"—whereby partners act together in concord[82]—when he decreed that the male should rule over the female.[83] The decree also points to BG's distinction between marital sex and the sexual union that Adam and Eve share, the construct of marital sex both reflecting male rule over the female and Yaldabaoth's rape of Eve.

This distinction is extended in the texts' contrast between the offspring that are born from the Chief Ruler's rape of Eve as compared

---

78. See SRJ BG 51.8–20 // II 19.18–32.
79. SRJ BG 52.4 // III 25.6. II 20.15–16 (no parallel in IV), says Insight was "sent *through* his beneficent Spirit."
80. SRJ BG 52.20–53.3. III 24.25–25.5 and II 20.9–14 contain some variants. The most notable occurs in II. 20.14 where the "body" ($\sigma\tilde{\omega}\mu\alpha$) is qualified as "soul-full" ($\psi\nu\chi\iota\varkappa\acute{o}\nu$) and "perceptive" ($\alpha\acute{\iota}\sigma\theta\eta\tau\acute{o}\nu$).
81. See King, *Secret Revelation of John*, 107, on Adam, Eve, and Seth following the pattern of the divine realm. Cf. SRJ BG 34.19–36.2 // III 12.24–13.19 // II 8.28–9.14, where the divine Adam and Seth are proliferated in the divine realms.
82. The concord that marks proliferation in the divine realm is not named as such, though it is exemplified in the way in which it occurs (BG 26.15–36.15 // III 6.2–14.9 // II 4.19–9.24 // IV 6.19–14.6).
83. SRJ BG 61.10–15 // III 30.24–31.1 // II 24.1–3 // IV 37.8–11. See earlier note about the ambiguity regarding the pronoun of the actor in II and IV.

to the birth of Seth, which occurs through Adam's recognition of his essence. Through this recognition, Seth is born "just as . . . in the race [γενεά] which is in heaven, in the [divine] realms"[84] and in "the likeness of the Child of the Human [ⲡϣⲏⲣⲉ ⲙ̄ⲣⲱⲙⲉ],"[85] whereas the product of Yaldabaoth's rape of Eve are rulers.[86] In addition, it is through Seth that the "human beings of the race [γενεά][87] of the eternal, enlightened, perfect Human" come to be.[88] This follows the Genesis text, as after Seth's birth Genesis returns to the story of the beginning, saying, "This is the book of the origin of human beings. On the day that God made Adam, he made him according to divine image; male and female he made them, and he blessed them. And he named their name 'Adam/ Humankind' on the day that he made them" (Gen 5:1–2; cf. Gen 1:26–27 LXX). As in Genesis, the emphasis after the birth of Seth in SRJ is on the blessing of humans made in the image of God and those that are to follow in this image.

Though Eve fades from the story line at this point in the narrative, the difference in the modes of proliferation between partners (whether of those in the upper or lower realms) is once again brought into relief through the manuscripts' retelling of the Noah story. After the Insight of Light awakened the generation of the human, the Chief Ruler knew that they surpassed him in their thought. In order to "restrict their plan" the rulers "begot Fate"[89] in an effort to make "the whole creation

---

84. SRJ BG 63.14–16; cf. III 32.8–9 // II 25.2 // IV 38.29–30.
85. Also, "the Son of Man."
86. SRJ II 25.1 // IV 38.27–29.
87. SRJ II 27.3–4 // IV 43.15: "perfect [τέλεοιν] race [γενεά]"; III 36.25: "immovable race" (ⲧⲅⲉⲛⲉⲁ ⲉⲧⲉⲙⲉⲥⲕⲓⲙ).
88. SRJ BG 71.10–13 // III 36.23–37.1 // II 28.3–5 // IV 43.14–7.
89. SRJ BG 72.2–4 // III 37.6–7 // II 28.11–14 // IV 43.24–29. Both II and IV add that Fate was begotten when, "together they committed adultery with Wisdom [σοφία]," or it is also possible that the text may say, "they committed adultery with one another's wisdom." This second reading was a suggestion in a June 2015 correspondence from Michael Williams, who adds, "Maybe [this reading] also is problematic grammatically, but it seems to me to fit the irony in the text. How would they be committing adultery with the Wisdom who by this point in the narrative is playing a positive, salvific role?" I find this reading intriguing, especially given Yaldabaoth's copulation with ἀπόνοια/madness (BG 39.45) or ignorance (III 16.7–8) "who was with him" providing a kind of precedent for this reading. I also wonder if it is possible that they are committing adultery with the power of "Wisdom" created by Yaldabaoth (BG 44.3 σοφία; II 12.24 ⲙ̄ⲧⲣⲙ̄ⲛ̄ϩⲏⲧ). The question I would raise regarding this is that in all other instances, the Greek is used in II to refer to Wisdom of the divine realm. Stroumsa views this episode as "a parallel description of the rape of a feminine figure by the demiurge and his 'authorities.' . . . Here the seduction attempt is successful."

. . . blind that they might not know God who is above them all. And because of the fetter [ᴍⲡⲣⲉ] of forgetfulness their sins were hidden, for they are bound with measures and times and moments: for it was lord [ⲝⲟⲉⲓⲥ] over all."[90] Next, the Chief Ruler "planned to bring a flood over the human creation." But the Insight of Light/the light of Foresight "taught Noah. And he proclaimed to the whole offspring, that is, the children of the humans." While not everyone listened to him, Noah and others from the "immovable generation" are saved.[91] As his plans keep failing, the Chief Ruler decides to plot again. This time:

> He sent his angels to the daughters of men so that they might raise a seed [σπέρμα], to be a respite for them. And at first they were not successful, but when they did not succeed, they gathered together again and made another plan. They created a despicable spirit [πνεῦμα] in the likeness [ⲉⲓⲛⲉ] [imitation-μίμησις III] of the Spirit [πνεῦμα] who had descended so that through it they might pollute [ⲥⲱⲱϥ] the souls [ψυχή]. And the angels changed their own likenesses [ⲉⲓⲛⲉ] into the likeness [ⲓⲛⲉ] of each one's mate, filling them with the spirit [πνεῦμα] of darkness [ⲕⲁⲕⲉ], which they mixed with them and with wickedness [πονηρία]. They brought gold, silver, a gift, and copper and iron and metal and every sort of thing belonging to these classes. And they beguiled [ⲥⲱⲕ] the human beings who had followed them into great anxiety by leading them astray [ⲥⲱⲣⲙ̄] into much error [πλάνη]. And they grew old without having enjoyment. They died without having found any truth and without having known [ⲥⲟⲩⲱⲛ] the God of Truth. And thus the whole creation became enslaved [ϭⲁⲩⲁⲛ] forever, from the foundation [καταβολή] of the world [κόσμος] until now. And they took [ⲝⲓ][92] women; they begot [ⲝⲡⲟ] children out of

The archons 'made a plan' and 'committed adultery' with Sophia 'with whom the Gods are united and the demons and all the generations until this day,'" Stroumsa, *Another Seed*, 62. In this view, it would clearly be a rape, but as backed by adultery laws (see Treggiari, *Roman Marriage*, 262–319), if Wisdom is considered partnered (as she would be to her consort), this could still be considered adultery.

90. SRJ II 28.27–32 // IV 44.13–20. BG 72.2–7 // III 37.6–10 simply says, "He made a plan [with his powers BG]. He [they BG] begot Fate, and bound the gods of the heavens and angels by measures and times and moments the gods of the heavens and the angels and demons and humans that all might be in its fetter [ᴍⲡⲣⲉ]: for it was lord [ⲝⲟⲉⲓⲥ] over all." Cf. Gal 4:8–10: "When you were ignorant of God, you were enslaved to gods that by nature are not gods. But now that you have come to know God, or rather be known by God, how can you return again to those powerless and bankrupt elements? How can you want to be enslaved by them again? You are observing special days and months and measures and years." See Kahl, *Galatians Re-Imagined*, 220–22, 283, 253nn47 and 48.

91. SRJ BG 72.12–73.18 // III 37.16–38.10 // II 28.34–29.15 // IV 44.22–45.14. On the "immovable race" in SRJ, see Michael Williams, *The Immovable Race: A Gnostic Designation and the Theme of Stability in Antiquity* (Leiden: Brill, 1985), esp. 103–40.

92. SRJ BG 75.4 // II 30.7 // IV 46.17; III 39.5 ⲉⲙⲁϩⲧⲉ. While ⲝⲓ is a less forceful verb, ⲉⲙⲁϩⲧⲉ certainly

darkness [ⲕⲁⲕⲉ] according to the likeness [ⲉⲓⲛⲉ] of their spirit. And their hearts became closed and hardened by the hardening of the despicable spirit until now. (SRJ II 28.32–30.11)[93]

Here the text seems to indicate that those in the lineage of Adam and Eve did not become vessels for the ruler's "counterfeit spirit" since the rulers must go to extremes with the "daughters of men" to control the fate of humanity—or at least attempt to control it.[94] But ultimately, the texts say that this attempt, too, was thwarted as the Mother-Father "takes form in her seed" (BG/III)[95] or Christ/Foresight "changed into my seed" (II/IV),[96] continuing to intervene on behalf of humanity to "set her seed upright."[97]

has resonances with the seizing of the Sabine women. This word is also used in RoR 88.1 and OnOrig 116.16 and 117.3 in relation to Eve's rape.

93. Cf. SRJ BG 72.11–75.10: "They brought them gold [ⲛⲟⲩⲃ], silver [ⲉⲁⲧ], gifts [δῶρον], and metals [μέταλλον] of copper [ⲉⲟⲙⲛ̄ⲧ], iron [ⲡⲉⲛⲓⲡⲉ], and every sort [γένος]. They beguiled [ⲥⲁⲕⲟⲩ] them into temptation [πειρασμός] [distractions/περισπασμός III] so that they would not remember [ⲙⲉⲉⲩⲉ] their immovable [ⲁⲥⲕⲓⲙ] Foresight/Pronoia [πρόνοια]. They took [ⲭⲓⲧⲟⲩ] them and begot [ⲭⲡⲟ] children out of darkness [ⲕⲁⲕⲉ] through their counterfeit [ἀντίμιμον] spirit [πνεῦμα]. It closed [ⲧⲱⲙ] their hearts [ⲉⲏⲧ]. They became hard [ⲛⲟⲩⲁⳋⲧ] by the hardening [ⲛⲟⲩⲁⳋⲧ] of the counterfeit [ἀντίμιμον] spirit [πνεῦμα] until now." Cf. also Rom 8:1–8, 14–22.

See also, King, *Secret Revelation of John*, 108, 327n31, on the relationship of this passage to Gen 6:1–4 and Enochic literature; Birger A. Pearson, "Jewish Sources in Gnostic Literature," in *Jewish Writings of the Second Temple Period: Apocrypha, Pseudepigrapha, Qumran Sectarian Writings, Philo, Josephus*, ed. Michael E. Stone (Assen: Van Gorcum, 1984), 443–81; and Stroumsa, *Another Seed*, 19–38. While Stroumsa's intertextual connections are extremely valuable, I do not always agree with his interpretations. For example, in relation to this passage, Stroumsa sees a "contamination between two traditions attested in Jewish literature" (37–38). First, he sees the shape-shifting of the angels into the women's husbands as "slavishly copied from its source ,*The Testament of Reuben*, making little sense in the context of SRJ. Second, he sees an uncritical borrowing in "the mention of the gold and silver, gifts and metals, etc. . . . This can be easily recognized as derived directly from the description of the angels' fall in 1 Enoch 8:1, for although it was significant in the early version of the myth (where the origins of evil and of moral depravation were linked to the origins of civilization), this element appeared as a mere literary vestige in the Gnostic story, without any special function." In both these instances, I would argue, that they *do* fit the overall pattern of the story: Yaldabaoth is consistently plotting against humanity, and here the angels share his shape-shifting attributes (BG 42.10–13 // III 18.9–12 // II 11.35–12.4 // IV 18.25–19.4). Following King's analysis of the connection between the rulers and the Roman emperors (*Secret Revelation of John*, 157–73) and my analysis in chapter 4, it seems that this criticim of "evil," "moral depravation," and "civilization" is integral to the ethical stance of SRJ. What is of extreme importance in Stroumsa's analysis is his comment, "It can therefore be safely assumed that the author—or the redactor—of SRJ knew and used the Jewish traditions embodied in various pseudepigraphic works and integrated them into his own version of the myth" (38). Cf. Elaine Pagels, "Christian Apologists and 'The Fall of the Angels': An Attack on Roman Imperial Power?" *HTR* 78.3–4 (1985): 301–25.

94. SRJ BG 72.3–10 // III –37.6–13 // II 28.11–32 // IV 43.24–44.20.

95. SRJ BG 75.10–13 // III 39.11–13.

96. SRJ II 30.11–13 // IV 46.23–26.

97. SRJ BG 76. 4–5 // III 37.20–21: "she was [rectifying] her deficiency"; no parallel in II or IV.

The Rape of Eve in the Reality of the Rulers[98]

The Reality of the Rulers is framed as a teaching treatise sent to unknown persons by an unknown person, initially writing in the first person. The words of the "great apostle" from Colossians 1:13 and Ephesians 6:12 are invoked as a kind of epitaph at the beginning of the work, the writer stating, "I have sent you this writing because you have asked about the nature of the authorities," before immediately jumping into the story.[99]

The author begins by saying that the "chief of the authorities is blind," and, in his "power, ignorance, and arrogance," he proclaimed, as in SRJ, "I am God; there is no other but me."[100] This "boast rose up to Incorruptibility, and a voice answered from Incorruptibility and said, 'You are wrong, Samael'—which means 'blind god.'"[101] Through his words Samael cast out his power and "pursued it down to chaos . . . by the hand of Faith Wisdom," who "established each of his offspring according to its power, after the pattern of the eternal realms above."[102]

Incorruptibility then looks down upon the waters where her image appears and with which the authorities fall in love. Whereas in the Secret Revelation of John the rulers create Adam in an attempt to illuminate themselves, in the Reality of the Rulers the rulers keep falling in love/lust with the female spirit, first seen in this image of Incorruptibility in the waters.[103] But, like the Insight of Light in SRJ,

---

98. For general introduction to and analysis of the Reality of the Rulers, see: Bentley Layton, "The Hypostasis of the Archons or The Reality of the Rulers," *HTR* 67.4 (1974): 351–425; Layton, "The Hypostasis of the Archons, Part II," *HTR* 69.1–2 (1976): 31–101; Roger Bullard, "Introduction," and Bentley Layton, trans., "The Hypostasis of the Archons," in *Nag Hammadi Codex II,2–7 together with III,2*, Brit. Lib. Or. 4926(1), and P.Oxy. 1, 654, 655: With Contributions by Many Scholars*, ed. Bentley Layton, 2 vols., NHS 20, 21 (Leiden: Brill, 1989), 1:220–59; Tardieu, *Trois mythes*; Barc, *L'Hypostase des Archontes, Traité*; and Ingvild Sælid Gilhus, *The Nature of the Archons: A Study in the Soteriology of a Gnostic Treatise from Nag Hammadi (CGII, 4)*, Studies in Oriental Religions 12 (Wiesbaden: Harrassowitz, 1985). The translation is my own in primary consultation with Layton. See also King, "Ridicule and Rape,"11–14, specifically on the rulers' rape of Eve.
99. RoR 86.20–27.
100. RoR 86.30–31. Cf. SRJ BG 44.14–15 // II 13.8–9 // IV 20.22–24; Exod 20:5; 34:14; Deut 5:6–7; 32:39; Isa 45:5–6; 46:9; Joel 2:27.
101. RoR 86.27–87.4. See chapter 4 on Samael.
102. RoR 87.4–11.
103. Cf. Gilhus, *Nature of the Archons*, 23, 42.

Incorruptibility is not graspable, for "what is only of soul cannot grasp (ⲧⲉϩⲉ . . . ⲁⲛ) what is of spirit."[104] Despite the rulers' ignorance of this fact—that is, what is of soul cannot grasp spirit—the rulers plot together and create a human of earth so that the image of the female they saw in the waters might be its partner (ϣⲃⲣⲉⲓⲛⲉ) and fall in love (ⲙⲉⲣⲓⲧ)[105] with it. And when she falls in love the rulers can then try to grasp/rule (ⲉⲙⲁϩⲧⲉ) her.[106] After they mold the human, they manage to breathe a soul into him, but they continue huffing and puffing to no avail and cannot give him the spirit that will make him rise.[107]

The Spirit sees the human lying on the ground and descends, making its home within him, and the human becomes "a living soul [ⲯⲩⲭⲏ ⲉⲥⲟⲛϩ]."[108] The Spirit names him Adam, because he is lying on the ground. Following Genesis 2:19–20, the rulers gather all of the animals and birds of the world together to see what Adam will name them (which he does with the help of a voice from Incorruptibility),[109] and then place him in paradise so he might tend the garden,[110] telling him he may eat from every tree but the Tree of Knowledge of good and evil.[111] The rulers then plot with one another again, making a deep sleep (ⲃⲱϭⲉ) fall upon Adam, which the text calls "ignorance" (ⲙⲛ̄ⲧⲁⲧⲥⲟⲟⲩⲛ).[112] Much as in SRJ, the rulers violate Adam's bodily integrity and "opened his side like a living woman," presumably extracting the Spirit, though the text states that they "built up his side with some flesh in place of her, and Adam had only a soul."[113] While it does not say that the rulers created a woman, this is clearly implied as RoR continues: "the spiritual woman came to him and spoke with

---

104. RoR 87.15–20; cf. SRJ BG 59.6–12 // III 29.12–17 // II 22.28–32 // IV 35.14. Again, note Daphne, whom Apollo cannot grasp or catch, at least not until her transformation (*Met.* 1.473–544).

105. See Layton, *Nag Hammadi Codex II, 2–7*, 1:238n on 87.35–88.1 reconstruction.

106. RoR 87.23–88.1; cf. SRJ III 39.5, ⲉⲙⲁϩⲧⲉ.

107. RoR 88.7–10; cf. Gen 2:7: "And the Lord God [יהוה אֱלֹהִים; LXX θεός] formed the human from dust of the ground, and breathed into his face the breath of life; and the human became a living being [LXX, ψυχὴν ζῶσαν]."

108. RoR 88.11–15; cf. LXX Gen 2:7, ψυχὴν ζῶσαν.

109. RoR 88.16–24; cf. Gen 2:19.

110. RoR 88.24–25; cf. Gen 2:8, 15.

111. RoR 88.26–32; cf. Gen 2:16–17.

112. RoR 89.3–7; cf. Gen 2:21a: "So the Lord God [יהוה אֱלֹהִים; LXX, θεός] caused a deep sleep [תרדמה; LXX, ἔκστασις] to fall upon the human, and he slept."

113. RoR 89.8–11; cf. Gen 2:21b. Again, see King, "Book of Norea," 70, on Adam's "surgical violation."

him saying, 'Arise, Adam!'" Adam sees her and says, "You have given me life. You will be called Mother of the Living."[114] In these lines it is the word of the spiritual woman that is efficacious, causing Adam to stand.[115]

When the authorities[116] see Adam's partner (ϣвρϵιнϵ), that is, the woman, they become disturbed (ϣτορτρ̄) and lust (мϵριτϲ̄)[117] after her. Instead of entrapping Incorruptibility by inciting her to lust (мϵριτ) after the human they produced, they fall prey to their own plot by lusting after the spiritual woman. The divine realm and the rulers are contrasted with each other, as it is the divine that intervenes to help rather than lust like the rulers. The Spirit endows Adam with power rather than trying to exercise power over him. In their lust, the authorities then say to one another, "'Come, let us cast [ноγχϵ] our seed [σπέρμα] in her,' and they pursued [διώκω][118] her."[119] Upon hearing these plans, the spiritual woman laughs at them "because of their foolishness [мн̄τατθητ] and blindness [мн̄τвλλϵ].[120] And in their grasp [τοοτογ] she became a tree [ϣнн], and left before them a shadow [ϩαιвϵϲ] of herself that resembled [ϵινϵ] her.[121] And they defiled

---

114. RoR 89.11–17; cf. Gen 3:20. For the Aramaic wordplay regarding Eve's name in this section (though RoR does not call her "Eve" here) see Layton, "Part II," 55–56n57; Gilhus, *Nature of the Archons*, 67; Birger A. Pearson *Gnosticism, Judaism, and Egyptian Christianity* (Minneapolis: Fortress Press, 1990), 44–46; and Pheme Perkins, *Gnosticism and the New Testament* (Minneapolis: Fortress Press, 1993), 22–24.

115. Cf. the efficaciousness of the divine word in Gen 1.3–30.

116. It is difficult to know if the authorities (ἐξουσία) are meant to be separate entities from the rulers or not.

117. Crum, 156a–b, "desire, love."

118. Cf. SRJ III 29.14–17, "And in a [desire he (the Chief Ruler) wanted to bring] her out from his [rib]. Insight/Epinoia is that (sort of thing) that cannot be grasped [ατταϩος]. The darkness pursued [διώκω] her light but it did not catch [ταϩϵ] the light." Again, cf. Daphne and Apollo.

119. RoR 89.17–25; cf. SRJ BG 62.3–8 // II 24.8–16.

120. See RoR 86.27; and especially 87.3–4 and 94.25–26, where the Chief Ruler is called "'Samael'—which is 'god of the blind.'" For a comparative reading of 86.27–87.4 and 94.12–26, see Gilhus, *Nature of the Archons*, 6–8. Cf. SRJ II 11.18 // IV 18.2. See also Bernard Barc, "Samaël—Saklas—Yaldabaôth: Recherche sur la genèse d'un myth gnostique," in *Colloque international sur les textes de Nag Hammadi*, ed. Bernard Barc (Quebec: Presses de l'Université Laval, 1981), 123–50. For additional information on Samael as the angel of Rome, see Ioan P. Culianu, "The Angels of the Nations and the Origins of Gnostic Dualism," in *Studies in Gnosticism and Hellenistic Religions Presented to Gilles Quispel on the Occasion of His 65th Birthday*, ed. R. van den Broek and M. J. Vermaseren, Etudes préliminaires aux religions orientales dans l'Empire romain 91 (Leiden: Brill, 1981), 78–91; and "Samael," JewishEncyclopedia.com. For the unedited full-text of the 1906 *Jewish Encyclopedia*, see www.jewishencyclopedia.com/articles/13055-samael.

121. Only in SRJ parallel in II and IV—see II 24.13–15, "And when the Foresight of all things noticed (it), she sent some and they snatched Life out of Eve." The Rulers also try to pursue Insight—BG

[ϫⲟϩⲙⲉⲥ][122] her abominably [ⲥⲱϥ].[123] And they defiled [ϫⲱϩⲙ̄] the seal [σφραγίς] of her voice [ⲥⲙⲏ],[124] and so they convicted [κατακρίνω] themselves through the form they had shaped in their own image [ⲉⲓⲛⲉ]."[125]

Here the spiritual woman is a trickster, escaping the grasp of the rulers through her transformation, but as with the extraction of the spiritual part of Adam, this is not a benign dissociation.[126] While the rulers in their "foolishness and blindness" have raped the form made in their own image and convicted themselves through this gross act of violence, Eve is left as a shadow, an empty shell of flesh, as after her transformation she is simply called "the woman of flesh (σαρκική)."[127] Not only do they rape her, but they also defile or rape (ϫⲱϩⲙ̄) "the seal [σφραγίς] of her voice [ⲥⲙⲏ]." While the text does not explicitly state the reasons behind the raping of the seal of her voice, or exactly what the seal of her voice is, it seems possible that this is a punishment for exposing the chief of the authorities through the voice,[128] whether this is the voice that comes from Incorruptibility to help (βοήθεια) Adam[129] or the spiritual woman's voice which causes Adam to rise.[130]

59.6–12 // II 22.28–32. Cf. Ovid, *Met.* 1.543–67 on the transformation of Daphne into a tree, and *Met.* 1.700–708 on the transformation of Syrinx into reeds.

It is argued that Eve here is transformed into the Tree of Life, though the text does not offer a concrete identification. Layton argues this on the basis of the wordplay between "life" and "Eve" in the Aramaic ("Part II," 57). Gilhus (*Nature of the Archons*, 24, 69–72) offers three reasons: (1) because it is not mentioned with the Tree of Knowledge (presumably she is referring to RoR 88.24–89.3, where Adam is given the prohibition to eat) which "has not yet come into existence"; (2) because of the difference between RoR and OnOrig—in RoR Eve becomes a tree, in OnOrig she goes into an existing tree, then becomes it (OnOrig 116.28–32); and (3) because the expulsion of Adam and Eve from the garden follows the Genesis narrative, where they are expelled because of the Tree of Life (70). These are all substantive arguments for identifying Eve and the Tree of Life, yet the text remains ambiguous because it is silent. I think there is still a possibility that Eve should be identified with the Tree of Knowledge, particularly given the association with Eve and knowledge in both SRJ and RoR as well as her association in all three texts with knowledge of the divine realm.

122. Crum, 797b–798a, "defile, pollute" // μιαίνω: LSJ, s.v. μιαίνω "stain, sully, defile, dishonor a woman."
123. Crum, 378a, "defile, pollute, abomination." The word ⲥⲱⲱϥ has the same semantic range as ϫⲱϩⲙ̄.
124. The act of "defiling the seal of her voice" could indicate oral rape.
125. RoR 89.23–30; cf. SRJ BG 62.8 // III 31.10 // II 24.15–16 // IV 37.27–28.
126. See King, "Ridicule and Rape," 12–14, citing Curran, "Rape and Rape Victims"; see the discussions on Daphne, Io, and Syrinx in chapter two above, "One Loves, the Other Flees . . ." Cf. Williams, *Rethinking "Gnosticism,"* 120–23.
127. RoR 90.2.
128. RoR 86.32–87.4: This is the voice from Incorruptibility that names the Chief Ruler "Samael" because he is blind.

The defiling of her voice may also be used as a way to silence Eve, to stop her from speaking out and naming the violence of the authorities so that it is both an act to punish and silence her.[131] They have raped every part of her, reducing her to nothing but flesh, and so it is also crucial to recognize that this is a gang rape by the rulers. This is made clear with the plural that is used at every point in describing those responsible for raping Eve.

After Eve's rape, the "female spiritual presence," presumably moving from Adam to Eve to the tree, then

> came in the shape of the serpent [ⲅⲁϥ], the instructor [ⲣⲉϥⲧⲁⲙⲟ].[132] And it taught [ⲧⲁⲙⲟⲟⲩ] them, saying, "What did he [say to] you all? Was it, 'You may eat from every tree in the garden [παράδεισος], but do not eat from [the tree] of knowledge [ⲥⲟⲩⲱⲛ] of evil [ⲅⲟⲟⲩ] and good [ⲛⲁⲛⲟⲩϥ]?'"[133] The woman of flesh [σαρκική] said, "Not only did he say, 'Do not eat,' but also, 'Do not touch it. For the day you all eat from it, with death you all will die.'"[134] And the serpent ⲅⲁϥ], the instructor [ⲣⲉϥⲧⲁⲙⲟ], said, "With death you all shall not die, for he said this to you out of jealousy [φθονέω]. Rather your eyes will open and you all will be like gods [ⲛⲟⲩⲧⲉ], knowing [ⲥⲟⲟⲩⲛ] evil [ⲅⲟⲟⲩ] and good [ⲛⲁⲛⲟⲩϥ]."[135] And the female instructor [ⲣⲉϥⲧⲁⲙⲟ] was taken away from the serpent [ⲅⲁϥ], and she left it behind as a thing of the earth [ⲣⲙ̄ⲛ̄ⲕⲁⲅ]. And the woman of flesh [σαρκική] took from the tree and ate, and she gave to her husband as well as herself.[136] And thus these beings that possessed only a soul [ψυχικός], ate.[137] And their imperfection [κακία] became apparent in their ignorance [ⲙ̄ⲛ̄ⲧⲁⲧⲥⲟⲟⲩⲛ]. They knew

---

129. RoR 88.17–18.

130. RoR 89.11–13.

131. For a classic treatment of this, see Judith Herman, *Trauma and Recovery* (New York: Basic Books, 1992), 7–8, 29. See also Curran, "Rape and Rape Victims."

132. Again, for the Aramaic wordplay, see Layton, "Part II," 55–56n57; Pearson, *Gnosticism, Judaism, and Egyptian Christianity*, 44–46; and Pheme Perkins, *Gnosticism and the New Testament*, 22–24.

133. Cf. Gen 3:1.

134. Cf. Gen 3:2–3. When the authorities initially give this instruction, it is to Adam alone, before Eve is extracted from him.

135. Cf. Gen 3:4–5.

136. Cf. Gen 3:6.

137. Note that when Adam only possessed a soul earlier in the narrative, he could not move until the Spirit came. This is true in SRJ as well; see BG 50.15–51.1 // III 23.14–19 // II 19.13–14 // IV 29.22–24.

[ⲉⲓⲙⲉ][138] that they were stripped of the spiritual [πνευματικόν],[139] and they took fig leaves and bound them upon their loins.[140]

This section of the Nature of Rulers closely follows the Genesis narrative, though it recasts the role of the serpent through the broader framing of the story—the serpent in this text is a representative of both the divine realm and the spiritual Eve as opposed to its connection with Yaldabaoth as in SRJ.[141] Here the spiritual woman, this time in the form of the serpent, comes to help her material counterpart, whom she left in the wake of the rulers' violence. The spiritual woman/serpent urges Eve and Adam to eat, which does not give the spirit back to them but allows them to see their circumstances under the rulers for what they are, to know they had been stripped of the spiritual, providing them with an opportunity to find what has been taken away.[142] Adam and Eve exist in a paradox of knowing that they do not know. Yet they understand that they are spiritually naked, and this *does* effect a change in them, one that, as the text continues, contains the potential both for salvation and a return to spirit in the human realm. While this potential is not immediately realized, it will resurface through the birth of Eve's children with Adam.

At this point, closely following Gen 3:8–14, the Chief Ruler, once

---

138. Crum, 771b, "know, understand." The words γινώσκω and γνῶσις are included in its semantic range.
139. In SRJ BG 52.11–13 // II 20.5–7, the rulers "knew that he [Adam] was naked [ⲕⲏⲕ ⲁϩⲏⲩ] of evil [κακία]"; and cf. BG 57.15–19: "They issued this commandment [ἐντολή] against him so that he might not look up to his perfection and realize [νοεῖν] that he was naked [ⲕⲱⲕ ⲁϩⲏⲩ] of his perfection [ⲭⲱⲕ]." Cf. also SRJ II 23.25–35: "Through her [Foresight] they tasted the perfect knowledge. In the form of an eagle, I appeared on the Tree of Knowledge, which is the Insight from the pure, enlightened Foresight, so that I might teach them and awaken them from the depth of the sleep. For they were both in a fallen state and they recognized their nakedness. Insight appeared to them as light, awakening their thought."
140. RoR 89.31–90.19; cf. Gen 3:7. They do not cover themselves in SRJ II 23.33 and IV 36.30–37.1 and only "recognize their nakedness."
141. In addition to the radically different role of the snake (the association of Eve and the snake in RoR is most likely based on Aramaic puns [Layton, "Part II," 55–56; Gilhus, *Nature of the Archons*, 67]), the eating and the tree occur in two separate sections in SRJ. The first deals with the serpent, who teaches them about "desire, pollution, and destruction," and it is the Savior who "set them right so that they would eat" (BG 57.8–58.10 // II 22.3–18). In the second section, Epinoia (Insight)/Christ teaches them to "eat of knowledge" (BG 60.19–61.5 // II 23.25–33).
142. The semantic range of κακία includes "hurt or damage done or suffered" (LSJ) and "a state involving difficult circumstances, trouble, misfortune" (BDAG). In this way, it is possible that they not only recognize the κακία within them (i.e., being stripped of the spiritual), but the κακία done to them by the rulers—and these are really one and the same.

again ignorant of what had transpired, asks where Adam is, and Adam says that he was afraid because he realized he was naked, that is, stripped of the spiritual, the element that the rulers keep trying to grasp through their continued violations of their creation. The ruler knows Adam and Eve are hiding because they have eaten from the tree, and, as in the Genesis narrative, Adam blames the woman, whom the ruler curses, and the woman, in turn, blames the serpent.[143] Continuing to follow the Genesis narrative, the rulers[144]

> [turned] to the serpent [ᴢoq] and cursed [coүᴢⲱp] its shadow [ᴢⲁⲓвєc], [so that it was] powerless, not knowing [cooүⲛ] that it was a form they themselves had shaped.[145] From that day, the serpent [ᴢoq] was under the curse [cⲁᴢoүє] of the authorities [ἐξουσία]. The curse [cⲁᴢoү] was on the serpent [ᴢoq] until the perfect [τέλειος] human was to come.[146] They turned to their Adam and took him and cast him from the garden along with his wife.[147] For they have no blessing [cⲙoү], since they too are under the curse [cⲁᴢoүє].[148] And they threw humanity into great distraction and a life of grief, so that their people might be devoted to worldly things and might not have the time to be occupied with the holy Spirit.[149]

Just as the rulers have violated themselves by violating Eve, the text emphasizes their ignorance of cursing their own form, their own creation, that is, the "shadow."[150] If this is true of the serpent—that they have cursed their own form—the same would seem to hold for both Adam and Eve, for here they have cursed their own creation as well.[151] It is striking that while Adam, Eve, and the serpent are all under

143. RoR 90.19–31.
144. This is an ambiguous "they" in the Coptic, without a clear antecedent.
145. This is the second time that the text (the first in relation to the rulers' rape) implicates the rulers in hurting their own creation. This seems to reflect the logic, or illogic as the case may be, of domination and occupation. It also says something about the idea of reciprocity, when one does not realize that the harm they cause to others is actually harming themselves. They are literally desecrating pieces of themselves.
146. Cf. Gen 3:14–15. Here, again, the serpent is completely dissociated from the role it plays with Yaldabaoth in SRJ.
147. Cf. Gen 3:23–24.
148. Cf. Gen 3:15–19. So the curse affects all three, even though the text only states that the woman was cursed in RoR 90.30 and the serpent was cursed in 91.32.
149. RoR 90.32–91.11.
150. Cf. RoR 89.26, where the spiritual Eve leaves her shadow (ᴢⲁⲓвєc) behind as she transforms into the tree.
151. Though in their creation Adam and Eve are clearly endowed with something that does not come from the rulers.

the curse, presumably all three, including the serpent, will be free of it once the perfect human comes, which indicates that it is not just humanity but the rulers' broader creation that will become free.[152]

After they have been cursed and cast from the garden, Eve gives birth to two sons: Cain through the rulers' rape and Abel through Adam.[153] While the text simply states that Eve "bore Cain, their son," Eve becomes pregnant and bears Abel when Adam "knows" her. As in SRJ, the Coptic word for "sex" is cooγn, "to know,"[154] and it is used in relation to Adam, Eve, and the birth of Abel, but is absent from the birth of Cain.[155] While this is a popular euphemism for sex throughout the Bible, it is important to note that the word is primarily used in RoR in relation to knowledge and ignorance: Adam is the only one who "knows" Eve; the rulers defile (ϫⲱϩⲙ̄) her. This is illustrated later in RoR, when Eve's fourth child, Norea, tells the rulers in 92.24–25 that they did not "know" (coγⲱn) her mother but "knew" (coγⲱn) their own partner/counterpart (ϣⲃⲣⲉⲓⲛⲉ)—that which was like them.[156] In this way RoR, like SRJ, contrasts the relationship between Adam and Eve—a relationship based on knowledge and mutuality, as the text names them partners/counterparts/co-likenesses (ϣⲃⲣⲉⲓⲛⲉ)—with that of the rulers who lust after her, violate her, and do not know her. Importantly, Adam and Eve are named as partners before Eve's rape when they still possess their spiritual aspects, and then again after they eat from the Tree of Knowledge, an indication that eating from the tree is connected with their renewed knowledge of and partnership with each other.[157]

The relationship of the rulers to humanity is further reflected in the relationship between their son, Cain, and Adam and Eve's son,

---

152. This seems to indicate the possibility that the entire earth will be lifted from the curse, that even that which is without spirit will be lifted from the curse.
153. Because the text simply calls Cain, "their son," it is impossible to know if this is referring to "their" as the rulers or "their" as Adam and Eve. Most likely (cf. Layton, "Part II," 61; and Gilhus, *Nature of the Archons*, 24, where she notes the omission of πάλιν, which is found in LXX Gen 4:25), and in my reading, Cain is a product of the rulers' rape of Eve, especially given his moniker the Cain "of flesh [σαρκικός]" (RoR 91.20), when he kills Abel.
154. SRJ II 24.35 // IV 38.25, ⲛ̄ⲙⲉ; BG 63.12, coγⲱn.
155. RoR 91.11–14.
156. See below and the epilogue on the difficulties and complexities of Norea's statement here.
157. RoR 87.35; 89.19; 91.31 for Adam and Eve as ϣⲃⲣⲉⲓⲛⲉ, and note below.

Abel. Again, the text follows Genesis closely in relating the story of the offerings of Cain and Abel—Abel's offerings were accepted by God (ⲛⲟⲩⲧⲉ) (and here God seems to be God and not the rulers),[158] while Cain's were not. And just as Samael pursues (διώκω) his power to chaos, and the rulers pursue (διώκω) the spiritual woman, so too, the Cain "of flesh [σαρκικός]" pursues (διώκω) his brother Abel.[159]

Next, specifically following Genesis 4:25, "Adam [knew (ⲥⲟⲟⲩⲛ)] his partner [ϣⲃⲣⲉⲓⲛⲉ][160] Eve, and she became pregnant and bore [Seth] to Adam. And she said, 'I have given birth to [another] person through God [ⲛⲟⲩⲧⲉ], in place of Abel.'"[161] The text makes it clear that the birth of Seth, resulting from Eve's union with Adam, occurs through *God*, thus making sure that this birth is in no way associated with the rulers. The Reality of the Rulers again uses the verb "to know" (ⲥⲟⲟⲩⲛ) to describe their sexual union and refers to Adam and Eve as partners (ϣⲃⲣⲉⲓⲛⲉ). Eve becomes pregnant again, this time giving birth to Norea[162] of whom she says, "He has borne [ϫⲡⲟ] for me a

---

158. Cf. Layton, "Part II," 61, 88. "God: our author or editor abandons the terms of his [*sic*] own narrative in favor of those of the Biblical account, which is summarized here (i.e. in RoR). Quite possibly Sabaoth the *dikaios theos* is meant" (88). See chapter 4 of this study.

159. RoR 91.11–30̄; cf. Gen 4:1–15.

160. See RoR 87.35, which describes Adam in relation to Incorruptibility, with whom the authorities became enamored; 89.19, which describes the spiritual Eve in relation to Adam; 91.31 (here) and 92.25, which describe the carnal woman (Eve?). In 92.25 Norea uses this word to say they did not violate her mother, but their own creation. I wonder if this points to an effective change for Eve after she eats the fruit. But cf. Gilhus, *Nature of the Archons*, 62, who reads that either Adam or God is the parent of Norea with the spiritual Eve and not the material Eve. I think this is a difficult logic to follow if Eve is indeed the tree. There is no indication in the text that it is not the material Eve who parents Norea. Norea's statement is much more likely pointing to a substantive change in Eve after eating the fruit.

161. RoR 91.30-33; cf. Gen 4:25. Birger A. Pearson notes, "The birth of Seth, 'through God,' is narrated in a way that reflects the use both of Gen 4:25 and 4:1 (originally of Cain!)" ("Revisiting Norea," in King, *Images of the Feminine in Gnosticism*, 269).See also Pearson, "The Figure of Seth in Gnostic Literature," in *The Rediscovery of Gnosticism: Proceedings of the International Conference on Gnosticism at Yale, New Haven, Connecticut, March 28-31, 1978*, vol. 2, *Sethian Gnosticism*, SHR 41 (Leiden: Brill, 1981), 479: "[I]t is to be noted that Gen 4:1 is reflected here, too, in the saying attributed to Eve: 'I have borne [another] man through God.' Cf. Gen 4:1 (LXX)." While the LXX uses θεός, the Hebrew in 4:1 is יְהוָה, which is generally translated throughout the LXX as κύριος. In 4:25, both אֱלֹהִים and θεός are used, respectively. I will argue this more thoroughly in chapter 4, but at this juncture I want to note that it is highly possible that RoR, as well as SRJ and OnOrig, is embellishing this difference—a difference based on the two different names of God used throughout the two tellings of the Adam and Eve narratives in the Hebrew Bible—in their retellings of the Genesis narrative.

162. On Norea, see Birger A. Pearson, "The Figure of Norea in Gnostic Literature," in *Proceedings of the International Colloquium on Gnosticism, Stockholm, August 20-25, 1973*, ed. Geo Widengren, Filolgisk-filosofiska serien 17 (Stockholm: Almqvist & Wiksell; Leiden: Brill, 1977), 143–52; Pearson, chapter 5, "The Figure of Norea in Gnostic Literature," in *Gnosticism, Judaism, and Egyptian Christianity*,

virgin [παρθένος] to help [βοήθεια][163] many human generations [γενεά]."
Norea is described in the text as "the virgin [παρθένος] whom the forces
[δύναμις] did not defile [ⲭⲁⲣⲙⲉⲥ]."[164] The birth of Norea seems to
reinstate the spiritual nature of humanity that was lost through the
rulers' machinations. This is indicted by the text, stating that,
immediately after her birth, "humanity began to multiply and
improve."[165] Just as Eve was sent as a helper to Adam, then forced
to split her spiritual from her material aspect in the face of rulers'
violence, the material Eve's process of returning to knowledge is
constantly coaxed forward by her spiritual counterpart and partner,
who moves from Eve to tree to serpent. Eve gains knowledge by eating
the fruit, knowledge of herself, knowledge of her partner, and
knowledge of her world. All this knowledge brings her full circle to
bear a child that will help the human generations.

After Norea's birth, the story quickly turns to her encounter with
Noah and the ark. Norea[166] approaches Noah, wanting to board the ark,
and he refuses her. Norea, exhibiting great power, blows on the ark
and it burns up[167]—here Norea's breath is more potent than even the
rulers, whose breath could only endow Adam with a soul and could
not make him arise.[168] After this display, the rulers come to Norea
wanting to seduce (ἀπατάω)[169] her, and their chief says to her, "Your
mother Eve came to us." Norea responds, "You are the rulers ἄρχων]
of darkness [ⲕⲁⲕⲉ]! You are accursed [ⲥⲅⲟⲩⲟⲣⲧ]! And you did not know
[ⲥⲟⲩⲱⲛ] my mother, it was your female counterpart [ϣⲃⲣⲉⲓⲛⲉ] that you
knew [ⲥⲟⲩⲱⲛ]. For I am not from you, rather I come from the world

---

75–85. See also King, "Ridicule and Rape"; King, "Book of Norea"; Anne McGuire, "Virginity and
Subversion," in King, *Images of the Feminine in Gnosticism*, 239–58; Pearson, "Revisiting Norea,"
265–75.

163. Cf. RoR 88.18—A voice comes from Incorruptibility to "help" Adam.

164. RoR 91.34–92.3.

165. RoR 92.3–4.

166. In RoR 92.4–18 referred to as "Orea."

167. RoR 92.4–18; cf. Brian Glazer, "The Goddess with a Fiery Breath: The Egyptian Derivation of a
Gnostic Mythologoumenon," *Novum Testamentum* 33.1 (1991): 92–94.

168. See RoR 88.3–10 on the ineffectualness of the rulers' breath.

169. This is what the serpent does to Eve in 90.31 and its parallel in Gen 3:13 LXX. ἀπατᾶν/ἀπάτη is also
used in SRJ BG 56.1–57.6 // III 27.7–28.5 // II 21.19–36 // IV 33.4–34.2 to connect the deception of
the rulers with the deception of the tree. Here the theme of seduction/desire is transferred from
the serpent to the rulers in RoR.

above."[170] Here Norea names the violence the rulers have perpetrated, particularly against Eve, and places the blame squarely on them. The rulers' words and actions undoubtedly say more about them than about Eve and reverberate back on themselves—just as they have throughout RoR—since (as Norea and the reader/hearer know) they have violated that part of Eve that is from them. But this self-incrimination also points a difficulty of the text: that although the rulers' actions actually serve to implicate them, what does this framing say about the material Eve? For it is the material Eve who is also called their "counterpart" (ⲱⲃⲣⲉⲓⲛⲉ) even though she in no way reflects the rulers—the material Eve who, blameless, is still the one who suffers the violence of their act.

The "arrogant [αὐθάδης] ruler [ἄρχων]" then says to Norea "cruelly [τολμάω],[171] 'You must service [ⲣ̄-ⲃⲱⲕ][172] us, as your mother, Eve, did'"[173] Here, the ruler names Eve for what she was to them—a slave. Though the text never frames her as such, she is seen this way only in the rulers' perception of her. And it is this misguided perception that the rulers want Norea to embody as well. But Norea turns and cries out in a loud voice "to the Holy One, the God of all things, 'Rescue me [βοηθέω] from these unrighteous [ἀδικία] rulers [ἄρχων] and rescue [ⲛⲁϩⲙⲉⲧ] me from their hands! Now!" And the angel Eleleth, or Understanding, intervenes.[174]

Through Norea's bold words and daring she breaks the cycle of

---

170. RoR 92.18–26. McGuire reads "Norea's confrontation with the Rulers as a confrontation between two modes of power, each of which has a distinctly sexual and social force. In the *Hypostasis of the Archons*, the confrontation of archontic and spiritual power is symbolized in a series of encounters in which the Rulers of this world attempt to grasp the female spiritual power. Twice their efforts take the form of attempted rape. In its representation of the struggle between the Rulers and the female manifestations of the Spirit, the *Hypostasis of the Archons* creates a world in which issues of power are directly linked to issues of gender. Throughout the narrative, the Rulers display their power in efforts to dominate and defile. Norea displays her virginal power, by contrast in the ability to resist, subvert, and rename the Archons who would falsely claim to rule Norea, her children, and the entire world" ("Virginity and Subversion," 241).
171. LSJ, s.v. τολμάω: "dare, to have cruelty to do a thing"—the above translations are both odd, maybe, "He dared her," or "He cruelly said. . . ."
172. Crum, 301–b, "servant, slave," often corresponding to the Greek δοῦλος, δουλεύω, though also ἐργάζομαι. Here both Norea and Eve are compared to slaves, implying a kind of sexual slavery. A more forceful translation of this might be, "You must be a slave to us as your mother Eve was."
173. RoR 92.27–31.
174. RoR 92.32–93.3. Cf. SRJ BG 34.2–3 // III 12.12 // II 8.18 // IV 13.13 where Eleleth is the fourth light over the fourth generation or realm.

violation that the rulers try to perpetuate with her. While much interpretation focuses on her status as a virgin, it is crucial to note the text's gloss, which calls her the one "whom the powers did not defile."[175] They were not able to defile her because she could see them for what they truly were. Norea could see their violence clearly, and she had the audacity to cry out for help.[176]

Not only does Norea stop the cycle of violence the rulers begin with Eve, but she learns about who she is and where she has come from by asking Eleleth to teach her "about the [power [ϭⲟⲙ] of] these authorities [ἐξουσία]." She asks: "[How] did they come into being? With what kind of nature [ὑπόστασις]? Of what material [ὕλη]? Who created [ⲧⲁⲙⲓⲟ] them and their power [δύναμις]?"[177] By answering her questions Eleleth gives Norea the tools necessary to overcome the authorities, if not externally, at least internally until "the time when the true [ἀληθινός] human in modeled form [πλάσμα], reveals [ⲟⲩⲱⲛϩ] the existence of [the spirit of] truth [ἀλήθεια], which the Father has sent" to "free [ⲛⲟⲩϫⲉ ⲉⲃⲟⲗ] them from the bondage [ⲙⲣⲣⲉ] of the authorities' [ἐξουσία] error [πλάνη]."[178] Eleleth's words indicate that Norea is not yet free of the constraints the rulers have imposed on the world—no one will be truly free until the true human comes—but, nonetheless, she has already shown through her boldness and knowledge that she is not subject to the rulers though she remains in their world.

The text never says whether Norea ever has sex, but it does refer to her children[179]—though it does not indicate if these children are to be understood as biological or spiritual. Her status as παρθένος, a maiden, does not exclude the possibility of mutual relationships, both physical

---

175. RoR 91.35–92.3.
176. One way of approaching this scene is through the lens of intergenerational trauma—something those living in the aftermath of the destruction of the Jerusalem temple—or more generally all those conquered, occupied, or displaced by the Romans—could understand. On intergenerational trauma, see Françoise Davoine and Jean-Max Gaudillère, *History beyond Trauma*, trans. Susan Fairfield (New York: Other Press, 2004); Gabriele Schwab, *Haunting Legacies: Violent Histories and Transgenerational Trauma* (New York: Columbia University Press, 2010); M. Gerard Fromm, ed., *Lost in Transmission: Studies of Trauma across Generations* (London: Karnac Books, 2012).
177. RoR 93.11–94.2.
178. RoR 96.28–35. For the entirety of Eleleth's teaching to Norea, see 94.2–96.28, where Eleleth's teaching returns to the story at the beginning of RoR and elaborates upon it.
179. RoR 96.19. Eleleth refers to Norea and her offspring being from the Father; cf. 92.3–4, where, immediately after her birth, "humanity began to *multiply* and improve."

and spiritual—in fact, there no longer seems to be a bifurcation or split between the material and spiritual in the person of Norea as there was for Adam and Eve. What the term παρθένος does signify is Norea's ability to maintain her integrity (physically, mentally. and spiritually), to speak out on behalf of herself, and to cry out for help—and for that help to come. While Norea's characterization as both παρθένος and the one "whom the rulers did not defile" might seem to serve as a negative contrast to Eve's characterization, this is not the case, nor does the text engage in victim blaming. At every turn, RoR lays the accountability for Eve's rape on the rulers: the rulers are responsible for it, and this is never questioned. The text is clear that, despite this horrific violation, Eve went on not only to have a mutual sexual relationship with Adam—a relationship based on partnership with and knowledge of one another—but, through this relationship, to bear the children who belonged to and carried on the legacy of the world above. Through both her actions and her offspring, Eve continually embodies and bridges the divine and human realms, whether in her spiritual aspect or her material.

The Rape of Eve in On the Origin of the World[180]

On the Origin of the World, like the Reality of the Rulers, begins as a first-person teaching treatise to known persons by an unknown person. Here the goal of the text is to prove that something "existed before chaos," and the story that follows is about the "first work" and the generation of the universe.[181] Closest in plot to the Reality of the Rulers—though in its proliferation of the divine and material realms it is more similar to the Secret Revelation of John—On the

---

180. For general introduction to and analysis of On the Origin of the World, see Painchaud, *L'Écrit sans titre*; Hans-Gebhard Bethge, "Introduction," and Hans-Gebhard Bethge, Bentley Layton, and the Societas Coptic Hierosolymitana, trans., "On the Origin of the World," *Nag Hammadi Codex II,2–7*, 2:11–134; and Tardieu, *Trois mythes*. For those interested in possibilities regarding redaction criticism, see particularly Louis Painchaud, "The Redactions of the Writing Without Title (CG II5)," *Second Century: A Journal of Early Christian Studies* 8.4 (1991): 217–34. (In the works of Painchaud and others this text is referred to as the "Writing Without Title," because the tractate is without a title and interpreters feel that On the Origin of the World is not really descriptive of the text.) Translations are my own, in consultation with Bethge and Layton.
181. OnOrig 97.24–98.11.

Origin of the World contains many significant differences from RoR and unique attributes as well.[182] On the Origin of the World begins by saying, "After the order of the immortals was brought to completion out of the infinite, a likeness flowed from Faith—it is called Wisdom." From Faith Wisdom, "a thing with no spirit" comes into being, "a ruler ... lion-like in appearance, androgynous ... and ignorant of where he came from," named Yaldabaoth.[183]

Yaldabaoth creates and orders his world, and "[a]fter the heavens were established, along with their powers and their entire government [διοίκησις], the Chief Parent exalted himself, and he was glorified by the whole army of angels. And all the gods and their angels praised and glorified him. And he was delighted and boasted again and again and said to them, I don't need anything." And then, as in both SRJ and RoR, he said, "I am God, and there is no other but me."[184] Faith hears this impious boast and says in anger, "You are wrong, Samael. . . . There is an immortal human of light who existed before you and who will appear to your modeled forms." She tells him that his world will eventually dissolve to nothing, and then, revealing her likeness in the waters, withdraws to her light.[185]

Upon hearing the voice of Faith, Yaldabaoth's son, Sabaoth, repents. Faith Wisdom pours light upon him and he becomes enlightened. Sabaoth is eventually established in the heavens by Faith Wisdom, and is sent Faith's daughter, Life, as a companion to teach him. Yaldabaoth envies his son and becomes angry, distressed, and ashamed because of his transgressions. But, despite knowing that there were others that existed before him, he acted the fool and shouted, "If anything existed before me, let it appear so that we may see its light!" And a light appears with a human likeness within it—and Yaldabaoth was amazed and ashamed.[186]

---

182. See both Painchaud (*L'Écrit sans titre*) and Tardieu (*Troismythes*) for comparative work on RoR and OnOrig.
183. OnOrig 97.24–100.9.
184. OnOrig 103.10–13. Cf. RoR 86.30–31; SRJ BG 44.14–15 // II 13.8–9 // IV 20.22–24; Exod 20:5; 34:14; Deut 5:6–7; 32:39; Isa 45:5–6; 46:9; Joel 2:27.
185. OnOrig 100.29–103.32.
186. OnOrig 103.32–108.9.

No one could see the light with the likeness except for Yaldabaoth and his Foresight. When Foresight sees the messenger, she falls in love with him (ⲙⲉⲣⲓⲧ), but he hates her. This messenger is called "Adam of Light," which the text says means "the enlightened human of blood." From this blood, Eros appears, and when the gods and angels of Yaldabaoth see Eros, the fall in love. From this love, pleasure blooms from the earth; then from the blood, creation blooms, creating paradise and its trees of life and knowledge.[187]

After "two days" the Adam of Light withdraws from chaos, but before he does so the authorities see him and laugh at the Chief Parent for his lie that, "I am God. No one exists before me!" The authorities approach the Chief Parent and ask if the Adam of Light is "the god who ruined our work." The Chief Parent replies, "Yes. If you do not want him to be able to ruin our work, come, let us create a human being out of earth according to the image of our body and according to the likeness of this being, to serve us, so that when he sees his likeness he might fall in love with it. Then he will no longer ruin our work, and we shall make those born from the light our slaves [ϩⲙϩⲁⲗ] for this entire age."[188]

All of this occurs "according to the Foresight of Wisdom" so that humanity will appear after the likeness of the Adam of Light and condemn the rulers. Wisdom Life anticipates the creation of their human and "laughed at their decision, because they are blind and they ignorantly created him against their own interests. They did not know what they were about to do."[189] Wisdom Life then creates her own human first, so that her human "might instruct their modeled form how to disregard them and thus to escape them."[190] On the Origin of the World is unique in that Eve is not created from Adam but is the daughter of Wisdom, a being fully created by and sent from the divine realm.[191] Eve is also called Life, "the instructor," and—by the

---

187. OnOrig 108.9–112.17. The proliferation of life on the earth is told further through the story of Eros and Psyche—love for Eros continuing to cause blood to pour forth and create life.
188. OnOrig 111.29–113.5.
189. OnOrig 113.6–16.
190. OnOrig 113.17–20.
191. OnOrig 113.17–114.15; 115.30–36. See Benjamin H. Dunning, "What Sort of Thing Is This Luminous

authorities—"the beast," as she "would lead their modeled forms astray."[192]

As Wisdom Life creates her human, that is, Eve, the rulers complete Adam, but they abandon him "as a lifeless vessel, since he was formed like an untimely birth with no spirit in him." Forty days later, Wisdom Life sends her breath into the soul-less Adam causing him to move. The rulers see him and are disturbed. Next, Wisdom sends her daughter, Life, called Eve, who sees her partner (ϣⲃⲣⲉⲓⲛⲉ) lying on the ground and says, "Adam, live! Arise from the ground!" Immediately her word (ϣⲁϫⲉ) becomes a work (ἔργον), and Adam rises and opens his eyes calling her "Mother of the Living."[193] Here, as in RoR 89.11–13, this "word [ϣⲁϫⲉ] became a work [ἔργον]" and is efficacious, having the power to cause Adam to stand.[194] When the authorities saw the effect of Eve's word, realizing their "modeled form [i.e., Adam] was alive [ⲟⲛϩ]

Woman? Thinking Sexual Difference in On the Origin of the World," *JECS* 17.1 (2009): 55–84. Dunning discusses sexual difference in OnOrig, noting that the text does not conceive of "sexual difference or the creation of the first female human being as secondary, derivative, or otherwise a figure of lack" (60–61). On the complications of this particular passage, see ibid., 71–73, esp. n55. Again, for the Aramaic wordplay, see Layton, "Part II," 55–56n57; Pearson, *Gnosticism, Judaism, and Egyptian Christianity*, 44–46; and Pheme Perkins, *Gnosticism and the New Testament*, 22–24.

192. OnOrig 113.17–114.15: "So she anticipated them and created her own human first so that he might instruct their modeled form how to disregard them and thus to escape them. The birth of the instructor happened like this. When Wisdom let a drop of light fall, it flowed onto the water, and immediately an androgynous human being appeared. She first formed that drop into a female body. Afterwards, she formed it into a body in the likeness of the mother which had appeared. She finished it in twelve months. An androgynous human being was born, whom the Greeks call Hermaphrodite, and whose mother the Hebrews call the Eve of Life, which means the female instructor of Life. Her child is the one born who is lord.

Afterwards, the authorities called it 'the beast' to cause it to lead their modeled forms astray. The meaning of 'the beast' is 'the instructor,' for it was found to be the wisest of all creatures. Eve is the first virgin, and she gave birth to her first child without a man. She was her own midwife/physician. For this reason she is held to have said:

I am part of my mother, and I am the mother.
I am the wife, I am the virgin.
I am pregnant, I am the physician.
I am the comforter of birth pains.
My husband birthed me, and I am his mother,
And he is my father and my lord.
He is my power,
he speaks his desires reasonably.
I am becoming,
But I have given birth to a human lord."

193. OnOrig 115.36–116.8.
194. OnOrig116.3. The word is efficacious throughout OnOrig's creation account as well; see OnOrig 100.15; 100.17; 100.34; 101.11; 102.14; 104.1; Cf. the efficaciousness of the divine word in Gen 1.3–30.

and had arisen [ⲧⲱⲟⲩⲛ] . . . they were very disturbed [ϣⲧⲟⲣⲧⲣ̄]," and sent seven of the archangels to investigate the situation.[195]

They go to Adam and see Eve speaking with him, asking one another, "Who is this enlightened woman? She is like [ⲓⲛⲉ] the likeness [ⲉⲓⲛⲉ] that appeared to us in the light [ⲟⲩⲟⲉⲓⲛ]. Come, let us grab [ⲉⲙⲁϩⲧⲉ] her and cast [ⲛⲟⲩϫⲉ] our seed [σπέρμα] into her so that she becomes defiled [ϫⲱϩⲙ][196] and unable to ascend to her light [ⲟⲩⲉⲓⲛ]. And those whom she bears will be subject to us [ὑποτάσσω]."[197] It seems their purpose in raping her is to defile her in order to accomplish two things. The first is to prevent her from ascending to her light, that is, the divine realm,[198] and the second, to make those born to Eve subject to the rulers, authorities, and angels.[199]

In a radical move compared with the other two Genesis elaborations (though somewhat resonant with SRJ's challenge of the hierarchical relationship between man and woman), OnOrig says that they put a sleep (ⲃ̄ϣⲉ) on Adam and "teach [ⲥⲉⲃⲟⲩ] him in his sleep [ϩⲓⲛⲏⲃ] that she came from his rib [ⲥⲡⲓⲣ] so that the woman [ⲥϩⲓⲙⲉ] may be subjected [ὑποτάσσω], and he may be lord [ϫⲟⲉⲓⲥ] over her."[200] With this

---

195. OnOrig 116.8–11.

196. ϫⲱϩⲙ: OnOrig 116.17; 117.5, 7, 9, 13, 14; 118.15; 124.25. RoR 89.27 (2x); 89.28; 92.3, 28. SRJ BG 62.8 // III 31.10 // II 24.15 // IV 37.27 (reconstruction).

197. RoR 116.11–20.

198. Cf. OnOrig 112.10–13: "When the Adam of Light wished to enter his light, which is the eighth heaven, he could not do so because of the poverty [i.e., materiality] that had mixed with his light." This mixing is what the rulers hope to achieve by raping Eve.

199. Cf. OnOrig 117.15–18: "First she [Eve] became pregnant with Abel by the Chief Ruler. And she gave birth to other children by the seven authorities and their angels."

These reasons contrast with SRJ, where in BG and III the Chief Ruler rapes Eve "because he was filled with senselessness [BG]/ignorance [III] and wanted to sow his seed in her," and where II and IV do not make the reason explicit, but simply say that "Yaldabaoth was filled with ignorance" (SRJ BG 62.5–7 // III 31.7–9; II 24.12 // IV 37.21–23). All four SRJ manuscripts, however, note that Cain and Abel, the rulers born from the Chief Ruler's rape of Eve, are meant to rule over humanity, just as the children of their rape in OnOrig (technically, "rule [ἄρχειν] over the tomb," i.e., body [SRJ BG 63.9–12 // III 32.4–6 // II 24.32–34 // IV 38.21–24]). In addition, in SRJ, Eve is a creation of the rulers, made in an attempt to extract the Insight of Light from Adam (SRJ BG 59.6–15 // III 29.12–20 // II 22.28–35 // IV 35.8–17). Both differ from RoR, where the creation of Eve is linked to the "plotting" (ϣⲟϫⲛⲉ) of the rulers, though there is no specific reason given for her creation (RoR 89.3–11). In RoR they become disturbed (ϣⲧⲟⲣⲧⲣ̄) and lust (ⲙⲉⲣⲉⲓⲧⲥ̄) after her, saying, "Come, let's cast [ⲛⲟⲩϫⲉ] our seed [σπέρμα] in her," and pursue (διώκω) her (RoR 89.17–25). The Reality of the Rulers does not specifically say anything regarding the rulers' purpose or reason for raping Eve, though the idea of subjugation does arise later in the text where the rulers claim that Eve was "a slave" to them (RoR 92.30–31).

200. OnOrig 116.20–25; cf. Gen 2:21–22; 3:16. On Adam's "sleep," cf. RoR 89.3–7, "And the deep sleep [ⲃ̄ϣⲉ] that they 'caused to fall upon him and he slept' is ignorance"; SRJ BG 58.13–19 // III 29.1–7

statement, OnOrig frames the creation of Eve from Adam as a lie to justify the subjugation of women to men, just as their rape—an act of subjugation in and of itself—is meant to subject those whom Eve bears to the rulers. The use of ὑποτάσσω in both 116.19 and 116.24–25—the only two instances of the word in the entire text—emphasizes the parallelism between these two acts as well as linking the constructs of gender and subjugation. Here, the rulers attempt to establish a mimetic parallel between their violent, power driven relationship to Eve and Adam's relationship to her.[201]

The text then describes Eve's response to the rulers saying, "Eve, being a power [δύναμις], laughed at their decision. She blinded [ϩⲗⲁⲥⲧⲛ̄][202] their eyes and stealthily left her likeness [ⲉⲓⲛⲉ] with Adam. She entered [ⲃⲱⲕ ⲉϩⲟⲩⲛ] into the Tree of Knowledge [γνῶσις] and remained [ϭⲱ] there. They went after her [ⲟⲩⲱϩ ⲛ̄ⲥⲱⲥ][203] her, and she revealed to them that she had entered [ⲃⲱⲕ ⲉϩⲟⲩⲛ] the tree and had become a tree. Then, becoming very fearful [ϣⲱⲡⲉ ϩⲛ̄ ⲟⲩⲛⲟϭ ϩⲣ̄ⲧⲉ], the blind ones [ⲃⲣ̄ⲣⲉ] fled [ⲡⲱⲧ ⲉⲃⲟⲗ]."[204] Here, somehow the rulers are made aware of Eve's transformation—which they are not in the other texts—but their knowledge of her transformation causes them to become so fearful that she creates a stupor (ⲃϣⲉ) in them, from which they must recover. The word used for "stupor," ⲃϣⲉ, is the same word initially used for "sleep" above when the rulers/authorities/angels want to plant the lie of female subordination to man into Adam. By causing a sleep to fall upon the rulers, Eve uses their own tricks against them to aid in her escape.

// II 22.20–25 // IV 34.28–35.3: "And he [the Chief Ruler] put a trance [ⲃϣⲉ, II, ἔκστασις] over Adam. . . . It is not as Moses said, 'He put him to sleep,' but it was his perception that he veiled." Both RoR and SRJ associate this sleep with ignorance; OnOrig "clarifies" what this ignorance entails.

In SRJ, it is the serpent who teaches them about "desire, pollution, and destruction," and the Savior who "set them right so that they would eat" (BG 57.8–58.10 ⲉⲓⲁⲧⲉ // II 22.3–18 and IV 34.5–19 ⲥⲃⲃⲟⲟⲩ). Also see Livy 1.9.14, where the women are "taught" by Romulus.

201. Again note SRJ BG 63.10–12 // III 32.4–6 // II 24.32–34 // IV 38.21–24, where Cain and Abel are meant to rule over humanity.

202. Crum, 671b, "mist, covered her eyes, like tears & she was blinded, overshadowed, darken."

203. Crum, 506b, the first Greek synonym for ⲟⲩⲱϩ ⲛⲥⲁ ("put after, follow") is ἀκολουθέω, "follow one, go after or with him, freq. of soldiers and slaves" (LSJ).

204. OnOrig 116.25–33. Cf. RoR 89.24–26; Ovid, Met. 1.543–67, on the transformation of Daphne into a tree and Met. 1.700–708 on the transformation of Syrinx into reeds.

When the rulers, authorities, and angels have recovered from this stupor created by Eve, they see:

the likeness [ⲓⲛⲉ] of this woman with him. They were disturbed [ⲁⲩⲧⲟⲣⲧⲣ̄], thinking [ⲙⲉⲉⲩⲉ] she was the true [ἀληθινή] Eve. And they acted cruelly [τολμάω]. They entered her [ⲉⲓ ⲉⲃⲟⲩⲛ ⲱⲁⲣⲟⲥ][205] and possessed [ⲉⲙⲁϩⲧⲉ] her and cast [ⲛⲟⲩϫⲉ] their seed [σπέρμα] down upon her [ⲉϩⲣⲁⲓ ⲉⲭⲱⲥ]. They acted upon her wickedly [πανοῦγρος]. They not only defiled [ⲭⲱⲣⲙ] in natural [φυσικῶς], but abominable ways [ⲥⲱⲱϥ].[206] They defiled [ⲭⲱⲣⲙ̄] the seal [σφραγίς] of her first voice [ϩⲣⲟⲟⲩ], which had said to them "What exists before you?"—intending to defile [ⲭⲱⲣⲙ] those who might say at the completion [συντέλια] [of the age] that they were born of the true [ἀληθινός] human through the word [ⲱⲁϫⲉ].[207]

In this portion of the narrative, the "blind rulers," who are both literally made blind by Eve and are also metaphorically blind due to their actions,[208] are, as in RoR, tricked by the spiritual Eve into thinking

---

205. I have pushed the translation of this phrase here to reflect the physicality of Eve's rape here, based on the somewhat ambiguous combination of words used in the phrase, generally translated as "They came to her. . . ." The verb ⲉⲓ generally means to "come or go" generally corresponding to the Greek ἔρχομαι (Crum, 70a). When followed by the preposition ⲉϩⲟⲩⲛ the combination of ⲉⲓ ⲉϩⲟⲩⲛ generally means to "come in or enter" and corresponds to the Greek εἰσέρχομαι, though it is used in Matt 26:60 for προσέρχομαι (Crum, 72a–b). While the NRSV translates Matt 26:60 as "many false witnesses came forward," this could easily be translated as "many false witness came in," given that the phrase references "entering into" legal proceedings (Crum 72a–b). In OnOrig, the phrase ⲉⲓ ⲉϩⲟⲩⲛ is used six times (98.7–6; 115.8; 119.20; 120.30; 121.7; 123.2) and in five instances is translated in NHC as "enter." In OnOrig 120.30 it is translated as "come to," referring to the rulers' worries that Adam will "come to the Tree of Life" as he did the Tree of Knowledge, but interestingly, NHC translates the same phrase in OnOrig 121.7 as "went in to," referring to the rulers' *entering* the Tree of Life and surrounding it with their creatures to protect it. Here, though the translation of 120.30 (that the rulers "came to" the Tree of Life) seems to make more sense, the translators have opted to retain the lexical meaning.
   On the Origin of the World 117.4 becomes ambiguous with the addition of the preposition ⲱⲁ- generally meaning "to or toward," and corresponding to πρός, but also used for εἰς, ἕως, and ἐπί (Crum, 541b–532a). Following ⲉϩⲟⲩⲛ (indicating "to inside or inward," Crum, 685b), that is, ⲉϩⲟⲩⲛ ⲱⲁ- generally corresponds to πρός (Crum, 686a). The difficulty here is whether the combination of ⲉⲓ ⲉϩⲟⲩⲛ or ⲉϩⲟⲩⲛ ⲱⲁ- should have precedence. The other two instances of the combination ⲉⲓ ⲉϩⲟⲩⲛ ⲱⲁ- occur in OnOrig 116.34 and 118.17 where the rulers approach, "come up to," in the first instance Adam, confronting him about Eve, and in the second to give Adam and Eve the prohibition to eat from the tree. These particular occurrences seem to reflect the use of with verbs of motion giving it the meaning of "upon or against" (LSJ s.v. πρός B.3), indicating in these verses the particular confrontation between the rulers and Adam and Eve. In addition, the definitions of the compound verb προσέρχομαι include "approach" (LSJ I.1); "come in" (LSJ II); and "sexual intercourse" (LSJ III). Given the range of all three words in the clause, the translation of (ⲉⲓ ⲉϩⲟⲩⲛ ⲱⲁⲣⲟⲥ) as "entered in" fits squarely within the semantic range of the definition.
206. Crum, 378b–379a, "pollution, abomination, βδέλυγμα, ἀσέλγεια, μόλυνσις."
207. OnOrig 116.3–117.11.
208. OnOrig 103.18: "'You are wrong, Samael,' which means 'blind god'"; 113.14: ". . . because they [the rulers]]are blind and they ignorantly created (Adam) against their own interests."

that she is her likeness, which she has stealthily left by entering and becoming the Tree of Knowledge. The Eve that the rulers rape is not, in fact, "really" Eve. Then, in the most graphic depiction of her rape of the three Genesis elaborations, OnOrig says, "They entered her and possessed her and cast their seed down upon her. They acted upon her wickedly. They not only defiled in natural, but abominable ways." Again, as in RoR, this is a gang rape of Eve with multiple actors "wickedly" raping her body.

The text also describes the rulers' actions as one of "possession." The word used for "possess" is ⲉⲙⲁϩⲧⲉ, which has a wide semantic range. Among its meanings are "to grasp, rule, detain, and possess."[209] Here the rulers, authorities, and angels act out upon Eve's body the things they have taught Adam in his sleep: that the woman should be subjected to man and that man should be lord over her.[210] ⲉⲙⲁϩⲧⲉ is used three other times in the text and always in relation to Life/Eve.[211] Compared with the spiritual women in SRJ, RoR, and OnOrig, this Eve is "graspable."[212]

Next, as in RoR,[213] OnOrig says, "They defiled [ⲝⲱϩⲙ̄] the seal [σφραγίς] of her first voice [ϩⲣⲟⲟⲩ], which had said to them 'What

---

209. Crum; 9a–b.
210. Cf. SRJ BG 61.10–15 // III 30.24–31.1; and SRJ II 23.37–24.3 // IV 37.7–11.
211. The first time it is used is in 115.18 after Wisdom Life sends her breath into Adam causing him to move. When the rulers see him with this newly endowed breath, they become disturbed (ϣⲧⲟⲣⲧⲣ̄—the same effect that incites their rape of Eve—117.1), and they rush toward him and grab (ⲉⲙⲁϩⲧⲉ) him, saying to the breath within him, the breath of Wisdom Life, "Who are you and where did you come from?" Next, ⲉⲙⲁϩⲧⲉ is used in 116.16 as the rulers premeditatedly form their plan against Eve, that is, to rape her, and then in 117.3, where they execute this plan. Cf. RoR 88.1; also SRJ BG 42.9 // III 18.8: "These (the rulers and powers) are the ones who rule [ⲁⲙⲁϩⲧⲉ] the world [κόσμος]"; BG 65.17 // III 33.14 // II 25.33 // IV 40.8: The immovable race is "not ruled [ⲁⲙⲁϩⲧⲉ] by anything"; BG 71.17 // III 37.4 // II 28.8; 28.11 // IV 43.21; 43.24: The Chief Ruler makes a plan to "seize" or "rule" (ⲁⲙⲁϩⲧⲉ) the thought of the "perfect race"; III 39.5: The angels of the Chief Ruler "seize" (ⲁⲙⲁϩⲧⲉ) the "daughters of men."
212. ⲁⲙⲁϩⲧⲉ/ⲉⲙⲁϩⲧⲉ (with this meaning) is only used at RoR at 88.1, where the rulers form their plan to "seize" Eve—though this word is not used during the act of rape itself. In SRJ it is used several times, but not in conjunction with the seizure of Eve. In III 39.5 (and only in this manuscript) it is used in the "seizing" of the daughters of humans. In III 37.4 // BG 71.17 // II 28.8 // IV 43.21 and II 28.11 // IV 43.24 where the Chief Ruler realizes that Adam and Eve have surpassed him in knowledge and he wants to "seize" or "restrict" their plan of wisdom through his ignorance. The last place the word occurs in SRJ is in III 16.4 // BG 38.19–39.1 // II 10.24, where he "seizes" a place to create his realms. Here, as with RoR and SRJ, it is only a part of Eve that is graspable—but in contrast to the other texts, she is a creation of the divine realm and so it would seem that her likeness hails from there as well.
213. RoR 89.28–29.

exists before you?' intending to defile [ⲭⲱⲣⲙ] those who might say at the completion [of the age] that they were born of the true [ἀληθινός] human through the word [ϣⲁⲝⲉ]." The rulers, authorities, and angels seem to defile "the seal of her voice" for several reasons. The first is to punish the voice that both spoke out against them and brought things into being—whether it is the voice of Pistis that told Samael the "blind god" he was wrong[214] or the voice that became "a thing" or "a work," thus causing Adam to stand.[215] The second reason is to halt the speech of those born of the true human through the word—for it is the word or speech that brings these children into being which they are trying to silence, and additionally the verbal witness of those children concerning their true parentage. The rulers, authorities, and angels are trying to punish words that speak the truth as they attempt again and again to cast the truth as a lie.[216] This process is parallel to the silencing logic of sexual violence, which often covers the survivor in a shroud of silence and also hopes to cast their words, cast their truth telling as a lie, thus attempting to cast the perpetrator as the victim.[217] Importantly, in the three Genesis retellings, this recasting—either blaming the victim, or casting the perpetrator as victim—never occurs: the rulers and their actions are always laid bare, named as evil and manipulative and self-serving—there is no equivocation on these points.

The text continues exposing the rulers' actions: "And they erred. They did not know [ⲥⲟⲟⲩⲛ] they defiled [ⲭⲁⲣⲙ̄] their own body [σῶμα]. The authorities and their angels had defiled [ⲭⲁⲣⲙ̄ϥ] the likeness [ⲉⲓⲛⲉ] in every way. First [Eve] became pregnant with Abel by the Chief Ruler.[218] And she gave birth to other children by the seven authorities and their angels."[219] As with RoR, OnOrig is explicit about the fact that the rulers have raped their own body, rather than defiling the spiritual

214. OnOrig 103.15–18.
215. OnOrig 115.36–116.5.
216. See chapter 1 in this study regarding Calgacus's speech, particularly where he says, "To rob, slaughter and rape they give the false name of empire; they make desolation, they call it peace" (Tacitus, *Agricola* 30.4–31.3).
217. Again, see Herman, *Trauma and Recovery,* 7–8, 29.
218. Cf. Gen 4:1–2, where Abel is born after Cain.
219. OnOrig 117.12–18.

Eve.²²⁰ This is foreshadowed in both texts as well when the Eve laughs at and mocks them²²¹ again exposing their blindness and ignorance.²²² The text also makes explicit the trickster qualities inherent in the characterization of Eve, allowing a portion of her to escape the violence and violation of the rulers. But although the text allows a portion of Eve to escape the rape, what the rulers do to Eve's body is called "wicked" (πανοῦγρος) and the text condemns it: the rulers are still accountable for their violent actions.

In a significant departure from the Genesis story line, Eve first gives birth to Abel through her rape by the Chief Ruler, and then gives birth "to other children [ϣΗⲣⲉ] by the seven authorities [ἐξουσία] and their angels [ἀγγελος]."²²³ Here again the multiple rapes endured by Eve are highlighted, as well as the fact that this is a gang rape perpetrated by multiple levels of beings that make up the government (διοίκησις)²²⁴ of Yaldabaoth's realm. Eve is literally violated by all of the levels of the world's "government," exposing not only the violences perpetrated by individuals, but the exploitation, subjugation, and violence of the entire system and structure created by the rulers.

Abel is the only child named in the text, and only this one time; there is no Cain. On the Origin of the World, then, states that all of this occurred—that is, the children resulting from the rulers', authorities', and angels' rape of Eve—"according to the Chief Parent's Foresight, so that the first mother might bear within her every seed [σπέρμα], mixed [ⲧⲏⲣ] and joined [ἁρμόζω] with the fate [εἱμαρμένη] of the world [κόσμος] and its schemas [σχῆμα], and justice [δικαιοσύνη]."²²⁵ But, as noted earlier, already a counterplan (οἰκονομία) "came into being regarding Eve, so that the modeled forms of the authorities might become enclosures of the light.²²⁶ Then it [the light] would condemn [κατακρίνω] them through their modeled forms."²²⁷ Despite the rulers'

---

220. RoR 89.29–31; 92.23–25.
221. Crum, 320b–321a.
222. OnOrig 116.25–26; RoR 89.23–25.
223. Note that Cain is conspicuously absent from OnOrig.
224. OnOrig 103.4.
225. OnOrig 117.18–24. Cf. SRJ BG 72.2–4 // III 37.6–7 // II 28.11–14 // IV 43.24–29 on the begetting of fate as well as Gal 4:8–10.
226. Cf. OnOrig 113.10.

intentions to control humanity and to make it subject to them, the divine intervenes, using the rulers' actions to engender their own undoing.

"The offspring of the earthly [χοϊκός] Adam multiplied and filled (the earth), and acquired within itself all of the knowledge obtained by the soul-ful [ψυχικός] Adam, but they were all in ignorance [ⲙⲛ̄ⲧⲁⲧⲥⲟⲟⲩⲛ]." When the rulers noticed this and "had seen him and the woman who was with him in error [πλανάω] and ignorance [ⲙⲛ̄ⲧⲁⲧⲥⲟⲟⲩⲛ], like farm animals [ⲧⲃⲛⲏ], they rejoiced [ⲣⲁϣⲉ]."[228] Here OnOrig describes Adam and Eve as being like farm or domesticated animals,[229] which seems to stress the rulers' idea that humanity is subject to them (cf. 116.15–25). But despite this seeming subjugation, the rulers were once again disturbed (ϣⲧⲟⲣⲧⲣ̄) because "they knew [ⲉⲓⲙⲉ] that the immortal [ⲁⲧⲙⲟⲩ] human would again surpass [παραβαίνω] them[230] yet they would still have to fear [ⲣⲟⲧⲉ] the woman who became a tree."[231] Then they said to one another, "Perhaps this is the true [ἀληθινός] human, this one who blinded[232] us and taught [ⲧⲥⲉⲃⲟⲛ] us that she who was defiled [ⲭⲁϩⲙⲉⲥ] is like [ⲓⲛⲉ] him, and so we shall be conquered [ϫⲣⲟ]!"[233]

Fearing that rather than subjugating humanity they will be conquered by it, the seven rulers again plot (συμβούλιον) with one another and go to Adam and Eve "in fear" (φόβος), and, following Genesis, say to Adam, "You may eat [ⲟⲩⲱⲙ] the fruit of every tree

---

227. OnOrig 117.24–28.

228. OnOrig 118.2–9.

229. Crum, 400b. It is interesting to note that they are viewed by the rulers as "farm animals" before they eat from the tree.

230. ⲛ̄ⲧⲁⲣⲟⲩⲉⲓⲙⲉ ϫⲉ ⲡⲣⲱⲙⲁ ⲛ̄ⲁⲧⲙⲟⲩ ϥⲛⲁⲣ̄ⲡⲁⲣⲁⲃⲁ [παραβαίνω] ⲁⲛ ⲉⲣⲟⲟⲩ ⲁⲗⲗⲁ ⲉⲩⲛⲁⲣ̄ⲡⲕⲉⲣ̄ ϩⲟⲧⲉ ϩⲏⲧⲥ̄ ⲛ̄ⲧⲉⲛⲧⲁⲣ̄ ϣⲏⲛ. . . . NHC translates this as "When they learned that the immortal man was not going to neglect them, rather that they would even have to fear the female creature that had turned into a tree. . . ." I have opted to translate this phrase assuming that the alternate spelling of ⲁⲛ for ⲟⲛ is being used here, and that rather than a negative particle should be rendered as the adverb "again." Of the six times the particle is used in OnOrig it occurs four times with the ⲁⲛ spelling (ⲁⲛ: 98.8; 98.34; 111.15; 122.28; ⲟⲛ: 120.30; 122.13). Additionally, immediately following this, the rulers are clearly frightened that they will be conquered, that is, surpassed. It is also possible, however, that they are no longer worried that Adam will surpass them, but simply worried about Eve, given the use of ἀλλά.

231. OnOrig 118.10–12.

232. Cf. esp. OnOrig 116.27, where Eve blinds the rulers and is raped, also 120.4.

233. OnOrig 118.13–16.

created for you all in paradise, take care and do not eat from the Tree of Knowledge [γνῶσις]. If you eat, you will die." This encounter gives Adam and Eve "a great fright [φόβος], and they withdrew up to their authorities."[234] Then the serpent appears, recast as in RoR, whom OnOrig names "the wisest of all creatures" and the "instructor"[235]—though the authorities call it "the beast" (θηρίον) as it leads "their modeled forms astray." The serpent-instructor sees the likeness of the mother, Eve, and says to her:

"What did God say to you all? Was it, 'Do not eat from the Tree of Knowledge [γνῶσις]?'" She said, "He not only said, 'Do not eat from it,' but 'Do not touch it, or you will die.'"[236] He said to her, "Do not be afraid. In death you all will not die. For he knows [cooyn] that when you eat from it, your minds [νοῦς] will become sober [νήφω] and you will become like gods [ⲛⲟⲩⲧⲉ], knowing [cooyn] the difference that exists between evil [πονηρός] humans and good [ἀγαθός]. He said this to you in jealousy [φθονέω] so that you would not eat from it."[237]
Eve had confidence in the words [ϣⲁϫⲉ] of the instructor [ⲣⲉϥⲧⲁⲙⲟ]. She gazed at the tree and saw that it was beautiful [ⲛⲉⲥⲱϥ] and grand [ⲗⲉϩⲗϩ], and she loved [ⲙⲉⲣⲓⲧϥ] it. She took some of its fruit and ate it. And she gave some to her husband [ϩⲁⲓ] also, and he ate it, too. Then their minds [νοῦς] opened [ⲟⲩⲱⲛ]. For when they had eaten, the light [ⲟⲩⲟⲉⲓⲛ] of knowledge [γνῶσις] enlightened [ⲣ̄ ⲟⲩⲟⲉⲓⲛ] them. When they clothed themselves with shame [ϣⲓⲡⲉ], they knew [ⲉⲓⲙⲉ] that they were stripped naked of knowledge [γνῶσις]. When they became sober [νήφω], they saw that they were naked and they loved [ⲙⲡ̄ⲣⲉ] each other. When they saw that those who molded them had the form of beasts [θηρίον], they loathed [σικχαίνω] them. They understood [ⲉⲓⲙⲉ] much.[238]

Here, the earthly Adam and Eve become enlightened, just as the Adam of Light (ⲟⲩⲉⲓⲛ, 108.2-24) and the enlightened (ⲧⲉⲉⲓⲣⲙⲟⲩⲉⲓⲛ) Eve

234. OnOrig 118.16-24; cf. Gen 2:16-17.
235. OnOrig 118.24-26: "Then came the wisest of all creatures, who was called "the Beast"; OnOrig 113.35-114.4: "Her child is the one born who is lord. Afterwards, the authorities called it 'the beast' to cause it to lead their modeled forms astray. The meaning of 'the beast' is 'the instructor,' for it was found to be the wisest of all creatures"; RoR 31-33: "Then the female spiritual presence came in the shape of the serpent, the instructor. And it taught them . . ."; cf. Gen 3:1, 14. Again for the Aramaic wordplay see Layton, "Part II," 55–56n57; Pearson Gnosticism, Judaism, and Egyptian Christianity, 44–46; and Pheme Perkins, Gnosticism and the New Testament, 22–24.
236. Cf. Gen 3:1-3.
237. Cf. Gen 3:4-5.
238. OnOrig 118.27-119.18; cf. Gen 3:7. Here everything is unmasked and honor becomes shame and shame becomes honor.

(116.12–15), and the fullness of the plan presented by the text comes to fruition. The earthly Adam and Eve's enlightenment is expressed in their mutual love for each other, as opposed to the one-sided love exhibited throughout much of OnOrig.

The verb me, "to love," is used primarily in two other scenes. The first is when the Chief Parent's Foresight sees the human likeness in the light after the Chief Parent says, "If anything existed before me, let it appear, so that we may see its light!" (107.36–108.2). She falls in love with this human likeness, "but he hated [мосте] her because she was in darkness [каке]. She desired [оуωϣ] to ensnare [ϭολϫc̄][239] him, and she was not able. When she was unable to heal her love [меειε], she poured out [пωρτ][240] her light [оуоειν] upon the earth."[241] Somehow this action of Foresight's is connected with the creation of blood, but how and why is not made explicit by the text. Regardless, from this blood Eros appears, with whom "all the gods and their angels" fall in love (меριτ 109.10), and which results in *eros* being "dispersed in all the creatures of chaos" (109.15).[242]

Again, though the text does not explicitly say how, this love toward Eros is connected with "the blood that was shed upon the earth," with many trees sprouting from this blood and "all kinds [κατά γένος], having within them their seed from the seed [σπέρμα] of the authorities [ἐξουσία] and their angels [ἄγγελος]."[243] Much as the rulers', authorities',

239. Crum, 814a–b, "entangle, ensnare, cling, adhere."
240. OnOrig 104.4: Pistis pours out some of her light on the immortal human; 109.27: a grapevine sprouts from the blood poured over the earth; 111.9: Psyche loves Eros and pours her blood upon him and the earth and the first rose sprouts; 111.19: the virgin daughters of Foresight/Pronoia become enamored of Eros and pour their blood upon him and the earth and different kinds of every plant sprout containing the seed of the authorities and their angels; 123.10: when the seven rulers were cast from heaven to earth they instruct humans, among other things, in the worship of idols and pouring of blood; 126.8: where the earth is intoxicated with the spilling of blood. What does this say about the connection between blood, desire, and empire? SRJ II 14.5 // BG 47.2 // III 21.6: the Spirit pours spirit upon the "Mother" to correct her deficiency; BG 73.17 // III 38.9: darkness pours over the earth (in the Noah scene). Not found in RoR.
241. OnOrig 108.14–19. It is not entirely clear how Foresight's light functions; it is clearly not the light from above, as the text says that the "Adam of Light," means "the enlightened human of blood" (108.20–22) and the text says later that he could not ascend to his light because his light was mixed with poverty (112.11–13).
242. OnOrig 109.1–16. See Patricia Cox Miller, "'Plenty Sleeps There': The Myth of Eros and Psyche in Plotinus and Gnosticism," in *Neoplatonism and Gnosticism*, ed. Richard T. Wallis and Jay Bregman, Studies in Neoplatonism 6 (Albany: State University of New York Press, 1992), 223–38, on the myth of Eros and Psyche embedded within OnOrig.

and angels' rape of Eve occurs "so that the first mother might bear within her every seed, mixed [ⲧⲏⲣ] and joined [ἁρμόζω] with the fate [εἱμαρμένη] of the world [κόσμος] and its schemas [σχῆμα], and justice [δικαιοσύνη],"[244] this "love" causes an intermingling or mixing so that, at this point, the vegetative life that has sprouted contains the seed of the lower realm.

After these trees are created, the text speaks about the creation of paradise by Justice. It describes the appearance of the Tree of Life by God's (ⲛⲟⲩⲧⲉ) will/desire (ⲟⲩⲱϣ) and the Tree of Knowledge, which is next to it and has "the power [δύναμις] of God [ⲛⲟⲩⲧⲉ]."[245] As in 119.6-9, the Tree of Knowledge is described as "beautiful" (ⲛⲉⲥⲱⲟⲩ) and "grand" (ⲗⲉⲣⲗⲣ̄). The text then quotes from an unknown book called the Sacred Book, which says, "You are the Tree of Knowledge [ⲡϣⲏⲛ ⲛ̄ⲧⲅⲛⲱⲥⲓⲥ], which is in paradise, from which the first human ate [ⲟⲩⲟⲙⲟ̄]. You opened [ⲟⲩⲏⲛ] his mind [νοῦς], and he loved [ⲙ̄ⲡ̄ⲣ̄ⲉ] his partner [ϣⲃⲣⲉⲓⲛⲉ], and condemned [κατάκρινω] the other [ⲕⲉ-], strange [ἀλλότριος] likenesses [-ⲉⲓⲛⲉ] and loathed [σιχαίνω] them."[246] These earlier lines directly parallel Eve and Adam's encounter with the tree as Eve and Adam eat (ⲟⲩⲱⲙ) (119.10-11); their minds (νοῦς) open (ⲟⲩⲱⲛ) (119.11-12), they love (ⲙ̄ⲡ̄ⲣ̄ⲉ) each other (119.16) and loathe (σιχαίνω) (119.18) those who modeled them.

These passages directly connect the proliferation of vegetative life with the awakening of Adam and Eve through their eating from the tree, bringing the text full circle from the unrequited love of Foresight, which occasions the lush proliferation of the earth. Furthermore, Eve and Adam's love for each other and partnership (ϣⲃⲣⲉⲓⲛⲉ) provide a contrast not only with the unrequited, one-sided "love" that brings about the creation of the plant world but particularly with the violent, one-sided "love" that brings about the creation of humans through the rulers' rape of Eve. This unrequited and one-sided love, at times better

243. OnOrig 109.25-110.1.
244. OnOrig 117.20-24. Again, cf. SRJ BG 72.2-4 // III 37.6-7 // II 28.11-14 // IV 43.24-29; Gal 4:8-10.
245. OnOrig 110.2-20.
246. OnOrig 110.18-111.1. This phrase reproduces the imperial rhetoric of "otherness," "foreignness," through reversal.

identified as lust, is intimately connected to the rulers, authorities, and angels and their attempt to capture and contain what is not theirs. Though they scheme to do this again and again, that which they wish to capture and contain, remains, as in SRJ and RoR "ungraspable."[247]

It is with deep irony that the one thing that the rulers are able to grasp, the earthly Eve, makes all that they wish to grasp forever ungraspable. Their act of violence in grasping and possessing the earthly Eve, raping her to create bodies that they hope to subjugate, becomes their undoing. Their bodies become containers of the light, conduits of enlightenment, unmasking the rulers and allowing humanity to see them as they truly are. And these enlightened bodies seem to come through the mutual love that Adam and Eve share after eating the fruit from the tree—the light moving from one being to the next until Adam and Eve themselves become enlightened, becoming the counterparts of the Adam of light and the spiritual Eve. Though the enlightenment that occurs through the Tree of Knowledge restores something that is lost, it still does not protect Adam and Eve from the rulers' wrath. They are cursed, cast from paradise to earth, and their life spans are cut short. Nonetheless their enlightenment/light does not end but will be passed on to their children.

The Rape of Eve

While each of these three versions of Eve's rape contains unique elements, they at the same time share a common story. Again, it is important to reiterate that I am not claiming either some kind of ur-

---

247. Painchaud notes this contrast between Adam and Eve's "spiritual love," which is reflected in their relationship as ϣⲃⲣⲉⲓⲛⲉ, and that of the "passionate love" of Foresight for the Human of Light (*L'Écrit sans titre*, 444). He notes that this difference—that is, that Adam and Eve's love is spiritual—is seen particularly in the fact they do not engender children. I think it is difficult to claim that Adam and Eve do not engender children through this love. While children of Adam are mentioned before the eating of the tree 118.2–6, who are in ignorance (possibly alluding to their births before the eating of the fruit), the children of Eve are mentioned 120.6–7 as being under the curse, and additionally Adam and his descendants are mentioned again in 122.5–6. The text then goes on, though there are several lacunae, that there are descendants of the spirit-ful, soul-ful, and earthly humans (122.7–9). Though Painchaud's reading is plausible based on the actors, I think it is unlikely. Nevertheless, I am in total agreement with his insight into the partnership between Adam and Eve in contrast to that of the rulers (here particularly regarding Foresight) and would extend (and have extended) this to both SRJ's and RoR's framing of Adam and Eve as well.

story or the primacy of one story or the dependence of one story upon another; I want to recognize and highlight the common threads that are contained in all three of these elaborations of the Genesis narrative.[248] Though there are differences between the texts, I have identified seven primary themes that provide a scaffolding for all three of the stories. I will address these themes one by one.

First, in all three narratives, Eve embodies something from the divine realm that is sent to help and enliven Adam. In SRJ this is seen particularly through the connection between Eve and Insight, who is initially sent from the divine realm to Adam and hidden inside him, and subsequently appears beside him in the woman the Chief Ruler shapes from Adam in an attempt to grasp Insight.[249] While Insight resides inside Adam she "awakens his thinking,"[250] and when she appeared beside him, Adam "became sober from the drunkenness of darkness,"[251] and she "uncovered the covering on his mind."[252] As in SRJ, in RoR, the Spirit is sent to Adam from the divine realm and makes "its home within him," and he becomes a "living being."[253] Next, this spirit seems to be extracted as the rulers open his side "like a living woman" and build "up his side with some flesh in place of her," leaving him with only a soul."[254] The spiritual woman then comes to Adam and tells him, "Arise!" and Adam proclaims to her, "You have given me life." Differing from SRJ and RoR, Eve in OnOrig is in no way derivative of Adam but is instead created by Wisdom Life to instruct Adam.[255] The rulers have left Adam lying on the ground, abandoned, when Eve is sent to him by Wisdom. Eve sees him and, much as in RoR, says to him, "Adam, live! Arise from the ground!" Adam immediately rises, opens

---

248. Through engaging the narrative of the rape of Eve, I am certain that this is a pivotal moment for understanding each of the three texts. While significant similarities and differences have been tracked in this chapter between SRJ, RoR, and OnOrig, I believe much more work needs to be done both on the individual texts and synoptically in order fully to trace the investments of the individual texts and where they overlap and diverge from one another as wholes.

249. SRJ BG 53.4–54.9; 59.6–16 // II 20.14–31; 22.28–23.2 // III 24.6–26.3; 29.12–21 // III 31.15–32.5; 35.7–22.

250. SRJ BG 55.17–18 // II 21.16 // III 27.3–4 // IV 32.26–33.1.

251. SRJ BG 59. 20–21 // II 23.8 // IV 35.30–31 // In III 30.1–2 Adam "became sober from the drunkenness of death."

252. SRJ BG 60.1–2 // II 23.6–7 // III 30.2–3 // IV 35.26–30.

253. RoR 88.11–15.

254. RoR 89.3–11.

255. OnOrig 113.17–20.

his eyes and declares, "you have given me life."[256] Because of these works, which both help and enliven Adam, in all three texts he names the divinely sent Eve "Mother of the Living."[257]

Second, the ruler/s, or some configuration of the beings "ruling"[258] the world, decide to rape Eve. In SRJ, Adam and Eve have withdrawn from Yaldabaoth when he curses them and declares that "the husband is to rule over [the woman.]" The Chief Ruler then sees Eve standing near Adam and "was full of ignorance" and "wanted to raise up a seed in her."[259] In RoR, the authorities (who seem to be the same as, or at least overlapping with, the rulers)[260] come to Adam and see "his partner speaking with him." The authorities become "disturbed" by this sight and say to one another, "Come, let's cast our seed in her," and then chase her.[261] In OnOrig, the authorities hear that Adam has arisen and send seven archangels to investigate. As in RoR, they go to Adam and see the woman speaking with him.[262] Because, unlike in SRJ and RoR, Eve is not derivative of Adam but a creation of the divine Wisdom Life, they do not know where this woman has come from and ask one another who she is.[263] She reminds them of "the likeness that appeared ... in the light," and they say to one another, "Come, let us grab her and cast our seed into her so that she becomes defiled and unable to ascend to her light. And those whom she bears will become subject to us."[264] In addition, a sleep is brought on Adam, and he is taught that Eve came from his rib so that, much as in SRJ, "the woman might be subjected,

---

256. OnOrig 115.27–116.8.
257. SRJ BG 60.15–16 // III 30.13–14. In II 23.23–24 // IV 36.15–17, she is given this appellation as well, but not specifically by Adam. In the SRJ manuscripts, this is connected to Insight's role of setting right the Mother (i.e., Wisdom, BG)/her deficiencies (II // III // IV). See RoR 89.15; OnOrig 116.7; cf. Gen 3:20.
258. I place "ruling" in quotation marks here, as all of the texts emphasize that, while the rulers exert undue influence over creation, the divine realm regularly influences and intervenes in the world continually as part of the process of the rulers undoing. The texts often refer to both the actions of the rulers and interventions by the divine as part of the divine plan—that is, all will be used for the rulers' undoing.
259. BG 61.8–62.7 // III 30.23–31.9; II 23.35–24.12 // IV 37.4–23 simply say that Yaldabaoth "was full of ignorance," and do not mention that he "wanted to raise up a seed," in Eve.
260. On this, see Gilhus, *Nature of the Archons,* 37, 37n79.
261. RoR 89.17–23.
262. OnOrig 116.8–13.
263. OnOrig 116.13; cf. 113.17–114.15.
264. OnOrig 116.13–20.

and he may be lord over her."[265] In each of these three texts, though illustrated in different ways, Eve's rape is closely intertwined with subjugation—both of woman to man and humanity to the rulers. The Reality of the Rulers is the least explicit about the connection between Eve's rape and the larger subjugation of humanity, but this connection can be seen as the rulers connect their rape of Eve to sexual slavery and demand that her daughter occupy the same position.[266] Both SRJ and OnOrig make this connection very clear by explicitly linking the act of rape to man ruling over woman. This subjugation is extended to the rest of humanity in SRJ when Cain and Abel, offspring of Yaldabaoth's rape of Eve are given rule over human bodies by Yaldabaoth[267] and in OnOrig where the rulers state that those whom Eve bears will be subject to them.

Third, in each text the spiritual portion of Eve splits off or dissociates from her material aspect. In SRJ this splitting, found only in manuscripts II and IV, occurs as divine Foresight sees "the enlightened Insight of Life" in Eve and "sent certain ones and they snatched Life out of Eve" before the Chief Ruler is able to rape her.[268] The Secret Revelation of John is unique in that the divine intervenes on Life's behalf and she does not seem to be an agent in this splitting or dissociation, as in the other two texts. In RoR, as the authorities chase Eve, she laughs at them "because of their foolishness and blindness."[269] As they seem to catch up with her, in "their grasp she became a tree, and left before them a shadow of herself that resembled her."[270] On the Origin of the World presents the most elaborate version of this theme. It says that Eve, being a power, laughs at the rulers, authorities, and angels as she does in RoR. Eve then blinds them, leaves "her likeness with Adam," and enters the Tree of Knowledge, remaining there.[271] Again, while there are significant differences between the three texts, all three posit some

---

265. OnOrig 116.20–25.
266. RoR 92.30–31.
267. SRJ BG 62.8–63.12 // II 24.16–34 // III 31.10–32.6 // IV 37.28–38.26.
268. SRJ II 24.10–15 // IV 37.19–26. In both BG and III it does not seem that Insight and Eve occupy the same space at this point in the text. See the section in this chapter on SRJ.
269. RoR 89.23–25.
270. RoR 89.25–26.
271. OnOrig 116.25–30.

kind of splitting, where the spiritual aspect of Eve is separated from her material aspect, each seeming to do this in an attempt to save a portion of Eve from the violence of the rulers.

Fourth, the ruler or rulers rape Eve. All three texts use the same Coptic word, ϫⲱϩⲙ, to describe this act of sexual violence.[272] The Secret Revelation of John contains the sparsest narrative of Yaldaboath's rape, simply saying in all four manuscripts, "The Chief Ruler defiled her."[273] The only additional thing about the Ruler's rape that can be inferred from the text is that he raped her multiple times, as two children, Cain and Abel, were born of the rapes.[274] While RoR' description is more detailed, it relates the rulers' rape of Eve in three clauses: "And they defiled her abominably. And they defiled the seal of her voice, and so they convicted themselves through the form they had shaped in their own image."[275]

There are several additional elements in RoR' description that are not found in SRJ's. First, rather than a rape solely perpetrated by the Chief Ruler, this is a gang rape of Eve, with multiple actors indicated by the plural subject "they." In addition, RoR calls the rape "abominable," showing clearly how the text views Eve's rape. Further, not only have they raped Eve's body, but they have raped "the seal of her voice." Through these actions, RoR is clear that the rulers/authorities have convicted themselves through their violence against the woman they had formed.

On the Origin of the World, again, is closer in plot line to RoR, but it contains several further elaborations. Like RoR, OnOrig is explicit in its view of the rulers' authorities' and angels' gang rape of Eve, initiating this scene with the words "they acted cruelly."[276] The text then describes their act in horrific detail: "They entered her and possessed her and cast their sperm down upon her. They acted upon her wickedly. They not only defiled in natural but abominable ways.

---

272. SRJ BG 62.8 // III 31.10 // II 24.15 // IV 37.27; RoR 89.27; 89.28; OnOrig 117.5; 117.7; 117.9.
273. SRJ II 24.15–16 // IV 37.27–28; BG 62.8 // III 31.10 simply say, "he defiled her."
274. SRJ BG 62.8–20 // II 24.15–25 // III 31.10–20 // IV 37.27–38.12.
275. RoR 89.27–31.
276. OnOrig 117.2.

They defiled the seal of her first voice, which had said to them 'What exists before you?' intending to defile those who might say at the completion [of the age] that they were born of the true human through the word."[277] On the Origin of the World is unequivocal in naming the horror and violence of the rulers' actions and their reasons for doing so. On the Origin of the World, too, is clear that the actions of the rulers serve to convict themselves, as it closes this scene saying, "And they erred. They did not know they defiled their own body. The authorities and their angels had defiled the likeness in every way."[278] Again, while the three texts differ in their telling of the rulers' rape, of the utmost import is the fact that none of the three texts blames or shames Eve in any way—these violent actions reflect only upon the rulers.

Fifth, some kind of encounter or "eating" of knowledge occurs, resulting in a change in both Eve and Adam. The Secret Revelation of John's account of Adam's and Eve's "eating of knowledge" differs most significantly from the other two texts. In SRJ, they "eat" before Eve's rape and their eating is occasioned by either Insight or Christ, rather than by the serpent.[279] Codex III relates that Insight taught them from the tree as an eagle to "eat of knowledge,[280] while in Codices II and IV, Christ enacts this eating of knowledge along with Insight and Foresight.[281] Regardless of the actors involved, both Adam and Eve gain insight through the actions of Insight/Christ/Foresight that lead to both recognition and awakening.

The Reality of the Rulers and OnOrig have more in common with each other than with SRJ, but they have a different narrative strategy in terms of this theme. In RoR the "female spiritual presence"—which resided in Adam, caused him to rise, then became the tree—now comes "in the shape of a serpent, the instructor," to teach them.[282] The serpent is recast as a helper and encourages Eve to eat from the tree,

---

277. OnOrig 117.2–11.
278. OnOrig 117.12–15.
279. See the discussion of this above.
280. SRJ II 30.17–21. SRJ BG 60.19–61.7 parallels II but says, "Reflection taught *him* about knowledge. From the tree, in the form of an eagle, she taught *him* about knowledge, so that *he* might remember his fullness for *both* were in a fallen state of ignorance."
281. SRJ II 23.25–35 // IV 36.20–37.4.
282. RoR 89.31–33.

and the Eve "of flesh" takes from the tree and eats giving it to her husband as well.[283] The text then says, "And thus these beings that possessed only a soul, ate. And their imperfection became apparent in their ignorance. They knew that they were stripped of the spiritual, and they took fig leaves and bound them upon their loins."[284] As in SRJ, in RoR Eve and Adam eat (though here that actually eat the fruit rather than just metaphorically "eating knowledge"), and they have a revelation concerning both their ignorance and their nakedness, which in RoR is linked to their knowledge that they have been stripped of their spiritual aspect.

In a similar manner, in OnOrig "the instructor,"[285] here called "the wisest of all creatures," and also "the beast" by the rulers,[286] comes to Eve.[287] Again, as in RoR, the instructor urges Eve to eat, and she eats, then giving some to Adam, who eats as well.[288] Upon their eating of the tree, OnOrig contains an array of elements found in both SRJ and RoR. As in SRJ, their minds open (SRJ frames this as Adam's mind becoming uncovered)[289] and they become enlightened (in SRJ Insight appears to them as light to awaken their thinking).[290] On the Origin of the World also says that they became sober upon eating, as in SRJ, where Adam becomes sober upon seeing the woman who was created from his side.[291] And, again, as in SRJ and RoR, Adam and Eve realize their nakedness, though here this nakedness is connected with being naked of knowledge. On the Origin of the World adds that Adam and Eve love each other and recognize that, rather than the instructor,

283. RoR 90.6–14.
284. RoR 90.14–19.
285. Named as such in OnOrig 119.7; 114.3.
286. OnOrig 118.25; cf. 113.35–114.4, here it seems as if "the beast" either is identified with the Eve of Life or is her child. (It is difficult to tell if the antecedent "her" in the following passage is meant to signify Wisdom/Wisdom Life or the Eve of Life. If it is the former, it seems as though "the beast" should be identified with Eve, which makes sense given her moniker of "instructor" in 115.34, as well.): "Her child is the one born who is lord. Afterwards, the authorities called it "the beast" to cause it to lead their modeled forms astray. The meaning of 'the beast' is 'the instructor,' for it was found to be the wisest of all creatures."
287. OnOrig 118.24–28.
288. OnOrig 118.32–119.11.
289. SRJ BG 59.20–21 // II 23.8 // IV 35.30–31 // III 30.1–2.
290. SRJ II 23.33–35 // IV 37.1–4.
291. SRJ BG 59.18–21.

it is the rulers who are beasts. While once again OnOrig is the most detailed, there are resonant themes throughout the three narratives, each showing some kind of change effected in both Eve and Adam through the eating of (the tree of) knowledge.

Sixth, there is a recognition of partnership, a knowledge and love between Eve and Adam that provide a counterpoint and an alterative template to her rape by the rulers; and, seventh, intimately connected with the sixth element, children are born from this union who will ensure the salvation of humanity in a world ruled by the rulers and their minions. In SRJ, this knowledge of Adam's partnership with Eve is first recognized when Insight uncovers his mind, and he knows his essence (BG), co-essence (III), and partner (II/IV), and declares "This is indeed bone of my bones, and flesh of my flesh."[292] This same recognition occurs for Adam later in the text despite the fact that the Chief Ruler has declared that the husband should rule the woman,[293] that the Chief Ruler has raped Eve,[294] and that intercourse has been created through his act of rape.[295] Instead of mimicking the power dynamics the Chief Ruler has enacted, Adam, just as he had earlier when the woman appeared beside him, "knew his essence," that is, Eve.[296] From this "knowledge" Seth is born according to the race of those in the divine realm,[297] and through this act of (pro)creation the spirit is then sent to humanity to both awaken it and make it resonant with the perfection of the divine realms.[298] In all four versions of SRJ, Adam "knows"[299] Eve. He knows his own essence or counterpart, and he does not defile her or reproduce the violence and dominance instituted by the Chief Ruler's act of rape. Because of this act of knowing—a knowledge brought to Eve and Adam through Insight—they are able to bring a child into the world following the path

292. SRJ BG 60.1–7, οὐσία; III 30.2–6, συνουσία; II 23.5–11 // IV 35.26–36.4 ϣⲃⲣ̄ ⲛ̄ⲣⲱⲧⲣ̄. Cf. Gen 2:23.
293. SRJ BG 61.10–12 // III 30.24–25.
294. SRJ BG 62.8 // III 31.10 // II 24.15–16 // IV 37.27–28.
295. SRJ BG 63.1–4 // III 31.21–23 // II 24.26–27 // IV 38.13–15.
296. SRJ BG 63.12–13; III 32.6–7: Adam "knew his lawlessness." See discussion above. II 24.35–36 // IV 38.25–26: "And . . . Adam knew the likeness of his own foreknowledge."
297. SRJ BG 63.14–16 // II 24.36–25.2 // III 32.7–9 // IV 38.27–30.
298. SRJ BG 63.26–64.13 // II 25.2–16 // III 32.9–22 // IV 38.30–39.15.
299. SRJ BG // III, ⲥⲟⲩⲱⲛ. II/IV, ⲛ̄ⲙⲉ=ⲉⲓⲙⲉ.

of those in the divine realm, a child who will proliferate awakening rather than instigate forgetfulness in the human realm.

In much the same manner, RoR refers to the spiritual woman as Adam's partner,[300] when she causes him to arise and gives him life.[301] After the authorities rape of Eve and Adam and Eve eat from the tree, the text says that Adam "knew"[302] his wife or woman, emphasizing their partnership through knowledge; she then gave birth to Abel. Then, when Abel has been killed by "the Cain of flesh," that is, the rulers' son by Eve, Adam again "*knew his partner* Eve"—directly connecting knowledge and partnership—"and she became pregnant and bore Seth."[303] Eve declares that she has born this new person "through God."[304] Finally comes the birth of Norea, the one born "to help many human generations."[305] Here again, RoR shifts the sexual dynamics of domination and defilement instigated by the rulers and authorities, shifting the sexual relationship to reflect one of knowledge and partnership—a knowledge and partnership that ultimately result in renewed relationship between the divine and human realms.

These dynamics are once again seen in OnOrig. Eve, the daughter of Wisdom Life, sees her life-less and spirit-less "partner"[306] on the ground and grieves for him, already exhibiting a connection between partnership and feelings of understanding and care between the two.[307] On the Origin of the World then narrates explicitly the connection between Adam and Eve's eating of the tree, the knowledge they have gained, and their relationship with each other when it states that they "loved each other."[308] While the offspring of Adam and Eve are not embodied in a specific person as in SRJ and RoR, that is, Seth and Norea, the text is clear that their offspring are part of the divine plan of salvation, saying, "Wisdom sent her daughter Life, called Eve, as

300. RoR 89.19, ϣⲃⲣⲉⲓⲛⲉ.
301. RoR 89.13–16.
302. RoR 91.13–14, ⲥⲟⲩⲱⲛ.
303. RoR 91.30–32, ⲥⲟⲟⲩⲛ (reconstruction), ϣⲃⲣⲉⲓⲛⲉ.
304. RoR 91.32–33.
305. RoR 92.34–93.2.
306. OnOrig 116.1, ϣⲃⲣⲉⲓⲛⲉ.
307. OnOrig 115.36–116.2.
308. OnOrig 119.6–16.

an instructor to make Adam, who had no soul, arise so that those he would engender might become vessels of light."[309] To these humans who were born,[310] the Father sends "the blessed little innocent spirits" to "the world of corruption" in order to "annul the rulers of corruption through the modeled forms [i.e., human beings]," of the authorities.[311] Where these spirits "appear in the world of corruption, first they reveal the pattern of incorruptibility as a condemnation of the rulers and their powers."[312] And when "the blessed ones appeared in enlightened form, they appeared in different ways. And each one of them, starting out in their own land, revealed their knowledge to the *ekklesia* [i.e., assembly or church] that was revealed in the molded forms of corruption."[313] So, here as well, the relationship between Adam and Eve is marked by mutuality and love, in stark contrast to the violent domination exhibited by the rulers and their minions. It is the offspring, born of this union, who will ultimately lead to the rulers' undoing.

While each of the three Genesis cosmogonies narrates these themes somewhat differently, these seven themes nonetheless permeate each of the tellings and provide a common arc to the three stories. In each, a helper from the divine is sent to the Adam created by the rulers through the person of Eve, enlivening him and connecting him with the spirit. And while Eve's spirit is split from her material counterparts in the wake of her rape by the rulers, the spiritual Eve continues to intercede on behalf of her counterparts, continuing to partner with them. In this way, the spiritual Eve brings knowledge and enlightenment to the earthly Adam and Eve, enabling them to establish a relationship that is not based on the violent and exploitative model of sexual domination enacted by the rulers but one that is marked by the values of knowledge, mutuality, and help exhibited by the divine realm. This shift from violence to mutuality allows both Eve and Adam,

---

309. OnOrig 115.30–36.
310. OnOrig 123.34–124.2.
311. OnOrig 124.5–12; cf. 124.21–25.
312. OnOrig 124.18–21.
313. OnOrig 124.25–30.

and those born from their relationship of mutuality, to participate with the divine in the unmaking of the violent structures they have been subjected to. These continual and dynamic dances between the divine and human realms serve to realize a restoration rather than a return—there is no return to a primordial paradise for Eve, Adam, or the divine realm itself, but there is a dynamic movement forward together, and an insistence that a world structured on mutuality and care, rather than violence and domination, will effect an end of a world marked by the malice of the rulers.

Conclusion

The rape of Eve pericopes provide a starkly different portrayal of sexual violence from that of the Roman narratives explored earlier in this study. What I mean by this is that, while the Secret Revelation of John, the Reality of the Rulers, and On the Origin of the World actually portray the *same* sexual violence and the *same* power dynamics as those found in the Roman texts addressed in chapters 1 and 2, their *conclusions* about these dynamics are radically different. In the Genesis elaborations, as in the Roman myths, women are a means to an end and sexual violence is justifiable *for the rulers*, but women are *not* a means to an end *nor* is sexual violence justifiable *for the texts in their entireties*, i.e. while the rulers are perpetrators of sexual violence the texts actively name and confront their violence.

The Eve presented in SRJ, RoR, and OnOrig exists in relationship to Ilia, raped by a god and called a slave—Ilia, who is treated as little more than a conduit to incubate the founder of Rome and left to languish in prison or exile, or to submit to the river Anio in the face of her shame once her task of ensuring Rome's inception is complete. Eve exists in relationship to Sabines, stolen and raped to furnish the Romans with wives, children, and land, their families and fatherlands subjugated under the rule of Romulus. Eve exists in relationship to Lucretia, whose envy-motivated rape prompted her to kill herself rather than live with its shame. Eve exists in relationship to Verginia, whose father would rather that she be killed by his own hand than suffer the shame of slavery and rape. And Eve exists in relationship to Io, raped then transformed into a farm animal so her rapist could hide his adultery; in relationship to Syrinx, who while escaping her rapist was transformed into his instrument; and in relationship to Daphne, who, though escaping her rape, still lost her life, forever to become her would-be rapist's symbol of victory.[314]

I use the word *relationship* here consciously, because, while Eve's story is different, there is something of all these women and of their analogue the nations, in the story of Eve. Eve, like Ilia, is raped by a god, called a slave, and is a conduit to incubate children—some who will harm, but others who will save. Eve, like the Sabines, is "seized" in RoR and OnOrig, and in all three texts serves to furnish the Chief Ruler and others with progeny both to continue their reign and to have people to rule. Like Lucretia, Eve in OnOrig feels shame, but it is not a shame brought on by the shameful acts of her rapists; it is an understanding that to feel shame is to be "stripped naked of knowledge," that is, to be like the rulers. Like Verginia, Eve is constantly under threat from those

---

314. While Michael A. Williams argues that some of the gendered imagery in these texts is "inherited," rather than "conscious" (["Variety in Gnostic Perspectives on Gender," in King, *Images of the Feminine in Gnosticism*, 1988], 2–22, here 8), and that in a text such a RoR specifically (though I can imagine interpreters extending this to SRJ and OnOrig), there is not "evidence that the author is particularly interested in Eve qua female" (9–10; quotation from 10), I would argue that given the embeddedness of rape in Roman narratives of origin—particularly in relation to women—that turning the story of Eve into a rape narrative *is* meant to say something specific about gender, gendered relationships, and hierarchical powers of domination. King also notes in relationship to RoR, "The concluding speech of Eleleth clearly shows that there is no intention in the text to initiate a social program for the overthrow of patriarchy; the ideal of the text is a return to the legitimate rule of the father and the son. Yet while gendered language is not primarily aimed at criticism of gendered social roles, it does point to the social world, not to change or redeem it but to expose it" ("Book of Norea," 76). While I agree with her point on certain levels, that is, the prominence of the father and son, particularly at the end of the text, I do wonder if the complicated gender dynamics in the text do point to change through their exposure. Would nonpatriarchal rule simply entail a woman being "on top"? It seems to me that dismantling patriarchal culture has less to do with who is "on top," than with particular types of power dynamics and relationality—gendered power dynamics and relationality that are constantly being undercut in certain ways throughout the text. This is not to discount some of the mimetic moves vis-à-vis Roman culture that occur in the text but to note that the gender dynamics at play—with Eve, with her relationship to Adam, with the way in which her spirit plays the trickster, with Norea—do not simply replicate the status quo. See Ross S. Kramer, "A Response to Virginity and Subversion: Norea against the Powers in the Hypostasis of the Archons," in King, *Images of the Feminine in Gnosticism*, 261: "In contrast, then, to Williams [the above essay in the same volume] analysis of the gendered language in the Hypostasis of the Archons, Norea's gender, and that of her female ancestors (and perhaps her female descendants as well), *is* significant, if not in the intention of the author (to which we have virtually no access), then certainly in the possibility of its interpretation by its readers."

who would rape and enslave her, but this does not spell her death. And, like Daphne, Eve became a tree. But for Eve, her transformation truly saved her (though not her body from the rulers' rape); the tree is not her prison but is what leads to her enlightenment. For Eve, her tree is the conduit for mutual relations with her partner, Adam—a partner who has never violated her or wielded power over her—and she births children, saviors, who are born of that mutual love.

While Eve is clearly subject to the same forces as the women in the Roman myth through the actions of the rulers, in SRJ, RoR, and OnOrig these forces are clearly named as evil and unjust.[315] The rulers' actions are never justified through denials of hubris or claims that seizure and rape are honorable: these are not the power dynamics operative in the plan of the divine realm. The Secret Revelation of John and OnOrig are particularly explicit on this fact. The Secret Revelation of John states that the Chief Ruler's decree that the male should rule over the female was proof that he did not understand "the holy design."[316] On the Origin of the World is even more explicit, saying that they put Adam to sleep to teach him the lie that Eve "came from his rib so that woman may be subjected, and he may be lord over her."[317] These notions name the dynamics active between Mars (and/or Amulius) and Ilia, the Romans and the Sabine women, Claudius and Britannia, Apollo and Daphne, Io and Jupiter, and all the other pairings explored thus far—and it is these very dynamics that SRJ claims are against the "holy design" and that Orig.World declares are a lie of the rulers.[318]

One of the ways in which the Genesis cosmogonies thwart the machinations of the rulers is by positioning Adam and Eve as embodied amalgams of the divine realm and the worldly rulers. While they are subject to the effects of the worldly rulers, they inhabit the trickster

315. Even though much ambiguity is opened up by the Ovidian texts, they do not perform this function as overtly as do SRJ, RoR, and OnOrig. While the Ovidian texts open up spaces for different types of logic, and critique can enter from the ambiguities and ambivalences he employs, he does not engage in the same type of clear critique as the three Genesis cosmogonies—he allows spaces for different types of readings.
316. SRJ BG 61.10–15 // II 30.24–31.1; cf. II 24.1–3 // IV 37.8–11.
317. OnOrig 116.20–25.
318. The Reality of the Rulers does display these dynamics but in a more implicit way. See the discussion in this chapter on RoR.

position—often through the aid of the divine realm—most clearly seen through Eve's insight into the rulers' planned violation of her and her ability to thwart their plan, at least partially.[319] It is in this moment that they are "tricked" into violating themselves and their creation. This trickster quality is also seen clearly in the way all three texts recast the Genesis narrative surrounding both Eve and Adam, and additionally in RoR and OnOrig, where the serpent becomes the purveyor of wisdom, knowledge, and insight. In contrast, in Ovid's humans, who are also creatures of heaven and earth,[320] this trickster quality becomes violent through figures like Lycaon, who tries to fool Jupiter through his cannibalistic feast, causing the destruction of humanity, or through the justification of domination as man turns to god (often through anticipated apotheosis). This transformative and trickster quality also becomes tragic in the figures of Daphne and Syrinx, whereby their transformation into vegetative life, while saving them from sexual violations, delivers them, as exploitable objects, into the hands of their would-be rapists.

Another striking feature of these retellings of Genesis is their psychological sophistication in terms of the rulers' rape of Eve. Much contemporary literature on trauma notes the attendant occurrence of splitting, dissociation, and/or rupture with acts of violence. Eve's story, particularly in RoR and OnOrig, follows this process closely. As Eve's body is about to be violated, she becomes aware of the rulers' plans for her. With this knowledge, her spirit leaves—dissociates or splits—from her body, leaving a portion of herself protected from the rulers' violence. Later, through the eating of the fruit, this split-off portion becomes reintegrated, allowing Eve to see reality for what it is and to experience mutual sexual relationships in the aftermath of the violence done to her. In many ways, as explored earlier, Adam also goes through this process of splitting and reintegration as his body is violated in SRJ and RoR in order to extract the spiritual element, which

---

319. This is particularly clear in RoR and OnOrig, but occurs in the snatching of Life from Eve by Foresight in SRJ II // IV as well. It is also important to note that the material Eve is not saved—she indeed is raped by the rulers.
320. Ovid, *Met.* 1.76–88.

is for him, as well, reintegrated as the divine woman moves from him, to Eve, to the knowledge from which he eats.[321]

This shifting dynamic between splitting and integration can also be read on a more social and systemic level. If the rulers in these texts are meant to represent the imperial powers of the world who have brought humanity into error and subjugation, this process also follows the insights of those such as W. E. B. Du Bois, Frantz Fanon, and Homi Bhabha, who each in a different way, address the splitting of the colonized mind.[322] The splitting that occurs for both Adam and Eve—especially given the political critiques of each of the three texts—is a function of the rulers malice and violence. This violence resonates profoundly with Calgacus's speech, worth quoting again:

> Rapists of the world, now that the earth betrays their encompassing devastation, they ransack the sea. If the enemy is rich, they are greedy; if poor, they encircle them. Neither east nor west has satisfied them—they alone covet equally want and wealth. To rob, slaughter and rape they give the false name of empire; they make desolation, they call it peace. Children and kin are by nature each one's dearest possessions. They are snatched from us by conscription to be slaves elsewhere: our wives and sisters, even if they escape the enemy's wantonness, are violated in the name of friendship and hospitality. Our goods and fortunes go for tribute; our lands and harvests in requisitions of grain; our hands and bodies themselves are shattered through clearing forest and swamp in the midst of insult and lash. Those born into slavery are sold once and for all and moreover are fed by their masters, but Britannia pays for her enslavement daily and feeds the enslavers. And as in the household the newest among the slaves is a mockery to his fellow-slaves, so in a world long used to slavery, we, the newest and most worthless, are marked out for destruction. (Tacitus, *Agricola* 30.4–31.3)[323]

The Secret Revelation of John, the Reality of the Rulers, and On the

321. Cf. Curran, "Rape and Rape Victims"; and King, "Ridicule and Rape."
322. See W. E. B. Du Bois, *The Souls of Black Folk* (1953; repr., New York: Signet Classic, 1995); Bhabha, *Location of Culture*; Fanon, *Black Skin, White Masks*; and Fanon, *Wretched of the Earth*. While the use of these theorists may be anachronistic, it is worth noting Warren Carter's important treatment of the dynamics of assimilation and resistance in his *John and Empire: Initial Explorations* (New York: T&T Clark, 2008), as well as the edited volume by Richard A. Horsley on the use of James C. Scott's, *Domination and the Arts of Resistance: Hidden Transcripts* (New Haven: Yale University Press, 1990) in biblical studies, *Hidden Transcripts and the Arts of Resistance: Applying the Work of James C. Scott to Jesus and Paul*, Semeia Studies 48 (Atlanta: Society of Biblical Literature, 2004).
323. Translation in consultation with Lopez, *Apostle to the Conquered*, 109; and Tacitus, *Agricola*, LCL.

Origin of the World each name this violence—the sexual violence, the greed and wealth, the condition of enslavement and—though in different ways—name the hypocrisy of empire while also seeking to imagine ways to overcome its effects, envisioning a future based on the ideals and mercy of the divine realm.

The story of the rape of Eve is a pivotal moment in all three texts. It is the point in which the rulers engage in their most heinously violent act against humanity, exposing themselves and unveiling their nature as malevolent, arrogant, and ignorant. Rather than successfully sowing the seeds of their dominance, they sow the seeds of their own undoing. The rulers' act of rape is not justified, as it is in the Roman myths, but is used to provide a conduit for the light and knowledge of the divine realm to be passed to generations of humans, whether through Seth, Norea, or simply as conduits for the light.

This moment of extreme violence also provides the starkest contrast between the divine realm's logic of benefaction, mercy, and mutuality that marks its power—not power over but power with—and the violent, oppressive, and exploitative "benefaction" of the rulers. Through trusting the words of the spiritual woman, whether Insight or Eve, and eating knowledge, Adam and Eve experience a relationship with each other that mimics the mutuality exhibited in the divine realm rather than the exploitative power relationships that mark the world of the rulers—and the Roman narratives of sexual violence and colonization.

Though these texts present a utopian and idealized possibility of the future,[324] they are far from naïve. The Secret Revelation of John seems to speak of contemporaneous realities as it relays the rulers bringing precious metals and gifts to "beguile the human beings who had followed them into great anxiety by leading them astray into much error. And they grew old without having enjoyment. They died without having found any truth and without having known the God of Truth. And thus the whole creation became enslaved forever, from the foundation of the world until now."[325] Similarly, in OnOrig, as the rulers

---

324. On the utopian impulse of SRJ, see King, *Secret Revelation of John*, 157–73.
325. SRJ II 29.30–30.7; cf. SRJ BG 72.11–75.10: "They brought them gold [ⲛⲟⲩⲃ], silver [ϩⲁⲧ], gifts [δῶρον], and metals [μέταλλον] of copper [ϩⲟⲙⲛ̄ⲧ], iron [ⲡⲉⲛⲓⲡⲉ], and every sort [γένος]. They beguiled

try to shorten the life span of humans in an attempt to overpower them once again, they end up only being able to subtract ten years, which, the text states, "are spent in pain and weakness and evil distractions. And so life has turned out to be, from that day until the completion of the age."[326] Far from an idealized "present," the texts reveal the world, just as eating the fruit allows Eve and Adam to see the rulers for the beasts they are: the texts attempt to lead the readers/hearers to knowledge that will allow them to unmask the machinations of the rulers in the world around them.

The critique of unbridled political power in these three texts is substantial. They name the violence and malice of the rulers in no uncertain terms. The juxtaposition of Eve's story with that of Ilia, the Sabines, Lucretia, and Verginia; with the Vestals and the nations; and with Daphne, Io, and Syrinx, bring these startlingly different ideological frames into clear relief. Through these juxtapositions the similarities in their themes and content emerge; through these juxtapositions the connections between Romulus, Mars, and Sextus; Apollo, Jupiter, and Pan; and the rulers are made palpable. But, despite the insistence of the Secret Revelation of John, the Reality of the Rulers, and On the Origin of the World regarding the ongoing reality of imperial oppression, these works also point to and espouse another way—a way in which ethical and mutual relationships can be established with the help of the divine realm, a way in which violence does not get the final word.

[cⲁⲕⲟⲩ] them into temptation [πειρασμός] [distractions/περισπασμός III] so that they would not remember [ⲙⲉⲉⲩⲉ] their immovable [ⲁⲥⲕⲓⲙ] Foresight/Pronoia [πρόνοια]. They took [ϫⲓⲧⲟⲩ] them and begot [ϫⲡⲟ] children out of darkness [ⲕⲁⲕⲉ] through their counterfeit [ἀντίμιμον] spirit [πνεῦμα]. It closed [ⲧⲱⲙ] their hearts [ϩⲏⲧ]. They became hard [ⲛⲟⲩⲱⲧ] by the hardening [ⲛⲟⲩⲱⲧ] of the counterfeit [ἀντίμιμον] spirit [πνεῦμα] until now." Also cf. Rom 8:1–8, 14–22.
326. OnOrig 121.13–27.

4

"And so they convicted themselves . . ."

The Rulers and Resistance

In this chapter, I draw together some of the overarching thematics explored in the first three chapters in terms of the characterizations of the rulers. This chapter will explore three different aspects of these themes. First is an exegetical proposal regarding the use of Genesis in the Secret Revelation of John, the Reality of the Rulers, and On the Origin of the World, particularly the way in which the names of God within the two creation narratives of Genesis frame both the deities and divine and material realms in the elaborations. I trace names of God within the Genesis narrative in conjunction with the corresponding elaborations in SRJ, RoR, and OnOrig to propose a significant connection between the Chief Ruler, Yaldabaoth, and the ruling structure of the Roman Empire. Second is an analysis of the rulers in the three cosmogonies in relation to the Roman and Ovidian texts, particularly looking at the correspondence of characterization. Finally, I turn to the relationship between the divine and worldly households, particularly in relation to SRJ, but within RoR and OnOrig as well, to explore the ways in which the texts both replicate and reappropriate themes within the Roman milieu to make new kinds of meaning. Through these thematics, this chapter explores the rape of Eve in relation to this imperial framing and address the interventions it makes into the imperial paradigm of gender and violence.

God, the Rulers, and Genesis

One of the most important aspects of the Secret Revelation of John, the Reality of the Rulers, and On the Origin of the World is their creative employment of the creation narratives of Genesis.[1] Each of these texts contains a double creation—one of the divine realm and one of Yaldabaoth's material world. In terms of the three Genesis cosmogonies this double creation has generally been emphasized in two ways. The first is that the elaborative strategy of the Secret Revelation of John, the Reality of the Rulers, and On the Origin of the World is based on a reading of the two creation narratives of Genesis itself: the first story, the Elohist narrative comprises Genesis 1:1–2:3 and the second, the Yahwist narrative, begins at 2:4 and contains an additional narrative of creation, including the Adam and Eve story.[2] The Elohist narrative then corresponds to the creation of the divine realm while the Yahwist narrative corresponds to the creation of the material world.[3] The second hypothesis, particularly illustrated in the elaborative strategy of SRJ, though possibly read in RoR and OnOrig,

---

1. For example, on SRJ, see King, *Secret Revelation of John*, 215–22; on RoR, see Gilhus, *Nature of the Archons*, 21–36, who provides a comprehensive comparison of RoR and Gen 1:1–6:22; and on OnOrig, see Painchaud, *L'Écrit sans titre*, 410–22, 435–39.
2. For a good introduction to and overview of source criticism in the Pentateuch, see John J. Collins, "The Nature of the Pentateuchal Narrative," chapter 2 in his *Introduction to the -ebrew Bible: Second Edition* (Minneapolis: Fortress Press, 2014), 49–68. Hal Taussig has emphasized this aspect of the three texts in his teaching since I began studying with him in the fall of 2006. Secondary literature tends to apply this double narrative to the creation of the human rather than the creation of the upper and lower realms—particularly in connection with "primal androgyny" and sexual difference. See, e.g., Kristen E. Kvam, Linda S. Schearing, and Valarie H. Ziegler, *Eve and Adam: Jewish, Christian, and Muslim Readings on Genesis and Gender* (Bloomington: Indiana University Press, 1999), for a swath of primary texts along with some commentary; Boyarin, *Carnal Israel*; Pagels, *Adam, Eve, and the Serpent*; Dunning, "What Sort of Thing Is This Luminous Woman?, 55–84; but see Dahl, who notes, "The omission of large portions of Genesis 1 in these texts is all the more remarkable because most of them follow the biblical account more closely from the creation of man onward.... The concentration upon Gen 1:1-3, 1:26-27, and 2:7 makes it clear that the origin of mankind, not the origin of the world, is the focus of interest" ("Arrogant Archon," 697). See also below.
3. For example, see Gilhaus, who also sees these two creation narratives employed in RoR, reading

is that the elaborative strategy employs a Platonic, double reading of both of the Genesis creation narratives together.[4] Though here I engage the first elaborative strategy, the two are not mutually exclusive.

To reiterate, it is the emphasis on two distinct creation narratives—that of the divine realm and that of the earthly or material realm—that is most important. While SRJ, RoR, and OnOrig figure the Elohist and Yahwist creation narratives in distinct ways, there is one central element that runs through all three of these elaborations in terms of the divine and material realms: the contrast between the supreme deity/God and the creator and ruler of the material world, Yaldabaoth. An analysis of these three elaborations of Genesis in conjunction with Genesis itself[5] shows that this distinction between the God of the divine realm and the "god" of the material realm is a function not simply of the two creation accounts but of the two distinct deities who create in the Genesis narrative—specifically their relationship in terms of their Hebrew names and Greek translations.[6]

Scholars hypothesize that several strands of tradition were merged to create the Genesis narrative. This is seen both in the two tellings of creation and the two different names used for God in each: Elohim (the Elohist tradition or E) and YHWH (the Yahwist tradition or J). In the first creation account, or E, which comprises Genesis 1:1–2:3, the creative deity Elohim (אֱלֹהִים) is translated in the LXX as θεός (God).

the second creation narrative of Genesis in 87.11–92.32, then reading the first narrative as Sophia's creation of her emanation of the divine realm in 94.4–96.17 (*Nature of the Archons*, 21–36).

4. See King, *Secret Revelation of John*, 191–214, 221–24 and King, "Reading Sex," 521. See also Richard T. Wallis, ed., *Neoplatonism and Gnosticism* (Albany: State University of New York Press, 1992).

5. This initial hypothesis rests on the use of the scholarly editions of the Septuagint (LXX –Rahlfs-Hanhart, *Septuaginta*) and the Masoretic Text (MT—*BHS*). While these are a useful starting point, this hypothesis will continue to benefit from additional research on variants within both Hebrew and Greek manuscripts, particularly of Genesis, in addition to various manuscripts of the Hebrew Bible in its Coptic translation. While this hypothesis will be greatly strengthened by further research in these areas, the scope of this project does not allow for a full investigation—a dissertation or book length project in its own right. These caveats aside, my initial forays into this area have garnered enough material to convince me that these correlations were too strong to overlook at this juncture given the other intertextual connections made throughout this study between the Genesis elaborations and Roman myths.

6. See Dahl, "Arrogant Archon"; and Nils A. Dahl and Alan F. Segal, "Philo and the Rabbis on the Names of God," *Journal for the Study of Judaism in the Persian, Hellenistic, and roman Period* 9 (1978): 1–28.

Beginning in Gen 2:4, the second creation narrative, the tetragrammaton is added to Elohim (אֱלֹהִים יְהוָה) and is generally translated into Greek as κύριος ὁ θεός (inscribed as "the Lord God" in English versions) in the LXX. Additionally, beginning with the birth of Cain in Gen 4:1, the Hebrew Bible exclusively uses the tetragrammaton (יְהוָה) on its own, which generally (but not in every instance) corresponds to the use of κύριος on its own in the LXX. After this, a combination of these three different configurations are used (i.e., God, Lord, the Lord God). Here, I am not particularly interested in redactional criticism. What does interest me are the interpretational potentials that become possible when the gaps and disjunctures of this patchworked text are utilized by the three Genesis cosmogonies to make particular types of meaning.

Returning to the names of God in Genesis, there is consistency between the Hebrew Bible and the LXX regarding the first creation narrative of Genesis (1:1–2:3) in terms of the name of the deity, with the Hebrew Bible using Elohim (אֱלֹהִים) exclusively and the LXX exclusively using θεός.[7] In the Yahwist creation narrative the compound YHWH Elohim is used exclusively by the Hebrew Bible in the Eden narrative (2:4–3:24), except when the serpent and Eve are speaking, and here Elohim is used alone. In this second creation narrative, the correspondence between the MT and the LXX regarding the name of God (YHWH Elohim/ κύριος ὁ θεός/the Lord God) is not always consistent but is frequent.[8] Over half of the instances of YHWH Elohim

---

7. Gen 1:1, 2, 3, 4 (2x), 5, 6, 7 (2x), 8 (2x), 9, 10 (2x), 11, 12, 14, 16, 17, 18, 20, 21 (2x), 22, 24, 25 (2x), 26, 27 (2x), 28, 29, 31; 2:2, 3 (2x).

8. The variants in usage are as follows: when the serpent speaks, there is absolute correspondence between the use of "God" alone: MT אֱלֹהִים; LXX θεός: Gen 3:1, 3, 5 (2x); in seven instances the MT uses the "Lord God" and the LXX simply uses "God": MT אֱלֹהִים יְהוָה; LXX θεός (Gen 2:4, 5, 7, 9, 19, 21; 3:22), and there are thirteen instances of absolute correspondence, where both use the "Lord God": MT אֱלֹהִים יְהוָה; LXX κύριος ὁ θεός (Gen 2:8, 15, 16, 18, 22; 3:1, 8 (2x), 9, 13, 14, 21, 23).

Obviously, one of the difficulties with this type of textual analysis is that it is only possible to work from the *extant* manuscripts (and again, here, I am only working with the BHS and *Septuaginta*), and it is impossible to know the full range of variants that once existed, that is, versions with more or less correspondence. In addition, it is impossible to know exactly what language the writers of the three cosmogonies were working in. (It is generally posited that SRJ, RoR, and OnOrig were originally written in Greek (see NHC), but the work of both Layton and Pearson regarding the Aramaisms in the texts (Layton, "Part II," 55–56n57; Pearson *Gnosticism, Judaism, and Egyptian Christianity*, 44–46) and the diasporic Jewish community throughout the empire raise the possibility that the writers may have had contact with Aramaic or Hebrew

have the parallel of κύριος ὁ θεός in the LXX.[9] Notable among these correspondences are the following: the creation of the plants in Eden (2:8); the placement of Adam in Eden (2:15); the command not to eat from the tree (2:16–17); the creation of Eve as a helper for Adam (2:18–23); the entry of the deity into the garden and questioning of Adam (3:8–9); the cursing of the serpent, the humans, and the earth (3:14); and the banishment from Eden (3:23). While only half of these correspond in both the LXX and Hebrew Bible, it is important to remember that in every occurrence[10] in Genesis 2:4–3:24 in the MT, the compound YHWH Elohim is used. Moreover, each of the instances of YHWH Elohim above, when utilized in the Genesis elaborations, corresponds to the deeds of the rulers or their minions.

The creation of plant life only occurs in On the Origin of the World: 109.1–111.28 narrates the creation of plant life, which is initiated through unrequited love of the rulers' Foresight for the divine image that appeared in the light of the heavens (the Adam of Light).[11] This light appears after the Chief Parent saying, "I am god. There is no other but me,"[12] then subsequently challenges the divine realm saying, "If anything existed before me, let it appear so that we may see its light."[13] The totality of plant life comes to fruition in OnOrig 111.21–28, where "every plant bloomed from the earth, different kinds, and they

---

versions of Genesis. In addition, those writing, translating or copying the text may have been familiar with or using Coptic versions as well. Scribes, as the scholarly class, may have also had access and knowledge to versions in all three languages (see William V. Harris, *Ancient Literacy* [Cambridge: Harvard University Press, 1989], 176). And, most importantly, as Dahl notes, "Hebrew or Aramaic names and etymologies are so common in our gnostic sources that at least some elements of the gnostic Genesis interpretation must go back to exegetes who were more familiar with the original languages of the Jewish Scriptures than was Philo" ("Arrogant Archon," 700). Evidence of these complexities can be seen in the variants listed in the *Septuaginta* itself. Genesis 2:4 is the first instance where YHWH Elohim occurs in the Hebrew Bible. While the majority of the LXX manuscripts listed simply contain the word θεός, there are several manuscripts that have κύριος ὁ θεός, reflecting YHWH Elohim found in the MT.

9. YHWH Elohim is used a total of twenty times in Gen 2:4–3:23, and in ten of these the LXX uses κύριος ὁ θεός, the eleventh example being the variant found in 2:4.
10. Barring the words between the serpent and Eve, where "God" is consistently referred to rather than the "Lord God."
11. OnOrig 108.12–24.
12. OnOrig 107.30–31. On this phrase and Isaiah, see Maia Kotrosits, "Social Fragmentation and Cosmic Rhetoric" (paper presented at Westar Institute, Christianity Seminar, Spring Meeting, 2014); and Dahl, "Arrogant Archon," 703.
13. OnOrig 107.36–108.2.

contained the seed of the authorities and their angels." In the midst
of this, OnOrig narrates the creation of the Tree of Life and the Tree
of Knowledge—though they are created by the true God, rather than
through the rulers or their minions.[14] Of particular note is the way in
which the presence of these trees is framed in the Genesis narrative
itself. Genesis 2:9 states, "Out of the earth the Lord God (MT)/God (LXX)
made to grow every tree that is pleasant to the sight and good for food,
and the Tree of Life is in the midst of paradise and the Tree of the
Knowledge of Good and Evil."[15] Likewise, in both the MT and the LXX,
it is unclear who the creator of these trees actually is, as the Trees of
Life and Knowledge appear in a separate clause from the one preceding
where the Lord God creates trees more generally. It seems that OnOrig
may play on this ambiguity. If, in fact, a version of the LXX was used
that simply had God/θεός, this again is contrasted to the Lord God/
κύριος ὁ θεός, who creates Eden in 2:8. Both of these interpretations
highlight the ways in which OnOrig remains close to the Genesis text
in its complex elaboration of the creation of the plants in Eden.[16]

The placement of Adam in paradise by the rulers[17] has a
straightforward correspondence with the use of the Lord God (אֱלֹהִים
יְהוָה/κύριος ὁ θεός) in Genesis 2:15. All three texts also narrate the
prohibition to eat from the Tree of Knowledge by the Lord God found in
2:16–17. Both RoR and OnOrig, again, follow the text of Genesis 2:16–17
in a quite straightforward manner, though in OnOrig the prohibition is
given to both Adam and Eve.[18] While SRJ still follows the narrative of

---

14. OnOrig 110.2–29.
15. Gen 2:9: ויצמח יהוה אלהים מן־האדמה כל־עץ נחמד למראה וטוב למאכל ועץ החיים בתוך הגן ועץ הדעת טוב
ורע; LXX: καὶ ἐξανέτειλεν ὁ θεὸς ἔτι ἐκ τῆς γῆς πᾶν ξύλον ὡραῖον εἰς ὅρασιν καὶ καλὸν εἰς βρῶσιν καὶ τὸ
ξύλον τῆς ζωῆς ἐν μέσῳ τῷ παραδείσῳ καὶ τὸ ξύλον τοῦ εἰδέναι γνωστὸν καλοῦ καὶ πονηροῦ.
16. The Secret Revelation of John utilizes the other side of the ambiguity within Gen 2:9, connecting
the first and second clauses in 2:9, that is, to the Lord God. In this regard, the Tree of Life functions
in an opposite manner to the way it functions in OnOrig. Concerning the Tree of Life, the Savior
tells John, "their tree is impiety. Their fruit is an incurable poison and their promise is death for
him. And their tree they planted is 'the Tree of Life.' I will teach you all about the mystery of
their life. It is their counterfeit spirit which comes from them, which seeks him out that he might
not know his perfection. That tree is of this kind: its root is bitter and its branches are shadows
of death, and its leaves are hatred and deception and its perfume is an ointment of evil; and its
fruit is the desire of death, and its seed drinks from darkness. Those who taste it, Hades is their
dwelling place" (SRJ BG 56.6–57.7 // II 21.22–22.2 // III 27.11–28.6 // IV 33.8–34.5).
17. SRJ BG 55.19–20 // III 27.4–6 // II 21.16–18 // IV 33.1–3; RoR 88.24–26; and OnOrig 115.27–29.
18. Gen 2:16–17: "And the Lord God commanded the man/Adam, 'You may eat for food of every tree

Genesis closely, it differs in that it is not precisely the tree that Adam is prohibited from eating but rather Insight, as the text says, "But the tree which they call 'to know good and evil' is the Insight of the light, about whom they gave the commandment, 'Do not taste of it,' that is 'do not listen to her,' since they gave the commandment against him so that he might not look up to his perfection and perceive that he was stripped naked of his perfection."[19] In SRJ, Insight is connected with the tree as the rulers are the creators of the garden following YHWH Elohim in the MT.[20]

The creation of Eve as a helper for Adam (Gen 2:18) is followed most closely by SRJ and RoR, but all three (including OnOrig) seem to elaborate their narratives by drawing on the Elohist creation narrative in Genesis 1:26a and 1:27, as Insight/Eve is sent from the divine realm.[21] In SRJ, Insight, also called Life, is sent from the divine realm from the Father as a helper ($\beta o \eta \theta \acute{o} \varsigma$) to Adam[22] and is hidden within him.[23] The Chief Ruler then wants to extract this power from Adam and makes a form in "the shape of a woman."[24] Insight, who now resides in the woman created by the ruler, lifts the covering from Adam's mind and he recognizes his essence, declaring as in Genesis 2:23, "Indeed this is the bone of my bones and flesh of my flesh."[25] Similarly, it is the Spirit

in the garden; but of the Tree of Knowledge of Good and Evil you (sg. MT; pl. LXX) shall not eat, for in the day you eat of it you (sg. MT; pl. LXX) shall die.'"

RoR 88.24–32: "And the rulers commanded him, saying, 'You may eat from every tree in the garden, but do not eat from the Tree of Knowledge of Good and Evil. Do not touch it, for the day you all eat from it, you will surely die.'"

OnOrig 118.16–23: "They said to him, 'You all may eat the fruit of every tree created for you in paradise, but guard yourselves and do not eat from the Tree of Knowledge. If you eat you will die.'"

19. SRJ BG 57.8–19 // II 22.3–8 // III 28.6–14 // IV 34.5–9. See also the discussion of this in chapter 3.
20. See n. 17 above on the Tree of Life in SRJ.
21. Gen 1:26a, 27: "Then God said, 'Let us make human in our image, according to our likeness. . . . And God created human in the image of God, in the image of God he created it; male and female he created them." (This translation combines elements of both the MT and LXX versions: ויברא אלהים את־האדם בצלמו בצלם אלהים ברא אתו זכר ונקבה ברא אתם; LXX versions of 1:27: καὶ ἐποίησεν ὁ θεὸς τὸν ἄνθρωπον, κατ' εἰκόνα θεοῦ ἐποίησεν αὐτόν, ἄρσεν καὶ θῆλυ ἐποίησεν αὐτούς.
22. SRJ BG 52.4–53.11 // II 20.14–19 // III 25.6–11. The Chief Ruler is actually tricked by the divine realm into breathing his own power, received from his mother, Wisdom, into Adam's body.
23. SRJ BG 53.18–19; 59.6–7 // II 20.25; 22.28–29 // III 25.17–18; 29.12–13 // IV 31.24–25; 35.8–9. These scenes also seem to draw on MT/LXX Gen 1:30, where everything has "in itself the breath/soul of life" (LXX: ἔχει ἐν ἑαυτῷ ψυχὴν ζωῆς) and MT/LXX Gen 2:7: "And the Lord God/God formed human, dust from the earth, and breathed into his face a breath of life [πνοὴν ζωῆς] and the human became a living soul [ψυχὴν ζῶσαν]."
24. SRJ BG 58.1–12; 59.7–15 // II 22.18–19; 22.29–36 // III 28.25–29.1; 29.13–20 // IV 34.26–27; 35.14–19.

in RoR who is sent to Adam and also dwells within him.[26] The Reality of the Rulers, following Genesis 2:21 closely, then says that the rulers "opened his side like a living woman. And they built up his side with some flesh in place of her."[27] As in SRJ, here too it seems as though the spirit that resided in Adam has been extracted, as the text says that after she was created Adam was left with only a soul. Additionally, the woman is referred to as "the spiritual woman"—the woman who causes Adam to stand.[28] On the Origin of the World differs significantly in that Eve is not a creation of the rulers in this text but a creation of the divine realm,[29] though, as in portions of the other two texts, she is both named "instructor" to Adam[30] and is the one who enables him to stand.[31]

What is most significant in these elaborations of Eve's creation, as noted earlier, is their use of both the Yahwist creation story of Gen 2:18–21 and the Elohist story from Genesis 1:26a and 1:27. If the three texts are indeed reading the Elohist creation narrative as a narrative of the divine realm and the Yahwist creation narrative as a narrative about the material realm, through the figure of Eve, these two stories intersect. Eve—in SRJ, RoR, and OnOrig—begins as a spiritual helper from the divine realm, whether she is called "Insight," "the spiritual woman," or simply Eve. This spiritual Eve then corresponds to the creation of "male and female" found in Genesis 1:27.[32] In all three of the Genesis retellings there is an attempt, then, to grasp this spiritual

---

25. SRJ BG 60.1–7 // III 30.2–6 // II 23.6–11 // IV 35.26–36.4.
26. RoR 88.13–15. Again, cf. Gen 1:30; 2:7 in both the MT and LXX; see also n. 24 above.
27. RoR 89.7–10; Gen 2:21: "And the Lord God caused a deep sleep to fall upon the human and he slept; then he took one of his ribs and closed up its place with flesh."
28. RoR 89.10–11.
29. Cf. Gen 1:27: "male and female he created them."
30. OnOrig 113.33; 114.3; 115.33.
31. OnOrig 115.34–116.5.
32. Gilhaus sees the two Genesis accounts of the creation of man and woman in 1:26–27 and 2:7 as being woven together in RoR 87.23–88.19 (Nature of the Archons, 23–24). The first creation narrative is often associated with "primal androgyny" (see, e.g., Boyarin, Carnal Israel, 35–46; Wayne A. Meeks, "The Image of the Androgyne: Some Uses of a Symbol in Earliest Christianity," Journal of the History of Religions 13 [1973]: 165–208), but see also Gilhaus (Nature of the Archons, 93), who links the distinction between the two creations of Adam as found in Philo, On the Creation of the World 134 and Allegorical Interpretation I, 31 and the two Eves as found in RoR.

woman sent from the divine realm—in SRJ and RoR initially through the creation of the material woman, and in all three through Eve's rape.

The next scene contained in both the Genesis text (3:1–5) and the three elaborations is the entry of the snake. This is the one scene in the Yahwist narrative that exclusively uses Elohim in the Hebrew, thus creating an ambiguity regarding the name of God—that is, the actor—in this portion of the text. This portion of Genesis is not followed as closely by SRJ, but SRJ seems to draw on Genesis 3:1a, where the serpent is a creation of the Lord God (אֱלֹהִים יְהוָה/κύριος ὁ θεός), which connects the serpent with the Chief Ruler. It is the Savior in SRJ, rather than the serpent, who teaches Adam and Eve to eat of the Tree of Knowledge, which is the Insight of light. Instead, the serpent teaches them about "the sowing of desire, defilement, and destruction" —exactly what the Chief Ruler "teaches" Eve through his rape of her.[33] In contrast to SRJ, both RoR and OnOrig closely follow the dialogue between the serpent and Eve found in Genesis 3:1–5, but in these two texts the serpent carries the presence of the spiritual woman or spiritual Eve and is thus identified with the divine realm—and the instruction to eat.[34]

The elaborative logic that RoR and OnOrig follow in relation to the name of God in the Genesis narrative can be seen clearly in its plot moves. As addressed above, in Genesis 2:16–17, the Lord God (אֱלֹהִים יְהוָה/κύριος ὁ θεός) gives the prohibition to eat from the Tree of Knowledge, and this corresponds to the ruler/s giving the prohibition in RoR and OnOrig as well.[35] In Genesis 3:1, then, the serpent asks Eve, "Did God [אֱלֹהִים/θεός) say, 'You shall not eat from any tree in

33. SRJ BG 57.8–58.7 // II 22.3–15 // III 28.6–23 // IV 34.6–21. Cf. SRJ II 24.28–29 // IV 38.16–17, where after Eve's rape the Chief Ruler "planted [χω] a seed [σπορά] of desire [ἐπιθυμία] in her who belongs to Adam"; and SRJ BG 63.5–6 // III 31.23–24, where this "desire [ἐπιθυμία] for seed [σπορά]" was planted in Adam himself. Here the Chief Ruler has planted it for the purpose of creating bodies through intercourse and in conjunction with his "counterfeit spirit"—a plan that is thwarted when Adam and Eve recognize and know each other, birthing Seth following the generative pattern that occurs in the divine realm (SRJ BG 63.14–16 // III 32.8–9 // II 24.25–25.2 // IV 38.25–30); see discussion in chapter 3.
34. RoR 89.31–90.12; OnOrig 118.24–119.6.
35. RoR 88.26–32; OnOrig 118.16–24; cf. SRJ BG 57.8–19 // III 28.6–15 // II 22.3–8 // IV 34.6–9, here the Tree of Knowledge is actually the Insight of Light whom the rulers do not want Adam and Eve to "eat of," that is, obey.

the garden'?" In RoR, the serpent also asks this question, using an ambiguous "he" at this point—that is, "What did he [say to] you all? Was it, 'You may eat from every tree in the garden, but do not eat from [the tree] of knowledge of evil and good'?" but OnOrig follows Genesis more closely, saying, "What did God say to you all? Was it, 'Do not eat from the Tree of Knowledge'?" While the text of RoR is ambiguous with its use of "he," the serpent's question to Eve in OnOrig seems somewhat ironic—it is clearly not God who prohibited Adam and Eve from eating of the tree, but the rulers, just as it is the Lord God (אֱלֹהִים יְהוָה/κύριος ὁ θεός) and not God (אֱלֹהִים/θεός) who issued the prohibition in Genesis.

Eve responds to the serpent in both RoR and OnOrig in the same manner as in Genesis, saying, yes it was "he," used by both texts, who told us, "'Do not eat,' but also, 'Do not touch it. For the day you all eat from it, with death you all will die.'"[36] It is difficult to tell who the Eve of flesh/the shadow Eve, thinks this "he" is. On some level Eve knows it is the ruler/s who told her this, but in both of these texts the Chief Ruler also claims to be God, quoting Isaiah and saying, "I am God, and there is no other but me."[37] At this point, Eve's state of being in RoR is described as being "ignorant" and "stripped of the spiritual," while OnOrig describes her as "stripped naked of knowledge."[38] In this state, it is possible that Eve (and Adam) are not clear about who God really is and who the rulers are. By eating the fruit of the tree—as the serpent says—they will become like gods, like the divine, which is exactly what the text urges. It is only after eating from the tree that Eve realizes that they are "ignorant" and "stripped of the spiritual";[39] it is only after eating from the tree that they saw "that those who molded them had the form of beasts," and "they loathed [σιχχαίνω] them."[40] Even so, the Genesis elaborations carefully follow the name of God through the Genesis text.

Only RoR and OnOrig fully narrate the entry of the deity into the

---

36. Gen 3:2–3; RoR 90.2–5; OnOrig 118.30–32: "'Do not eat from it,' but 'Do not touch it, or you will die.'"
37. OnOrig 103.10–12; RoR 86.30–31.
38. Implied in both by RoR 90.15–17 and OnOrig 119.14–15.
39. RoR 90.15–17.
40. OnOrig 119.15–18.

garden and the questioning of Adam (3:8–9); the cursing of the serpent, the humans, and the earth (3:14); and the banishment from Eden (3:23). Both generally follow the Genesis narrative, where, again, the rulers correlate to the use of the Lord God (יְהוָה אֱלֹהִים/κύριος ὁ θεός) throughout this section. SRJ relays a very sparse version of the narrative, but it too corresponds to the Genesis narrative: Yaldabaoth sees that Adam and Eve "withdrew from him and he cursed them. And, in addition, he adds about the woman that the husband is to rule over her [Gen 3:16], for he does not know the mystery which came to pass through the holy decree from on high. . . . And he cast them out of paradise."[41]

After the Eden narrative, Genesis 4:1 relates the birth of Cain. While this is an instance in which the LXX uses θεός, it is the first instance in which the Hebrew Bible uses YHWH alone. Both SRJ and RoR, the two of the three cosmogonies that contain Cain and Abel,[42] agree that Cain is the product of the rape by the rulers; and he is specifically referred to in RoR as the Cain "of flesh," connecting him directly to the rulers' realm.[43] Genesis then moves to the birth of Abel, where there is no mention of any deity—and in SRJ and OnOrig, Abel is the child of Yaldabaoth, while in RoR, he seems to be the child of Adam.[44]

---

41. SRJ BG 61.7–15; 61.18–62.1 // II 23.35–24.3; 24.6–7 // III 30.22–31.1; 31.4–5 // IV 37.4–11; 37.13–14.
42. In SRJ Cain and Abel are rulers meant to rule over humanity, while in RoR Cain exemplifies the characteristics of the rulers in his murder of Abel.
43. See Stroumsa, *Another Seed*, 38–53, on a variety of sources and traditions regarding the "non-Adamic" children of Eve, particularly in terms of Cain. Stroumsa notes four possibilities for the interpretation of Gen 4:1b, "and she [Eve] conceived and bore Cain, saying, 'I acquired a man from the Lord,'" the first being that, "Gen 4:1b could be interpreted as meaning that Cain was the son of Sammael and Eve. . . . The utterly antinomian 'Cainites' also adopted this view, but with a twist; the Tetragrammaton in Gen. 4:1 was not understood by them as referring to the lesser deity (the demiurge, Sammael, but rather—as in Jewish or Christian exegesis—to the supreme Lord God, thus giving Cain divine ancestry" (50–51).
44. See Stroumsa, who notes, "Abel was often seen in the same light as Cain"; that is, his position vis-à-vis the rulers and Adam and Eve vacillates (*Another Seed*, 51). Additionally, in Gen 4:3, where Cain makes his offering to the Lord, it is only "the Lord" (i.e., יְהוָה and κύριός) in both the Hebrew Bible and the LXX.[44] The Hebrew Bible continues to use YHWH exclusively throughout the rest of the Cain and Abel story, though the LXX is very inconsistent concerning which name it uses in this portion of the text.[44] This inconsistency corresponds in many ways to the inconsistency of the actor (i.e., the divine realm or Yaldabaoth) in these portions of the three cosmogonies.
When Cain kills Abel in RoR 91.21–30, it seems as if God is the one who is speaking with Cain. Layton suggests that it might be Sabaoth ("Part II," 61) but, given that Cain is being held accountable for actions that mimic the rulers, it could be that, through following the Genesis narrative, the God of the divine realm has slipped in.

Of extreme significance is the correspondence of the name of the deity in regard to the birth of Seth in all of the texts. In 4:25, Adam and Eve have sex and she says, "For God has raised up for me another seed instead of Abel, whom Cain killed." Both the Hebrew and the LXX unequivocally use the term Elohim/God (i.e., אֱלֹהִים and θεός)—the first time that Elohim has been used exclusively in the Hebrew Bible since the first creation account in Genesis 1:1–2:3. Additionally, אֱלֹהִים and θεός are used exclusively in the retelling of the first creation narrative in 5:1–2, where God (אֱלֹהִים and θεός) creates human beings (5:1a), made in the image of God (אֱלֹהִים and θεός), male and female, and are blessed (5:1b–2a). Immediately after this, Genesis 5:3 states that Seth was made according to the form/likeness and image of his father. This follows closely the interpretations of Seth as a savior figure connected with the divine realm, most particularly in SRJ, but in RoR as well.[45] In addition, it is at this point in RoR that the creation narrative is also retold, the narrative redoubling back on itself just as in the Hebrew Bible.[46]

The only major deviation from the framing of the rulers and the correspondence of the name of the deity in the Hebrew Bible/LXX occurs in 6:2 and 6:4, where Genesis says the "sons of God used to go into the daughters of humans." In this instance, in both the Hebrew Bible and the LXX "God" (i.e., אֱלֹהִים and θεός) is used, whereas the three cosmogonies make this part of Yaldabaoth's plot.[47] These verses then lead into the Noah section (Gen 6:5–8:1), where there is a high level of inconsistency regarding the name of the deity in both the Hebrew Bible and in the LXX, which could help to explain the two very different versions of the Noah story found in SRJ and RoR.

The above analysis shows that in the Genesis elaborations there is a general correspondence between those places in Genesis where the deity is named Elohim/God (i.e., אֱלֹהִים and θεός) and the divine realm

---

45. Seth is not found in OnOrig.
46. Also of note regarding the genealogy in chapter 5 is that, when it gets to Noah in 5:29, Noah's father, Lamech, says of him that he will bring respite from the ground that "the Lord [יְהוָה]/Lord God (κύριος ὁ θεός)] has cursed." This, then, has internal consistency with the curses of "the Lord God" in 3:14–19.
47. Here the cosmogonies seem to be drawing more heavily from Enochic traditions. See Stroumsa, *Another Seed*, 35–38.

and those in which the deity is referred to as the "Lord God" (אֱלֹהִים יְהוָה/κύριος ὁ θεός) or "the Lord" (יְהוָה/κύριος) and the rulers. Again, while these correspondences follow the MT more closely than they follow the LXX, for the most part, these correspondences generally hold true for the LXX as well. As noted earlier, scholars tend to think that SRJ, RoR, and OnOrig were originally written in Greek, and there are still high concentrations of Greek/Copto-Greek in all three texts. In addition, it seems that the LXX is the reference point for quotations of the Hebrew Bible in each of the three texts (while also exhibiting influences from non-Greek traditions). Given the exploration above, the translation of יְהוָה as κύριος makes for an interesting political interpretational possibility, one that moves away from interpretations of Yaldabaoth as the God of the Hebrew Bible and toward an interpretation of Yaldaboath as connected with the rulers of the Roman Empire.

In order to lay this argument out clearly, there are three significant points to note. First, in Philo's exegetical strategy, he identifies the two names of God with different aspects of God, "*theos* (the equivalent of *Elohim* in LXX Greek) represented the beneficent, gracious and creative power of God while *kyrios* (the equivalent of the tetragrammaton in LXX Greek) stood for the royal, ruling or punishing power," because of "the association of *kyrios* with governmental authority in Greek."[48] Rather than being simply "two powers" or aspects of God as in Philo, Elaine Pagels highlights in her reading that the Valentinians[49] use "'Lord' to designate Yahweh, as 'God' designates the Father" in their exegesis of Paul.[50] Here, rather than being two aspects of the one God, the designation of "Yahweh" and "God," *through the Greek*, is bifurcated into two separate beings.

Second, it has been well established in New Testament literature that many of the titles used for Jesus in the New Testament have

---

48. Dahl and Segal, "Philo and the Rabbis," 1–2: "he reversed the midrashic scheme" whereby Elohim was associated with justice and the tetragrammaton with the beneficent, gracious, and creative power of God.

49. I think this category, like many others associated with extracanonical texts, often oversimplifies the dynamics within the texts it wishes to explicate.

50. Pagels, *Gnostic Paul*, 15 and 36n10: "Cf. Against Heresies 3.5.1–10.5 for Irenaeus' refutation."

political currents running through them. Titles such as Lord (κύριος), Son/Child of God (υἱὸς τοῦ θεοῦ), Savior of the World (σωτὴρ τοῦ κόσμου) were used to describe the Roman emperors and were appropriated by the early Jesus communities to describe Jesus and his alternate kingdom/empire, that of God (βασιλεία τοῦ θεοῦ). The word κύριος is generally used for the English terms "lord" or "master" but was also the word used to describe the gods, particularly in the East, which had a high incidence of deifying its rulers.[51] Because of this, the term κύριος often referred to the deified rulers of the East, and through the Ptolemies' imperial reign the idea of the deified ruler gained traction in the West.[52] This led to the term being used for Roman emperors beginning with Augustus, and for rulers more generally.[53]

Third, the moniker of Samael, found in all three of the Genesis cosmogonies,[54] is identified not only with both the serpent and Satan in rabbinic and other Jewish sources[55] but also with the archangel of Rome.[56] As Ioan Culianu explicates:

> We already came across the name Sammael in the Ethiopian and the Latin fragmentary version of the Ascension of Isaiah. The name also occurs in Jewish texts not earlier than the IIIrd cent. A.D., as *Bereshît rabba*, *Tanhuma* and *3 Enoch*. In all this later evidence, he is identified with the angel of Edom (Rome). According to an older tradition, the name Sammael is given [to] the Angel of Death, who already receives the title of *kosmokrator* from R. Eliezer b. R. Jose Haggelilil (c. 150). It is likely that Sammael was one of the most repellent heavenly beings for the Jewish intelligentsia at the end of the Tannaim. This is also proved by an etymological attempt to make his name descend from *sam ¢êl*, "God's poison." The Prince (*archon*) of the Roman people is also frequently given the title of "Prince of the World" (*sar ha-olam, archon tou kosmou*).[57]

51. See S. R. F. Price, *Rituals and Power: The Roman Imperial Cult in Asia Minor* (New York: Cambridge University Press, 1984).
52. See Beth Severy, *Augustus and the Family at the Birth of the Roman Empire* (New York: Routledge, 2003), 113–18.
53. See Michael Peppard, *The Son of God in the Roman World: Divine Sonship in Its Social and Political Context* (New York: Oxford University Press, 2011), esp. 9–30, for a good overview of the overlapping titles for Jesus and the emperor.
54. SRJ II 11.18 // IV 18.2; RoR 87.3; 94.25; OnOrig 103.18.
55. Stroumsa, *Another Seed*, 48.
56. Culianu, "Angels of the Nations."
57. Ibid., 84.

In view of these three points, one can postulate that the crafters of these texts were drawing on the meaning of κύριος within the broader culture in their interpretation of the Genesis narrative, and thus the entire framing of these texts is an explicit and overt critique of Roman Empire and emperors rather than a veiled one.[58] In all three texts, the rulers (ἄρχων—another word that in Greek has significant political connotations)[59] are framed as ignorant, unjust, and violent—which is how certain constituencies in conquered and occupied Roman lands often experienced their rule.[60] Though the Roman rulers claimed a peaceful reign, the violence, intimidation, and displacement used to maintain this peace made it ironic—the lofty ideals with which the empire framed itself were a type of double-speak for those under its rule. The peace of the empire meant war for those subjugated by it, justice meant injustice, wisdom meant ignorance.[61] While this type of rule spanned especially the growing edges of the empire, it is one that can be seen significantly in the context of the Jesus followers. The Jesus tradition is rooted not only in Jesus's crucifixion by the Roman imperial authorities through Pilate but in the Roman occupation of Israel and the sacking of Jerusalem. While this type of violence was a wider Roman imperial policy not limited to the region, the experience of those in Israel would have been enough for these types of

---

58. King's work (*Secret Revelation of John*) has convincingly shown how the juxtaposition of the lower realm and realm of the true God creates a social critique of Roman imperial system—a critique that can be extended to include the other two texts as well.

Interestingly, Dahl almost makes the leap to this conclusion, but cannot quite manage it. After connecting the "arrogant Archon's" statement, "I am god . . . ," and explicating it in terms of Isaiah 14 ("an ironical lamentation for the king of Babylon" [703]), Ezekiel 23 (the oracle in Ezekiel "directed against the prince [nāgîd, ἄρχων] of Tyre, who said, 'I am a god' [Ezek 28:2, 9]," [703]) and noticing that "various adversaries were depicted as haughtier rulers who claimed to be divine or were acclaimed as gods: Nebuchadnezzar in Judith (3:8; 6:12); Antiochus Epiphanes in Daniel (11:36f); Pompey in the *Psalms of Solomon* (2:28f); Caligula in Philo (*Gaium* 22, 74–80, 93–97, 118, 162); Herod Agrippa in Acts (12:21–23) and Josephus (*Ant.* 19.8.2 §344–50); Nero in the *Sibylline Oracles* (5.33–35, 137–54, 214–21) and in the *Ascension of Isaiah* (4:6–8)" (704), he concludes: "What is unique is that they [the writers of the texts] cast the Creator of the world himself into the role of the arrogant ruler who claims that he is God and that there is no other. We can say that the theme was remythologized. The mythopoetic polemic is *not directed against an earthly ruler*" (705; emphasis added).

59. LSJ, s.v. ἄρχων: "*ruler, commander*; II as official title, *chief magistrate, the authorities, consul*; 2 *governor* of a dependency or province; of a Roman *governor*; 3 generally, *magistrate, official*."

60. Obviously, this is a more complicated dynamic than that presented here; see chapter 1 in this study.

61. Cf. Tacitus, *Agricola* 30.4–31.3.

characterizations. Given the framing of the rulers in the Secret Revelation of John, the Reality of the Rulers, and On the Origin of the World, it seems much more likely that these rulers are meant to correlate with the κύριοι of the Roman Empire than with the God of the Hebrew Bible.[62]

Representations of the Rulers

Despite substantial differences between the three Genesis cosmogonies, there is an overwhelmingly consistent portrait in all three regarding the rulers, authorities, and powers of Yaldabaoth's world. They are given a wide array of unbecoming descriptors, including violent, beastly, deceptive, lustful, arrogant, power-hungry, greedy, wealth obsessed, self-serving, war-mongering, unjust, foolish, jealous, and ignorant—and, topping it all off, they think they are gods. These characterizations are remarkably similar to the ways in which the rulers (and gods) are portrayed in the Roman founding narratives discussed at the beginning of this study.

The king, Amulius, after killing his brother's sons to remain king, uses deception and violence to both "imprison" Rhea Silvia under the guise of honor and to rape her—if it was indeed him—by masking his appearance. In addition, Amulius's actions were motivated by his self-serving lust for power, as Dionysius articulates them, showing his "contempt for justice."[63] If it was not Amulius but rather Mars who raped her, even if his rape lacked deception, it certainly did not lack violence. The warlike violence of Mars passing from one generation to the next, these same attributes are seen in King Romulus's deception of his neighbors, luring them to a festival to steal their women and force them to become Roman wives. Romulus then uses war and retaliation in the face of their neighbors' resistance to take the lands of the

---

62. This hypothesis and this analysis require further work, occasioning further questions, particularly around the long-held view that texts such as the three Genesis cosmogonies in this study are anti-Semitic, directly attacking Israelite religion. If these texts are as indebted to Jewish sources, textual traditions, and rabbinic materials as they seem to be in this analysis, and are instead focused primarily on imperial critique, much new thinking must be done in terms of situating these texts in their wider mileu.
63. DH 1.76.

ravaged women's kin, gaining wealth, power, and colonies under the guise of peace and concord. These characteristics are echoed in the story of Lucretia, where the son of the king, Sextus Tarquinius, lusts after the wife of another. Not only does he lust, but he threatens her by forcing her into one of two options: she can let him rape her or he can kill both her and her slave, posing their dead bodies together and accusing her of adultery. In the end, Sextus's machinations result in both her rape and her death.[64] Finally, there is Verginia, caught in the lust and machinations of Appius Claudius, sentenced to death rather than violation.

In the *Metamorphoses*, there is an analogue to the characterizations of these human rulers in the Roman founding texts, but the picture Ovid paints extends to his characterizations of the gods, the line between human and divine slipping as each is compared to, and sometimes turns into, the other. Jupiter's disproportionately violent responses, his lust, deception, and self-serving nature are illustrated in both the stories of Lycaon and Io. Jupiter punishes the entirety of humanity for the crimes of one man; and, as Lycaon, Io is turned from human to beast, but here on account of Jupiter's own crime as he tries to mask his deceitful deception from Juno.

Apollo is characterized as arrogant and lustful, and his actions are "laughable" in many of the same ways as the rulers of the Genesis cosmogonies. Just as the spiritual Eve laughs at the rulers when they finally catch "her," Apollo, too, is laughable as he finally catches "Daphne," only to be seen canoodling with a tree. Such arrogance, lust, and laughability are also seen in the story of Pan and Syrinx, as Pan mistakes Syrinx for the goddess, displaying not only his lust but his ignorance, and she, too, slips through his fingers.[65] Just as Daphne and Syrinx slip through the fingers of their would-be rapists, the Insight of the Light and the spiritual Eve are ungraspable. Further, in an amazing symmetry with the beastly "gods" of SRJ, RoR, and OnOrig, Ovid characterizes both the Romans chasing the Sabines in

---

64. See the full discussion of Rhea Silvia, the Sabines, and Lucretia in chapter 1.
65. See the full discussion of Lycaon, Io, Daphne, and Pan and Syrinx in chapter 2.

the *Ars* and Apollo chasing Daphne in the *Metamorphoses* as predator chasing prey—both the Romans and Apollo are compared to beasts as they chase their victims to rape them, the same type of beasts as the worldly rulers who rape Eve.[66]

Jupiter is also laughable in the way he attempts to deceive his wife, Juno; and not only does he act like a beast, he actually becomes one, shape-shifting to deceive—just like Yaldabaoth and his angels, who go to beguile the daughters of humans.[67] In book 6 Arachne captures the full range of Jupiter's beastly, shape-shifting pattern of violence on her woven tapestry:

> Arachne shows Europa tricked by Jove in semblance of a bull upon the sea. . . . Asterie is shown in eagle's grip, and Leda, lying under swan's wing; Arachne shows how, in Satyr's guise, Jupiter filled Antiope with twins; how, as Amphitryon, he hoodwinked you, Alcmena; and how Danaë was deceived by a golden shower; Aegina by a flame; how Mnemosyne was cozened by a shepherd and Proserpina, child of Demeter, was ruined by a many-colored serpent. (6.103–14)[68]

Additionally, this shape-shifting is seen in the transformation of Julius Caesar and Augustus from men to gods, which in the thought world of the cosmogonies would be akin to Yaldabaoth's claim, "I am god." Not only is Augustus transformed into a god by the Ovidian text, but he is specifically connected to the gods Jupiter and Apollo. He is connected particularly to Jupiter through the Palatine hill metaphor, and to Apollo through the laurel, which guards his house, and in the final book of the *Metamorphoses* in which the state gods become his household gods and Ovid looks forward to Augustus's own apotheosis.[69] These stories resonate deeply with the characterizations of the rulers

---

66. BG 37.20–21 // III 15.11 describes Yaldabaoth as having "the face of a serpent and the face of a lion," and II 10.9 describes him as "a lion-faced dragon."
    RoR 87.27–29: "Now the rulers . . . body . . . they have . . . female . . . is . . . with the face of a beast."
    OnOrig 100.1–9: From Faith Wisdom, "a thing with no spirit" comes into being, "a ruler . . . lion-like in appearance, androgynous . . . and ignorant of where he came from," named Yaldabaoth.
    OnOrig 119.17–18: "they saw that those who molded them had the form of beasts."
67. SRJ BG 72.11–75.10 // II 28.32–30.11.
68. Translation, Charles Martin.
69. See the full discussion of the Augustan ending of the *Metamorphoses* in chapter 2.

in the cosmogonies as emperors are conflated with gods; gods turn into beasts; and gods rape the objects of their desire.

Imperial Rule in the Genesis Cosmogonies

As with other aspects of the texts, each of the three Genesis cosmogonies reflect imperial critique in both unique and overlapping ways.[70] The Reality of the Rulers tends to reflect imperial critique mostly in its characterization of the rulers, but I believe it does so more directly in two particular instances. The first is where the rulers frame Eve's rape as her slavery or service to them (a slavery to which Norea replies with a resounding no—she will not be subject to this system).[71] This framing resonates particularly with Calgacus's speech, as he speaks of the enslavement of the peoples by the empire,[72] as well as with the imagery of individual captives and captive personifications of lands.[73] The second is when RoR refers to the kingless or emperor-less generation/the generation without king or emperor.[74] This designation indicates that freedom from the rulers' subjugation is central to the salvific plan of the divine realm, exemplified particularly in the knowledge, sight, and refusal of Norea—ignorance and blindness the marks of those still under the rulers' control.

The Secret Revelation of John and On the Origin of the World contain more direct references, in addition to their characterization of the rulers. In SRJ, Cain and Abel, the offspring of Yaldabaoth's rape of Eve, are set up as rulers to subjugate humanity.[75] Humanity is also beguiled into temptation and trouble by the rulers and their minions through

---

70. The seeds for this analysis are found, for example, in the works of Hans Jonas, *The Gnostic Religion: The Message of the Alien God and the Beginnings of Christianity*, 3rd ed. (Boston: Beacon Press, 2001); Kurt Rudolph, *Gnosis: The Nature and History of Gnosticism*, trans. Robert McLachlan Wilson (San Francisco: Harper & Row, 1984); and Walter Wink, *Cracking the Gnostic Code: The Powers in Gnosticism*, SBL Monograph Series 46 (Atlanta: Scholars Press, 1993). Because of the insistence on the bifurcation of the material and spiritual in the interpretation of these texts, however, these interpreters seem unable to notice what I perceive as the fullness of the texts' engagement with the material world/reality.
71. RoR 92.30–31; 92.32–93.2.
72. Tacitus, *Agricola*, 30.4–31.3.
73. See the discussion in chapter 1.
74. RoR 97.4.
75. SRJ BG 63.11–12 and parallels.

the gifts of gold, silver, copper, iron, and other metals.[76] Ultimately this is how "the whole creation became enslaved forever, from the foundation of the world until now."[77] As Stroumsa notes, the Enochic text from which these lines are drawn is a direct critique of civilization.[78] This depiction resonates with Revelation's cargo list in 18:11–13—which begins with listing gold and silver and ends with the bodies and souls/lives of humans—and also Galatians 4:8–9, where Paul states, "When you were ignorant of God, you were enslaved to gods that by nature are not gods. But now that you have come to know God, or rather be known by God, how can you return again to those powerless and bankrupt elements? How can you want to be enslaved by them again?" In addition, it reflects Ovid's portrait of the Iron Age in the *Metamorphoses,* where the mining of metals both produces the tools of war and is the cause of war.[79] The Secret Revelation of John makes clear that the conditions of subjugation, slavery, and violence are conditions of life under the reign of the rulers.

The conclusion of OnOrig is far more vivid, as it names the hallmarks of imperial religion in connection with the gods of the world. The demonic messengers of the seven rulers instruct "humankind in many kinds of error and magic and potions and idol worship and spilling blood and altars and temples and sacrifices and libations to all the daemons of the earth."[80] Additionally, the rulers create humanity to "make those born from the light our slaves,"[81] emphasizing this through the rape of Eve as the rulers violate her not because of lust but to both defile her and make her bear children who will be subject (ὑποτάσσω) to them.[82] Just as Eve's children will be subject to the rulers, so too will they tell Adam the lie that Eve should be subjected (ὑποτάσσω) to him.[83] Here the connection between sexual violence and

---

76. SRJ BG 74.11–75.1 and parallels.
77. SRJ II 30.4–7 // IV 46.13–16.
78. Stroumsa, *Another Seed,* 37–38, though he does not see this aspect of Enoch reflected in the investments of SRJ.
79. Ovid, *Met.* 1.127–50.
80. OnOrig 123.4–12. See Lillie, "Rape of Eve."
81. OnOrig 113.3–4.
82. OnOrig 116.19–20.
83. OnOrig 116.21–25.

subjugation, so clearly illustrated in the imperial texts—most thoroughly in the story of the rape marriage, and conquest of the Sabines—is distinctly named.

Divine and Human Households

Michael Williams and Karen King both emphasize the similarities between the divine household in SRJ, consisting of Father, Mother, and Son, and the traditional hierarchical and patriarchal Roman household.[84] While this imagery is not nearly as prevalent in RoR and OnOrig, there still remain mentions of the Father and Son.[85] Though both Williams and King see this divine household as "idealized" in comparison with the everyday reality of the Roman family, King particularly stresses that in SRJ the rupture in the divine realm follows from Wisdom's independent act of creation. Without consent or approval from either the invisible Spirit (i.e, the Father) or her male counterpart, Wisdom disrupts the harmony and *concordia* of the divine realm.[86] With Williams's and King's important insights in terms of the *paterfamilia* and the patriarchal and hierarchical residue in the divine family, I would like to extend their readings and ask what these approaches might yield if we start from a different vantage point.

In the Republic, *pater patriae* was a designation given to those who saved Rome "from invaders or conspirators, or . . . the lives of many citizens."[87] This designation was also associated with Romulus, who was "father of the city and of *virtus*" (Propertius 4.10).[88] Before being officially given the title *pater patriae* in 2 BCE by the Senate (the title was inscribed on the quadriga in Augustus's forum, outside the temple of Mars), the role of father was one that Augustus cultivated. This

---

84. Williams, *Rethinking "Gnosticism,"* 154–60; King, *Secret Revelation of John,* 125–28.

85. RoR (father) 86.21; 87.22; 88.11, 34; 96.12, 20, 35; 97.15, 17; (son) 97.18; OnOrig (father only) 124.5, 14; 125.8; 127.11; cf. 125.14 λόγος—though the "word"/ϣⲁϫⲉ is always associated with divine female figures.

86. King, *Secret Revelation of John,* 89–94; King, "Reading Sex," 529; but see her analysis of the ways Wisdom's actions can be read against the text as parody, *Secret Revelation of John,* 125–26; "Reading Sex," 533–36.

87. Ando, *Imperial Ideology,* 399.

88. Zanker, *Power of Images,* 203; Severy, *Augustus and the Family,* 173; Ando, *Imperial Ideology,* 399. See also the discussion in chapter 1.

cultivation occurred in several arenas. One was in his role as moral exemplar not only within his family but for the Roman people as a whole through his moral legislation. An additional way, and one of the most striking, in which Augustus became Father of the Roman people was when he was voted to the position of *pontifex maximus*, moving the state shrine of Vesta to his home on the Palatine and adding the state gods to those of his own household. This fusion of public and private, state religion with Augustus's household was foregrounded in the discussion of the apotheosis of Caesar in Ovid's *Metamorphoses*.[89]

The metaphor of Rome as family is highlighted in Roman monuments such as the Ara Pacis, where Roman founding narratives like Aeneas, as ancestor of the Julian line, and Romulus, Father of Rome, are found in juxtaposition to the parading family of Augustus, along with people from senators to adopted foreign children and possibly personifications of the nations.[90] This constellation is also mirrored in Augustus's forum, which contained statues of Romulus and Aeneas, the portico of the nations, and the quadriga with the inscription "Father of the Fatherland."[91]

The relationship between Augustus's family and Rome was extended in connections between Livia, Augustus's wife, and *concordia*. Livia built a shrine to August Concord in her portico to celebrate her marriage to Augustus—*concordia* symbolizing marital concord, concord within the state (exemplified privately through the marriage laws and publicly in the end of the civil war and establishing of the Pax Romana), and also concord, through victory, with the nations.[92] In addition, Beth Severy notes that the peoples of the provinces worshiped not only the divine emperor but also members of his family.[93] The idea of Augustus's role as Father extended beyond Rome and is seen in inscriptions from

---

89. See the discussion in chapter 2; cf. chapter 1.
90. Severy, *Augustus and the Family*, 104–12; Zanker, *Power of Images*, 120–23, 158–59, 203–4. See also the discussion in chapter 1.
91. Zanker, *Power of Images*, 113–14, 129, 194–95, 201–5, 209–15. See also the discussions in chapters 1 and 2.
92. Severy, *Augustus and the Family*, 132–33; Lobur, *Consensus, Concordia*, 92.
93. Severy, *Augustus and the Family*, 113–14.

the eastern empire: a typical one naming Augustus "father of his fatherland and of the entire human race."[94]

These examples also weave thematically with the story of the Sabine women. As explored in chapters 1 and 2, with Romulus as the founding father, the Sabines story shows how marriage (i.e., the family) and conquest are inextricable. Indeed, the seizure and marriage of the women to the Roman men become a microcosm for the wider dynamics of conquest: as husband relates to wife, so too does Rome relate to its territories. The narratives of Livy and Dionysius, written during the Augustan era—an era marked by an appeal to origins in the wake of Actium and the refounding of the city—connect the flourishing of the city with marriage and conquest.[95] The Sabine women are spoils of necessity, a necessity for producing men who will perpetuate the Roman legacy, and their abduction is the impetus for conquest: the conquering of lands, the colonization of lands, and the subsuming of peoples under the dominion of Rome under the banner of concordia. Not only is the Sabines narrative an aetiology of Roman marriage and conquest, but it embeds within it the aetiologies of the Roman triumph and the temple of Jupiter Capitolina, along with the treachery of what occurs when the Vestals, who guarantee the integrity of Rome (and whose shrine has been moved to Augustus's home at the time of Livy's and Dionysius's writings), fail to do their duty. These aetiologies all arise from the Romans' initial act of violence: that of the capturing and raping of women through deception.[96]

The friezes in the Basilica Aemilia visually depict the stories of the Sabines and Tarpeia, with the echoes of these stories finding their way into the wider programmatic visual ideologies of Roman conquest. Combining Greek personifications of territories with the visual optics of triumph, whether actual triumphs or depictions of them, the objects of Rome's conquest begin to be portrayed as captive, female personifications. It is almost as if the Sabine women themselves become the symbols for the conquered nations of their kinsmen. But,

94. Ando, *Imperial Ideology*, 403; Severy, *Augustus and the Family*, 113–18.
95. See the discussion in chapter 1.
96. Again, see the discussion in chapter 1.

at the same time, these women are the wives of the founding father, the embodiment of *concordia* at home and abroad, the perfect representations of colonization and conquest.

Conversely, in SRJ, the divine household provides a foil and counterpoint to what could be thought of as the household of Yaldabaoth. Yaldabaoth and his world are based on a mimetic, yet deficient template of the divine realm. As the Invisible Spirit is the father of the divine realm, so too is Yaldabaoth the father of the material realm, begetting the rulers, authorities, and powers that will rule his world. Yaldabaoth mimics both Wisdom and the Invisible Spirit by creating on his own. But, in contrast to these divine beings, he creates out of madness, a loss of right perception,[97] as opposed to the noetic creation of the divine realm.[98] Sophia also creates noetically: "she thought a thought from herself,"[99] though she does so in "ignorance."[100] BG emphasizes that Yaldabaoth actually "copulated with madness," distinguishing his act from the begetting of the divine realm,[101] and his own world reflecting that act.

If these imperial constructs of father and family, marriage and conquest provide the template for the rulers of the world as described in the Secret Revelation of John, the Reality of the Rulers, and On the Origin of the World, what might the construct of the divine family, particularly in SRJ, be signifying in relationship to it? Again, there are several mimetic elements that occur between the divine household and the *paterfamilia*, particularly illustrated with the figures of father and mother at the top of the hierarchy and the divine realm itself ascribing to the ideal of concordia or harmony. These mimetic elements are also seen where the Father is called a "merciful benefactor,"[102] and Foresight/the Savior comes "seeking to put my household (οἰκονομία) in order."[103] But a key difference between the divine household and the

---

97. SRJ BG 39.5 // II 10.26 only, ἀπόνοια.
98. νοεῖν/νοῦς produces πρόνοια, ἔννοια, ἐπίνοια.
99. SRJ BG 36.17–18 // II 14.10–11 // II 9.26 ⲁⲥⲙⲉⲉⲩⲉ ⲉⲩⲙⲉⲉⲩⲉ ⲉⲃⲟⲗ ⲛ̄ⲣⲏⲧⲥ̄.
100. SRJ BG 38.6 // III 15.16 // II 10.14.
101. See King, *Secret Revelation of John*, 127.
102. SRJ BG 52.19 // III 24.25–25.1; cf. II 20.9–10 // IV 31.3–5, where it is the Mother-Father (μητροπάτωρ) who receives these designations. See also the *Res Gestae* for examples Augustus's own benefaction.

Roman/rulers' household, is that the divine household never operates through violence or threat of violence. Even Wisdom, who has caused this rupture, is taken back into the fold.[104] Though the divine household does operate under the virtues of consensus and *concordia*,[105] these operate in terms of a paradigm based on mutual power-with, rather than violent power-over.

It is this paradigm of mutuality that is exemplified in the relationship between Adam and Eve, whose family unit of Father, Mother, and Seth is the worldly parallel to the structure of the divine realm. This worldly household follows and is "just as" the divine.[106] The household of Eve, Adam, and Seth indicates a very concrete ideal: the relationship of the members of the household is based on recognition, mutuality, and consent—the exact opposite of the "relationship" enacted by Yaldabaoth as he rapes Eve. It is also significant that it is not a relationship based on marriage.[107] But instead, at least according to BG, that "marital [γάμος] intercourse" follows the pattern of Yaldabaoth's actions[108]—his desire for Eve, his rape of her, and the subsequent birth of his subjugating sons. While supposedly this "desire for seed" or "seed of desire" is planted within Adam and Eve respectively, this does not follow the pattern of their union: their union follows the pattern of the divine realm.[109]

The paradigm of what SRJ refers to as "marital intercourse" begins to be established just before Yaldabaoth's rape of Eve. When Adam and Eve withdraw from him after they "eat of knowledge," he curses them.

103. SRJ II 30.26–27 // IV 47.15; see Williams, *Rethinking "Gnosticism,"* 155–56.
104. SRJ BG 46.11–47.7 // III 21.1–11 // II 13.32–14.9 // IV 21.23–22.13.
105. See Lobur (*Consensus*, Concordia) on these virtues in the Roman world. For συμφωνεῖν/σύμφωνος/ⲭⲱⲛϩ in SRJ, see BG 37.7 // II 9.33; BG 37.9 // II 15.2 // II 9.35; BG 45.2–4 // II 13.16–17 // IV 21.2–3; BG 46.12 // II 13.35 // IV 21.25–26.
106. SRJ BG 63.14–16 // III 32.8–9 // II 25.2 // IV 38.29–30.
107. Here I am particularly thinking in terms of the legal status of marriage in Roman law which makes a woman subject to either her *paterfamilias* or her husband. It is important to note that there are many types of legal statuses for both men and women in the Roman world, which encompassed a range of relational possibilities not only with one another but with families of origin or adoption. See Treggiari, *Roman Marriage*, esp. 5–36, for a good overview of the subject, as well as Staples, who approaches the subject of Roman marriage through the stories of Ceres and Flora, the Sabine women, and Lucretia (*From Good Goddess to Vestal Virgins*, 59–93).
108. SRJ BG 63.1–2.
109. SRJ BG 63.5–6 // III 31.23–24, in Adam; II 24.28–29 // IV 38.16–17, in Eve. See the discussion in chapter 3.

BG and Codex III say that Yaldabaoth "adds [to this curse] concerning the female that the male should rule over her for he does not understand the mystery which came to pass from the design of the Holy Height."[110] This declaration makes clear that the construct of male over female does not actually regulate the divine realm. The Secret Revelation of John II frames this in a slightly different manner by saying, "He found the female preparing herself for her male. He was lord over her, for he did not understand the mystery which had come to pass from the holy design."[111] This passage is extraordinarily interesting. While it is impossible to know exactly what kind of "preparations" Eve was making, there is something, given what follows, that seems to imply sexual intercourse here—before Yaldabaoth has created it, before he has planted desire. What is more, in this entire passage, Adam and Eve are referred to together in the plural, they are a "they," while Yaldaboath is the "he" throughout. Consequently, it follows that Yaldabaoth is the one who "was lord over her," and not Adam, which emphasizes that the relationship of domination is borne out through his rape of Eve—it is not about sex as such.

The Coptic is somewhat ambiguous, with Eve referred to as ⲥϩⲓⲙⲉ, meaning female, woman, and wife, and Adam as ϩⲟⲟⲩⲧ, meaning male, man, and husband—making the specific status of the relationship between the two difficult to analyze fully. It could be argued that the text is referring to "husband and wife," in relation to its earlier quotation of Genesis 2:24, where "a man leaves his mother and father and clings to his wife,"[112] but both the Hebrew אִשָּׁה and the Greek γυνή have the same semantic range as the Coptic ⲥϩⲓⲙⲉ and thus give no indication of the "legal" status inherent in marriage. Instead, when Adam recognizes Eve, he recognizes not his ⲥϩⲓⲙⲉ but his οὐσία, his essence, which appears both in the Genesis 2:24 quotation and in the inception of Seth.[113] The only time γάμος is used in the text is in relation

110. SRJ BG 61.8–15 // III 30.23–31.1; see the discussion in chapter 3.
111. SRJ II 23.35–24.3 // IV 37.4–11; cf. Gen 3:16, and see the discussion in chapter 3.
112. SRJ BG 60.3–11 // III 30.3–10 // II 23.9–14 // IV 36.1–8.

to "marital intercourse."[114] ⲅⲁⲓ, the Coptic word for husband specifically, is used for husband in BG only when the messengers of the ruler take the shape of the "husbands" of the daughters of men to deceive and despoil them.[115]

The Reality of the Rulers and On the Origin of the World also contain the semantic ambiguities mentioned above. In addition, ⲅⲁⲓ is used for "husband" in both RoR and OnOrig when Eve gives the fruit to her husband and then one additional time in OnOrig in the so-called Hymn to Eve, where Eve is her own husband.[116] In general, when both of these texts speak of Adam and Eve's relationship, "counterpart" or "partner" is used.[117] The word γάμος is not used at all in RoR and is only used twice in OnOrig after the world is proliferated through female outpouring in response to unrequited love—in the section where woman follows earth, marriage follows woman, birth follows marriage, and death follows birth.[118] But it is never used in relationship to Adam and Eve.

Despite these ambiguities, all three of the Genesis retellings are clear that a different type of relationship occurs between Adam and Eve after they eat and are enlightened. Additionally, their relationship is not one predicated on traditional Roman marriage—though neither is it one devoid of sex. Especially given the connections between marriage and conquest and family in the Roman texts, it seems that SRJ uses the divine household as much as foil as mimetically to provide a model for right relationship between man and woman specifically, and more broadly between one another.

Conclusion: Resisting the Rulers

As I have shown throughout this chapter and in chapter 3, Eve and Adam's acquisition of knowledge has a corollary in the way Adam and Eve relate to each other in the expression of their knowledge and love,

113. SRJ BG 60.4 // II 30.4; cf. II 23.9, ⲉⲓⲛⲉ // IV 35.29, ϣⲃⲣⲉⲓⲛⲉ; and BG 63.13; cf. II 24.23 // 38.25–26: ⲉⲓⲛⲉ. III 32.7: ἀνομία.
114. SRJ BG 63.1–2.
115. SRJ BG 74.13; 74.12, possible reconstruction NHC.
116. RoR 90.14; OnOrig 114.11; 119.11.
117. See the discussion in chapter 3.
118. OnOrig 109.22–25.

in their sexual relationship. Their relationship not only subverts the hierarchical and violent relationships instigated and modeled by the rulers, but the knowledge they gain allows them to see the rulers and the structural malice that they perpetuate. This ability to see, in turn, causes them to act in a way contrary to the system that the rulers keep attempting to establish. Eve and Adam's actions, as evidenced by their sexual union, reflect the pattern of the divine realm, providing a template for the actions between humans in the world in opposition to the relational dynamics of the rulers. While SRJ, RoR, and OnOrig similarly represent this emphasis on praxis in the human realm through the actions of Adam and Eve, each of them contains additional, though different, ways in which they address it.

In RoR, this emphasis on praxis is seen in the actions of Norea. She is an exemplar of how people should act in the face of the rulers: they should resist them, they should refuse to participate in their actions, and they should not be afraid to ask for assistance. She embodies the knowledge gained by Adam and Eve through the eating of the fruit and thinks with clarity rather than the confusion hoisted on humanity by the rulers: she is not distracted by their worldly trappings of violence and lust. Norea has freed herself from "the bondage of the authorities error,"[119] by refusing to subject herself to them as their slave,[120] and this is the mark of the offspring of the divine realm.[121] While not addressing praxis as directly as the other two texts, Norea, by embodying the qualities of those who come from the Father, provides a model for humanity to follow.[122]

John directly asks Christ/the Savior in SRJ about who will be saved, asking if everyone's souls will go to "the pure light." The Savior responds that it is difficult for any but those from "the immovable race" to understand, but that the ones "upon whom the Spirit of Life descends . . . will be saved and become perfect."[123] These will be purified

---

119. RoR 96.30–31.
120. RoR 92.32–93.2.
121. RoR 96.23–24.
122. RoR 96.19–28.
123. SRJ BG 64.17–65.8 // III 32.26–33.7 // II 25.18–26 // IV 39.16–30.

from the "beguilements" (BG), "concerns" (II/IV), and "bonds" (III) of evil, and they will "attend to the incorruptible congregation without anger or envy or fear or desire or overindulgence."[124] Then John asks the Savior if those who fail to "do these works" might be saved. The Savior tells him that the Spirit has descended on everyone and where the Spirit is strong, it strengthens the soul so it cannot be led astray, but "those into whom the counterfeit spirit enters are beguiled by him and are led astray."[125] John finally asks what happens to those who do not "know" (соүшн/ммє). The Savior answers that these are the souls that have been led astray by the counterfeit/despicable spirit, which "burdens their soul and beguiles it to the works of evil and casts it into forgetfulness."[126]

And what are these works of evil that beguile? These are the works named when the rulers' messengers deceptively transform themselves into the likeness of the husbands of the daughters of humans for their "satisfaction," to raise offspring, and "to oppress them in the darkness [which comes] from evil."[127] These works include bringing them gold and silver and gifts and copper and iron and other metals; beguiling "them into temptation" (BG); and "leading them astray with many deceptions" (II/IV), "so that they would not remember their immovable Foresight" (BG/III).[128] These did not know the God of truth, becoming enslaved,[129] and their hearts became closed and hardened.[130] It is those in the "immovable race"—those who are not moved by the beguilement of the rulers and their seductive trappings; those whose hearts and minds are opened through knowledge, clear thinking, and mutual recognition; those who awaken—who can join entry into the immovable race: those who act like Adam and Eve after they eat the knowledge of Insight.[131]

---

124. SRJ BG 65.8–16 // III 33.7–13 // II 25.26–33 // IV 39.30–40.7.
125. SRJ BG 66.13–67.18 // III 33.23–34.18 // II 26.7–22 // IV 40.20–41.10.
126. SRJ BG 68.13–69.5 // III 35.2–10 // II 26.32–27.4 // IV 41.21–42.1.
127. SRJ BG 73.18–74.16 // III 38.10–24 // II 29.16–29 // IV 45.14–46.2.
128. SRJ BG 74.11–75.3 // III 38.21–39.4 // II 29.26–30.2 // IV 45.27–46.10.
129. SRJ II 30.4–5 // IV 46.12–13.
130. SRJ BG 75.7–8 // III 39.8–9 // II 30.9–10 // IV 46.19–21.
131. See Williams, *Immovable Race*, 103–40, on the immovable race in SRJ, and 172–73; and Williams, *Rethinking "Gnosticism,"* 195–96, on inclusive membership.

On the Origin of the World also portrays Adam and Eve as the paradigmatic humans of enlightenment, even though it, too, frames ethical action more in terms of what not to do by using the rulers as a model. Eve's and Adam's "minds are opened," after they eat, and "the light of knowledge enlightened them," as they realize that they had been "stripped naked of knowledge."[132] With these realizations, they not only "love each other," but see that the rulers are actually beasts.[133] On the Origin of the World emphasizes, "They knew much."[134] But the work is clear that true knowledge is not attained without a corresponding praxis as the final words of the entire text state, "For everyone must go to the place from which they have come. Indeed, by their acts πρᾶξις] and their knowledge [γνῶσις] each one will make their origin known [ⲥⲱⲗⲡ]."[135] This is not a praxis modeled by the rulers, or Augustus, but rather the divine realm.[136] And so, it is fitting that OnOrig speaks of the race without king/emperor who kings themselves in the mortal realm because they will "condemn the gods of chaos and their forces."[137] It seems that this race consists of those who step outside of the system created by the rulers of the world, the ones who live into the "work" of the "Word" (λόγος), which is "to make known what is unknown."[138]

Though OnOrig does speak of four different races that are different in their "chosenness" (ἐκλογή), this does not appear to be on the basis of their birth per se,[139] but rather seems to be based on their condemnation "of the gods of chaos and their powers" that mark the emperorless race mentioned above.[140] The ability to do this seems to lie with the same acquisition of knowledge Adam and Eve gain when they eat the fruit of the tree, allowing them to see the rulers as beasts. This ability to see clearly the workings of the world is the same "work"

---

132. OnOrig 119.11–15.
133. OnOrig 119.17–18.
134. OnOrig 119.18.
135. OnOrig 127.14–17. See Williams, *Rethinking "Gnosticism,"* 192–93.
136. The translation of *Res Gestae* in Greek is Πρᾶξις.
137. OnOrig 125.2, 6, 11–14. Cf. RoR 97.1–4.
138. OnOrig 125.14–16.
139. Though there is a lacuna at 124.33.
140. OnOrig 124.32–125.14.

(ⲣⲱⲃ) the Word is sent for: to reveal what is hidden. That this is indeed called "work" again points to the last lines of the book, which inextricably link actions and knowledge—right action not only proceeds from knowledge but is a confirmation that knowledge has been attained.

This idea of "race," whether in regard to the immovable race or that of the kingless/emperorless race, provides a stark contrast to Roman configurations of race, both in terms of who and how one could become Roman and in terms of the personifications of the nations.[141] This was not a race based on ethnicity or power differentials, on casting some as civilized and others as conquerable barbarians, but a race where admission was based on knowledge and praxis resonant with the values of care and mutuality exemplified by the divine realm. Admission to this race was the birthright of all who followed Adam and Eve and their offspring and who based their relationships not on the violent power dynamics perpetuated by the rulers but on knowledge and mutual recognition.

141. See Beard, *Roman Triumph*, 133–41; Ando, *Imperial Ideology*, 312; see also the discussion in chapter 1.

5

"But she could not be grasped . . ."

Thinking through the Rape of Eve

This chapter returns specifically to Eve and takes another look at the places where the three rape of Eve narratives converge and diverge, emphasizing thematic overlays common to the three Genesis cosmogonies and framing these within the larger discussions of the Roman narratives. Of particular importance are ways in which the rape of Eve narratives reframe and resist the dynamics of rape that take shape within the Roman narratives, but also the ways in which they reproduce these dynamics as they take on these texts, displaying their own ambivalences in relation to the complex dynamics of rape, gender, sexuality, and subjugation.

Connections and Disjunctions

Eve is a type of savior figure in each of the three texts; she is associated with the divinities of the divine realm and is the one who brings real life to Adam, her partner. Likewise, each text names her rape as a horrific display of the rulers' violence. All show a savvy psychological understanding of the effects of sexual violence in the complicated dissociation of Eve and also effect some kind of movement or reintegration of Eve after her rape. These three narratives are further connected by their shared emphasis on the mutual and sexual relationship between Adam and Eve after they eat. Finally, Eve is always named as the ancestor of those who will finally overcome the rulers. But, as is often true in the wake of violence, these themes are fraught with ambivalence. So, as I return to these themes, I also turn them, refracting different aspects and drawing out new complexities.

Eve's Association with the Divine Realm

Eve is always associated with the female actors of the divine realm and is sent from the divine realm as an emissary to help Adam. In SRJ BG/III, she is primarily associated with Insight, who was hidden in Adam but is released when the rulers try to grasp her, making Eve (though she is never named as such) from him.[1] As indicated in chapter 3, it is difficult to tell exactly what Insight's relationship with Eve is, especially in BG, but nonetheless the creation of Eve is associated with the enlightenment of Adam. In addition in Codices II/IV it seems that she is part of a constellation that includes Wisdom and Life sent from divine Foresight.[2] In RoR it is the Spirit, grammatically male in Coptic, that initially enlivens Adam. The text never explains specifically why Eve is created but says that after Adam was created he only had a soul. Then the "spiritual woman" appears, implying that the spirit that was in him has now moved to her. It is her words to him, enlivened by the spirit, that cause him to rise.[3] On the Origin of the World has the most complicated portrayal of Eve through the many interwoven connections between Faith, Wisdom, Life, and Eve. Eve is the daughter of Faith and is also the instructor, female in body but also androgynous and mother.[4] Wisdom Life sends her breath to Adam so he can move, and then Wisdom sends her daughter Life Eve to him directly—she is not created from Adam—so that he could arise and father vessels for

1. SRJ BG 53.4–59.19 // III 25.6–29.24.
2. See the discussion of SRJ in chapter 3.
3. RoR 87.10–15; 89.13. See the discussion of RoR in chapter 3.
4. OnOrig 113.21–114.15.

the light.[5] She then tells him to rise and "her word becomes a work," and indeed Adam rises.[6]

Eve is the embodiment of and conduit for the work of the divine realm. She is the one sent by it and the one who does its work. She bridges and connects the divine with the human, bringing enlivenment to the ones created by the rulers in the likeness or image of those from the divine realm. It is for these reasons that the embodied Eve becomes the partner of Adam, and Adam becomes the partner of Eve. But she is more than just his partner, she is his savior—and as Eve comes to save him, so too her actions set in motion the plan for the salvation of humanity.

Eve and the Violence of the Rulers

The rulers' rape is unequivocally named as violent in each of the three texts. The Secret Revelation of John has the least to say about this aspect of the text, BG articulating Yaldabaoth's "senseless folly" and "desire to sow a seed" in her, while Codex II simply says, "he was filled with ignorance" and "he defiled her."[7] In RoR, when the rulers saw her, they became "aroused and lusted after her." The Reality of the Rulers goes on to describe their rape, saying, "And they defiled her sexually. And they defiled the seal of her voice," then adding "and so they convicted themselves through the form they had shaped in their own image."[8] In OnOrig's even more elaborate version, when the rulers see her, they decide they want to "grab her and cast our sperm into her so that she becomes defiled and unable to ascend to her light." Additionally, they hope to create children through their violent act "who will become subject to us."[9] On the Origin of the World, like RoR, is explicit in describing her rape: "And they acted cruelly. They entered her and possessed her and cast their sperm into her. They acted upon her wickedly. They not only defiled her in natural but abominable

---

5. OnOrig 115.11–36.
6. OnOrig 116.1–4. See the discussion of OnOrig in chapter 3.
7. SRJ BG 62.5–8 // III 31.7–10 // II 24.12–16 // IV 37.21–28. See the discussion in chapter 3.
8. RoR 89.19–30.
9. OnOrig 116.15–20.

ways. They defiled the seal of her first voice, which had said to them 'What exists before you?' intending to defile those who might say at the completion of the age that they were born of the true human through the word." The text continues, saying that through this act "they erred. They did not know they defiled their own body. The authorities and their angels had defiled the likeness in every way."[10]

The violence done to Eve is horrific. In SRJ, Yaldabaoth is named as the father of both Cain and Abel, implying that this was not just a single violation, but many, over time. In both RoR and OnOrig, Eve is not violated by one but many: she is gang raped. In RoR, she is raped by all the authorities and then gives birth to "their son," Cain. In OnOrig, Eve suffers the same fate as in SRJ and RoR as she is raped not only by the Chief Ruler but also by the seven authorities—the entire system of government—then giving birth to Abel by the Chief Ruler, and seven other children through the seven authorities.[11]

The narration of Eve's rape is not only a powerful exposition on sexual violence but also a vital moment of social critique. Both SRJ and OnOrig are clear that through this act of sexual violence the rulers usher in a hierarchy between male and female that is not part of the divine plan. The Secret Revelation of John frames this as the male ruling over the female in BG, and the male being her lord in Codex II.[12] BG goes even further, saying that this act of violence by Yaldabaoth ushers in the construct of marital intercourse.[13] On the Origin of the World frames the hierarchical relationship between man and woman as a lie told to Adam by the rulers. This lie consisted of two parts: the first was that the woman was derivative of him, that she came from his rib; and this in turn would make him think she was subject to him and that he was her lord.[14]

This act of sexual violence ushers in not only gendered hierarchy but also wider structural subjugation. On the Origin of the World is clear

---

10. OnOrig 117.2–14.
11. See the discussion in chapter 3.
12. SRJ BG 61.10–15 // III 30.24–31.1 // II 24.1–3 // IV 37.8–3. Cf. Gen 3:16.
13. SRJ BG 63.1–3.
14. OnOrig 116.20–25.

that part of the "reasoning" for Eve's rape is for her to bear children that will be subject to the rulers. This statement is connected to the rulers' desire to create humans so "those born from the light" will become their slaves.[15] The link between sexual violence and slavery is seen also in RoR when the rulers confront Norea and tell her that she must be a slave to them as her mother Eve was.[16] These connections—linking power, sexual violence, and subjugation—explode the paradigms that form the basis of the Roman mytho-logic of deception and violence, rape and marriage, war and conquest discussed in chapter 1. The seizure and subordination, rape and subjugation of Eve mirror those of Ilia, the Sabines, Lucretia, and the nations. It is this paradigm—the paradigm of power, greed, and lust-based conquest—that Genesis cosmogonies both name and declare as evil.

Another area of social critique can be seen in both RoR and OnOrig as they emphasize the ways in which the rulers continually undermine and condemn themselves through their actions. This is particularly seen in the rape of Eve where the rulers are condemned for not understanding that they are violating their own body and are actually violating themselves, exposing themselves through their actions.[17] The Reality of the Rulers and OnOrig seem to be saying something very specific about the intersubjective nature of violence—that it reverberates back upon the one perpetrating it. Because of the claims of divine rule—where Yaldabaoth claims to be god, where emperors claim to be gods, where their sovereignty is seen as divine favor—these texts say that this is not true, and that eventually their own actions will be their undoing. While RoR notes the destruction of the rulers' world, it is more of a passing aside in the midst of describing what will come for the children of light, that is, the children of Norea.[18] But OnOrig describes the destruction of the rulers and their world in detail, where, with many resonances with Revelation, this violence ends up leading

---

15. OnOrig 113.4–5.
16. RoR 92.30–31.
17. RoR 90.30; OnOrig 117.12–14.
18. RoR 97.1–13.

to the wholesale destruction of the rulers and their world. As they have condemned themselves through Eve's rape, here too the rulers are ultimately responsible for their own destruction as they "wage war against one another, so that the earth is drunk with bloodshed" and they become "like volcanoes and consume one another until they are annihilated at the hand of" Yaldabaoth.[19] Whatever claims to a Golden Age or eternal rule the world rulers appeal to, these will pass, not only because, as Ovid seems to indicate in the *Metamorphoses*, the Golden Age is really more like the Iron Age, but because the rulers' violent actions can only lead to more violence, to their own undoing and destruction.

Eve, the Tree, and Dissociation

An integral part of Eve's rape by the rulers is the splitting, or dissociation, that occurs at the time of her rape. This splitting occurs in SRJ Codices II/IV, as Life is "snatched" from Eve by beings dispatched by Foresight, her dissociation initiated by beings other than herself.[20] In both RoR and OnOrig, Eve is clear about what the rulers are plotting and laughs at them. In RoR this "laugh" is prompted by the rulers' "foolishness and blindness," and the text says that "in their grasp, she became a tree."[21] On the Origin of the World simply says that she laughs at their decision because she is "a power." She then blinds them, leaving her likeness with Adam and entering into and becoming the tree of knowledge.[22]

Eve, like Daphne and Syrinx before her, manages to elude the grasp of those who wish to violate her. Yet the transformation or movement of the spiritual Eve to the tree also effects a corresponding transformation of her earthy counterpart. Like Daphne with Apollo and Syrinx with Pan, through her transformation, the earthy Eve remains behind to be held in the clutches of her pursuers. Daphne, Syrinx, and Eve all become shadows of themselves, and all are subjugated and used by those who desire them. These transformations

19. OnOrig 125.23–127.3.
20. SRJ II 24.13–15 // IV 27.23–26.
21. RoR 89.23–26.
22. OnOrig 116.25–32. See also the discussion in chapter 3.

mirror closely the dissociation that often occurs for those subjected to violence; the self splits in an attempt to protect itself from the violation. A corresponding dissociation can often be found in the colonial subject as well, subjected to the will of the colonizer.

This dissociation is not always a site of fracture but can also be a site of resistance. Dissociative states marked by trance, possession, mourning, and ecstasy are often used to say the unsayable, to say those things that are not possible to say in "everyday" consciousness.[23] Through this type of dissociation, spaces open that allow critique of the reigning powers, the powers that subjugate, the powers that imprison. Thus the foreclosure, disconnection, and fragmenting that often mark dissociation can be a conduit through which these aspects not only find voice, but allow, connect, and integrate.

Integration, Mutuality, and Sexuality: The Legacy of Eve

The resistant side of the dissociative process is articulated in each of the texts through the ways in which Adam and Eve partake of knowledge after the rupture between spirit and body created through the rulers' rape of Eve. Insight, who travels from the divine realm, to Adam, then to Eve, finally teaches them to eat of knowledge from the tree in SRJ. This power of Insight that allows Adam to see his essence within Eve is again activated after her rape and the subsequent birth of Cain and Abel, allowing him to know her—both spiritually and physically. This knowledge in turn leads to the birth of Seth, the one born following the generations of the divine realm, who, according to Codex II, is made in the image of the divine human. Through their union and their child, Adam and Eve heal the rupture, initially created through Wisdom and recreate the above in the below, paving the way for the knowledge of the divine realm to enter that of the human.

23. See, e.g., Erika Bourguignon, "Suffering and Healing, Subordination and Power: Women and Possession Trance," *Ethos* 34.4 (2004): 557–74; Samir Dayal, "Managing Ecstasy: A Subaltern Performative of Resistance," *Angelaki* 6.1 (2001): 75–90; Elizabeth Hegeman, "Ethnic Syndromes as Disguise for Protest against Colonialism: Three Ethnographic Examples," *Journal of Trauma & Dissociation* 14.2 (2013): 138–46; and Parita Mukta, "The 'Civilizing Mission': The Regulation and Control of Mourning in Colonial India," *Feminist Review* 63 (1999): 25–47.

In RoR it is initially the spirit that moves from the divine realm to Adam, and then transforms into a female spiritual presence as it moves from Eve to the tree and finally to the instructor, taking the form of the serpent. The instructor tells them to eat from the tree and exposes the rulers' prohibitions as lies, disclosing that eating will in fact open their eyes and bring them the knowledge. Eve eats, and then Adam. And indeed their eyes are open, and they understand the reality of ignorance and lack of spirit in which they dwell. Despite this, or maybe because of their knowledge of it, Adam and Eve still have the ability to know each other both physically and spiritually, this knowledge embodied as the text calls them "partners." Through this partnership and mutual knowing, Eve first gives birth to Seth, through God. Then Eve becomes pregnant a second time, giving birth to Norea, the one sent to help the generations of humankind.

On the Origin of the World tracks the movement of Faith's outpouring from Faith, to Wisdom, to Faith-Wisdom, then to Life, Wisdom-Life, and the instructor who is Life-Eve who is "the beast." Their overlapping and interwoven names reflect the flow and interconnectedness of these beings in the divine realm. This outpouring then flows through Eve to Adam and finally to the Tree of Knowledge. Here, "the wisest of creatures," the one "called 'the beast,'" the one identified earlier with Wisdom-Life's daughter, Life-Eve, approaches Eve, recognizing that she is the likeness of the mother.[24] The creature tells her that the words of the rulers are lies and that, when they eat, their mind will become sober and they will know the difference between evil and good humans. Eve trusts the instructor's words, and she eats and Adam eats. Then their minds are opened, and they become enlightened. Not only does this knowledge allow them to love each other, but it allows them to see the rulers as the beasts they truly are. The text says little about the children of Adam and Eve. Nevertheless, OnOrig is clear that Eve was sent to Adam so that those he would engender would become vessels for the light, and that Eve was part of this plan to make the rulers' human

---

24. OnOrig 118.24–29.

forms enclosures for the light so that these humans could condemn them. While Adam's children filled the earth, they were still under the control of the rulers—but these are the same children who will eventually hold the blessed spirits who bring knowledge to humanity. Through all of this, Adam and Eve are not only partners, but Wisdom Life names them as her counterparts, closing the loop from the rulers' rupture and reidentifying them with the divine realm.

Each of these texts insists that there is a difference between the paradigm of sexual violence marking the actions of the rulers and the mutuality existing between Adam and Eve. Unlike the Sabines—or their analogue, the nations—Eve and Adam are not forced to live in this paradigm of both hierarchical and gendered power relations. Through their clear seeing, they are truly able to become co-partners and co-creators with each other, in sharp contrast to the Roman power relations of domination that are masked in the double-speak of terms like *concordia* and *peace*. Somehow, despite the fact that the rulers' systemic violence continues to press upon them, Eve and Adam seek out and find a different model to enact. It is a model that allows them and their descendants to operate outside of the structural violence of the rulers while still living within it.

Violence and Ambivalence: Roman Narratives and the Rape of Eve

Much of the critique of the rulers seems to emerge from the fissures created by the ambivalence undergirding the Roman founding rape narrative. All of the Roman "histories"—whether in the Rhea Silvia, Sabines, or Lucretia and Verginia myths—display an underlying ambivalence surrounding issues of sexual violence and rape. These stories, used to reforge the history of Augustus's reign and usher in his renewal project, look forward to a golden age—though an age predicated on violence. The importance of these stories for Augustus himself is seen particularly in their employment in the Basilica Aemilia friezes in the Roman Forum. But whereas friezes like those in the Basilica Aemelia and sculptural programs of the defeated nations in places like Pompey's theater and Augustus's Hall of the Nations literally freeze this imagery and work to foreclose certain types of interpretations. The written works display ambivalences and fissures that cannot be foreclosed despite attempts to frame them in particular ways. Here, I would like to recall some of the details of the Rhea Silvia and Sabines stories explored in chapter 1, keeping in mind that the Sabines narrative functions as an aetiology not only for Roman marriage but for Roman conquest, triumph, and war-enforced peace.

Livy's narratives, most likely the earliest version of the myths explored in chapter 1, are probably the most ambivalent. For example, he speaks of Rome's founding as bound by fate, saying that the "great city" and "mightiest of empires" was "second only to that of the gods" (1.4.1). And yet, in almost the same breath, he expresses a type of compassion for Rhea Silvia and the violence perpetrated against her, whether Numitor's violence and crimes against her or those from perhaps Mars, as he says that "neither gods nor men protected [Rhea Silvia] herself or her children from the king's cruelty" (1.3.10–4.4). This holds true for Livy's version of the Sabine's story. Livy implies that the Romans' acts are "justified" because of their "longing and love" (1.9.16) for the abducted women and that the abduction is really the fault of their parents due to their "arrogance" and refusal to grant the Romans the right to intermarry (1.9.14). These justifications notwithstanding, Livy still refers to the Romans' act as an "injury" against their neighbors (1.3.1). Despite these ambivalences, the overall force of Livy's narrative of the Sabines is directed toward the privileges of Roman marriage for the abducted women (fellowship, citizenship, and progeny) (1.9.14)[25] and their embodiment of the Roman virtue of *concordia*[26]—statuses gained through an acquiescing to both the gender and colonial power differentials.

This trend can also be seen in Dionysius of Halicarnassus, where this ambivalence is seen more between the tellings of the Rhea Silvia and Sabines stories than within them individually. His telling of Rhea

25. See Treggiari, *Roman Marriage*, 4–5.
26. See Brown, "Livy's Sabine Women."

Silvia's story is fairly unequivocal in terms of the actions against her: he names the violence against the "slave girl," which was most likely perpetrated by a "suitor carried away by his love" or by Amulius, her plotting uncle, whose "purpose was to destroy her quite as much as to satisfy his desire." If it was indeed Mars who raped her, Dionysius refers to the result of his act simply as her "misfortune," calling him "the violator" (DH 1.76–77) Dionysius names the aggression against Ilia as such.

When it comes to the Sabines, however, Dionysius appears not only forgiving but encouraging of Romulus's actions: Romulus's force is justified due to necessity, endorsed by Numitor and the Senate, and was a violence without wantonness (DH 2.30.2). Dionysius seems to praise the Romans as he emphasizes that they did not violate the virgins in the night following their seizure (DH 2.30.4). Romulus then assures the women in their "despair" (this word Dionysius's only hint that there might be treachery involved) that the Romans seek only marriage, telling them that their seizure is an illustrious and ancient Greek custom of marriage (DH 2.30.5). The measuredness of Dionysius is transferred to the neighboring cities as well, for while some were enraged, others understood the Romans' reasoning and acted with moderation (DH 2.32.1).

Prior to the Sabines story, Dionysius has discussed, again with praise, the marriage laws enacted by Romulus. Central to these laws were that husband and wife were to share in all possessions and that the union was indissoluble (DH 2.25). Dionysius writes, "This law forced both the married women, having no other recourse or refuge, to conform themselves entirely to the temper of their husbands, and the husbands to rule their wives as necessary and inseparable property" (DH 2.25.4). If she was "moderate" and "obedient," a wife could expect to be a mistress (κυρία), as her husband was lord, and to be included in inheritance should he die. But if she did any "wrong the one wronged was her judge and entitled to decide the degree of her punishment" (DH 2.25.6). Other wrongs, such as committing adultery and drinking wine, were judged by her kin along with her husband: Romulus allowed both of these to be penalized by death (2.25.6). Throughout time, these offenses continued to be "met with merciless severity," but the "merits" of the law were great that no marriage was dissolved during a five-hundred and twenty year span in Rome (DH 2.25.7). Dionysius's overly laudatory framing of these displays of power and violence belie an uneasiness—an uneasiness that is clearly displayed in the unambiguous framing of the Rhea Silvia episode.[27]

This uneasiness is echoed in Plutarch's writings from a century later, where he introduces the Sabines narrative by assuring his readers, as did Dionysius, that the Romans' act was one not of wantonness but of necessity: the Romans have, in fact, honored the women as they carried them off (*Rom.* 9.4). This becomes a refrain as Plutarch repeats this in *Rom.* 14.6, stating again that the Romans "did not commit the rape out of wantonness, nor even with a desire to do mischief, but with the fixed purpose of uniting and blending the two people in the strongest bonds." These characterizations of Romulus and the Romans occur in stark contrast to the words Plutarch places in the mouths of the Sabine women as they enter the battlefield, placing their bodies between their warring fathers and husbands. Here the women implore, "have we done terrible or painful things to you, that we must suffer in the past, and must still suffer now, such cruel evils?" then unequivocally declare, "We were violently and lawlessly ravished away by those who now possess us" (*Rom.* 9.3).[28] With the Sabine women's words, the nature of the incident is reframed, emphasizing those aspects which it seems Plutarch wants to elide through his justification of the Romans' actions.

Plutarch's uneasiness is seen even more clearly in his comparison of Romulus and Theseus. Theseus's acts of rape are characterized as "transgressions," having "insufficient motive." Plutarch admonishes Theseus for taking too many women for his own use, and some when

27. This uneasiness may also point to an underlying double standard in the treatment of insiders (i.e. Rhea Silvia) versus outsiders (the Sabines)—though this in also interesting given Dionysius's status as a foreign Greek in Rome.
28. Plutarch does have them continue, exhibiting in many ways Livy's emphasis on *concordia*, as they women admonish their kin for their slow response to the Romans, with whom they are now bonded, then beg their kinsmen and husbands to cease their fighting (*Rom.* 19.4-5).

he was too old (*T&R* 6.1), also suspecting that Theseus's rapes are committed out of lust (ἡδονή) and wantonness (ὕβρις) (*T&R* 6.2). But when Plutarch turns to Romulus's rapes,[29] using the same language to justify his actions as in the story of the Sabines, his conclusions oppose those regarding Theseus:

> First, Romulus, although he carried off nearly eight hundred women, took them not all to wife, but only one, as they say, Hersilia, and distributed the rest among the best of the citizens. And second, by the subsequent honor, love, and just treatment given to these women, he made it clear that his deed of violence and injustice was a most honorable achievement, and one most adapted to promote political partnership. (Plutarch, *T&R* 6.2)

Theseus's acts of rape are judged harshly, while Romulus's are justified. Much of this seems to pivot on what constitutes dishonorable actions versus acceptable motives and honorable treatment of the women.[30] While it may be possible to follow Plutarch's logic in terms of his justification of the Romans, these types of juxtapositions strain the narrative, exposing the cracks and ruptures inherent in his text.

Whether seen as good, bad, or dangerous, the stories themselves also point to the ways in which the women in these narratives are active participants in their worlds and ultimately display some measure of control and self-possession of their bodies. The Sabine women use their bodies in an act of both defiance of and resistance to their husbands and fathers—they place themselves in the field of battle, making the best decision they can envision, for themselves and their children, in a horrific situation. By saving their husbands and fathers, they act on their own behalf in the best way they possibly can.

Lucretia's act, as well as Ilia's in the *Amores*, may be seen as even more controversial. While it is appalling on many levels to think that suicide was her only recourse, it is a denial of her personhood to refuse to acknowledge this as an act of self-possession as well. No one had forced this suicide upon her. It was her own choice. In the aftermath of violation, after the failure to be given a choice regarding the integrity

---

29. The word ἁρπάζω is used to describe both Theseus's and Romulus's actions (*T&R* 6.1–2).
30. Plutarch, *T&R* 6.2; *Rom.* 9.2; 19.6; 20.3.

of her own body, after not only being raped but threatened with deception and lies, deciding what to do with her body, even if that choice is death, might have been a way to regain control, might have been a way to end the torrent of pain.

As much as the texts attempt to foreclose these interpretational possibilities, they cannot be muted. While the Sabine women were supposed to signify the acquiescent side of *concordia*, they also embody courage, willfulness, and independence. While Lucretia's suicide is supposed to represent loyalty to family, chastity, and country, it can also represent a reclamation of self in the wake of possession by another. The texts may attempt to contain the women portrayed, but these women and the possibilities for reading them are not bound by the texts.

Whether intentional or not, all of these narratives, textual and visual, point to the paradox that the *Pax Romana* is predicated on violence, and that this interdependence makes for an uneasy and always precarious peace, a peace that is shot through and upheld with violence in much the same way as the Ara Pacis sits in the Field of Mars. Each shows how the use of violence, no matter how it is justified and for what ends, is part of an unending cycle of destruction, consolidation, and creation, each often existing in the same moment but viewed and experienced in extremely different ways depending on one's relationship to it. These multivalent aspects of violence create space, create fissures, where the texts are opened to ways of reading that ultimately allow their own undoing, while also encouraging others to appropriate these stories to create and voice opposite results.

These types of strategies can be seen both in the rape of Eve narrative and in the texts in which they are embedded. As discussed particularly in chapter 4, all three of the narratives draw on the thought-resources of their time and culture. Constructs like the *paterfamilias* and the Roman household are employed to shape the function of the divine realm, particularly in the Secret Revelation of John; virtues such as truth, justice, partnership, and concord are upheld. But at the same time the texts advocate for an idealized notion of these constructs and virtues. Just as Adam and Eve see clearly after eating the fruit and are no longer "blind" like the rulers, so too the Secret Revelation of John, the Reality of the Rulers and On the Origin of the World see clearly these structures and virtues and the ways in which Yaldabaoth's world embodies their corrupt counterparts. The texts lay bare the false claim that the empire of earth is "divinely" ordained: Yaldabaoth and his minions are neither gods nor legitimate rulers as he declares. In a world where, as the *Metamorphoses* and the Genesis cosmogonies illustrate, men can become gods and gods can act like fools, where the paragon of all that is virtuous fails to embody this virtue, the logic of the whole system begins to collapse upon itself.

At the same time, by drawing on these resources, the cosmogonies at times seem to embody that which they critique. Despite their strong critique of the rulers, an underlying ambivalence persists in the stories of Eve's rape as well. It is clear, when one looks at the overall schemas of the Genesis retellings, that even though the divine household does not function to the same hierarchically gendered extent as the traditional Roman *paterfamilias*, each of the texts still includes a Father-God who remains the sovereign patron who authorizes what happens below him. In SRJ, this is particularly apparent where the divine emanations need to ask permission before creating. This dynamic also arises in the Father/Son construct that, though minimal, is evoked at critical moments that clearly place the male line on top.

More specifically, this can be seen both in Eve's rape and in the ways that she recedes from each of the three texts in particular ways despite her pivotal and vital role. In each of the texts, Eve is subject to the rulers' violation and to her own dissociation. While the insights of the texts in terms of the psychological processes of violence, dissociation as resistance, and their insistence on naming the rulers' acts as evil remain crucial, these insights compete with the suggestion, seen specifically in RoR and OnOrig,[31] that this violence is a trickstery joke: Eve laughs at the rulers' blindness as they rape their own creation, condemning themselves. There is nothing in the texts that applauds

---

31. See chapter 3 regarding the "splitting" of Eve in SRJ.

the rulers for their actions, but this separation of the material from the spiritual carries with it a sense that the rape of Eve's body is somehow a lesser act of violence than if they had raped the spiritual Eve. This same sense of "humor" is often read into the Daphne and Syrinx tales, where the predatory gods are seen as bumbling and ultimately fail to grasp their prey. But little appears humorous as the text makes the spiritual Eve appear indifferent to her material counterpart.

Eve is also overshadowed in ways related to Adam and the birth their children. In SRJ, she can be read as simply existing in relationship to Adam, a conduit for his children. Both BG and Codex II emphasize this, with BG stating, "He knew *his* essence which is like *him*. Adam begot Seth," and Codex II saying, "When *Adam* knew the likeness of *his own* foreknowledge, *he* begot the likeness of the Child of the Human; *he* called him Seth."[32] In these lines, Eve is almost entirely written out of the parallel in Genesis 4:25 LXX on which they are based: "And Adam knew his wife Eve, and after she conceived, she bore him a son and she named him Seth, saying, 'God has raised up for me another seed in place of Abel, whom Cain killed.'" This erasure seems to occur so that Adam's begetting of Seth follows the pattern of begetting in the divine realm—one where begetting is done by a male father.[33] In OnOrig, after Adam and Eve eat from the tree and are cursed, she is referred to only once simply as "his woman/wife."[34] The only time Eve's children with Adam are mentioned is many manuscript pages later where the text says, "a multitude of beings had come into being through him, who had been formed from matter."[35] While Adam at least gets a generative nod, and somehow seems to conceive and birth these multitudes on his own, Eve is nowhere to be found.

At first glance, RoR seems slightly less ambivalent than SRJ and OnOrig, as Eve has a continued presence in at least a portion of the text. Adam "knew his woman/wife. *She* became pregnant again and gave birth to Abel."[36] Then, after Abel is killed by Cain, RoR, like SRJ,

---

32. SRJ BG 62.12–13 // II 24.35–36 // IV 38.25–27. See the discussion in chapter 3.
33. See the discussion in chapter 3.
34. OnOrig 121.5.
35. OnOrig 123.34–124.1.

follows Genesis 4:24 closely, saying, "Adam knew his *partner* (ϣⲃⲣⲉⲓⲛⲉ) *Eve*, and *she* became pregnant and bore [Seth] to Adam. And *she* said, '*I* have given birth to [another] person through God, in place of Abel'"[37]—retaining an active role in the text. She continues as the protagonist: "Eve became pregnant again, and she gave birth to [Norea]. And she said, 'He has produced for me a virgin to help many human generations.'"[38] Just as the voice from Incorruptibility came to help Adam, now Norea, from Eve, will come to help the human race.[39]

But beyond this, RoR displays a deep ambivalence as well. When the rulers witness the fiery power of Norea, they once again find an object for their desire. They tell her that her mother came to them—which, of course, she did not—but Norea, seemingly defending her, turns to them and says, "You are the rulers of darkness! You are accursed!" And then, in an act of the material Eve's denial she continues, "And you did not know my mother! It was your female counterpart that you knew for I am not from you! I come from the world above!" The last time Eve's name is uttered is through the mouths of the rulers who tell the daughter who denied her, "You must be a slave to us, as your mother, Eve, was." Finally, Norea is so threatened that she is forced to call for help, and for the first time in the text it is a male who is a savior.[40]

The Secret Revelation of John, the Reality of the Rulers, and On the Origin of the World name both the violence and hierarchical power structures that unwittingly seep into other parts of their narratives, exposing the ways in which violence and power shatter as well as the difficulties of disentangling their effects. These are texts that confront rape and power in a world where certain people, both men and women, were considered legitimately rapable, enslavable, conquerable. But, as the Roman narratives struggle unsuccessfully to *mask* the force of violence *they contain*, SRJ, RoR, and OnOrig struggle, at times

---

36. RoR 91.13–14.
37. RoR 91.30–33.
38. RoR 91.34–92.2.
39. See the discussion in chapter 3.
40. RoR 92.14–93.6. See the discussion in chapter 3 and the Epilogue.

unsuccessfully, *against* the force of the violence *they confront*, unintentionally reifying it.

While this reading of these three Genesis cosmogonies is technically valid, it is also both simplified and partial. For though it is true that the trickstery, spiritual Eve may abandon her fleshy counterpart, there is no equivocation about the nature of the rulers' act, a heinous act, which they ultimately perpetrate against themselves in their blindness and ignorance. The fleshy and material humans are never abandoned by the divine realm, but the divine keeps intervening on humanity's behalf: they are not left to the malice of the rulers. In fact, Foresight, Wisdom, Life, Eve, and Insight are constantly reaching out, displaying anything but indifference for material creation. The same is true of the Father, Son, Eleleth, and the Self-Generated One—though their actions are far less frequent and often remote.

Conclusion: Eve in the Aftermath

Eve in many ways embodies the complexities inherent in these larger stories themselves. Though she is able to regain something lost after her violence, she does not become what she was before her rape. Though she eats the fruit from the tree, she does not experience a return to some pure, unadulterated self. She becomes an amalgam of the material and spiritual, she inhabits her soul-stuff. It is not as if the violence and violation did not occur, but, by taking in all of the pieces that have been shattered, she has the ability to see, as if for the first time. She has enough space within her to harbor the magnitude of her experience, to begin to contact it with the support of the resources at hand. She is marked by the violation, but all she *is* is not collapsed into that one moment, that one experience. Her eating of the fruit constitutes not a fall but an opening, an opening to the possibility of seeing what has happened to her, of integrating it into her larger world, and living in that world by using that hard-won and painful knowledge. That knowledge, in turn, holds the possibility of changing into something new, holds the possibility of a becoming.

Here Eve finds "voice" not through speech—as she did earlier when she literally speaks Adam into the world of the living—but through her actions. It is through her sexuality, through her material body, through the pleasure of eating; it is through the recognition of herself in another, her recognition of another in herself, through her act of loving Adam, and Adam loving her back, that she expresses the return of her violated voice. Just as the process of the becoming of the world has been an expression of, a dialogical process between the divine and material worlds, so too Eve is an embodied expression of this complex and dialogical process between the divine and the material.

The weaving of the divine and material through the union of Eve and Adam expresses a truly remarkable feature of these texts: that much of their resistance to the violent power dynamics of the rulers is expressed through sexuality itself. The mutual sexual relationship of Adam and Eve expresses the best of the divine realm—as the rape of rulers expresses the worst of the world. The texts frame Eve and Adam, in their amalgamous material form, as the true heirs to divinity, and their children as its saviors. There is no stigma attached to Eve after her rape—the only ones that her rape reflects upon are her rapists, the rulers. She has not been defiled. Unlike Lucretia, she is not forced to take her life out of shame; she has not been made rulers' permanent slave or subject. Unlike the Sabine women and the nations, she is not forced to live out her life with her rapists. Eve's persistence in reaching toward life, in eating the fruit and claiming her knowledge—both the horrific and the beautiful—allows her to pass this legacy on to her clear-seeing, truth-naming children—Seth and Norea.

Epilogue

The Eve of the Secret Revelation of John, the Reality of the Rulers, and On the Origin of the World has much to say about gender and violence—issues that continue to this day. So many are still shaped by and bear Eve's legacy today—that broader legacy that has demonized her and often relegated her to a place of subordination, sin, and dangerous sexuality, to shame and slander. Yet the stories of her rape speak of her survival, perseverance, and salvific power, transforming Eve's legacy. In view of the murkier, more promising, and more complex portrait of Eve found in these three texts, in this epilogue I turn to another Eve figure to reframe issues of gender, violence, and legacy in these textual traditions: Eve's own daughter, Norea. It is Norea who extends her mother's role as helper from "man" (*adam*) to the entire human race.

Norea is the virgin, the self-possessed one who, inheriting the experiences and insight of her mother, cannot be defiled and possessed by the rulers. Norea is the one who wields the same fiery breath as Life in Eleleth's teaching tale—a fiery breath that for Life binds Yaldabaoth. For Norea, this breath is an affirmation of her own life in the face of Noah's refusal. It is this same fiery breath that causes the rulers to desire her, but it is Norea who, in many ways, binds the rulers in their own world as she embodies the hard-won knowledge of her mother and refuses to play a role in the rulers' ongoing cycle of violence: Norea binds the rulers as she names and exposes them for who they are. Norea binds them as she says no to their violence, as she says no to her own violation and enslavement. It is Norea who stops the rulers as she, faced with the imminent threat of violence, dares to cry out with her power and ask God for help—Norea, who refuses to be silent, whose "I" is unafraid to ask questions, for she knows there are answers that others need to hear.[1] Norea is the embodiment of her mother's legacy.

As the spiritual Eve embodies and imbues Adam with the qualities of the divine realm, Norea embodies and imbues the qualities that the divine desires for humanity as a whole. She extends the insight of both the spiritual and material Eves, seeing the rulers for who they are and naming them as such. She refuses to participate in their cycle of violence; she refuses to be their slave—and she breaks the intergenerational violence the rulers attempt to foist upon her. In these ways, Norea refuses humanity's accommodation to the rulers, whose actions are always ultimately destructive; she refuses to be a part of the enslavement and imprisonment that mark humanity in the world under the rulers and refuses it in the reality of her life as well. She continues to bear the insight of the fruit her parents ate from the tree.

Even with this strong characterization, there are ambivalences that mark Norea's story, just as they do Eve's. Three aspects of Norea's story in particular are sites of this ambivalence. These aspects include Norea's status as a virgin, her denial of Eve as her mother, and her rescue by a male. While each of the critiques associated with these sites has merit, as with the other stories considered, these critiques are only some of the many interpretational possibilities for Norea's story. But these critiques are important to understand alongside the other meaning-making possibilities these sites hold in order to grasp the fullness of the position that Norea embodies.

Norea's Virginity

It is possible to read Norea's virginity as a reversal or corrective of the establishment of sexuality in RoR both by the rulers and through the

---

1. See RoR 91.34–93.13.

relationship between Adam and Eve. In this way, the focus on Norea's virginity could be read as a rejection of sexuality. Similarly, Norea's virginity can be read in contrast to the defilement of her mother, Eve, rendering a negative comparison between Norea's purity and Eve's defilement. Though Norea's status as a virgin is emphasized, to relate this status to sexual purity is an oversimplification.

One argument for the sexual purity of Norea can be made through her birth itself. While it is likely that Norea is one of the children born through the union of Adam and Eve, the text is not explicit on this point. Though it is explicitly stated that Adam and Eve both parent Seth, in terms of Norea the text simply says, "Eve became pregnant again and bore Norea." Next, mirroring Eve's words after the birth of Seth, who came "through God," Eve says, "He has produced for me a virgin [παρθένος] to help [βοήθεια] many human generations [γενεά]." It is possible that the "he" in "he has produced for me a virgin" refers to God rather than Adam, but God is also present at the birth of Seth, who is clearly a product of the union of Adam and Eve, so there is no reason to preclude Adam—that is, her birth through intercourse—from the birth of Norea as well.[2]

Beyond this ambiguity, attempts to argue in favor of sexual purity become more complex. This complexity can be seen in another important intratextual echo that occurs in Eve's statement surrounding Norea's birth. She says, "He has produced for me a virgin [παρθένος] to help [βοήθεια] many human generations."[3] The only other actor in the text signified as virginal is the "virgin [παρθενικόν] Spirit [πνεῦμα]" who dwells with Incorruptibility.[4] Though it is difficult to know if these two "Spirits" should be identified with each other, it is also "the Spirit" who is sent to inhabit Adam and transform him into an enlivened being.[5] The other actor signified by βοήθεια in RoR is the voice that comes from Incorruptibility.[6] The virgin Spirit and

2. See RoR 91.30–92.4, on Seth, Norea, and Norea's virginity. If God was the parent of Norea, this would make Norea a savior-sibling of Jesus.
3. RoR 91.35–92.2.
4. RoR 93.30.
5. RoR 88.10–15; 89.11–17.
6. RoR 88.18.

Incorruptibility are then connected directly to Norea, as she is told that "those of her race" will call the place where the virgin Spirit and Incorruptibility dwell together, "home."[7] The significance of παρθένος and βοήθεια, then, seems to be to identify Norea with both the Spirit and Incorruptibility—the use of them pointing toward Norea's relationship with these intermediaries of the divine realm rather than her sexual status.

Furthermore, after Eve declares, "He produced for me a virgin," the narrator adds a gloss to this: "She is the virgin whom the forces did not defile."[8] The text is very specific about what qualifies this virginity—it is not sexual purity per se but remaining undefiled by the forces. It seems that this does not apply only to Norea, since Eleleth extends this to the emporerless race when he tells Norea that "these authorities cannot defile you or that race, for your [pl.] home is with Incorruptibility, where the virgin Spirit dwells."[9] Moreover, the term *defile* applies not only to sexual impurity but also to pollution and ritual uncleanliness.[10] Pollution seems the most apt way to describe the rulers actions as they subject humanity to their maliciousness, violence, and lust, throwing "humanity into great distraction and a life of grief, so that their people might be devoted to the things necessary to stay alive and might not have the time to be occupied with the holy Spirit."[11] In this vein, while RoR names what the rulers do to Eve as defilement, Eve is never described by the texts as defiled—defilement is solely associated with the rulers.[12] The resistant Norea is undefiled *not* because she has remained sexually pure, but because she has found a way to maintain her integrity and not be seduced or led astray, despite the violence of the rulers and the constraints and malice constantly directed toward herself as well as toward humanity as a whole.[13]

Finally, the text speaks of Norea's children[14]—as Norea carries on

7. RoR 93.27–32.
8. RoR 92.1–2.
9. RoR 93.27–32.
10. Crum, 797b–798a.
11. RoR 91.7–11.
12. This dynamic around defilement is true of SRJ and OnOrig as well.
13. There are many ways in which I feel that the characterization of Norea here is extremely idealized—what about those for whom crying out for help does not work? What about those who,

the legacy of Eve, so too, Norea's children issue from this lineage of hard-won knowledge and resistance. There is no way to know if RoR is referring to biological children or if instead these children are to be thought of as simply spiritual. The text does not foreclose either of these options. If indeed these are Norea's biological children who carry her spiritual nature, her virginity is related more to her integrity—physical, psychic, and spiritual—than to her sexual status, and this may be the case whether she has biological children or not.

Norea's Denial of Eve

After witnessing Norea's display of fiery power, the rulers go to meet her and the Chief Ruler says, "Your mother Eve came to us," and Norea responds, "You are the rulers of darkness! You are accursed! And you did not know my mother, it was your female counterpart that you knew! For I am not from you, rather I come from the world above!"[15] On the one hand, it cannot be denied that this is a rejection of the material Eve, and in certain ways a denial of the violence done to her by the rulers. Norea's words resonate closely with the actions of the spiritual Eve. Like the spiritual Eve, Norea abandons her material counterpart in her hour of need. But the rulers' rape of Eve is also their conviction, as the violence they perpetrate reverberates back on themselves as they defile their own body made in their image. Norea knows what they have done to Eve, and she both convicts them by naming them the "rulers of darkness" and curses them as they had cursed the serpent, Eve, and Adam.

Again, with the questions surrounding Norea's birth, which the vagueness of the text invites, it is possible that it was the spiritual Eve who birthed a child with God rather than Adam If this were so, this would actually cast Eve, like Mary and Norea, as a Christ figure! But the text does not make this distinction and simply calls her Eve. Given the flow and continuity of the text, however, it could only be the material,

despite their internal integrity, still experience violence at the behest of individuals and systems? This is why Norea cannot exist without Eve, and why both hold places of importance within RoR.
14. RoR 96.19–31.
15. RoR 92.18–26.

or possibly a post-eating reintegrated spiritual/material Eve who gives birth to Norea.

It is possible to imagine that Norea makes a distinction about her mother for another reason: that Eve is indeed not the same person she was at the time of the rape. From a psychological perspective, there are two salient points. First, of course, Eve will not be the same Eve after experiencing the violence of the rulers—indeed, how could she be? Second, the Eve who was raped is also not the same Eve once she has eaten the fruit. As the serpent said, through eating, their eyes were opened, they came to know good and evil, and they realized that they had been stripped naked of the spiritual. This knowledge changed them. While these interpretations may seem unlikely, the text does not foreclose their possibility.

Norea's Rescue by Eleleth

When the rulers begin to act on their threats, Norea cries out to God for help: "Rescue me [βοηθέω] from these unjust rulers and rescue me from their hands! Now!"[16] Here, the one who was named as helper is forced to plead for help from the divine realm. Norea's cries are heard by the divine realm and the angel Eleleth appears. Upon hearing her cry, Eleleth says to her, "Why are you calling to God? Why are you so daring [τολμάω] toward the holy Spirit?"[17] Norea's cry for help and the subsequent response from a male deity could be read as a usurpation of Norea's power, reproducing ancient paradigms where the "lower" female appeals to the "higher" male above her in the family system for protection. This strategy can also be argued in RoR, where the Father appears, asserting his will in a text where the female actors do most of the work. But, again, this is not the only way to read the passage.

First, Norea does not appeal to a male for protection—she does not cry out for "Father," but for "God,"[18]—and it is noteworthy that the first time the title "God" is used in the text is in relation to the image

16. RoR 92.33–93.2.
17. RoR 93.4–6.
18. Though, of course, if we subscribe to one of the alternate readings of Norea's birth, "God" could actually be her father.

that appeared to the rulers in the waters, the image of Incorruptibility. Second, Norea has just destroyed Noah's boat because he will not let her aboard: Noah, a man, is refusing to save her. Third, Norea's "daring" and "boldness" (τολμάω) here are contrasted to the "daring" and "cruelty" (τολμάω) of the rulers, who want Norea to be their sexual slave.[19]

Norea's cry for help shows an acute awareness of the rulers' character and the danger they pose: the powerful ones who rule the world are threatening her with sexual violence. Additionally, asking for help, especially in the face of violence, is an act of bravery rather than helplessness. Admonishing both Norea for her appeals for help and the text for its recourse to a male deity, while attempting to lay bare patriarchal paradigms, inadvertently reinscribes them by appealing to modern, hyperindividualistic paradigms that fail to see the ways in which human beings are dependent on one another and on the wider world at all times. This assessment also fails to recognize what we know about sexual violence and intimate violence—that so often what occurs under its threat and in its wake is silence. Norea's cry for help is not an indication of her need for a male figure to intervene but a profound act of caring for herself.

In RoR, Norea embodies Eve's legacy and exhibits the lessons so hard-won by her mother. Even if one thinks that Norea denies the carnal Eve, there is no doubt that she has learned from her experience as she cries out for help as the rulers try to perpetuate their cycle of violence upon her. In all three of the texts, Norea follows in her mother's legacy by continuing to parent the spiritual line, the ones without an emperor, the immovable race. Like her mother, Eve, she is the complex amalgam of matter, spirit, and soul; she is a mediator between the worlds talking to and connecting with both. Norea is bold and brave and knows when to ask for help. Norea, like Eve, sees the world clearly and never refuses to name her truth.

---

19. RoR 92.29–30.

Women and Violence and Early Christ/Jesus Movements

It is evident from the extant literature that the Romans did have an idea about rape—most clearly seen in Roman legislation making it illegal to rape a citizen of the empire. Even so, this legal "protection" did not extend to others, including non-citizens and slaves.[20] In addition, as the story of the Sabine women illustrates and historical evidence substantiates, rape was both a tool and a "spoil" of Roman conquest.[21] Despite sources that point to the widespread occurrence of sexual violence—on both the individual and the state (particularly military) levels—early writings of the Jesus/Christ movements rarely engage the subject.

Two instances in which the subject of rape does arise are in the Acts of Paul and Thecla and the Act of Peter. In the Acts of Paul and Thecla, "violent young men" (ἄνδρας νεωτέρους σοβαρούς) are sent by the physicians in the city "to ruin" (ἐπὶ τὸ φθεῖραι) Thecla because "she has the power of healing" (44:1).[22] Thecla is made aware of this impending violation by God's foresight[23] and enters "into a rock, alive, and it descended under the earth," saving her (44:2). This is an instance where rape is threatened but completely thwarted; there is no splitting or dissociation, as the entirety of Thecla—body, spirit, and soul—enters the rock: nothing is left of her to be violated. In addition, Thecla is allowed to reemerge from this position, continuing her life, both body and spirit, into old age.

In the Act of Peter,[24] Peter's "virgin [παρθένος] daughter" is saved by the Lord as he paralyzes and withers one side of her body, thus protecting her from "defilement and pollution and destruction" (ⲉⲩⲥⲱⲱϥ ⲙⲛ ⲟⲩϫⲱϩⲙ ⲙⲛ ⲟⲩⲧⲉⲕⲟ) by a man who abducts her wanting marriage (132.11-19; 135.1-13[25]). Peter is harangued for not healing his daughter while he is healing strangers in a crowd. To prove his healing

20. Dixon, *Reading Roman Women*, 49–51.
21. See chapter 1.
22. "The Acts of Paul and Thecla," trans. Celene Lillie in *ANNT*.
23. προνοίᾳ δὲ θεοῦ. Here, as in SRJ and OnOrig, divine Foresight is a salvific agent.
24. The manuscript and line numbers for the Act of Peter refer to BG 8502.4.
25. Pages 133-34 are missing from the manuscript.

prowess, Peter heals his daughter and then later returns her to the paralyzed and withered state in which she began. Peter defends his actions to the crowd, saying that her state not only saved her from her would-be ravisher but that she is better off paralyzed and withered than tempting (σκανδαλίζω) men (132.10). Peter's justification, then, is not only to spare her the disgrace of being raped, defiled, and shamed,[26] but more so to prevent her beauty from tempting other men. It is not the men's responsibility to check their temptation, but rather his daughter's responsibility to remain undesirable.

These two tales of rape escaped, have certain resonances with the story of Eve's rape by the rulers, but they also disclose numerous differences. Thecla, much like the spiritual Eve in RoR and OnOrig who becomes/enters into the tree, escapes into a rock as she is warned beforehand of her impending fate. In contrast to the case of Eve, this is not an instance of the splitting of her spiritual and material aspects. Thecla's whole being—both her spiritual and material aspects—manages to escape her would-be rapists as she enters the rock alive and is protected by the earth.[27] Likewise, Peter's daughter, like the spiritual Eve, is technically saved by her form, but this time her form retains its humanness. In much the same manner as Daphne and Syrinx, Peter's daughter is trapped by her form[28] and this is what keeps her from being raped. Also like Daphne, who is used to adorn and glorify Apollo, and Syrinx, who is continually available for Pan to play, Peter's daughter is a tool to be used—she a tool to demonstrate her father's healing power.

In contrast to Eve's story in the three Genesis elaborations, the emphasis in the stories of Thecla and Peter's daughter is their insistence upon the chastity of these at-risk women. In the Act of Peter, the daughter's chastity trumps her paralysis. Nothing is said of trying to change the man or men who would violate her—why could Peter not have healed their violent and possessive lust rather than

26. As with the rape of Eve, the Act of Peter uses ϫⲱⲣ̄.
27. Here, as in Rev 12:16, "And the earth came to help the woman."
28. I acknowledge the difficulties both in the text and in this reading, particularly surrounding ablism and dominant notions of beauty, but I also do not want to lose sight of the fact that Peter's daughter is transformed because the men cannot control themselves.

healing, then unhealing, his daughter? Why is she, and not the men, held accountable for her violation? In Thecla, too, Thecla is forced to hide in a rock and be sucked into the earth—nothing is done to curb to violence of her would-be rapists or to prevent them from attempting this kind of violence again.

This is the striking difference between these stories and that of Eve. While there is horror in the fact that Eve is not saved from her rape, she is also not blamed or judged for it: it is an act done to her through no fault of her own. In the SRJ, RoR, and OnOrig, the responsibility always and unequivocally lies with the rapist/s, whether it is the Chief Ruler, rulers and authorities, or rulers, authorities, and angels. Neither Eve's beauty nor her power nor even her partnership with Adam is used as a justification of her rape. Conversely, neither the Acts of Paul and Thecla nor the Act of Peter addresses the issue of attempted rape or the issue of sexual violence. Rather, these texts focus on the salvation of chastity. Whereas the focus of the Genesis cosmogonies is on condemning the violence of the rulers and Eve's salvation through her healing after violation. For both Thecla and Peter's daughter, the the narrative points toward a fear not of the violation itself but of what these women might become or even how they might be labeled after it: marked as sullied, stained, or defiled. Eve is never labeled in this way—these attributes remain with the rulers. The texts do not categorize Eve differently after the rape, nor is she shamed—in fact, she goes on, through her mutual relationship with Adam, to birth saviors, thus not only participating in her healing as she eats from the tree, but participating in the salvation of humanity.[29] In comparing these examples, and there are scant few more,[30] it seems that the rape of Eve stories in the Genesis cosmogonies may be the primary, if not the only, early Jesus/Christ texts that attend specifically to the issue of violence against women.

29. Otherwise, as King has suggested to me (personal communication, March 7, 2013)—might it be that conversations of rape are elided through conversations of chastity, as can be seen in both the New Testament and other early writings of the movement.
30. See Stroumsa, *Another Seed*, 17–70, for anything that might approach the content of these texts. The closest approximations may be found in Tertullian; see, e.g. his *Address to the Martyrs* 4.1–4 and *Monogamy* 17.2, on Lucretia's postrape suicide as pious example.

Women, Captives, and Slaves: Life under the Rulers

The Secret Revelation of John, the Reality of the Rulers, and On the Origin of the World all place an important emphasis on the subjugation of humanity under the reign of the rulers. This subjugation is illustrated particularly through the rulers' rape of Eve and is most clearly and succinctly articulated in OnOrig, where humanity is subjugated (ὑποτάσσω) to the rulers as woman is subjugated (ὑποτάσσω) to man.[31] This subjugation is also illustrated in all three texts through their insistence that humanity exists in a state of slavery and bondage in relationship to the rulers.[32] In these texts, the categories of woman, slavery, and bondage all implicate one another, much as they do in the gendered imagery of Roman conquest and particularly in the speech of Calgacus.[33]

The idea of enslaved humanity is found in both the Hebrew Bible and the Christian Testament, from Exodus to Paul, not only reflecting the reality of those enslaved within the institution of slavery itself but the condition of peoples under the rule of foreign empires.[34] While

31. Orig.World 116.19–20, 24–25.
32. SRJ BG 55.10–13 // III 26.20–23 // II 21.9 // IV 32.22–26: "This is the bond. This is the tomb of the form of the body with which the robbers had clothed the human, the bond of forgetfulness." BG 69.5–13 // III 35.10–18 // II 27.4–10 // IV 42.1–9: (II) "After it [the soul] comes out of (the body), it is handed over to the authorities who came into being through the ruler, and they bind it in chains and cast it into prison and consort with it until it awakens from forgetfulness and receives knowledge." BG 72.4–7 // II 37.8–10 // III 28.29–31 // IV 44.16–19: (II) "And because of the fetter for forgetfulness their sins were hidden. For they are bound with measures and times and moments." II 30.4–7 // IV 45.13–16: "And thus the whole creation became enslaved forever, from the foundation of the world until now."II 31.8–10 // IV 48.11–13: "And he said, 'Who is it that calls my name, and from where has this hope come to me while I am in the bonds of prison?'"RoR 30.31: "You must be a slave to us as your mother Eve was." 96.30–31: "it will be revealed after three generations and free them from the authorities' error."OnOrig 113.4–5: "we shall make those born from the light our slaves for this entire age." See Williams, Rethinking "Gnosticism," 123.
33. Calgacus's speech: "Rapists of the world, now that the earth betrays their encompassing devastation, they ransack the sea. If the enemy is rich, they are greedy; if poor, they encircle them. Neither east nor west has satisfied them—they alone covet equally want and wealth. To rob, slaughter and rape they give the false name of empire; they make desolation, they call it peace. Children and kin are by nature each one's dearest possessions. They are snatched from us by conscription to be slaves elsewhere: our wives and sisters, even if they escape the enemy's wantonness, are violated in the name of friendship and hospitality. Our goods and fortunes go for tribute; our lands and harvests in requisitions of grain; our hands and bodies themselves are shattered through clearing forest and swamp in the midst of insult and lash. Those born into slavery are sold once and for all and moreover are fed by their masters, but Britannia pays for her enslavement daily and feeds the enslavers. And as in the household the newest among the slaves is a mockery to his fellow-slaves, so in a world long used to slavery, we, the newest and most worthless, are marked out for destruction" (Tacitus, Agricola 30.4–31.3).

SRJ, RoR, and OnOrig draw on these biblical resources, what is most striking is that they, in much the same way as the Roman sources, pair enslavement both with acts of violence against women and the subjugation of women. Unlike, for example, Jeremiah 3:1-9, Ezekiel 23:1-30, and Revelation 18, where the figure of the woman as whore represents the sinful constellation of idolatry, subjugation, foreign rule, and accommodation, in SRJ, RoR, and OnOrig this constellation is represented by the male rulers who fashion themselves as gods, just as the imperial rulers who actually rule the nations. The rape of Eve, attempted rape of Norea, and the rape of the daughters of men show these women to be the victims of this rule rather than symbols of it, removing the shame of violence from those who suffer it and locating it in its proper place with the perpetrators.

In this way, sexual violence, slavery, and bondage are connected, as in the Roman texts, but here they become part of a constellation that functions in *opposition* to the rulers. This is why RoR and OnOrig frame those who follow the example of the divine as members of the "king-less" or "emperor-less" race.[35] This designation, while not identical, connects with SRJ's use of the "immovable race" to signify those who follow in the footsteps of the divine. These "races"[36] are the ones who remain unmoved by the machinations and seduction of the rulers: the ones who are not beguiled by the precious metals and gifts of the rulers; the ones who are not anxious or led astray; and those unenslaved by the rulers.[37] Those who belong to this "race" are the ones not brought to distraction and mired in the toil and competition of daily life;[38] the ones not distracted or led astray by magic or potions, idol worship, spilling blood, altars, temples, sacrifices and libations offered to the daemons of the earth.[39] These immovable and kingless

---

34. Exodus; Deuteronomy; Ezra 9:6–9; Isa 49:7; Ezek 34:27; Wis 1:4; Rom 8:21–22; Gal 4:3, 8–9; Philemon; Rev 18:1–13.
35. RoR 97.4; OnOrig 125.2; 125.6; 127.14.
36. For a discussion of the designation of race in the ancient world, see Denise Eileen McCoskey, *Race: Antiquity and Its Legacy* (New York: Oxford University Press, 2012); and Denise Kimber Buell, *Why This New Race: Ethnic Reasoning in Early Christianity* (New York: Columbia University Press, 2005).
37. RoR II 29.30–30.7; cf. SRJ BG 72.11–75.10.
38. RoR 91.3–11.
39. OnOrig 123.4–15.

ones are those who act in accordance with the ethics of the divine realm, rather than blindly following the way of the rulers.

While SRJ, RoR, and OnOrig all point to the ways in which humanity can resist the violent machinations of the rulers, one of their failings is that they cannot quite fully imagine a place on earth where the dynamics that are signified by the rulers cease to exist—thus participating in, inscribing, and reinscribing the spectacles of sexual violence, subjugation, imprisonment, and bondage.[40] So how might one reimagine a reality that seems to be and is presented and experienced as omnipresent? It is this violent, oppressive, and exploitative reality or orientation to it that I believe elicits the associations of life enfleshed with violence, slavery, and imprisonment. When bodies are held captive by the systems that surround them, it makes sense that their metaphors are those of constraint.

In SRJ, RoR, and OnOrig, the way out is not able to fully occur within the world itself,[41] but, in spite of this, these texts do not negate the world. This investment in the world is seen in all of the texts through their insistence on right action—OnOrig specifically ends with the words, "Indeed, by their actions [πρᾶξις] and their knowledge each one will make their origin known" (127.16–17). As noted in chapter 4, I think the word *praxis* here is telling, πρᾶξις being the Greek translation of *res gestae*—the title used to evoke the deeds of the great emperors and generals. While this praxis or right action is not laid out in overt terms, it is presented explicitly through the rulers' actions of subjugation, sexual violence, enslavement, and bondage—the rulers the exemplars of what *not* to do.

Women as Saviors

While a Father-God[42] may lie at the top of the hierarchical pyramid of

---

40. See Wendy S. Hesford, "Reading Rape Stories: Material Rhetoric and the Trauma of Representation," *College English* 62.2 (1999): 192–221.
41. BG 64.13–69.13 // III 32.22–35.18 // II 25.16–27.11 // IV 39.16–42.10; RoR 96.32–97.21; OnOrig 125.23–127.14.
42. Though Mother-Father (μητροπάτωρ is used in SRJ II 5.6; 6.16; 14.19; 19.17; 20.9; 27.23 and IV parallels.

the divine realm, "he"[43] is often overshadowed by the greater part of the salvific action that is initiated by the female actors—whether from the divine realm or the human. Even where the texts seem to rely on male savior figures, these instances are often coupled with the female presence:[44] In SRJ, the Savior is identified with and is Foresight;[45] in RoR, Eve causes Adam to rise through her speech;[46] the intercession of Eleleth comes at Norea's bold request, and his intervention does not strip her of her important place in the salvific plan.[47] While the "child/son" may be "over all things" the child is also "with everyone," and this is a generation "without king."[48] In OnOrig, although the "word" λόγος/ⲋⲁϫⲉ is associated with the immortal human[49] and the one "exalted above everyone,"[50] Faith-Wisdom brings the principle of the creative word into the world,[51] the word by which Sabaoth, the child of Yaldaboath, repents.[52] As in RoR, the word of Eve "becomes a work," and she causes Adam to arise;[53] and Eve has "confidence in the words of the instructor," so she and Adam eat from the tree and become enlightened.[54] Especially with the association between the manifestation of speech in both RoR and OnOrig, these female saviors, along with Wisdom, who is described in both of these texts as the curtain or veil, are clearly the mediators between the divine and material realms, as are Insight and Foresight in SRJ. This makes them comparable not only

---

43. The gendered conception of God, the holy invisible Spirit of SRJ, to my mind, is left up for grabs in particular ways as It (to use King's pronoun) is described in an apophatic manner in relation to what It is not and the beings that emanate from him can be viewed as amalgams of male and female, and as eschewing gender through their androgyny as well. They clearly inhabit a place of gender ambiguity/ambivalence. This ambiguity seems to be less present in the conception of the Father-God in RoR and OnOrig, but the texts spend little time meditating on the nature of the Father-God.
44. As I have consistently argued throughout this study, the mere presence of male figures cannot be uncritically equated with patriarchy.
45. SRJ II 30.11–31.31 // IV 47.23–49.13; cf. II 23.26–31 // IV 36.2–29.
46. RoR 89.11–17.
47. RoR 92.33–93.6.
48. RoR 97.13–21. These are Norea's children.
49. OnOrig 117.9–11.
50. OnOrig 125.14–19, identified here with a quotation from Mark 4:22 // Matt 10:26 // Luke 8:17; 12:2 // Thomas 5:2; 6:5–6.
51. OnOrig 100.1–18.
52. OnOrig 103.32–104.10.
53. OnOrig 115.36–116.5.
54. OnOrig 119.6–18.

to Wisdom as mediator in the Wisdom tradition but also to the Logos of the Gospel of John.

Despite the fact that some hierarchical patterns remain in place, they are of an order highly different from those espoused within the cultural and social status quo. While the Father, Christ, and the son/child are present in various ways, they are not the sole, or even the primary, conduit for salvation—indeed without the salvific powers of the female actors they could not play their part. The co-creative process so clearly related as the basis of the divine realm in SRJ is integral to the fabric of the co-creative process of salvation in the world. It is only through acting together in harmony with one another that salvation can be achieved. This is the mark of a nonpatriarchal paradigm. Again, it is not that there is no patriarchal residue present, but patriarchy is not the model or mode for which the texts are striving. In this model, power is not wielded and exercised from above but, instead, is authorized and granted in conjunction with those below, creating parity among all levels of the divine and human realms.[55]

This design provides a sharp contrast to a model of the household code management that undergirds the pastoral epistles' conceptions of both the divine and mortal families.[56] While this reading of the divine realm and its structure may be overly optimistic, King's poignant point of the operation of parody and the leakage of critique into the divine realm through Wisdom's actions, as well as the ways in which sexuality leaks upward into the divine realm, point to these types of interpretational possibilities in the texts.[57] If this type of leakage occurs in some areas, where else might it be possible? If the critique leveled by these texts is seen as a simple critique of the rulers and their power structures and if the egalitarian impulses of the texts are not seriously engaged as well, I believe we miss the point.

---

55. See Ta-Nehisi Coates, "The Myth of Police Reform," *The Atlantic Monthly,* April 15, 2015, www.theatlantic.com/politics/archive/2015/04/the-myth-of-police-reform/890057/ for his understanding of the difference between power and authority.

56. See chapter 4.

57. See King, "Reading Sex."

The Secret Revelation of John, the Reality of the Rulers, and On the Origin of the World all engage issues of gender, slavery, and bondage and the ways in which they are part and parcel of the imperial system of conquest, domination, and rule. As the Roman mythologies and ideologies unmistakably illustrate, gender subordination, ethnic subordination, and imperial colonialism are all embedded with and predicated upon one another. This is not to say that the Genesis cosmogonies address these issues perfectly, without ambivalence and without recourse to their social and cultural milieus, but they engage head-on the issues of deception, violence, and subordination—the very themes that come together and are highlighted in the Sabines narrative.

This is a salvation that comes not through a single male or Christ figure, or through a Father who acts alone, but through the totality of beings, female and male and genders in-between, who act in harmony with one another as they strive together for a more just world. In this way, these texts are not only about the subjugation of women, but confront the ways in which all of humanity—indeed all of creation—is violated and enslaved by the rulers. These are texts that point toward notions of collective salvation—just as the divine realm gets bound up in Wisdom's deficiency and creation of the material world, so too together they enact her and the world's salvation.

Healing and Salvation, Christ and Eve

Toward the end of the Gospel of John the disciples are found locked in a room, fearing that they too will face the fate of Jesus. Into this locked room, the risen Christ appears, and after he greets the disciples with the word "Peace," he bears the scars on his body for all to see. Though he has been resurrected, the reminder of his crucifixion at the hands of the rulers and authorities has not been erased; his disciples know it is Jesus because he knowingly bears the marks of the violence he has suffered. By acknowledging and baring his scars, not only he but also his followers move forward into new life—not a life as it was before but a life lived with the knowledge of all that has happened.

Through his resurrection, Jesus does not return to his former self, and the scars he continues to bear prove this. But, despite a death meant to penetrate and shame, Christ does not hold on to the shame of his violation. Instead he bears witness to the violence he endured and calls on his community to do the same.

As Christ, Eve is forced to bear violence that is meant to penetrate and shame, but neither does she hold the shame of her violation. She, too, is marked by the violence done against her, her spirit splitting from her body, and her body subjected to sexual violence. While Eve gains knowledge and insight in the wake of this violence—not a pleasant, easy, or trite knowledge but a deeply painful one—this knowledge does not erase the violence done but produces the possibility of facing it and creating space for something new.

As OnOrig's description of Eve's rape is the most detailed—and brutal—of the three texts, its description of her transformation after eating the fruit is also the most vivid. In the midst of her vicious violation, Eve shatters, her spirit rending herself from her body. But this part of her that has splintered from her being has not left her. Eve believes the words of the instructor, who is herself; she eats from the tree, who is herself; and then she shares this knowledge of herself with her partner, Adam. They become enlightened, knowing the difference between those who are good and those who are evil; and, while the text says they feel shame, it is not a shame brought on by violation but one in which they understand their ignorance and how easy it would be to follow in the footsteps of the rulers. But, because of this understanding, instead of reproducing the violent and subjugating relationship the rulers try to foist upon them, they become sober and love each other. They see the rulers for who they are and what they do, and they know much.

Eve's spirit continues to return and to help her—and not only her but her partner as well. Somehow in the midst of the shattering of her self, she has not abandoned herself, and this is because she is not shamed by the violence done to her. Shame is never brought upon her from the outside: not by the divine, not by Adam, and not by the text—they have not abandoned her either. While Eve cannot be the same—how could she be?—her scattered pieces keep getting drawn together. That part of her, that inviolable part of her, remains with her. Eve enters into a new relationship with herself, continually facing into her shattered self. And, while this relationship is born from the violence done to her, it is also the relationship that refuses to give this violence the final word.

Works Consulted

Adler, Eric. "Boudica's Speeches in Tacitus and Dio." *CW* 101.2 (2008): 173–95.

Ahl, Frederick. *Metaformations: Soundplay and Wordplay in Ovid and Other Classical Poets.* Ithaca, NY: Cornell University Press, 1985.

Albertson, Fred C. "The Basilica Aemilia Frieze: Religion and Politics in Late Republican Rome." *Latomus*, T.49, Fasc. 4 (1990): 801–15, esp. 806–9.

____. *Mars and Rhea Silvia in Roman Art.* Brussels: Latomus, 2012.

Alcock, Susan E. "The Reconfiguration of Memory in the Eastern Roman Empire." In *Empires: Perspectives from Archaeology and History,* edited by Susan E. Alcock, Terence N. D'Altroy, Kathleen D. Morrison, and Carla M. Sinopoli, 323–50. New York: Oxford University Press, 2001.

Alexander, Philip S. "The Fall into Knowledge: The Garden of Eden/Paradise in Gnostic Literature." In *A Walk in the Garden: Biblical, Iconographical, and Literary Images of Eden,* edited by Paul Morris and Deborah Sawyer, 91–104. Journal for the Study of the Old Testament: Supplement Series 136. Sheffield: JSOT Press, 1992.

Allen, Graham. *Intertextuality.* New Critical Idiom. New York: Routledge, 2000.

Althusser, Louis. *Lenin and Philosophy and Other Essays.* Translated by Ben Brewster. New York: Monthly Review Press, 1971.

Anderson, William S. *Ovid's Metamorphoses: Books 1-5.* Norman: University of Oklahoma Press, 1997.

Ando, Clifford. *Imperial Ideology and the Provincial Loyalty in the Roman Empire.* Classics and Contemporary Thought 6. Berkeley: University of California Press, 2000.

Arieti, James A. "Rape and Livy's View of Roman History." In *Rape in Antiquity:*

Sexual Violence in the Greek and Roman Worlds, edited by Susan Deacy and Karen F. Pierce, 209–29. London: Duckworth, 2002.

Arthur, Rose Horman. *The Wisdom Goddess: Feminine Motifs in Eight Nag Hammadi Documents.* Lanham, MD: University Press of America, 1984.

Asad, Talal. *On Suicide Bombing.* Wellek Library Lectures. New York: Columbia University Press, 2007.

Assmann, Jan. *Cultural Memory and Early Civilization: Writing, Remembrance, and Political Imagination.* 1st English ed. New York: Cambridge University Press, 2011.

Balsley, K. "Truthseeking and Truthmaking in Ovid's *Metamorphoses* 1.163–245." *Law and Literature* 23.1 (2011): 48–70.

Barc. Bernard. *L'Hypostase des Archontes: Traité gnostique sur l'origine de l'homme du monde et des archontes.* Bibliothèque Copte de Nag Hammadi, Section "Textes" 5. Louvain: Peeters, 1980.

____. "Samaèl—Saklas—Yaldabaôth: Recherche sur la genèse d'un myth gnostique." In *Colloque international sur les textes de Nag Hammadi,* edited by Bernard Barc, 123–50. Quebec: Presses de L'Université Laval, 1981.

____. "La taille cosmique d'Adam dans la literature juive rabbinique des trois premiers siècles après Jésus-Christ." *Revue des Sciences Religieuses* 49 (1975): 173–85.

Barc, Bernard, and Louis Painchaud. "La réécriture de l'Apocryphon de Jean à la lumière de l'hymne final de la version longue." *Le Muséon* 112 (1999): 317–33.

Barnard, Mary E. *The Myth of Apollo and Daphne from Ovid to Quevedo: Love, Agon, and the Grotesque.* Durham, NC: Duke University Press, 1987.

Barton, Carlin A. *Roman Honor: The Fire in the Bones.* Berkeley: University of California Press, 2001.

____. "Savage Miracles: The Redemption of Lost Honor in Roman Society and the Sacrament of the Gladiator and the Martyr." *Representations* 45 (1994): 41–71.

____. *The Sorrows of the Ancient Romans: The Gladiator and the Monster.* Princeton, NJ: Princeton University Press, 1993.

Beard, Mary. "Re-Reading (Vestal) Virginity." In Women in Antiquity: New Assessments, edited by Richard Hawley and Barbara Levick, 166–77. London: Routledge, 1995.

_____. *The Roman Triumph.* Cambridge, MA: Belknap Press of Harvard University Press, 2007.

_____. "The Sexual Status of Vestal Virgins." *Journal of Roman Studies* 70 (1980): 12–27.

Beard, Mary, John North, and Simon Price. *Religions of Rome.* Vol. 1, *A History.* New York: Cambridge University Press, 1998.

Benjamin, Jessica. *The Bonds of Love: Psychoanalysis, Feminism, and the Problem of Domination.* New York: Pantheon Books, 1988.

Bergoffen, Debra B. *Contesting the Politics of Genocidal Rape: Affirming the Dignity of the Vulnerable Body.* Routledge Research in Gender and Society 29. New York: Routledge, 2012.

Bethge, Hans-Gebhard. *"Vom Ursprung der Welt." Die fünfte Schrift aus Nag-Hammadi Codex II neu herausgegeben und unter bevorzugter Auswertung anderer Nag-Hammadi-Texte erklärt.* Theological Dissertation. Berlin, 1975.

Bhabha, Homi K. *The Location of Culture.* New York: Routledge, 1994.

Boatwright, Mary T. "Women and Gender in the Forum Romanum." *TAPA* 141.1 (2011): 105–41.

Böhlig, Alexander, and Pahor Labib. *Die koptische-gnostische Schrift ohne Titel aux Codex II von Nag Hammadi.* Deutsche Akademie der Wissenschaften zu Berlin, Institut für Orientforschung 58. Berlin: Akademie-Verlag, 1962.

Bömer, Franz. *P. Ovidius Naso Metamorphosen: Kommentar I-III.* Heidelberg: Winter, 1976.

Born, Lester K. "Ovid and Allegory." *Speculum* 9.4 (1934): 262–379.

Bourguignon, Erika. "Suffering and Healing, Subordination and Power: Women and Possession Trance." *Ethos* 34.4 (2004): 557–74.

Boyarin, Daniel. *Carnal Israel: Reading Sex in Talmudic Culture.* New Historicism 25. Berkeley: University of California Press, 1993.

_____. *Intertextuality and the Reading of Midrash.* Bloomington: University of Indiana Press, 1990.

Brakke, David. "The Seed of Seth at the Flood: Biblical Interpretation and Gnostic Theological Reflection." In *Reading in Christian Communities: Essays on Interpretation in the Early Church,* edited by Charles A. Bobertz and David Brakke, 41–62. Christianity and Judaism in Antiquity 14. Notre Dame, IN: University of Notre Dame Press, 2002.

Brison, Susan J. "Trauma Narratives and the Remaking of the Self." In *Acts of Memory: Cultural Recall in the Present,* edited by Mieke Bal, Jonathan Crewe, and Leo Spitzer, 39–54. Hanover, NH: University Press of New England, 1999.

Broek, R. van den. *Studies in Gnosticism and Alexandrian Christianity.* NHMS 39. New York: Brill, 1996.

Brown, P. G. McC. "Athenian Attitudes to Rape and Seduction: The Evidence of Menander, Dyskolos." *ClQ* 41.2 (1991): 533–34.

Brown, Robert. "Livy's Sabine Women and the Ideal of *Concordia.*" *TAPA* 125 (1995): 291–319.

Buell, Denise Kimber. *Why This New Race: Ethnic Reasoning in Early Christianity.* New York: Columbia University Press, 2005.

Bultmann, Rudolf. *The History of the Synoptic Tradition.* Translated by John Marsh. Oxford: Basil Blackwell, 1963.

Burke, Peter. "History as Social Memory." In *Memory: History, Culture and the Mind,* edited by Thomas Butler, 97–113. New York: Basil Blackwell, 1989.

Burrus, Virginia. *Saving Shame: Martyrs, Saints, and Other Abject Subjects.* Philadelphia: University of Pennsylvania Press, 2008.

Butler, Judith. *Frames of War: When Is Life Grievable?* London and New York: Verso, 2009.

———. *Precarious Life: The Powers of Mourning and Violence.* London and New York: Verso, 2004.

Cahoon, Leslie. "The Bed as Battlefield: Erotic Conquest and Military Metaphor in Ovid's *Amores.*" *TAPA* 118 (1988): 293–307.

Card, Claudia. *The Atrocity Paradigm: A Theory of Evil.* New York: Oxford University Press, 2002.

———. *Confronting Evils: Terrorism, Torture, Genocide.* Cambridge: Cambridge University Press, 2010.

———. "Rape as a Weapon of War." *Hypatia* 11.4 *Women and Violence* (Autumn 1996): 5–18.

Carey, C. "Rape and Adultery in Athenian Law." *ClQ* 45.2 (1995): 407–17.

Carter, Warren. *John and Empire: Initial Explorations.* New York: T&T Clark, 2008.

Caruth, Cathy. *Unclaimed Experience: Trauma, Narrative, and History.* Baltimore, MD: Johns Hopkins University Press, 1996.

Casper, Monica J. *Missing Bodies: The Politics of Visibility.* Biopolitics. New York: New York University Press, 2009.

Castelli, Elizabeth A. *Martyrdom and Memory: Early Christian Culture Making.* Gender, Theory, and Religion. New York: Columbia University Press, 2004.

Cavanaugh, William T. *The Myth of Religious Violence: Secular Ideology and the Roots of Modern Conflict.* Oxford: Oxford University Press, 2009.

Cavarero, Adriana. *Horrorism: Naming Contemporary Violence.* New Directions in Critical Theory. New York: Columbia University Press, 2009.

Centrone, Bruno. "Platonism and Pythagoreanism in the Early Empire." In *The Cambridge History of Greek and Roman Political Thought,* edited by Christopher Rowe and Malcolm Schofield, 559–84. Cambridge: Cambridge University Press, 2000.

Chaniotis, Angelos. *War in the Hellenistic World: A Social and Cultural History.* Malden, MA: Blackwell, 2005.

Charron, Régine. "The Apocryphon of John (NHC II, I) and the Graeco-Egyptian Alchemical Literature." *Vigiliae Christianae* 59.4 (2005): 438–56.

Chérix, Pierre. *Le concept de notre grand puissance: CG VI, 4: text, remarques philologiques, traduction et notes.* Orbis biblicus et orientalis 47. Göttingen: Vandenhoeck & Ruprecht, 1982.

Clarke, John R. *Roman Sex: 100 BC–AD 250.* New York: H. N. Abrams, 2003.

Cole, Susan Guettel. "Greek Sanctions against Sexual Assault." *CP* 79.2 (1984): 97–113.

Coleman, K. M. "Fatal Charades: Roman Executions Staged as Mythological Enactments." *Journal of Roman Studies* 80 (1990): 44–73.

Collins, John J. *Introduction to the Hebrew Bible: Second Edition.* Minneapolis: Fortress Press, 2014.

Connors, Catherine. "Ennius, Ovid and Representations of Ilia." *MD* 32 (1994): 99–112.

Coulthard, Glen Sean. *Red Skin, White Masks: Rejecting the Colonial Politics of Recognition.* Minneapolis: University of Minnesota Press, 2014.

Crislip, Andrew. "Envy and Anger at the World's Creation and Destruction in the Treatise Without Title 'On the Origin of the World' (NHC II,5)." *Vigiliae Christianae* 65.3 (2011): 285–310.

Culianu, Ioan P. "The Angels of the Nations and the Origins of Gnostic Dualism."

In *Studies in Gnosticism and Hellenistic Religions Presented to Gilles Quispel on the Occasion of His 65th Birthday*, edited by R. van den Broek and M. J. Vermaseren, 78–91. Études préliminaires aux religions orientales dans l'Empire romain 91. Leiden: Brill, 1981.

Curran, Leo C. "The Mythology of Rape." *The Classical World* 72.2 (1978): 97–98.

———. "Rape and Rape Victims in the *Metamorphoses*." In *Women in the Ancient World: The Arethusa Papers*, edited by John Peradotto and J. P. Sullivan, 263–86. Albany: State University of New York Press, 1984.

Dahl, Nils A. "The Arrogant Archon and the Lewd Sophia." In *The Rediscovery of Gnosticism: Proceedings of the International Conference on Gnosticism at Yale New Haven, Connecticut, March 28–31, 1978*. Vol. 2, *Sethian Gnosticism*, edited by Bentley Layton, 689–712. SHR 41. Leiden: Brill, 1981.

Dahl, Nils A., and Alan F. Segal. "Philo and the Rabbis on the Names of God." *Journal for the Study of Judaism in the Persian, Hellenistic, and Roman Period* 9 (1978): 1–28.

Das, Veena. "Commentary: Trauma and Testimony: Between Law and Discipline." *Ethos* 35.3 (2007): 330–35.

———. "Language and Body: Transactions in the Construction of Pain." *Daedalus* 125.1 *Social Suffering* (Winter 1996): 67–91.

———. *Life and Words: Violence and the Descent into the Ordinary*. Berkeley: University of California Press, 2007.

———. "Sexual Violence, Discursive Formations and the State." *Economics and Political Weekly* 31.35/37 (September 1996): 2411–23.

Davis, P. J. *Ovid and Augustus: A Political Reading of Ovid's Erotic Poems*. London: Duckworth, 2006.

———. "Ovid's Amores: A Political Reading." *CP* 94.2 (1999): 431–39.

Davoine, Françoise, and Jean-Max Gaudillère. *History beyond Trauma*. Translated by Susan Fairfield. New York: Other Press, 2004.

Dayal, Samir. "Managing Ecstasy: A Subaltern Performative of Resistance." *Angelaki* 6.1 (2001): 75–90.

Dench, Emma. *Romulus' Asylum: Roman Identities from the Age of Alexander to the Age of Hadrian*. New York: Oxford University Press, 2005.

Dixon, Suzanne. *Reading Roman Women*. London: Bristol Classical Press, 2001.

———. "Sex and the Married Woman in Ancient Rome." In *Early Christian Families in Context*, edited by David L. Balch and Carolyn Osiek, 111–29. Grand Rapids: Eerdmans, 2003.

Douglas, Mary. *Purity and Danger: An Analysis of Concepts of Pollution and Taboo.* New York: Routledge, 2002.

Du Bois, W. E. B. *The Souls of Black Folk.* 1953. Reprint, New York: Signet Classic, 1995.

Due, Otto Stein. *Changing Forms: Studies in the* Metamorphoses *of Ovid.* Copenhagen: Museum Tusculanum Press, 1974.

Dunning, Benjamin H. *Specters of Paul: Sexual Difference in Early Christian Thought.* Divinations. Philadelphia: University of Pennsylvania Press, 2011.

_____. "Virgin Earth, Virgin Birth: Creation, Sexual Difference, and Recapitulation in Irenaeus of Lyons." *Journal of Religion* 89.1 (2009): 57–88.

_____. "What Sort of Thing Is This Luminous Woman? Thinking Sexual Difference in On the Origin of the World." *JECS* 17.1 (2009): 55–84.

Eck, Werner. *The Age of Augustus.* 2nd edition. Malden, MA: Blackwell, 2007.

Enterline, Lynn. *The Rhetoric of the Body from Ovid to Shakespeare.* Cambridge: Cambridge University Press, 2000.

Fallon, Francis T. *The Enthronement of Sabaoth: Jewish Elements in Gnostic Creation Myths.* NHS 10. Leiden: Brill, 1978.

Fanon, Frantz. *Black Skin, White Masks.* Translated by Richard Philcox. 1967. Reprint, New York: Grove Press, 2008.

_____. *Wretched of the Earth.* Translated by Richard Philcox. 1963. Reprint, New York: Grove Press, 2004.

Farrell, Joseph. "The Ovidian Corpus: Poetic Body and Poetic Text." In *Ovidian Transformations: Essays on the Metamorphoses and Its Reception*, edited by Philip Hardie, Alessandro Barchiesi, and Stephen Hinds, 127–41. Supplementary Vol. 23. Cambridge: Cambridge Philological Society, 1999.

Fassin, Didier. *The Empire of Trauma: An Inquiry into the Condition of Victimhood.* Princeton, NJ: Princeton University Press, 2009.

Feeney, D. C. *Gods in Epic: Poets and Critics of the Classical Tradition.* New York: Oxford University Press, 1991.

Feldherr, Andrew. *Playing Gods: Ovid's* Metamorphoses *and the Politics of Fiction.* Princeton, NJ: Princeton University Press, 2010.

_____. *Spectacle and Society in Livy's History*. Berkeley: University of California Press, 1998.

Ferris, I. M. *Enemies of Rome: Barbarians through Roman Eyes*. Stroud: Sutton, 2000.

Fischer-Mueller, E. Aydeet. "Yaldabaoth: The Gnostic Female Principle in Its Fallenness." *Novum Testamentum* 32.1 (1990): 79–95.

Flemming, Johann, and Ludwig Radermacher. *Das Buch Enoch*. Griechischen christlichen Schriftsteller der ersten drei Jahrhunderte 5. Leipzig: J. C. Hinrichs, 1901.

Francese, Christopher. "Daphne, Honor, and Aetiological Action in Ovid's 'Metamorphoses.'" *CW* 97.2 (2004): 153–57.

Fratantuono, Lee. *Madness Transformed: A Reading of Ovid's* Metamorphoses. Lanham, MD: Lexington Books, 2011.

Fromm, M. Gerard, ed. *Lost in Transmission: Studies of Trauma across Generations*. London: Karnac Books, 2012.

Galinsky, Karl. *Augustan Culture: An Interpretive Introduction*. Princeton, NJ: Princeton University Press, 1996.

_____. *Ovid's* Metamorphoses: *An Introduction to the Basic Aspects*. Berkeley: University of California Press, 1975.

_____. "Ovid's Metamorphoses and Augustan Cultural Thematics." In *Ovidian Transformations: Essays on the Metamorphoses and Its Reception*, edited by Philip Hardie, Alessandro Barchiesi, and Stephen Hinds, 103–11. Supplementary Vol. 23. Cambridge: Cambridge Philological Society, 1999.

Gamel, Mary-Kay. "Performing Sex, Gender and Power in Roman Elegy." In *A Companion to Roman Love Elegy*, edited by Barbara Gold, 339–56. West Sussex, UK: Blackwell, 2012.

Geertz, Clifford. "Ideology as a Cultural System." In *Ideology and Discontent*, edited by D. E. Apter, 47–76. New York: Free Press, 1964.

Geiger, Joseph. *The First Hall of Fame: A Study of the Statues in the Forum Augustum*. Mnemosyne Supplements 295. Leiden: Brill, 2008.

Gero, Stephen. "The Seduction of Eve and the Trees of Paradise: Note on a Gnostic Myth." *HTR* 71.3–4 (1978): 299–301.

Gilhus, Ingvild Sælid. *The Nature of the Archons: A Study in the Soteriology of a Gnostic Treatise from Nag Hammadi (CGII, 4)*. Studies in Oriental Religions 12. Wiesbaden: Harrassowitz, 1985.

Giversen, Søren. "Apocryphon of John and Genesis." *Studia Theologica* 17.1 (1963): 60–76.

Glancy, Jennifer A. *Corporeal Knowledge: Early Christian Bodies.* New York: Oxford University Press, 2010.

____. "Violence as Sign in the Fourth Gospel." *Biblical Interpretation* 17.1–2 (2009): 100–117.

Glazer, Brian. "The Goddess with a Fiery Breath: The Egyptian Derivation of a Gnostic Mythologoumenon." *Novum Testamentum* 33.1 (1991): 92–94.

Gold, Barbara, ed. *A Companion to Roman Love Elegy.* West Sussex, UK: Blackwell, 2012.

Gordon, Avery. *Ghostly Matters: Haunting and the Sociological Imagination.* New ed. Minneapolis: University of Minnesota Press, 2008.

Greene, Ellen. "Travesties of Love: Violence and Voyeurism in Ovid 'Amores' 1.7." *CW* 92.5, *Power, Politics, & Discourse in Augustan Elegy* (June 1999): 409–18.

Halbwachs, Maurice. *On Collective Memory.* Heritage of Sociology. Chicago: University of Chicago Press, 1992.

Hallett, Judith P., and Marilyn B. Skinner, eds. *Roman Sexualities.* Princeton, NJ: Princeton University Press, 1997.

Hardie, Philip R. *Ovid's Poetics of Illusion.* Cambridge: Cambridge University Press, 2002.

____. *Virgil's Aeneid: Cosmos and Imperium.* Oxford: Oxford University Press, 1986.

Hardie, Philip, Alessandro Barchiesi, and Stephen Hinds, eds. *Ovidian Transformations: Essays on the Metamorphoses and Its Reception.* Supplementary Vol. 23. Cambridge: Cambridge Philological Society, 1999.

Harper, Kyle. *From Shame to Sin: The Christian Transformation of Sexual Morality in Late Antiquity.* Cambridge, MA: Harvard University Press, 2013.

Harrington, Carol. *Politicization of Sexual Violence: From Abolitionism to Peacekeeping.* Gender in a Global/Local World. Burlington, VT: Ashgate, 2010.

Harris, Edward M. "Did the Athenians Regard Seduction as a Worse Crime than Rape?" *ClQ* 40.2 (1990): 370–77.

Harris, William V. *Ancient Literacy.* Cambridge, MA: Harvard University Press, 1989.

_____. *War and Imperialism in Republican Rome 327-70 B.C.* Oxford: Clarendon Press, 1979.

Heath, John. "Diana's Understanding of Ovid's 'Metamorphoses.'" *CJ* 86.3 (1991): 233-43.

Hegeman, Elizabeth. "Ethnic Syndromes as Disguise for Protest against Colonialism: Three Ethnographic Examples." *Journal of Trauma & Dissociation* 14.2 (2013): 138-46.

Helmbold, Andrew K. "The Apocryphon of John: A Case Study in Literary Criticism." *Journal of the Evangelical Theological Society* 13.3 (1970): 173-89.

Hemker, Julie. "Rape and the Founding of Rome." *Helios* 12.1 (1985): 41-47.

Herman, Judith. *Trauma and Recovery.* New York: Basic Books, 1992.

Hesford, Wendy S. "Reading Rape Stories: Material Rhetoric and the Trauma of Representation." *College English* 62.2 (1999): 192-221.

_____. *Spectacular Rhetorics: Human Rights Visions, Recognitions, and Feminisms.* Durham, NC: Duke University Press, 2011.

Hexter, Ralph, and Daniel Selden, eds. *Innovations of Antiquity.* New York: Routledge, 1992.

Hinds, Stephen. "*Arma* in Ovid's *Fasti:* Part 1, Genre and Mannerism"; "Part 2, Genre, Romulean Rome and Augustan Ideology," *Arethusa* 25.1 (1992): 81-112, 113-53.

Holden, Antonia. "The Abduction of the Sabine Women in Context: The Iconography on Late Contorniate Medallions." *AJA* 112.1 (2008): 121-42.

Hollis, Adrian S. "Ovid, Metamorphoses 1.445ff.: Apollo, Daphne, and the Pythian Crown." *ZPE* 112 (1996): 69-73.

Horsley, Richard A. *Hidden Transcripts and the Arts of Resistance: Applying the Work of James C. Scott to Jesus and Paul.* Semeia Studies 48. Atlanta: Society of Biblical Literature, 2004.

Howell, Elizabeth F. *The Dissociative Mind.* Hillsdale, NJ: Analytic Press, 2005.

Jackson, Michael. *The Politics of Storytelling: Violence, Transgression, and Intersubjectivity.* Copenhagen: Museum Tusculanum Press 2002.

James, Sharon L. "Teaching Rape in Roman Love Elegy, Part II." In *A Companion to Roman Love Elegy,* edited by Barbara K. Gold, 549-57. West Sussex, UK: Blackwell, 2012.

Janssens, Yvonne. "L'Apocryphon de Jean." *Le Muséon* 83 (1970): 157–65; 84 (1971): 43–64, 403–32.

———. *La Prôtennoia trimorphe (NH, XIII, 1): Texte établi et présenté*. Bibliothèque copte de Nag Hammadi: "Textes" 4. Québec: Presses de l'Université Laval, 1978.

Jonas, Hans. *The Gnostic Religion: The Message of the Alien God and the Beginnings of Christianity*. 3rd ed. Boston: Beacon Press, 2001.

Kahl, Brigitte. "And she called his Name Seth . . . (Gen 4:25): The Birth of Critical Knowledge and the Unread End of Eve's Story." *Union Seminary Quarterly Review* 53 (1999): 19–28.

———. "Fratricide and Ecocide." In *Earth Habitat: Eco-Injustice and the Church's Response*, edited by Dieter Hessel and Larry Rasmussen, 53–68. Minneapolis: Fortress Press, 2001.

———. *Galatians Re-imagined: Reading with the Eyes of the Vanquished*. Minneapolis: Fortress Press, 2010.

Kahle, Paul. *Bala'izah: Coptic Texts from Deir el-Bala'izah in Upper Egypt*. London: Oxford University Press, 1954.

Kaiser, Ursula Ulrike. *Die Hypostase der Archonten (Nag-Hammadi-Codex, II,4): Neu herausgegeben, übersetzt und erklärt*. Texte und Untersuchungen zur Geschichte der altchristlichen Literatur 156. Berlin: de Gruyter, 2006.

Kampen, Natalie. "The Muted Other." *Art Journal* 47.1 (1988): 15–19.

———. "Reliefs of the Basilica Aemilia: A Redating." *Klio* 73 (1991): 448–58.

Kaplan, E. Ann. *Trauma Culture: The Politics of Terror and Loss in Media and Literature*. New Brunswick, NJ: Rutgers University Press, 2005.

Kennedy, Duncan F. "'Augustan' and 'Anti-Augustan': Reflections on Terms of Reference." In *Roman Poetry and Propaganda in the Age of Augustus*, edited by Anton Powell, 26–38. London: Bristol Classical Press, 1992.

Kilby, Jane. *Violence and the Cultural Politics of Trauma*. Edinburgh: Edinburgh University Press, 2007.

King, Karen L. "Approaching the Variants of the Apocryphon of John." In *The Nag Hammadi Library after Fifty Years: Proceedings of the 1995 Society of Biblical Literature Commemoration*, ed. John D. Turner and Anne McGuire, 105–37. NHMS 44. Leiden: Brill, 1997.

———. "The Body and Society in Philo and the Apocryphon of John." In *The

School of Moses: Studies in Philo and Hellenistic Religion; In Memory of Horst R. Moehring, ed. John Peter Kenney, 82–97. Studia Philonica Monographs 1. Atlanta: Scholars Press, 1995.

____. "The Book of Norea, Daughter of Eve." In *Searching the Scriptures.* Vol. 2, *A Feminist Commentary*, edited by Elisabeth Schüssler Fiorenza, 66–85. New York: Crossroad, 1994.

____, ed. *Images of the Feminine in Gnosticism*. Philadelphia: Fortress Press, 1988.

____. "Reading Sex and Gender in the *Secret Revelation of John*." *JECS* 19.4 (2011): 519–38.

____. "Ridicule and Rape, Rule and Rebellion." In *Gnosticism and the Early Christian World: In Honor of James M. Robinson*, edited by James E. Goehring, Charles W. Hedrick, and Jack T. Sanders, 3–24. Sonoma, CA: Polebridge, 1990.

____. *The Secret Revelation of John*. Cambridge, MA: Harvard University Press, 2006.

____. "Sophia and Christ in the Apocryphon of John." In *Images of the Feminine in Gnosticism*, edited by Karen L. King, 158–76. Philadelphia: Fortress Press, 1988.

____. "Toward a Discussion of the Category 'Gnosis/Gnosticism': The Case of the Epistle of Peter to Philip." In *Jesus in Apokryphen Evangelienüberlieferungen: Beiträge zu ausserkanonischen Jesusüberlieferungen aus verschiedenen Sprach- und Kulturtraditionen*, ed. Jörg Frey, 445–65. Wissenschaftliche Untersuchungen zum Neuen Testament 254. Tübingen: Mohr Siebeck, 2010.

Kleiner, Diana E. E. *Roman Sculpture*. New Haven: Yale University Press, 1992.

Kleinman, Arthur. "'Everything That Really Matters': Social Suffering, Subjectivity, and the Remaking of Human Experience in a Disordering World." *HTR* 90.3 (1997): 315–35.

Kleinman, Arthur, Veena Das, and Margaret Lock, eds. *Social Suffering*. Berkeley: University of California Press, 1997.

Knox, Peter E. "In Pursuit of Daphne." *TAPA* 120 (1990): 183–202, 385–86.

Kohl, Philip L. "Nationalism and Archaeology: On the Constructions of Nations and the Reconstructions of the Remote Past." *Annual Review of Anthropology*, no. 27 (1998): 223–46.

Konstan, David. "Narrative and Ideology in Livy: Book 1." *ClAnt* 5.2 (1986): 198–215.

Kotrosits, Maia. "Social Fragmentation and Cosmic Rhetoric." Paper presented at Westar Institute, Christianity Seminar, Spring Meeting, 2014.

Kramer, Ross S. "A Response to Virginity and Subversion: Norea against the Powers in the Hypostasis of the Archons." In *Images of the Feminine in Gnosticism,* edited by Karen King, 259–64. Philadelphia: Fortress Press, 1988.

Krause, Martin. "Zur Hypostase der Archonten in Codex II von Nag Hammadi." *Enchoria* 2 (1972): 1–20.

Krevans, Nita. "Ilia's Dream: Ennius, Virgil, and the Mythology of Seduction." *HSCP* 95 (1993): 257–71.

Kristeva, Julia. *Powers of Horror: An Essay on Abjection.* European Perspectives. New York: Columbia University Press, 1982.

Kuttner, Ann L. *Dynasty and Empire in the Age of Augustus: The Case of the Boscoreale Cups.* Berkeley: University of California Press, 1995.

LaCapra, Dominick. *History and Its Limits: Human, Animal, Violence.* Ithaca, NY: Cornell University Press, 2009.

———. *Writing History, Writing Trauma.* Parallax. Baltimore: Johns Hopkins University Press, 2001.

Laiou, Angeliki E., ed. *Consent and Coercion to Sex and Marriage in Ancient and Medieval Societies.* Washington, DC: Dumbarton Oaks Research Library and Collection, 1993.

Lavan, Myles. *Slaves to Rome: Paradigms of Empire in Roman Culture.* New York: Cambridge University Press, 2013.

Lawless, Elaine J. "Woman as Abject: 'Resisting Cultural and Religious Myths That Condone Violence Against Women.'" *Western Folklore* 62.4 (2003): 237–69.

Layton, Bentley. "The Hypostasis of the Archons, Part II." *HTR* 69.1–2 (1976): 31–101.

———. "The Hypostasis of the Archons or The Reality of the Rulers." *HTR* 67.4 (1974): 351–426.

———. *Nag Hammadi Codex II, 2–7: Together with XIII, 2*, Brit. Lib. Or.4926(1), and P.Oxy. 1, 654, 655: With Contributions by Many Scholars.* 2 vols. NHS 20–21. Leiden: Brill, 1989.

_____, ed. *The Rediscovery of Gnosticism: Proceedings of the International Conference on Gnosticism at Yale New Haven, Connecticut, March 28-31, 1978.* Vol. 2, *Sethian Gnosticism*. SHR 41. Leiden: Brill, 1981.

_____. "The Riddle of the Thunder (NHC VI,2): The Function of Paradox in a Gnostic Text from Nag Hammadi." In *Nag Hammadi, Gnosticism, and Early Christianity*, edited by Charles W. Hedrick and Robert Hodgson Jr., 37–54. Peabody, MA: Hendrickson, 1986.

Lazreg, Marnia. *Torture and the Twilight of Empire: From Algiers to Baghdad.* Human Rights and Crimes against Humanity. Princeton, NJ: Princeton University Press, 2008.

Lefkowitz, Mary R. *Women in Greek Myth.* 2nd ed. Baltimore: Johns Hopkins University Press, 2007.

Lévi-Strauss, Claude. *The Naked Man.* 1st U.S. ed. Introduction to a Science of Mythology 4. New York: Harper & Row, 1981.

Levithan, Josh. *Roman Siege Warfare.* Ann Arbor: University of Michigan Press, 2013.

Lewis, Nicola Denzey. *Introduction to "Gnosticism": Ancient Voices, Christian Worlds.* New York: Oxford University Press, 2013.

Leys, Ruth. *Trauma: A Genealogy.* Chicago: University of Chicago Press, 2000.

Lightfoot, J. L. "The Roots of 'Daphne.'" *Hermathena* 168 (Summer 2000): 11–19.

Lillie, Celene. "The Rape of Eve: Exploring the Social-Historical Context of the 'Gnostic' Myth." Paper presented at the Annual Meeting of the Society of Biblical Literature, New Orleans, Louisiana, 2009.

Lincoln, Bruce. *Death, War, and Sacrifice: Studies in Ideology and Practice.* Chicago: University of Chicago Press, 1991.

_____. *Discourse and the Construction of Society: Comparative Studies of Myth, Ritual, and Classification.* New York: Oxford University Press, 1989.

_____. "Gendered Discourses: The Early History of 'Mythos' and 'Logos.'" *History of Religions* 36.1 (1996): 1–12.

_____. *Myth, Cosmos, and Society: Indo-European Themes of Creation and Destruction.* Cambridge, MA: Harvard University Press, 1986.

_____. "The Rape of Persephone: A Greek Scenario of Women's Initiation." *HTR* 72.3/4 (1979): 223–35.

____. *Religion, Empire, and Torture: The Case of Achaemenian Persia, with a Postscript on Abu Ghraib*. Chicago: University of Chicago Press, 2007.

____. *Theorizing Myth: Narrative, Ideology, and Scholarship*. Chicago: University of Chicago Press, 1999.

Lively, Genevieve. *Ovid's* Metamorphoses: *A Reader's Guide*. London: Continuum, 2011.

____. "Teaching Rape in Roman Elegy, Part I." In *A Companion to Roman Love Elegy*, edited by Barbara Gold, 542–48. West Sussex, UK: Blackwell, 2012.

Lobur, John Alexander. *Consensus, Concordia and the Formation of Roman Imperial Ideology*. New York: Routledge, 2008.

Logan, Alistair H. B. *Gnostic Truth and Christian Heresy: A Study in the History of Gnosticism*. Edinburgh: T&T Clark, 1996.

____. "John and the Gnostics: The Significance of the Apocryphon of John for the Debate about the Origins of the Johannine Literature." *Journal for the Study of the New Testament* 43 (1991): 41–69.

Lopez, Davina C. *Apostle to the Conquered: Reimagining Paul's Mission*. Minneapolis: Fortress Press, 2008.

Luttikhuizen, Gerard P. "The Creation of Man and Woman in The Secret Book of John." In *Creation of Man and Woman: Interpretations of the Biblical Narratives in Jewish and Christian Traditions*, edited by Gerard P. Luttikhuizen, 140–55. Themes in Biblical Narrative 3. Leiden: Brill, 2000.

____. "Critical Gnostic Interpretations of Genesis." In *Exegetical Encounter between Jews and Christians in Late Antiquity*, edited by Emmanouela Grypeou and Helen Spurling, 75–86. Jewish and Christian Perspectives 18. Leiden: Brill, 2009.

____. "The Evaluation of the Teaching of Jesus in Christian Gnostic Revelation Dialogues." *Novum Testamentum* 30.2 (1988): 158–68.

____. *Gnostic Revisions of Genesis Stories and Early Jesus Traditions*. NHMS 58. Leiden; Boston: Brill, 2006.

MacRae, George W. "The Ego-Proclamation in Gnostic Sources." In *The Trial of Jesus: Cambridge Studies in Honour of C. F. D. Moule*, edited by Ernst Bammel, 122–34. Studies in Biblical Theology 2/13. Naperville, IL: Alec R Allenson, 1970.

____. "The Jewish Background of the Gnostic Sophia Myth." *Novum Testamentum* 12.2 (1970): 86–101.

Martin, Dale B. *The Corinthian Body*. New Haven: Yale University Press, 1999.

Martin, François. *Le livre d'Hénoch traduit sur les textes éthiopien*. Documents pour l'étude de la Bible. Paris: Letouzey et Ané, 1906.

Mattingly, David J. *Imperialism, Power, and Identity: Experiencing the Roman Empire*. Miriam S. Balmuth Lectures in Ancient History and Archaeology. Princeton, NJ: Princeton University Press, 2011.

____. *An Imperial Possession: Britain in the Roman Empire 54 BC-AD 409*. New York: Allen Lane, 2006.

McCoskey, Denise Eileen. *Race: Antiquity and Its Legacy*. New York: Oxford University Press, 2012.

McGuire, Anne. "Virginity and Subversion: Norea against the Powers in the Hypostasis of the Archons." In *Images of the Feminine in Gnosticism,* edited by Karen L. King, 239–58. Philadelphia: Fortress Press, 1988.

____. "Women, Gender, and Gnosis in Gnostic Texts and Traditions." In *Women and Christian Origins,* edited by Ross Shepard Kraemer and Mary Rose D'Angelo, 257–99. New York: Oxford University Press, 1999.

McInerney, Maud Burnett. *Eloquent Virgins from Thecla to Joan of Arc*. New Middle Ages. New York: Palgrave Macmillan, 2003.

Meyer, Marvin, ed. *The Nag Hammadi Scriptures: The International Edition*. New York: HarperCollins, 2007.

Miles, Gary B. "The First Roman Marriage and the Theft of the Sabine Women." In *Innovations of Antiquity,* edited by Ralph Hexter and Daniel Selden, 161–96. New York: Routledge, 1992.

Millar, Fergus. "Ovid and the *Domus Augusta*: Rome Seen from Tomoi." *Journal of Roman Studies* 83 (1993): 1–17.

Miller, John F. *Apollo, Augustus, and the Poets*. New York: Cambridge University Press, 2009.

____. "Ovid and Augustan Apollo." *Hermathena* 177/178 (2004/2005): 165–80.

Miller, Patricia Cox. "'Plenty Sleeps There': The Myth of Eros and Psyche in Plotinus and Gnosticism." In *Neoplatonism and Gnosticism,* edited by Richard T. Wallis and Jay Bregman, 223–38. Studies in Neoplatonism 6. Albany: State University of New York Press, 1992.

Mukta, Parita. "The 'Civilizing Mission': The Regulation and Control of Mourning in Colonial India." *Feminist Review* 63 (1999): 25–47.

Myerowitz, Molly. *Ovid's Games of Love*. Detroit: Wayne State University Press, 1985.

Nagel, Peter. *Das Wesen der Archonton aus Codex II der gnostischen Bibliothek von Nag Hammadi: Koptischer Text, deutsche Übersetzung und griechische Rückübersetzung, Konkordanz und Indizes*. Wissenschaftliche Beiträge der Martin-Luther Universität Halle-Wittenberg 1970/6. Halle: Martin-Luther-Universität Halle-Wittenberg, 1970.

Naguib, Saphinaz-Amal. "The Martyr as Witness: Coptic and Copto-Arabic Hagiographies as Mediators of Religious Memory." *Numen* 41.3 (1994): 223–54.

Nicolet, Claude. *Space, Geography, and Politics in the Early Roman Empire*. Translated by Hélène Leclerc. Ann Arbor: University of Michigan Press, 1990.

Nicoll, W. S. M. "Cupid, Apollo, and Daphne (Ovid. Met. 1.452ff)." *CQ* 30.1 (1980): 174–82.

Nikiprowetzky, Valentin. *Philon d'Alexandrie: De Decalogo*. Les oeuvres de Philon d'Alexandrie 23. Paris: Cerf, 1965.

Noonan, J. D. "Livy 1.9.6: The Rape at the Consualia." *CW* 83.6 (1990): 493–501.

Ogilvie, Robert M. *A Commentary on Livy: Books 1-5*. Oxford: Clarendon, 1965.

Otis, Brooks. *Ovid as an Epic Poet*. 2nd ed. Cambridge: Cambridge University Press, 1970.

Ovid. *Amores*. Translated by A. S. Kline. http://poetryintranslation.com/PITBR/Latin/AmoresBkIII.htm#_Toc520536662.

——. *The Art of Love and Other Poems*. Translated by J. H. Mozley. Revised by G. P. Goold, vol. 2. LCL. Cambridge, MA: Harvard University Press, 1929, 1979.

——. *Fasti*. Translated by James G. Frazer. Revised by G. P. Goold, vol. 5. LCL. Cambridge, MA: Harvard University Press, 1931, 1996.

——. *Heroides* and *Amores*. Translated by Grant Showerman. Revised by G. P. Goold, vol. 1. LCL. Cambridge, MA: Harvard University Press, 1914, 1977.

——. *The Metamorphoses*. Translated by Charles Martin. New York: W. W. Norton, 2004.

_____. *The Metamorphoses*. Translated by Frank Justus Miller. Revised by G. P. Goold, vols. 3–4. LCL. Cambridge, MA: Harvard University Press, 1916, 1984.

Packman, Zola Marie. "Call It Rape: A Motif in Roman Comedy and Its Suppression in English-Speaking Publications." *Helios* 20.1 (1993): 42–55.

Pagels, Elaine. *Adam, Eve, and the Serpent*. New York: Random House, 1988.

_____. "Christian Apologists and 'The Fall of the Angels': An Attack on Roman Imperial Power?" *HTR* 78:3–4 (1985): 301–25.

_____. "Exegesis and Exposition of the Genesis Creation Accounts in Selected Texts from Nag Hammadi." In *Nag Hammadi, Gnosticism, & Early Christianity*, edited by Charles W. Hedrick and Robert Hodgson Jr., 257–85. Peabody, MA: Hendrickson, 1986.

_____. *The Gnostic Paul: Gnostic Exegesis of the Pauline Letters*. 1975. Reprint, New York: Continuum, 1992.

_____. "Pursuing the Spiritual Eve: Imagery and Hermeneutics in the Hypostasis of the Archons and the Gospel of Philip." In *Images of the Feminine in Gnosticism*, edited by Karen L. King, 187–206. Philadelphia: Fortress Press, 1988.

Painchaud, Louis. *L'Écrit sans titre: Traité sur l'origine du monde (NH II, 5 et XIII, 2 et Brit. Lib. Or. 4926 [1])*. Québec: Presses de l'Université Laval, 1995.

_____. "The Literary Contacts between the Writing Without Title On the Origin of the World (CG II,5 and XIII,2) and Eugnostos the Blessed (CG III,3 and V,I)." *Journal of Biblical Literature* 114.1 (1995): 81–101.

_____. "The Redactions of the Writing Without Title (CG II5)." *Second Century: A Journal of Early Christian Studies* 8.4 (1991): 217–34.

_____. "Le sommaire anthropogonique de L'Ecrit sans titre (NH II, 117:27–118:2) à la lumiere de 1 Cor 15:45–47." *Vigiliae Christianae* 44. 4 (1990): 382–93.

_____. "The Use of Scripture in Gnostic Literature." *JECS* 4.2 (1996): 129–46.

Parker, Holt N. "Why Were the Vestals Virgins? Or the Chastity of Women and the Safety of the Roman State." *American Journal of Philology* 175.4 (2004): 563–601.

Parrott, Douglas M. *Nag Hammadi Codices III,3–4 and V,1 with Papyrus Berolinensis 8502,3 and Oxyrhynchus Papyrus 1081: Eugnostos and The Sophia of Jesus Christ*. NHS 27. Leiden: Brill, 1991.

Parry, Hugh. "Ovid's *Metamorphoses*: Violence in a Pastoral Landscape." *TAPA* 95 (1964): 268–82.

Pearson, Birger. "The Figure of Norea in Gnostic Literature." In *Proceedings of the International Colloquium on Gnosticism, Stockholm, August 20-25, 1973,* edited by Geo Widengren, 143–52. Filolgisk-filosofiska serien 17. Stockholm: Almqvist & Wiksel, 1977.

_____. *Gnosticism, Judaism, and Egyptian Christianity.* Minneapolis: Fortress Press, 1990.

_____. "Jewish Sources in Gnostic Literature." In *Jewish Writings of the Second Temple Period: Apocrypha, Pseudepigrapha, Qumran Sectarian Writings, Philo, Josephus,* edited by Michael E. Stone, 443–81. Assen: Van Gorcum, 1984.

_____. "Revisiting Norea." In *Images of the Feminine in Gnosticism,* edited by Karen L. King, 265–75. Philadelphia: Fortress Press, 1988.

_____. "She Became a Tree: A Note to CG II, 4:89, 25–26." *HTR* 69.3-4 (1976): 413–15.

Peppard, Michael. *The Son of God in the Roman World: Divine Sonship in Its Social and Political Context.* New York: Oxford University Press, 2011.

Perkins, Judith. "The 'Self' as Sufferer." *HTR* 85.3 (1992): 245–72.

_____. *The Suffering Self: Pain and Narrative Representation in the Early Christian Era.* New York: Routledge, 1995.

Perkins, Pheme. *Gnosticism and the New Testament.* Minneapolis: Fortress Press, 1993.

_____. "Irenaeus and the Gnostics: Rhetoric and Composition in Adversus Haereses Book One." *Vigiliae Christianae* 30.3 (1976): 193–200.

_____. "On the Origin of the World (CG II,5): A Gnostic Physics." *Vigiliae Christianae* 34.1 (1980): 36–46.

Pétrement, Simone. *A Separate God: The Christian Origins of Gnosticism.* Translated by Carol Harrison. San Francisco: HarperSanFrancisco, 1990.

Pleše, Zlatko. *Poetics of the Gnostic Universe: Narrative and Cosmology in the Apocryphon of John.* NHMS 52. Leiden: Brill, 2006.

Powell, Anton, ed. *Roman Poetry and Propaganda in the Age of Augustus.* London: Bristol Classical Press, 1992.

Price, Robert M. "Amorous Archons in Eden and Corinth." *Journal of Unification Studies* 2 (1998): 19–34.

Price, S. R. F. *Rituals and Power: The Roman Imperial Cult in Asia Minor*. New York: Cambridge University Press, 1984.

Quispel, Gilles. "The Demiurge in the Apocryphon of John." In *Nag Hammadi and Gnosis: Papers Read at the First International Congress of Coptology (Cairo, December 1976)*, edited by R. McL. Wilson, 1–33. NHS 14. Leiden: Brill, 1978.

Rasimus, Tuomas. "The Serpent in Gnostic and Related Texts." In *Colloque international "L'évangile selon Thomas et les textes de Nag Hammadi," Québec, 29-31 mai 2003*, edited by Louis Painchaud and Paul-Hubert Poirier, 417–71. Bibliothèque copte de Nag Hammadi: Études 8. Québec: Presses de l'Université Laval, 2007.

Richlin, Amy, ed. *Pornography and Presentation in Greece and Rome*. New York: Oxford University Press, 1992.

———. "Reading Ovid's Rapes." In *Pornography and Presentation in Greece and Rome*, edited by Amy Richlin, 158–79. New York: Oxford University Press, 1992.

Robbins, Vernon K. *Exploring the Texture of Texts: A Guide to Socio-Rhetorical Interpretation*. Valley Forge, PA: Trinity Press International, 1996.

———. *Tapestry of Early Christian Discourse: Rhetoric, Society and Ideology*. New York: Routledge, 1996.

Rosaldo, Renato. "Imperialist Nostalgia." *Representations* 26 (1989): 107–22.

Rudd, Niall. *Lines of Enquiry: Studies in Latin Poetry*. Cambridge: Cambridge University Press, 1976.

Rudolph, Kurt. *Gnosis: The Nature and History of Gnosticism*. Translated by Robert McLachlan Wilson. San Francisco: Harper & Row, 1984.

Salzman-Mitchell, Patricia B. *A Web of Fantasies: Gaze, Image, and Gender in Ovid's Metamorphoses*. Columbus: Ohio State University Press, 2005.

"Samael." JewishEncyclopedia.com: The unedited full-text of the 1906 *Jewish Encyclopedia*, www.jewishencyclopedia.com/articles/13055-samael.

Scarry, Elaine. *The Body in Pain: The Making and Unmaking of the World*. New York: Oxford University Press, 1985.

Schenke, Hans-Martin. *Das Thomas-Buch: Nag-Hammadi-Codex II,7*. Berlin: Akademie-Verlag, 1989.

Schofield, Malcolm. "Epicurean and Stoic Political Thought." In *The Cambridge History of Greek and Roman Political Thought*, edited by Christopher Rowe and Malcolm Schofield, 435–56. Cambridge: Cambridge University Press, 2000.

Schwab, Gabriele. *Haunting Legacies: Violent Histories and Transgenerational Trauma.* New York: Columbia University Press, 2010.

Scoppola, Francesco, ed. *Palazzo Altemps Guide.* Milan: Electa, 2012.

Scott, James C. *Domination and the Arts of Resistance: Hidden Transcripts.* New Haven: Yale University Press, 1990.

Segal, Alan F. *Two Powers in Heaven: Early Rabbinic Reports about Christianity and Gnosticism.* Studies in Judaism in Late Antiquity 25. Leiden: Brill, 1977.

Segal, Charles. "Ovid's Metamorphic Bodies: Art, Gender, and Violence in the 'Metamorphoses.'" *Arion* 5.3 (1998): 9–41.

_____. "Violence and the Other: Greek, Female, and Barbarian in Euripides' Hecuba." *TAPA* 120 (1990): 109–31.

Severy, Beth. *Augustus and the Family at the Birth of the Roman Empire.* New York: Routledge, 2003.

Sharrock, Alison R. "Intratextuality: Texts, Parts, and (W)holes in Theory." In *Intratextuality: Greek and Roman Textual Relations,* edited by Alison Sharrock and Helen Morales, 1–42. New York: Oxford University Press, 2000.

_____. "Ovid and the Politics of Reading." *MD* 33 (1994): 97–122.

_____. *Seduction and Repetition in Ovid's* Ars Amatoria 2. Oxford: Clarendon, 1994.

_____. "Womanufacture." *Journal of Roman Studies* 81 (1991): 36–49.

Sissa, Giulia. *Sex and Sensuality in the Ancient World.* New Haven: Yale University Press, 2008.

Skinner, Marilyn B. *Sexuality in Greek and Roman Culture.* Ancient Cultures. Malden, MA: Blackwell, 2005.

Skjelsbæk, Inger. *The Political Psychology of War Rape: Studies from Bosnia and Herzegovina.* War, Politics and Experience. New York: Routledge, 2012.

Smethurst, S. E. "Women in Livy's 'History.'" *Greece & Rome* 19.56 (1950): 80–87.

Smith, Andrea. *Conquest: Sexual Violence and Genocide.* Brooklyn: South End Press, 2005.

Smith, Jonathan Z. *Imagining Religion: From Babylon to Jonestown.* Chicago Studies in the History of Judaism. Chicago: University of Chicago Press, 1982.

_____. *Map Is Not Territory: Studies in the History of Religions.* Studies in Judaism in Late Antiquity 23. Leiden: Brill, 1978.

_____. *Relating Religion: Essays in the Study of Religion.* Chicago: University of Chicago Press, 2004.

Smith, R. R. R. "Imperial Reliefs from the Sebasteion at Aphrodisias." *Journal of Roman Studies* 77 (1987): 88–138.

_____. "*Simulacra Gentium*: The *Ethne* from the Sebasteion at Aphrodisias." *Journal of Roman Studies* 78 (1988): 50–77.

Solodow, Joseph B. "Livy and the Story of Horatius, 1.24–26." *TAPA* 109 (1979): 251–68.

Sontag, Susan. *Regarding the Pain of Others*. New York: Picador, 2003.

Staples, Ariadne. *From Good Goddess to Vestal Virgins: Sex and Category in Roman Religion*. London: Routledge, 1998.

Stem, Rex. "The Exemplary Lessons of Livy's Romulus." *TAPA* 137.2 (2007): 435–71.

Stirrup, Barbara E. "Techniques of Rape: Variety of Wit in Ovid's 'Metamorphoses.'" *Greece & Rome* 24.2 (1977): 170–84.

Strong, Donald Emrys. *Roman Art*. Harmondsworth: Penguin Books, 1988.

Stroumsa, Gedaliahu A. G. *Another Seed: Studies in Gnostic Mythology*. NHS 24. Leiden: Brill, 1984.

Sugirtharajah, R. S., ed. *The Postcolonial Biblical Reader*. Malden, MA: Blackwell, 2006.

_____. *Voices from the Margin: Interpreting the Bible in the Third World*. 3rd ed. Maryknoll, NY: Orbis Books, 2006.

Takács, Sarolta A. *Vestal Virgins, Sibyls, and Matrons: Women in Roman Religion*. Austin: University of Texas Press, 2008.

Tanner, Laura E. *Intimate Violence: Reading Rape and Torture in Twentieth-Century Fiction*. Bloomington: Indiana University Press, 1994.

Tardieu, Michel. *Écrits gnostiques: Codex de Berlin*. Paris: Cerf, 1984.

_____. *Trois mythes gnostiques: Adam, Éros et les animaux d'Égypte dans un écrit de Nag Hammadi (II,5)*. Paris: Études Augustiniennes, 1974.

Taussig, Hal. "Melancholy, Colonialism, and Complicity: Complicating Counterimperial Readings of Aphrodisias's Sebasteion." In *Text, Image, and Christians in the Graeco-Roman World: A Festschrift in Honor of David Lee Balch*, edited by Aliou Cissé Niang and Carolyn Osiek, 280–95. Eugene, OR: Pickwick, 2012.

_____, ed. *A New New Testament: A Bible of the 21st Century Combining Traditional and Newly Discovered Texts*. New York: Houghton Mifflin Harcourt, 2013.

Taussig, Michael T. *Shamanism, Colonialism, and the Wild Man: A Study in Terror and Healing*. Chicago: University of Chicago Press, 1986.

Thompson, D. L. "The Meeting of the Roman Senate on the Palatine." *AJA* 85 (1981): 335–39.

Thompson, James Westfall. "The Alleged Persecution of the Christians at Lyons in 177." *American Journal of Theology* 16.3 (1912): 359–84.

Till, Walter C. *Koptische Grammatik: Saïdischer Dialekt; Mit Bibliographie, Lesestücken und Wöterverzeichnissen*. Leipzig: Otto Harrassowitz, 1955.

Toynbee, Jocelyn M. C. *The Hadrianic School: A Chapter in the History of Greek Art*. London: Cambridge University Press, 1934.

Treggiari, Susan. *Roman Marriage: Iusti Coniuges from the Time of Cicero to the Time of Ulpian*. Oxford: Clarendon, 1991.

Trumbower, Jeffrey A. "Traditions Common to the Primary Adam and Eve Books and On the Origin of the World (NHC II.5)." *Journal for the Study of the Pseudepigrapha* 14 (1996): 43–54.

Turner, John D. "The Gnostic Threefold Path to Enlightenment: The Ascent of Mind and the Descent of Wisdom." *Novum Testamentum* 22.4 (1980): 324–51.

Turner, John D., and Anne McGuire, eds. *The Nag Hammadi Library after Fifty Years: Proceedings of the 1995 Society of Biblical Literature Commemoration*. NHMS 44. Leiden: Brill, 1997.

Vaillant, Andre. *Le livre des secrets d'Énoch: Texte slave et traduction française*. Paris: Institut d'études slaves, 1952.

Vandiver, Elizabeth. "The Founding Mothers of Livy's Rome: The Sabine Women and Lucretia." In *The Eye Expanded: Life and the Arts in Greco-Roman Antiquity*, edited by F. B. Titchener and R. F. Moorton Jr., 206–32 Berkeley: University of California Press, 1999.

Vasaly, Ann. "Personality and Power: Livy's Depiction of the Appii Claudii in the First Pentad." *TAPA* 117 (1987): 203–26.

Walcot, Peter. "Plutarch on Women." *Symbolae Osloenses: Norwegian Journal of Greek and Latin Studies* 71.1 (1999): 163–83.

Waldstein, Michael. "The Providence Monologue in the Apocryphon of John and the Johannine Prologue." *JECS* 3.4 (1995): 369–402.

Waldstein, Michael M., and Frederik Wisse, eds. *The Apocryphon of John: A*

Synopsis of Nag Hammadi Codices II,1, III,1, and IV,1 with BG 8502,2. NHMS 33. Leiden: Brill, 1995.

Wallis, Richard T., ed. *Neoplatonism and Gnosticism.* Albany: State University of New York Press, 1992.

Walters, Jonathan. "Invading the Roman Body: Manliness and Impenetrability in Roman Thought." In *Roman Sexualities,* edited by Judith P. Hallet and Marilyn B. Skinner, 29–43. Princeton, NJ: Princeton University Press, 1997.

Weil, Simone. "The Iliad, Poem of Might." In Simone Weil, *Intimations of Christianity among the Ancient Greeks.* New York: Routledge, 1957.

Welburn, Andrew J. "Identity of the Archons in the 'Apocryphon Johannis.'" *Vigiliae Christianae* 32.4 (1978): 241–54.

Wheeler, Stephen Michael. *Narrative Dynamics in Ovid's* Metamorphoses. Tübingen: Gunter Narr, 2000.

Whittaker, C. R. *Rome and Its Frontiers: The Dynamics of Empire.* New York: Routledge, 2004.

Wildfang, Robin Lorsch. *Rome's Vestal Virgins: A Study of Rome's Vestal Priestesses in the Late Republic and Early Empire.* New York: Routledge, 2006.

Wilkinson, L. P. *Ovid Recalled.* Cambridge: Cambridge University Press, 1955.

Williams, Michael A. "Higher Providence, Lower Providences and Fate in Gnosticism and Middle Platonism." In *Neoplatonism and Gnosticism,* edited by Richard T. Wallis and Jay Bregman, 483–507. Studies in Neoplatonism 6. Albany: State University of New York Press, 1992.

_____. *The Immovable Race: A Gnostic Designation and the Theme of Stability in Late Antiquity.* Leiden: Brill, 1985.

_____. *Rethinking "Gnosticism": An Argument for Dismantling a Dubious Category.* Princeton, NJ: Princeton University Press, 1996.

_____. "Uses of Gender Imagery in Ancient Gnostic Texts." In *Gender and Religion: On the Complexity of Symbols,* edited by Caroline Walker Bynum, Stevan Harrell, and Paula Richman. 196–227. Boston: Beacon Press, 1986.

_____. "Variety in Gnostic Perspectives on Gender." In *Images of the Feminine in Gnosticism,* edited by Karen L. King, 2–22. Philadelphia: Fortress Press, 1988.

Wink, Walter. *Cracking the Gnostic Code: The Powers in Gnosticism.* Society of Biblical Literature Monograph Series 46. Atlanta: Scholars Press, 1993.

Wintermute, Orval S. "A Study of Gnostic Exegesis of the Old Testament." In

The Use of the Old Testament in the New and Other Essays: Studies in Honor of William Franklin Stinespring, edited by James M. Efird, 241–70. Durham, NC: Duke University Press, 1972.

Woolf, Greg. "Inventing Empire in Ancient Rome." In *Empires: Perspectives from Archaeology and History,* edited by Susan E. Alcock, Terence N. D'Altroy, Kathleen D. Morrison, and Carla M. Sinopoli, 311–22. New York: Oxford University Press, 2001.

Wright, Neil. "Creation and Recreation: Medieval Responses to *Metamorphoses* 1.5–88." In *Ovidian Transformations: Essays on the Metamorphoses and Its Reception,* edited by Philip Hardie, Alessandro Barchiesi, and Stephen Hinds, 68–84. Supplementary Vol. 23. Cambridge: Cambridge Philological Society, 1999.

Zanker, Paul. *The Power of Images in the Age of Augustus.* Translated by Alan Shapiro. Ann Arbor: University of Michigan Press, 1988.

Zissos, Andrew. "The Rape of Proserpina in Ovid 'Met.' 5.341–661: Internal Audience and Narrative Distortion." *Phoenix* 53.1/2 (1999): 97–113.

Žižek, Slavoj. *Violence: Six Sideways Reflections.* Big Ideas/Small Books. New York: Picador, 2008.

Index of Subjects, Writings, and Names

emperors, 112, 196n93, 253–54;
in Secret Revelation of John,
xiv, 1n2, 4, 6–7, 10, 13, 14n36,
17–18, 179, 180n4, 181, 182n10,
184, 185n32, 185n34, 186n40,
186n42, 188n51, 192n77, 193n81,
196n93, 197, 209, 226–28, 233,
235, 237–39, 241–42, 243n4,
246n16, 255, 259–60, 261n84,
261n86, 264, 266, 275–76,
286–87, 289, 293, 303, 308; and
subjugation, 19, 143, 145,
213n199, 214, 218, 219, 226, 237,
259–60, 273, 276–77, 303–5, 308

Sabines narrative, 29, 30n22, 42, 50,
52n78, 59n94, 77, 80, 89n162,
102, 103, 118–19, 144, 155n115,
263, 282, 284, 308; as aetiology,
44, 103, 263, 282; of
colonization, 36, 45, 49, 54, 61,
65, 71n119, 118, 176, 238, 263; of
marriage, 263, 282; of triumph,
29n17, 49, 51, 52n77, 53–54,
57–58, 63–64, 71n119, 78, 103,
104, 107, 108n214, 109, 127n13,
129n20, 138, 146n76, 147–49,
156, 166n166, 173n198, 176n200,
263, 271n141, 282; *caritas* and,
46–47, 76, 77n123, 86; concord
and, 68–70, 76–77, 104, 123, 182,
193, 193n82, 256, 262, 286; men
and, 3, 5n11, 12, 16, 24–25, 27,
28, 37–38, 41n51, 42n52, 43n53,

45, 48–50, 52, 55–56, 69, 72n120,
82n136, 83, 88, 102, 144, 169,
214, 304; Pax Romana and, 145,
262, 286; women and, 38–41, 43,
49, 50, 59–60, 66, 71, 72, 80, 82,
84, 101, 102; abduction of, 62, 76,
95, 105, 105n205, 282; and
battlefield, 21, 29n17,19, 71–74,
82n136, 84n143, 85, 87, 103,
144n67, 284

Samael, 197, 199n120, 200n128, 205,
210, 215n208, 217, 254
Sebasteion, Aphrodisias, 23,
108n216, 112, 113, 114n235,
115–17, 123
Secret Revelation of John, xiv, 1n2,
4, 6–7, 10, 13, 14n36, 17–18, 179,
180n4, 181, 182n10, 184,
185nn33–34, 186n40, 186n42,
188n51, 192n77, 193n81, 196n93,
197, 209, 226–28, 233, 235,
237–39, 241–42, 243n4, 246n16,
255, 259–60, 261n84, 261n86,
264, 266, 275–76, 286–87, 289,
293, 303, 308, 322
serpent, the, 2–3, 5n11, 128–29,
179n1, 182, 190n70, 191n70,
201–4, 206, 214n200, 220, 228,
236, 242n2, 244, 245, 249–50,
258, 280, 297, 298
Seth, 14n36, 190n69, 191, 192n72,
193, 194, 205, 230–31, 238,
249n33, 251–52, 265–66, 279–80,
288–89, 291, 295

Index of Selected Authors

Ahl, Frederick, 128

Albertson, Fred C., 24n5, 95, 104

Allen, Graham, 7n13

Althusser, Louis, 22n2, 127n12

Ando, Clifford, 54n81

Arieti, James A., 88n159

Barc, Bernard, 180n4, 199n120,

Barton, Carlin A., 132n29, 141n55

Beard, Mary, 51n77, 103, 121n250,
149n91, 155n113

Bhabha, Homi K., 9n22, 237

Boatwright, Mary T., 44n54, 100,
101n187

Boyarin, Daniel, 5n11, 7, 8, 11,
242n2, 248n32

Brown, Robert, 47n65, 49n74, 58,
59n92, 59n96, 66n111, 66n113,
76n123

Buell, Denise Kimber, 304n36

Bultmann, Rudolf, 9n21

Cahoon, Leslie, 21n1

Cox Miller, Patricia, 221n242, 326

Culianu, Ioan P., 199n120, 254

Curran, Leo C., 8n16, 127n12

Dahl, Nils A., 14n37, 243n6

Das, Veena, 9n22, 12n30

Davis, P. J., 126n4

Dench, Emma, 36n40, 103

Dixon, Suzanne, 11n27

Douglas, Mary, 35n35

Dunning, Benjamin H., 211n191

Eck, Werner, 111n231, 148n89

Fallon, Frances T., 183n16

Fanon, Frantz, 9n22, 237

Feeney, D. C., 126, 145

Feldherr, Andrew, 44n54, 77n124,
126n5, 167

Ferris, I. M., 108n215

Fratantuono, Lee, 125n1

Galinsky, Karl, 85n145, 126n4,
126n6

Gamel, Mary-Kay, 21

347